THE INDONESIAN CRISIS

A Human Development Perspective

edited by

ARIS ANANTA

ISEAS

INSTITUTE OF SOUTHEAST ASIAN STUDIES
Singapore

First published in Singapore in 2003 by
Institute of Southeast Asian Studies
30 Heng Mui Keng Terrace, Pasir Panjang
Singapore 119614

E-mail: publish@iseas.edu.sg
Website: www.iseas.edu.sg/pub.html

ISEAS Library Cataloguing-in-Publication Data

The Indonesian crisis : a human development perspective / edited by Aris Ananta.
1. Financial crises—Economic aspects—Indonesia.
2. Financial crises—Social aspects—Indonesia.
3. Manpower policy—Indonesia.
4. Indonesia—Economic conditions—1997-
I. Ananta, Aris.
HB3815 I41 2003 sls2002034326

ISBN 981-230-171-2

Typeset by International Typesetters Pte. Ltd.
Printed in Singapore by Seng Lee Press Pte. Ltd

Contents

Acknowledgements

This book emanated from a workshop on "Socio-economic Conditions during the Indonesian Crisis" organized by the Department of Economics and Centre for Advanced Studies, National University of Singapore, in 2000. The workshop was made possible with a grant from the Faculty of Arts and Social Sciences, National University of Singapore. Nine out of the sixteen chapters in this book are revised versions of the papers presented at the workshop. The remaining chapters were solicited for publication in this volume.

The editor would like to acknowledge the Department of Economics, National University of Singapore, for having provided a conducive environment to conduct the workshop and to begin the editing of the book.

The editor owes a special debt to the Institute of Southeast Asian Studies, Singapore, for its encouragement and for providing facilities to carry out the major part of the editing and completion of this volume. Special appreciation goes to all the authors for their contributions. The authors would also like to acknowledge the comments from anonymous referees on the draft of this book. Finally, Mrs. Roselie Ang deserves a special mention for her dedicated efforts in improving the readability of this book.

List of Contributors

Adrian Panggabean is a Lecturer at the University of Indonesia. At the time his chapter was written, he was Vice-President of Equity Research and Southeast Asian Economist at Nomura Singapore Limited. His research covers public finance, institutional economics, and macroeconomics.

Aris Ananta is a Senior Research Fellow at the Institute of Southeast Asian Studies, Singapore. His current works cover labour mobility in Southeast Asia and human development in Indonesia. He is also Professor in the University of Indonesia.

Budi Utomo is the Country Director of the Population Council in Indonesia. He is also a Lecturer in the School of Public Health, University of Indonesia. His interests and research works cover broad topics of reproductive health issues, including child health and nutrition. He is also working on issues related to HIV risk behaviour and capacity building in a decentralized health programme.

Daksini Kartowibowo is a Junior Researcher at the Demographic Institute, University of Indonesia. She has been working mainly on the welfare of population, including those related to labour, gender, and population mobility. Her research has mostly involved directly observing the society.

David Djaelani Gordon is the Programme Director of Yayasan Harapan Permati Hati Kita, a drug addiction and treatment recovery community and foundation, based in Ciawi, Bogor, Indonesia. He has been closely associated with drug users and the addict community since 1957. His knowledge about addicts, his training as a transpersonal psychologist, and his intensive and cumulative experience with various recovery centres in the United States and other countries has served him well in working with addicts, in both the practical and theoretical senses.

David Ehrmann is Consultant to the Central Independent Monitoring Unit (CIMU) of the Indonesian Scholarship and Grants Programme (SGP) in Jakarta. The SGP is one component of the Indonesia Social Safety Net programme.

Djoko Hartono is Consultant to the Central Independent Monitoring Unit (CIMU) of the Indonesian Scholarship and Grants Programme (SGP) in Jakarta.

Iwan J. Azis is Professor at Cornell University and the University of Indonesia. He has published on various subjects. The recent ones include modelling counterfactual policies during the crisis (MIT Press) and contrasting the IMF's perspectives and alternative policies on the crisis.

Josep Jelahat is Assistant Lecturer at the Nusa Cendana University in Kupang, the capital of East Nusa Tenggara in eastern Indonesia. He has been extensively involved in various government-sponsored research projects throughout the province of East Nusa Tenggara.

Joyce Djaelani Gordon is a Psychologist, and founder of the Yayasan Harapan Permata Hati Kita (Yayasan KITA), a drug addiction and treatment recovery community based in Ciawi, Bogor, Indonesia. She has been actively involved in various health NGOs since 1984, including the Indonesian Planned Parenthood Association and Friends of Youth in Jakarta, as well as international NGOs such as Program for Appropriate Technology in Health (PATH), Project Concern International (PCI), CARE, WHO, and John Snow. She also teaches Social Intervention at Atmajaya University in Jakarta.

Linda Low is an Associate Professor in the Department of Business Policy, National University of Singapore. Her research interests and publications cover the political economy aspects in the Asia Pacific and ASEAN, on the subjects of trade, services, regionalism, human resource development, public sector economics, privatization, social security, and comparative economic development.

Maribeth Erb is an Associate Professor in the Department of Sociology, National University of Singapore. She has been doing research in western Flores since the early 1980s, and has been recently interested in the development of tourism there.

Muhadjir Darwin is the Director of the Master's Programme in Public Administration at Gadjah Mada University, Indonesia, and also a senior researcher at the Centre for Population and Policy Studies in the same university. His research interest focuses on violence against women and institutional improvement of local government.

Muhammad Chatib Basri is Associate Director for Research at the Institute of Economic and Social Research, Faculty of Economics, University of Indonesia. He is also a Lecturer in the Faculty of Economics, University of Indonesia. He has research interests in the area of international trade, macroeconomics, and political economy.

Nur Hadi Wiyono is Junior Researcher at the Demographic Institute, Faculty of Economics, University of Indonesia. He is also the managing editor of *Warta Demografi*, a bi-monthly magazine on population and development in Indonesia. His research interests include population mobility, child labour, and gender.

Riwanto Tirtosudarmo is Senior Research Fellow at the Centre for Social and Cultural Studies, Indonesian Institute of Sciences, Jakarta. He has published in both scientific and popular journals on the politics of population mobility in Indonesia. The latest publication is *The Geographic Mobility and the Emergence of Ethnic Politics in Indonesia* (forthcoming). He is currently conducting research on the political demography of ethnicity in Indonesia, and preparing a book *From Colonization to Nation State: The Political Demography of Indonesia.*

Santo Koesoebjono is a Research Fellow at the Netherlands Interdisciplinary Demographic Institute (NIDI). He is currently conducting research on international migration (Erasmus University/ University of Amsterdam). He also has research interests on ageing and the labour force.

Setiadi is a Lecturer at the Faculty of Cultural Science and Faculty of Geography, Gadjah Mada University, Indonesia. He is also a researcher at the Centre for Population and Policy Studies in the same university. His recent research interests include issues such as governance and decentralization, international migration, policy of internally displaced persons, and the impact of the economic crisis on rural people.

Solita Sarwono is currently assigned as a consultant in Indonesia in a World Bank project on health. Her main interests include gender training, women empowerment, education, reproductive health, and ageing.

Sri Harijati Hatmadji is Executive Secretary of the Ministry of Women Empowerment. She is also a Lecturer in the Faculty of Economics, University of Indonesia, and Senior Researcher at the Demographic Institute, Faculty of Economics, University of Indonesia. Her research interest is on gender and development.

Sukamdi is the Associate Director of the Centre for Population and Policy Studies at Gadjah Mada University, Indonesia, and has been very active in some professional organizations. His research interests cover issues such as governance and decentralization, informal sectors, population quality, and international migration.

Tirta Nugraha Mursitama is pursuing his Master's degree at the Graduate School of Management, Gakushin University in Tokyo, with specialization in Technology Management of Japanese Multinational Corporations. Before studying in Japan, he worked with the Tim Pengendali JPS [Team of Social Safety Net Monitoring] during the period 1997–2001.

Tubagus Feridhanusetyawan is a Senior Economist and Head of the Department of Economics at the Centre for Strategic and International Studies, Indonesia, and a Lecturer in the Post-Graduate Programme, University of Indonesia, as well as a Research Associate in the Division of Economics, Research School of Pacific and Asian Studies, Australian National University. His interests cover international economics, labour economics, and applied macroeconomics.

PART I

Introduction

1

WHAT DO WE LEARN FROM THE CRISIS?
Insights on Human Development in Indonesia during 1997–99

Aris Ananta

Introduction

Economic development can be seen simply as sustainable economic growth over a long period. This is the narrowest definition of economic development, often equivalent to the concept of economic growth, which emphasizes capital accumulation. Without high economic growth, no development of social issues such as education and health can take place. This narrow definition of economic development has a special advantage as it is relatively easy to measure the dynamics of national income.

Development can also be seen as structural and qualitative changes in the economy. Therefore, this concept of development covers not only monetary variables, but also social variables. Sen (1999) goes even further. He sees development as "a process of expanding the real freedoms that people enjoy". This freedom depends on variables such as gross national product (GNP), industrialization, and technological advance, but freedom also depends on other determinants such as social and political rights. However, it is not easy to measure this kind of development.

Since 1990, the United Nations Development Programme (UNDP) has advocated the concept of human development. In its *Human Development Report 1991*, it mentions that for a very long time the question had been centred on the growth of the economy. However, they argue that the question should focus rather on the welfare of the people.

Human development involves much more than national product. It aims to create an environment in which "people can develop their full potential and lead productive, creative lives in accord with their needs and interests" (UNDP, 2001). People are seen as the wealth of the nation and development is to expand the choices available to the people, thus giving them more freedom to choose. Economic growth is very important, but it is only one of the means of increasing freedom.

Every year the UNDP publishes a special report, with a different emphasis, on the progress of human development in all countries of the world. The UNDP recommends HDI (human development index) as a measurement of development, which is relatively easy to follow. HDI is defined as comprising human capital (measured by education and health) and purchasing power (measured by parity purchasing power). It suggests that HDI should replace the conventional way of measuring development, which is based on the dynamics of economic growth.

This volume follows the tradition of the UNDP, in seeing development from the point of view of human development. It is hoped that this will contribute to a better understanding of human development in Indonesia during 1997–99, in the early part of the Indonesian economic crisis. It is not within the scope of this book to show the impact of the crisis on human development. Neither is it to provide the most recent information on human development and the related issues. The period 1997–99 has been taken as a base because most of the data on that period are available, and hence a more thorough analysis can be carried out. This book has also been enriched by the variety of approaches used by the authors.

Part I provides an economic background to the discussion on human development and serves as an illustration of the conventional way of looking at development. Not only does it describe the overall current macroeconomic condition, but it also explains the long economic structural transformation occurring since the beginning of the New Order era. It also provides a quantitative simulation analysis, showing the social impact of the financial crisis.

Parts II and III enter the core of the discussion on human development, with Part II focusing on human capital and Part III on purchasing power. One feature of this volume is the broad treatment of the concept of human capital. It includes not only education and health, but also covers labour mobility and freedom from fear. The discussion on purchasing power focuses on the Social Safety Net programme which has been seen as a very important means to help the poor cope with the crisis. The discussion is preceded by a study of the change in urban consumer prices. Part III also examines what happened to the labour market, including the change in earnings and labour productivity.

With the rapidly changing situation in Indonesia, it is important to understand how human development has progressed in Indonesia within the emerging contextual settings. Part IV starts with a discussion on the business relationship between Indonesia and Singapore. Singapore is a small but rich country, and it has acted as an important linkage for Indonesian integration in the world market. The emerging lucrative business in illegal drugs is also discussed. Ironically, this business may have helped the recovery of the Indonesian economy. Following this discussion is the issue of old people, especially its impact on health and the economy, which is an emerging problem worth examining in the human development of Indonesia. Finally, the meaning of development itself is studied by looking at development experiences in Flores, a small island in Indonesia.

It is interesting that what happened during the Indonesian crisis has some similarities with what happened in the United States during the Great Depression in the 1930s. The degree may be different, but some lessons may be learned from the Great Depression to better understand the recent Indonesian crisis. In the next section of this chapter some features of the Great Depression which may resemble those during the recent Indonesian crisis are highlighted. Following this is a discussion on how the Indonesian people perceived the crisis, and the prospects of economic recovery. Next is a discussion on human capital; and purchasing power. Then follows an analysis of the emerging contextual settings before the chapter closes with a recommendation on "people-centred development".

The chapter concludes that, as during the Great Depression, the recent Indonesian crisis may simply aggravate the already precarious situation. Yet, as also in the Great Depression, the suffering is perhaps not as dramatic as some people (both Indonesians and non-Indonesians) may have perceived it. It is ironic that, similar to the war during the Great Depression, it is possible that the money spent on controlling riots and chaos as well as leakage from various programmes might have facilitated the recovery of the Indonesian economy. However, this kind of recovery does not contribute to people-centred development, which puts the quality of people's lives as the object of development and treats income as simply one of the means of improving the quality of life. Yet, with the experiences of the Great Depression and East Asia before its rapid growth, the current gloomy and uncertain situation in Indonesia does not necessarily mean dim prospects for a peaceful and prosperous Indonesia in the future.

Finally, more work should follow this study on human development during the crisis. The crisis has taught a very important lesson: that it is not easy to provide a prescription for the prevention of a crisis, but even more difficult, one for development.

The Great Depression

> Poverty and insecurity are painful enough even to one accustomed to them from childhood: but when a person suddenly and almost without warning finds himself thrust from comfort and self-sufficiency into need and the arms of charity, an immeasurably worse shock ensues.
>
> ... the catastrophic banking situation, the shattered moral and nation-wide fear. Everybody was panicked and hoarding. The prevailing hardship had caused strikes, riots, communist propaganda and frustration on the industrial system. Violence occurred in both urban rural areas. Some demonstration had resulted in death and injuries. Attacks on civil liberty were mounting, directed particularly against communists, African Americans, aliens, and strikers. Some meetings were broken up, prohibited; demonstrators were arrested, and strikers were suppressed by violence (Enzler 1939).

The above may sound like a description of the current Indonesian crisis. But Hill (1988) wrote:

> ..., the world was a very uncertain place in the 1930s. For many, any hope of economic recovery appeared uncertain. Revolution, war, and other forms of significant social transformation were all thought quite likely. The very core of Western society was challenged and the challenge was an enduring one.

Indeed, the three paragraphs describe some conditions during the Great Depression in the 1930s.

Furthermore, Kennedy (1999) has shown that the Great Depression resulted in many Americans, in particular the farmers, African Americans, and recent immigrants, having to live at subsistence level. Yet, for those people, the Depression was simply another ordeal of fear and security that they had experienced before.

Woodward (1999) wrote:

> At wages of $1 a day miners subsisted on a diet suggesting that of domestic animals. Emaciated children who never tasted mild wandered the streets, some shoeless in winter, too poorly clad to go to school. Milch cows dried up for lack of feed, and starving horses dropped in

> their harness. More surprising than the people's despair was their prevailing submissiveness.

Nevertheless, Kennedy wrote that the Great Depression only made many Americans a little harder than usual. Poverty was already endemic long before the start of the Great Depression. Even during the boom period of the 1920s, about forty million Americans, consisting of virtually all non-Whites, most of them elderly, and the majority of the rural population, had to eke out a very low subsistence life.

He concluded that the Great Depression was not simply a crisis, but it also revealed the fundamental structural inequalities in American society before the Great Depression. The old and poor were among the hardest hit by the Depression, but it is wrong to conclude that the Depression had caused them to suffer. The Depression simply aggravated the already precarious condition.

The newly poor also suffered much during the Great Depression. They were the white-collar classes who had enjoyed prosperity during the boom. Suddenly, they slipped from security, self-sufficiency, and pride to uncertainty, dependency, and shame.

Interestingly, the Great Depression in the United States, which started in 1929, began to end during World War II (1942–45). During the war, the Depression was only a distant, painful memory for many Americans on the home front. The war provided jobs for the decade-long unemployed labour force; it also created 3.25 million jobs for the new entrants (half of them women) to the labour force. These new entrants would not have joined the labour force during peacetime.

> I felt like something had come down from heaven. I went from forty cents an hour to a dollar an hour... At the end of the war I was making two seventy-five an hour... I couldn't believe my good fortune... I was able to buy some working clothes for a change, buy suit... It just made a different man out of me... After all the hardships of the Depression, the war completely turned my life around (a shipyard labourer in Portsmouth, Virginia, as cited by Kennedy [1999], p. 644).

Indeed, Kennedy also maintained that the war had created a consumer's paradise. Franklin Roosevelt, the then President of the United States, warned that the country could not afford to sustain the growing economy from the war production; yet, what the United States did was to expand military production. Fortunately, because of the many unutilized resources during the Depression, the military production was not done at the expense of civilian production. Military production increased together with civilian production. At the end of the 1930s, almost 90 per cent of Black families and nearly half of White families were still living in poverty. About 14 per cent of the labour force was unemployed. After the war, almost nobody was unemployed.

The huge expenditure for the war-related production was consistent with the Keynesian view that large government spending would increase aggregate demand and hence improve the economy, regardless of the "utility" of the spending. The act of spending itself was good for the recovery of the economy from the prolonged and deep depression. Kennedy described that in the following twenty-five years after the war, the American economy created about twenty million new jobs. In less than a generation, the number of people belonging to the middle class more than doubled. The war had really changed the American people. It had brought back and even rapidly boosted economic welfare.

The Indonesian Crisis

During the boom period before the crisis some people enjoyed prosperity and had rising expectations. They had many plans for the years ahead. Suddenly and unexpectedly, they faced a dramatic crisis. They might have talked about poverty before, but they had never experienced being poor. Then, they experienced being poor, though in absolute terms they were still better off than subsistence level. However, they suffered a sudden dramatic drop in their relative welfare, and they did not know when this declining situation would end. It was like riding a roller-coaster without knowing when it would stop. These people mostly belonged to the élite, such as academicians, politicians, bureaucrats, business people, journalists, and people who worked in the non-governmental organizations (NGOs). They had a political voice and now they talked about poverty.

The above paragraph could best describe the crisis situation in Indonesia, especially in the first year (August 1997 until July 1998). Papanek and Handoko (1999) observe that it was the first time since the 1960s that the Indonesian middle class had been hit so hard. They posit that the large drop in welfare in such a short time could create a politically dangerous situation for the government. The drop in welfare, happening especially after a long, steady, booming economy, had destroyed most of their aspirations.

Cameron (1999) also supports the thesis that the upper income group had suffered the largest percentage drop in welfare. Using a simulation model, Azis (Chapter 4) has shown how the financial crisis hit the urban households, especially the rich, the hardest. Yet, the persistently high interest rates may have benefited the middle and high-income groups. He also found that the levelling of the consumption pattern had helped people to cope with the crisis.

Using a nation-wide quick survey in 1998, Sumarto, Wetterberg, and Pritchett (1999) have similarly found that there was no association between pre-crisis poverty and the severity of the crisis. Many regions which had been relatively rich had also been hard hit but they did not reach the level of absolute poverty, or of the traditionally poor areas. They found that the impact was more an urban phenomenon.

Kutanegara (1998) found that in Srihardjo (Central Java), it was the middle and upper classes who complained much about the crisis. The lower classes, who might have suffered more in absolute terms, was more quiet. Sukamdi and Setiadi (Chapter 11) describe people in rural Central Java as more accepting of the recent crisis because it was not something new for them. They already had the coping mechanism for such a crisis.

In 1998, in a village in Jatinom, Central Java, Indonesia, a respondent said

> "*Padha bae... sithik dicakake sithik, okeh dicakake okeh*" (It is no difference. When we have little, we consume little; when we have a lot, we consume a lot.) (Abdullah 1998, as cited in Sukamdi and Setiadi in Chapter 11).

The crisis started in August 1997 as a financial one. Until November 1997, the situation was still similar to that in other countries, such as Korea and Thailand. However, from December 1997 until May 1998, the financial crisis turned into a social, political, and economic crisis. By June 1998, it was a total crisis. The economic decline had been so rapid that there was a complete loss of confidence. For example, in mid-January 1998, when the rupiah declined rapidly to 10,000 per U.S. dollar, the middle-class flooded the markets buying everything, especially rice, cooking oil, milk, sugar, and noodles. The month of January 1998 also witnessed a massive bank run when people tried to withdraw their money from the banks. During June-December 1998, social and political problems became more pronounced than economic problems (Feridhanusetyawan 2000). The economy then hit bottom, to the 1995 level, in the last three quarters of 1998 (McLeod 2000).

Yet, from the structure of production and employment and, in particular, manufacturing and trade sectors, Basri (Chapter 3) has found few early warning signs during the pre-crisis period. The structural changes in the economy before the crisis had been consistent with the general (stylized) facts. He has concluded that there is little evidence that the pre-crisis structural changes led to the crisis.

In general, during the first two years of the crisis, there were two extreme views about the crisis, especially at the beginning. Mubyarto (2000), as cited in Sukamdi and Setiadi (Chapter 11), mentioned the existence of these two views. The first was that it was "not that bad". People, especially among the middle and lower-income classes, were still having an attitude of "business as usual". Both the traditional and modern markets were as crowded as before the crisis. Traffic was still bad, or worse, indicating the "busy" activities of the people.

The second was the doomsday view, which saw the situation as catastrophic and devastating. This was usually macroeconomic and financial in nature. The *rupiah* had dropped drastically, prices of goods had skyrocketted, the banking system had collapsed, a huge number of workers had lost their jobs, and incomes had declined dramatically. Policy recommendations, including those from the International Monetary Fund (IMF), may have led to this doomsday scenario.

Not surprisingly, with the doomsday view, estimates produced in early 1998 were very pessimistic. The International Labour Organization (ILO), for example, estimated that 50 per cent of the Indonesian population lived below the poverty line in 1998. The Indonesian Central Board of Statistics revealed an estimate of 39 per cent in mid-1998, much higher than the 11 per cent in 1996. If the estimates were correct, the situation in 1998 would have resembled Indonesia in the 1970s. It would have been a dramatic increase from 17.7 per cent in 1996.

Later data, however, show that there were only 24.2 per cent of the population living below the poverty line in December 1998. This was an increase but not as much as estimated earlier. It even declined to 18.17 per cent in August 1999 (Badan Pusat Statistik, 2000), and 15.2 per cent in February 2001.[1]

The macroeconomic situation had also been predicted to be dreadful: the economy would contract by 20 per cent and the inflation rate would reach 100 per cent in 1998 (Hill 1998). It turned out that the economy contracted by only 13.8 per cent and the inflation rate was only 77.63 per cent. The situation in 1998 was very bad, but not as bad as had been estimated earlier.

In early 1998, ILO (1998), in its foreword, also provided an informed guess that unemployment would be more than 20 per cent in 1998. However, the ILO task-force estimated that it would be 10.0 per cent, lower than the estimates provided by the Ministry of Manpower (14.8 per cent) and BAPPENAS (13.6 per cent). Later data (Badan Pusat Statistik 2000) show that the actual rate was only 4.68 per cent in 1997.

It rose a little to 5.46 per cent in 1998, and 6.39 per cent in 1999. It should be noted, however, that the unemployment rate cannot be used as a measure of poverty or of the economic crisis in Indonesia. In a country such as Indonesia, where there is no unemployment benefit/ insurance and the importance of the informal sector is still substantial, the unemployment rate tends to be small. The rising unemployment rate may imply that people can better afford to be unemployed. Indeed, the rate had been rising during the boom period, 1990–95.

Policy-makers had also projected a nightmare scenario for education. As mentioned by Hartono and Ehrman (Chapter 7), in early 1998 both the Ministry of Education and the BAPPENAS (National Board of Development Planning) had agreed that the impact of the crisis on education was very severe. The Ministry of Education projected that the enrolment rates would decline from 72 per cent in 1997/98 to 57 per cent in 2001/02 for junior secondary schools, and from 40 per cent to 23 per cent for senior secondary schools. The results were much better than that feared by the government and lending agencies. Hartono and Ehrman show that there was no significant drop in the enrolment rate.

The panic also brought on much concern over the social aspects of the crisis. Sukamdi and Setiadi (Chapter 11) show how the government then tried to introduce some breakthrough programmes to cope with the problem of poverty caused by the crisis, while Ananta and Siregar (1999) has described how the social programme was one of the major causes of fiscal burden during the crisis. Mubyarto (2000), cited in Sukamdi and Setiadi, has argued that the inaccuracy in the estimation led to the doomsday view, reflected by the panic attitude among experts, policy-makers, and people in the international donor agencies.

Economic Recovery

As shown by Panggabean (Chapter 2), Indonesia has started its economic recovery since 1999. After a growth rate of minus 13.0 per cent in 1998, the market expected the gross domestic product (GDP) growth rate to be still negative in 1999. It turned out that it rose 0.9 per cent. The market made another underestimation of economic growth in the year 2000. In early 2000, it predicted that growth would be only 3.0 per cent, but it turned out to be 4.8 per cent for the year. Surrounded by global recession and uncertainty, Indonesia managed a growth rate of 3.3 per cent in 2001. It was the second highest growth rate in the Asia-Pacific, after China.

Panggabean maintains that the main engines of growth in 2000 were the commerce and manufacturing sectors. The growth had been pushed by both private consumption and investment. Soesastro (2001) has argued that the recovery was initially contributed by the rise in domestic consumption and followed by the rise in exports. Investments had also risen. However, all of them were small-scale industries and the crisis had not destroyed the infrastructure of these small industries. The recovery was also characterized by the emergence of new entrepreneurs in small enterprises with low risks. These enterprises had actually existed in Indonesia for a long time, but they had been overshadowed by the "bright" and "big" businesses. On the other hand, the recovery of the sick economy also depends much on government involvement. The management of this "sick" economy is politically sensitive.

These small-scale businesses are what Soesastro calls healthy industries, as opposed to the "sick" industries in Indonesia. The healthy industries are those which do not depend much on the government and financial institutions. They have been growing rapidly in recent years and have been the main drivers of the economic recovery in Indonesia. These industries operate mostly on cash, that is, personal savings, and use almost no banking facilities. They are mostly small and medium-sized firms.

Soesastro (2002) has also shown the dynamics and resilience of Indonesian society during the year 2001. He has noted the continuous expansion of retail space, sale of cars and motor-cycles, renovation of office space, and a mini-boom in small and medium housing estates.

In the labour market, Manning (2000) has found that labour has been adjusting better than expected. He observes that the labour market leans more towards the neo-classical model, with flexible real wages. Real wages have declined sharply as a result of a rapid rise in price levels. The existence of the informal sector and agriculture, with flexible wages, has resulted in a better adjustment of the labour market in Indonesia.

However, there has also been a rising trend away from the neo-classical model in the labour market. The implementation of regional autonomy since the beginning of 2001 has motivated regional labour unions to demand higher minimum wages. Feridhanusetyawan (2001) has noted that the minimum wage has increased very rapidly, at about 26 per cent nationally during 2000–01. Furthermore, the increase in real wages has surpassed the increase in labour productivity. Based on some qualitative studies, the SMERU team (2001) has concluded that the enforcement of the minimum wage policy has benefited white-collar workers much more than blue-collar workers.

The continuous increase in minimum wage may endanger business in the formal sector. The slowing down of business in the formal sector will result in an increasing flow to the informal sector and depress earnings in the informal sector.

Soesastro (2001) has observed an emerging phenomenon of the decoupling of the economy from politics. Business goes on as usual, seemingly paying no attention to the political fighting and "security threats". Nevertheless, he has also concluded that Indonesia's economic recovery may still be fragile.

The Social Safety Net scheme, with the heavy inflow of international loans to Indonesia, may have significantly boosted domestic demand although the output may not necessarily have reached the target. The spending, the outpouring of money itself, may be "good" for the economy. It may be similar to the "benefit" of war, which ended the Great Depression in the United States.

Human Capital

In this volume, human capital is given a broader treatment, covering more than health and education. Elements such as labour mobility and freedom from fear are also included. Labour mobility is seldom discussed in the context of human capital development. However, labour mobility can also be seen as an investment in human capital (Sjaastad 1962; and Becker 1964). The ability to be mobile expands the human capacity of an individual. By being mobile, people are able to find better jobs and better places of residence, and therefore improve their welfare. Restrictions on mobility may therefore hinder the development of human capital.

In addition to the three elements of human capital, Djajanegara and Ananta (1986) have argued that "freedom from fear" is another important aspect of human capital. The feeling of fear can reduce the individual's capacity to produce. Similar to being healthy, being educated, and being able to move, freedom from fear is embedded in each individual, though it can be much affected by the surrounding. The terrifying and threatening situation in Indonesia in mid-1998 is just an example of how the surroundings might have implanted the feeling of fear among individuals. Ananta (2001) has argued that Indonesia should strive towards a "freedom-from-fear based economy", where "freedom from fear" should be counted as a public good, enjoyed by all, including the poor. With the absence of fear, people will be able to work more productively. Financial assistance may not be as important for small and medium-sized businesses as assistance in creating an environment that is free from fear, which may help them to grow in a healthy way. Large businesses may hire their own "security guards" to provide such as an environment, but the medium and especially small-sized firms do not have that luxury.

Kearney (2001) has reported that *preman* (gangster and thugs) controlled some day-to-day activities in Jakarta. They controlled almost all the major markets and bus stations. Some were harmless, merely collecting fees for directing the traffic. Others, however, forced stallholders to pay protection money. The stallholders had to pay protection money to various *preman* gangs, who visited them on a regular basis.

Darwin (Chapter 5) describes the riots that have taken place in Indonesia since the day of independence, in 1945. During the 1998–2000 period, riots increased both quantitatively and qualitatively. Indonesia did not experience a war during the crisis, but there were many sporadic riots and fighting, and even continuous internal wars in some regions, such as Maluku, Aceh, Papua, and East Timor. (Since 1999, East Timor has been no longer a part of Indonesia, but fighting has continued in west Timor.)

The turmoil was triggered by political disputes and religious fanaticism, ethnic or regional. At the same time, law enforcement has been weak. These riots have killed many people and caused much damage. Political fighting among élites since the fall of President Soeharto in 1998 has been escalating. All of these have involved large amounts of money, not necessarily from the government's budget or even planned by the government. They could stem from different opposing groups. Yuwono Sudarsono, a former Minister of Defence, believes that fighters coming to the war-torn Maluku island were recruited from the large pool of people with very low levels of earning. He said:

> If you have the money, you can always instigate or foment a demonstration, whether it's for two hours or two days, two weeks or two months (Chew 2000)

It is worth pondering here whether the riots and all the fighting among the political élites have created employment opportunities and how much they have contributed to the recovery. Indonesia is fortunate in that the chaos and riots were not nationally widespread. They were limited and concentrated in some parts of the region. Destruction can be seen in the affected areas, but the majority (not in the victim areas) might have enjoyed the impact of employment opportunities resulting from the chaos and riots. Further studies should be pursued on this issue.

It is also interesting to note that the threat of security usually alarms foreign investors, but does not necessarily deter domestic entrepreneurs. For the majority of domestic entrepreneurs, especially those with small and medium-sized firms, there may be no other choice than to continue their business. They cannot move abroad. They do not know how to do business outside Indonesia. Domestic entrepreneurs cannot afford to be put off by domestic politics. Some people may not care about politics and others may even ask: "Is there a crisis?"

The next crucial element of human capital is health. This is not limited to curative health, but includes preventive and promotive aspects. From the perspective of these aspects of health, an increase in national income through higher spending in the health sector may not necessarily be good for the economy. For example, growth in the pharmaceutical industry because of the rising number of sick people does not necessarily indicate that the health of the society is getting better. Human development gives a higher score to a healthy society, although the national income may be lower. In the long run, an economy with healthy people will be sustainable. Therefore, Indonesia should work towards a "health-based economy".

In terms of both infant and child mortality, Indonesia has been performing relatively well. Though there have not been any statistics on infant and child mortality during the crisis, Ananta and Kosen (2000) have speculated that the crisis had no effect on child and infant mortality. At least, they argue, the rates have not risen, except in the riot-torn areas, such as Aceh and Maluku.

On the other hand, Budi Utomo (Chapter 6) argues that the crisis has worsened the already deteriorating health status in Indonesia. A higher incidence of Vitamin A deficiency, as an illustration, has been seen during the crisis. Since early 1990, long before the start of the crisis, the health status in Indonesia had been declining. For example, one in three two-year-old children were underweight by an average of two kilograms, and stunted by five to seven centimetres. About half of the Indonesian children under five suffered from "hidden hunger" deficiencies of micronutrients, including Vitamin A, iron, and zinc.

Through the SSN (Social Safety Net) programme, the government has paid special attention to the health sector. In this chapter, Budi Utomo reveals the problems of implementing the SSN in general, and in the health sector in particular. The fund was distributed directly to the health providers at subdistrict and village levels, but they were not professionally ready to administer the fund for the needy. Most of them did not know what to do with the fund. Worse, there was a lack of co-ordination among related sectors and implementing organizations.

Education is the next crucial element in human capital. With better education, society will be more informed on what is happening around them, in the regions, as well as the global society. A knowledge-based economy is not simply one with a large proportion of its people having high skills; but it is also an economy where people are aware of what is happening around them. All agents of the economy must have as much information about the market as possible. Information should not be the privilege of those who have money. The government of Indonesia should work towards providing information for the poor so that they too can compete in the national, regional, and even global market.

Djoko Hartono and David Ehrmann (Chapter 7) show that there was no significant drop in enrolment in primary and junior secondary schools during the first three years of the crisis (1997/98, 1998/99, and 1999/2000). In fact, the enrolment in senior secondary schools has increased. Unlike in the health sector, they conclude that the scholarship and grants programmes introduced during the crisis by the government have helped to stem the decline in enrolment. However, it should be noted that Java and Bali experienced a decline in enrolment, but the rest of Indonesia has seen an increase in enrolment. Some shifts have been observed from private schools to public schools in the urban areas, and from general to Islamic schools in the rural areas.

Hugo (2000) has described how Indonesians have been increasingly using labour mobility as a means to find better job opportunities, both inside and outside the country. Therefore, it is reasonable to say that they used this mobility as one way to cope with the crisis. They moved to areas where the impact of the crisis was not as severe, or even to areas which benefited from the crisis.

Therefore, labour mobility may improve the well-being of those who are moving. However, migrants are usually the selected few from society. They have a relatively higher entrepreneurship spirit than those who do not move. These migrants then come to new areas and compete with the local people. It is not surprising that these newcomers often win in the competition with the locals. If the newcomers have different cultural, ethnic, and religious backgrounds from the local people, potential conflicts are likely to emerge.

Tirtosudarmo (Chapter 8) argues that the ethnic plurality and archipelagic geography of Indonesia have made labour mobility a very important element in the modernization of the country. However, the relationship between migrants and locals are not always harmonious. Sporadic incidents of social tensions and conflicts have been observed for a long time in Indonesia. During the crisis, Indonesia saw rampant ethnic and religious conflicts. Historically, the situation after the crisis may be the turning point of population mobility, when people start migrating (returning) from outside Java to Java. Ethnic mobility seems to have played an important role in the resurgence of politics of identity, as it has produced an atmosphere of uncertainty in the current political system, the realization of democracy, and civil society in Indonesia.

Purchasing Power

One of the most feared impacts of the crisis is the decline in real incomes, or purchasing power of the people, which is made up of both price and income. Because this volume is concerned with people as consumers, the discussion on purchasing power is focused on consumers, rather than producers. It first discusses changes in consumer prices in Indonesia during 1997–99. Owing to scarcity of data, Ananta, Kartowibowo, and Wiyono (Chapter 9) concentrate their analysis on changes in prices in the big cities of Indonesia. Another reason for the concentration on urban areas is that studies, such as that by Sumarto, Wetterberg, and Pritchett (1999), have shown that the crisis may be more an urban phenomenon.

They examine which urban consumers have suffered more. For example, the price of a simple lunch in the canteen in the University of Indonesia was 1,000 rupiah in June 1997, but became 2,500 rupiah in June 2000 — having increased by 150 per cent. On the other hand, the price of a "Kijang" (a relatively cheap family car) was 60 million rupiah in June 1977 and 120 million rupiah in June 2000, having increased by only 100 per cent. To buy a "Kijang" in 1997, people had to sacrifice 60 thousand simple lunches, but only 48 thousand simple lunches in 2000. In other words, relative to the simple lunch, the "Kijang" had become cheaper. Therefore, those whose budget was spent on simple lunches may have suffered more than those whose budget was spent on buying a "Kijang".

Using data on the consumer price index, they find that the impact of the creeping price was not much at the end of 1997. However, 1998 was strikingly different from 1997. Prices had risen rapidly. The year 1998 was the worst year of the crisis, but prices became more stable during 1999. The increase in price ranged from 35 per cent to minus 20 per cent in 1999, much lower than the maximum increase of 160 per cent and no decline in prices during 1998. Yet, it is difficult to say, for example, whether those who consumed "meat, fish, and eggs" had suffered relatively more than those who consumed "nuts, vegetables, and fruits". The pattern varies from one city to another.

One general pattern, however, exists in the comparison of trends in the prices of human capital (measured by education and health only) and the prices of food (including prepared food). The price of human capital has not risen as much as the increase in the price of food. The people whose budget is largely spent on food might have suffered more than those who spent more on human capital.

On the other hand, through personal observations in Jakarta they observed that those who worked in a more modern environment had suffered much. Their "quality of life" had declined. For example, an office worker in Jakarta (with a *sarjana* degree, equivalent to a Bachelor's degree) used to buy *Kompas* daily (a leading newspaper in Indonesia) and *Tempo* (a leading news magazine in Indonesia). *Kompas* cost 500 rupiah and *Tempo* 5,000 rupiah before the crisis. Then *Kompas* was priced at 1,500 rupiah, a 200 per cent increase, and *Tempo* at 10,000, a 100 per cent increase, during the crisis. She stopped buying both. She also changed her "lunch pattern." She then brought her own lunch, instead of buying lunch. She was fortunate because she breastfed her baby. Her neighbour, who did not breastfeed her baby, had suffered much more because of the rising prices of baby foods (including milk).

The second element of purchasing power is the income of the consumers. The crisis has prompted both policy-makers and international donor agencies to initiate programmes to help the people cope with the crisis. Hatmadji and Musitama (Chapter 10) discuss the Social Safety Net programme, which was created by the Indonesian Government to help reduce the "severe" social impact of the crisis. With funding from the World Bank and the IMF, the programme was started in fiscal year 1998/99. Announced in a presidential speech in front of the Parliament (DPR) on 15 August 1998, the SSN was meant to integrate special development programmes for reducing the impact of the crisis with the regular development programme to correct disparity, poverty, and backwardness. In the short run, the programme was supposed to be a rescue effort, to safeguard the people's consumption. In the long run, it is seen as a recovery programme, focusing on productive activities to bring the people's welfare back to the pre-crisis level.

Drawing on the experiences of many countries which have implemented the SSN programme, Graham (1994) has concluded that the implementation of this programme is strongly influenced by domestic politics, especially during an economic crisis which also involves political changes.

To whom should the money be given? Ideally, the money must go to the poor. However, the poorest and most vulnerable group in society are usually also those with the "poorest" political voice. Thus, their welfare carries little weight in political calculations. The sudden decline of welfare for those who were previously better off (before the crisis), but who may not be poor during the crisis, can be more important to the government because this group can be more vocal. Because of its political influence, this group may also refuse to take up jobs with lower pay. Furthermore, reaching the poorest and most vulnerable is also frequently more difficult, technically. The government may also pay more attention to those who are just a little below the poverty line. Helping them will reduce the number of people below the poverty line. This allocation may not be cost-effective, but it can be politically more feasible.

Subbarao et al (1997), also utilizing lessons from many countries, have provided an illustration of the politics involved in implementing SSN programmes. Public work usually has much political interest. Politicians may use the opportunity to garner support from certain groups, while bureaucrats may be threatened with losing their "power" over the programme to other agencies — which often implies that the bureaucrats may have to sacrifice opportunities to get more earnings. Furthermore, if the targetted groups — that is, the poor or the very poorest — are vocal or supported by vocal groups, they may refuse to do public work with lower wages although the low wages may be economically sufficient to revive the local economy, especially among themselves.

Subbarao et al. has also shown that many new public programmes were introduced just before the presidential election. Public works might have been implemented just to convince supporters that the newly elected government really would fulfil its promises made during the campaign period. Public works are also often implemented during times of social unrest.

It should be noted here that the ability of the government to campaign for the programme would determine its success, both in targetting at the poor and securing political support. Without such skill, an excellent programme might incite public protest, and even riots.

Hatmadji and Mursitama have concluded that the SSN programme in Indonesia is an illustration of a confusing and complicated social policy of the government, supported by international loans. They opined that the government, the Parliament, universities, and NGOs had not been prepared to carry out this emergency programme. A "project mentality" may have caused some "leakage" during the implementation of the programme.

However, despite the weaknesses, they argue that the SSN programme has been able to alleviate the poor people affected by the crisis. It has helped them to cope with the crisis. After two years of implementation, the programme has been shifted to the National Movement for Poverty Alleviation, a long-term strategy to fight poverty.

On another side, between 10 per cent and 14 per cent of the loans to the SSN programme may have been corrupted.[2] Sumarto, Suryahadi, and Widyanti (2001) found that a large number of poor had not received help from the programme. Instead, a high percentage of the funds had reached the non-poor. It is ironic that these leakages may have done something "desired", though not planned. The money which did not reach the poor had been used by those with a higher level of income, and therefore was likely to have been spent more on luxury goods. In turn, this could have induced the rising demand for such goods and services. These leakages might have been one of the contributing factors for the recovery in 1999, and hence might have indirectly helped to reduce poverty.

Though describing only the people in Central Java and Yogyakarta, Sukamdi and Setiadi (Chapter 11) try to show a different perspective of the suffering of the people during the crisis. The low-income group seemed to adjust better to the crisis. On the other hand, the intervention of the government (especially through the SSN programme) seemed to give the impression that the people were overwhelmed by the crisis and were not being fairly treated. An image was created that the people were poor and hence had to be helped — they had to receive charity. The programme thus produced a feeling of dependence among the people.

Sukamdi and Setiadi also question the notion of the vulnerability of the society during the crisis in rural Yogyakarta and Central Java. They show the difference in perception between the government and the society about the crisis. They describe the financial resilience of the rural people in Yogyakarta and Central Java. Yet, the programmes designed to "help" these people resulted in new problems in the form of social poverty. This social poverty had not been seen before the crisis because the poor people had always found ways to cope.

Using statistical data from the Central Board of Statistics, Feridhanusetyawan (Chapter 12) shows that the crisis had reduced real wages in the formal sector. Real wages declined by 34.2 per cent during 1997–98. The purchasing power in 1998 was equivalent to that in 1989/99, implying that the one-year crisis had wiped out the progress made in the previous seven years. Yet, people did not seem to reduce their consumption much; they used their savings to finance their consumption. Real wages rose 10.5 per cent in 1999, though this was still 27.2 per cent lower than that in 1997. On the other hand, he also shows that labour productivity declined by 1.1 per cent in 1999, and 14.7 per cent during 1997–99.

The year 1998, the worst time of the crisis, also witnessed a reversal from formalization to informalization, from urbanization to ruralization, and from industrialization to "agriculturalization". However, as pointed out by Ferdihanusetyawan, this reversal did not last long. The 1999 data indicated movement out from the informal sector, from the rural areas, and from agriculture.

It is also important to point out that open unemployment did not change much during the crisis. It rose from 4.7 per cent in 1997 to 5.5 per cent in 1998, and 6.4 per cent in 1999. The unemployment rate in Indonesia has always been low, but this rate is not necessarily positively correlated with poverty. Indeed, it may be negatively correlated with poverty.

There is no unemployment benefit/insurance, and hence, it is a luxury to be unemployed. Before 1990, the rates were less than 3 per cent. In other words, the change (or the rise) in unemployment rate is not an indicator of rising poverty in Indonesia. On the other hand, the rising unemployment rate may reflect an increasing rate of the labour force who could still afford to be unemployed. Good severance pay, the SSN programme, previous income, or help from friends and relatives may explain the rising unemployment rate.

Indonesia defines underemployment as including those who work less than 35 hours a week, regardless of whether they still need additional income or not. This rate does not reflect poverty, because "Who can afford working less than 35 hours a week?" Those who have good severance pay, high earnings per hour, personal wealth and previous income, or good financial support from spouses/ relatives, and friends may have enabled them to be underemployed. Being underemployed is a luxury, but not as luxurious as being openly unemployed.

During the "informalization" period mentioned before, it was difficult to "force' people to work less during 35 hours. It was more likely that they voluntarily worked less then 35 hours a week. Therefore, Badan Pusat Statistik (2000) has used a new method to estimate underemployment. They focus on those who work less than 35 hours a week and are still looking for other jobs.

As shown by Feridhanusetyawan, the so-defined underemployment decreased from 11.96 per cent in 1997 to 9.28 per cent in 1998, and rose to 12.63 per cent in 1999. The decrease in underemployment in 1998 may reflect the worst time of the crisis. People became less able to afford being underemployed. They attempted to work longer to compensate for the declining real earnings per hour. The small decline in 1999 was also consistent with the start of the recovery of the Indonesian economy, when people were better able to afford being underemployed.

Emerging Contextual Issues

In Part IV some emerging contextual issues are presented, which may have important implications on human development in Indonesia. The first is the importance of the relationship between Indonesia and Singapore. Low (Chapter 13) argues that Indonesia and Singapore cannot avoid globalization, new technology, and the new economy. The partnership between the big and small countries can benefit each other if interest is developed from both the private sector and the governments. The two countries have to establish confidence in working with each other before they can find other alliances. More knowledge and information on each other are important ingredients in fostering the relationship between the two countries. Yet, this relationship can only be built through the participation from the bottom, rather than simply relying on the initiatives of the political leaders and bureaucrats.

Low argues that Indonesia and Singapore can be a dynamic duo for two reasons. Firstly, because Singapore is relatively diminutive compared with Indonesia, its ability to help drive the Indonesian economy will be enhanced by bigger economies such as the United States. Secondly, Indonesia and Singapore should see their relationship as a positive sum game. They should try to diminish the stigma of a big but less developed Indonesia and a rich but arrogant Singapore.

The next important emerging issue is the illegal drug problem. In addition to its impact on health, its economic impact can be tremendous. The spending on these activities can in itself be a very lucrative business. Gordon and Gordon (Chapter 14) describe how the crisis has spurred the drug business. The illegal drug market has been a multi-million dollar business each day. With this conservative estimate, the amount of money circulating through the drug business can reach about 18,750 million rupiah per day. If their analysis is valid, then illegal drug activities may have helped the recovery of the economy. It is not impossible that this activity can be one of the determinants of the "buoyant" economy in Indonesia since 1999.

The next issue to be considered is demographic change. Indonesia's population used to be dominated by the young but it is now gradually ageing. Though it has not been as problematic as in the advanced countries, the ageing phenomenon will become more and more serious and a relevant contextual issue in Indonesia's development. Koesoebjono and Sarwono (Chapter 15) cite the experiences of the advanced countries and compare them with the limited experience of Indonesia to anticipate issues arising from an ageing population. They find paradoxes on this issue. On one hand, an increasing number and percentage of old people may mean a rising financial burden for society. These people no longer contribute to the economy but they still consume. They are therefore a burden to society. On the other hand, they can be used as reserve labour during labour shortages.

Indonesians want to continue respecting the elderly, but the proportion of the national budget spent on children under five years is still much higher than that spent on the elderly. Young people often leave their aged parents and pay little attention to their welfare. There are also cultural and institutional barriers to sending old people to institutions for the aged, despite the rising numbers of such care centres.

Overall, the rising number and percentage of old people in the population will change the condition of human development in Indonesia. The question of freedom from fear, health, education, population mobility, and purchasing power will soon have to be addressed with regard to the changing age composition of the population.

People-Centred Development

Erb and Jelahat (Chapter 16) reflect on their experiences while living and observing development in Flores, a small island in the eastern part of Indonesia, not far from East Timor. What they experienced may not represent what has happened in Indonesia as a whole; it only describes the experience in the "periphery" of Indonesia. Yet, their experiences are worth sharing.

They question the concept of economic growth as a measurement of development and suggest that Indonesia should not return to growth-oriented development. The policy for recovery from the crisis should not be measured by growth only. Otherwise, Indonesia will make the same mistake that it made before the crisis.

Indeed, as shown in this chapter, the growth rate of the Indonesian economy has been relatively good. Its performance was the second best in the Asia-Pacific during 2001. Soesastro (2002) has argued that

Indonesia has achieved recovery without any reform, and therefore the recovery may not be sustainable.

Erb and Jelahat recommend a sustainable economy based on local autonomy and community participation, instead of focusing on foreign investment and economic growth. They provide many "stories" from the field on how development had progressed in the thirty years before the crisis; and what hidden costs (including social costs) development had produced

The transmigration programme, to move people from Java to outside Java to help industrialization there, is just an example. It has produced environmental damage and ignored the rights of the local people. The same thing has happened in mining, logging, plantation, and tourism projects. All of these activities, indeed, have helped to produce growth, without giving attention to the social costs of the local residents.

Agriculture grew rapidly during the New Order period, when Indonesia advanced from an importer of rice at the beginning of the period to self-sufficiency in rice in the period 1979–85. However, what happened to individual farmers during this time was ignored. The success resulted in the pauperization of many land-holders, who were later forced to leave agriculture. The percentage of landlessness in Java rose 16 per cent during 1963–83, creating cheap labour for industrialization. Farmers became the captive supply of labour for the government through the village co-operative, the Koperasi Unit Desa (KUD). The KUD was supposed to be the safety net for the villagers during bad harvests. In fact, the KUD was used by corrupt officials, who forced farmers to sell their products to the KUD. As a result, some farmers moved to the urban areas to work for businesses whose products were primarily oriented for export, rather than for the rural people.

The picture painted by Erb and Jelahat seems to suggest the need for people-centred development in Indonesia, as also pointed out by Ananta (2001). They propose that the measurement of recovery should not simply hinge on macroeconomic and financial indicators. If the recovery and success of the economy are simply measured by, for example, economic growth (such as whether the growth rate is 5 per cent or higher), then Indonesia may suffer another crisis. Indonesia will simply return to the pre-crisis situation of high growth rates amidst all the problems associated with this before it plunges to another deep, or deeper, crisis. The people-centred development would focus on human development, covering freedom from fear, health, education, people mobility, and people's purchasing power. The measurement of recovery should be aimed at these five elements of human development.

For example, illegal drug activities may have helped the recovery of the economy, but the rising consumption of drugs, as discussed by Gordon and Gordon (Chapter 14), has reduced the status of the health of drug consumers and increased violence. Clearly, the growth of this activity is not recommended by people-centred development.

People-centred development does not ignore macroeconomic and financial indicators. It is not anti-growth. Growth is needed but the importance of the stability of the macroeconomic and financial sectors is also recognized. However, people-centred development includes many other aspects of development. People, rather than production, should be the centre of attention. Thomas et al (2000), for example, has mentioned that development should concern the quality of people's lives and the expansion of their ability to control their own destinies. They need much more than higher income per capita.

People-centred development is not against foreign investment and the international market, but it should emphasize the importance of utilizing the large Indonesian domestic market. The relatively low income per capita, combined with the large population, may imply a lucrative business for relatively cheap goods and services, including daily needs and services.

However, it should also integrate with the international economy through the consistent application of liberalization and a free market. Thirdly, development cannot proceed in a vacuum. Building good governance is thus another recommendation of people-centred development. Economic policies should be made taking into consideration the stage of governance.

Therefore, economic recovery and the progress of development should at least be measured by the performance of these aspects. Though growth does not need to stagnate, development can be at a slower pace but more sustainable. An annual economic growth rate of 4 per cent, for example, accompanied by improvement in various aspects of people-centred development, can be much better than a rate of growth of, say, 8 per cent but accompanied by deteriorating conditions in people-centred development.

In closing, it is worth noting what Root (1998) has argued, that the rapid growth in East Asia had been preceded by social chaos, war, and sometimes revolution. The Cold War had brought political uncertainty into East Asia. Governments had to make quick and effective decisions under a very volatile and risky political climate. As mentioned earlier, Hill (1988) has also posited that the Great Depression ended only with the beginning of World War II. It is wise to heed the warning from Hoover (1952) that the primary cause of the Great Depression was the war of 1914–18. In other words, World War I may have caused the Great Depression, but World War II is likely to have helped the economy to recover and boom.

Thus, the current uncertain situation in Indonesia does not necessarily mean a gloomy future for Indonesia. Of course, more chaos is not recommended. Quick, difficult, and effective decisions are needed to utilize this golden opportunity to make a more peaceful and prosperous Indonesia; otherwise, Indonesia may fall into a deeper crisis.

Notes

1. An estimate by the Central Board of Statistics, as cited by Feridhanusetyawan (2001).
2. The percentage was mentioned by James Wolfsenohn, the president of the World Bank, during his visit to Jakarta in 2000. See "Bank Dunia Menunda Pinjaman" [World Bank Postpones Loan], *Kompas*, 14 April 2001, pp. 1 and 11.

References

Ananta, Aris. "Policies for Sustainable Economic Development in Indonesia". In *Gus Dur and the Indonesian Economy*, edited by Anthony L. Smith, pp. 116–49. Singapore: Institute of Southeast Asian Studies, 2001.

Ananta, Aris, and Soewarta Kosen. "Health Financing for the Poor during the Indonesian Crisis". In *Health Economics in the New Era*, edited by John Kyriopoulos, Tryfon Beazoglou, and Dennis Heffley, pp. 59–78. Athens: National School of Public Health and Exandas Publisher, 2001.

Ananta, Aris, and Reza Siregar. "Social Safety Net Policies in Indonesia. Objectives and Shortcomings". *ASEAN Economic Bulletin* 16, no. 3 (December 1999): 344–59.

Badan Pusat Statistik. *Laporan Perekonomian Indonesia 2000. Angkatan Kerja, Konsumsi dan Kemiskinan Penduduk* [Report on Indonesia Economy 2000. Labour Force, Consumption, and Population Poverty]. Jakarta: Badan Pusat Statistik, 2000.

Becker, Gary S. *Human Capital*. New York: NBER, 1964.

Cameron, Lisa. "Survey of Recent Developments". *Bulletin of Indonesian Economic Studies* 35, no. 1 (April 1999): 3-40.

Chew, Amy. "Inside Story. Fight for Maluku". *Asiaweek*, 27 October 2000, pp. 50–54.

Christianto, I. "Hotels in Yogyakarta, Bali See Higher Occupancy". *Jakarta Post*, 22 October, 2000, p. 13.

Djajanegara, Siti Oemijati, and Aris Ananta. *Mutu Modal Manusia: Suatu pemikiran mengenai kualitas penduduk* [Quality of Human Capital: A thought on population quality]. Jakarta: Demographic Institute, Faculty of Economics, University of Indonesia, 1986.

Enzler, Clarence J. *Some Social Aspects of Depression*. Washington, D.C.: Catholic University of America Press, 1939.

Feridhanusetyawan, Tubagus. "Indonesia: In Search of the Source of Crisis". *Indonesian Quarterly* 28 No. 2 (second quarter 2000): 156–70.

________ . "Indonesia: Facing or Ignoring the Economic Reality?" Paper presented at the Fourteenth Workshop on Asian Economic Outlook, conducted by the Asian Development Bank, Manila, 11–12 December 2001.

Graham, Carol. *Safety Nets, Politics, and the Poor. Transition to Market Economies*. Washington, D.C.: The Brookings Institution, 1994.

Hill, Kim Quaile. *Democracies on Crisis*. Boulder: Westview Press, 1988.

Hill, Hal. "The Indonesian Economy: The strange and sudden death of a tiger". In *The Fall of Soeharto*, edited by Geoff Forrester and R. J. May, pp. 93–103. London: Crawford House Publishing, 1998.

Hoover, Herbert. *The Memoirs of Herbert Hoover: The Great Depression, 1929–1941*. New York: MacMillan, 1952.

Hugo, Graeme. "The Impact of the Crisis on Internal Population Mobility in Indonesia". *Bulletin of Indonesian Economic Studies* 36, no. 2 (August 2000): 115–38.

International Labour Organization. *Employment Challenges of the Indonesian Economic Crisis*. Jakarta: International Labour Organization, Jakarta Office, and United Nations Development Programme, 1998.

Jaffer, Mehru. "Hotel Owners Face Challenging Times with Optimism". *Jakarta Post*, 22 October 2000, p. 13.

Kompas daily. "Masyarakat Menyerbu Barang Konsumsi" [Society Invades Consumption Goods]". *Kompas* daily, 12 April 2000, pp. 1 and 11.

Kearney, Marianne. "Rule of Thugs". *Straits Times*, 10 April 2001, p. A-1.

Kennedy, David M. *Freedom from Fear. The American People in Depression War, 1929–1945*. New York: Oxford University Press, 1999.

Kutanegara, Pande Made. "Dinamika Kesejahteraan: Srihardjo dalam Masa Krisis [Welfare Dynamics: Srihardjo during Crisis]". Paper presented at the seminar on "Social Security and Social Policy". Yogyakarta: Population Studies Centre, University of Gadjah Mada, 28–29 November 1998.

Manning, Chris. "Labour Market Adjustment to Indonesia's Economic Crisis: Context, Trends, and Implications". *Bulletin of Indonesian Economic Studies* 36, no. 1 (April 2000).

McLeod, Ross H. "Survey of Recent Developments". *Bulletin of Indonesian Economic Studies* 36, no. 2 (August 2000): 5–40.

Panggabean, Adrian. "4Q00 GDP. Robust 4Q00 Boosts Full-Year Growth". *News Flash*. Hongkong: Nomura International, 20 February 2001.

Pangestu, Mari. "Seize Momentum, Ensure Change is in Right Direction". *Jakarta Post*, 21 December 2000, p. 20.

Papanek, Gustav F., and Budiono Sri Handoko. "The Impact on the Poor of Growth and Crisis. Evidence from Real Wage Data". Paper presented at a

conference on "Economic Issues Facing the New Government". Jakarta: Faculty of Economics, University of Indonesia, 18–19 August 1999.
Root, Hilton L. "Distinctive Institutions in the Rise of Industrial Asia". In *Behind East Asian Growth: The Political and Social Foundation of Prosperity*, edited by Henry S. Rowen. London: Routledge, 1998.
Sen, Amartya. *Development as Freedom*. New York: Anchor Books, 1999.
Soesastro, Hadi. " Regional Economic Outlook 2001. Indonesia: Another Crisis?" Paper presented at the Regional Outlook Forum, Institute of Southeast Asian Studies, Singapore, 5 January 2001.
———. "Indonesia under Megawati". Paper presented at the Regional Outlook Forum, Institute of Southeast Asian Studies, Singapore, 8 January 2002.
Subbarao, K. et al. *Safety Net Programs and Poverty Reduction. Lessons from Cross-Country Experiences*. Washington, D.C.: World Bank, 1997.
Sumarto, Sudarno; Asep Suryahadi; and Wenefrida Widyanti. "Design and Implementation of the Indonesian Social Safety Net Programs: Evidence from the JPS Module in the 1999 SUSENAS". Working paper. Jakarta: SMERU Research Institute, March 2001.
Sjaastad, Larry A. "The Costs and Returns of Human Migration". *Journal of Political Economy* 70 (supplement) (1962): 80–93.
SMERU team. "Wages and Employment Effects of Minimum Wage Policy in the Indonesian Labor Market". SMERU Research Report, October 2001.
Sumarto, Sudarmo, Anna Wetterberg and Lant Pritchett. "The Social Impact of the Crisis in Indonesia: Results from a Nationwide Kecamatan Survey". At www.worldbank.org, 1999.
Thomas, Vinod, et al. *The Quality of Growth*. New York: Oxford University Press, 2000.
United Nations Development Programme. *Human Development Report 1991*. New York: UNDP, 1991.
———. *Human Development Report 2001*. New York: UNDP, 2001.
Woodward, C. Van. "Editor's Introduction". In *Freedom from Fear: The American People in Depression War, 1929–1945*. New York: Oxford University Press, 1999.

2

MACROECONOMIC RECOVERY

Facts and Prospects

Adrian Panggabean

Is Recovery Sustainable?

The widely-held perception is that the economy has not improved. Yet, it may not be entirely true. If political headlines are used as proxy to the economy, this perception holds. In politics, as if the antagonism between President Wahid and the DPR (Parliament) is not enough, regional tensions (in Aceh, Maluku, Kalimantan, and West Timor), bomb explosions, and political scandals have made the rupiah a yo-yo currency, increasing the financial market's risk and driving inflation and interest rates upward. However, contradictory trends have dominated Indonesia since 1999 when signs of a continued recovery in the economy was seen amidst turbulent politics. Non-performing loans (NPLs) in banks, although still high, came down to 19 per cent in April 2001 from 27 per cent in September 2000, signalling an improvement on the economic front. We get a better picture if we use consumption or exports as a proxy to the economy. Trade figures have improved quite markedly; the industrial production index has shown improvement; there is a relatively high volume of vehicle sales — all these indicate improvements in the real economy.

This chapter aims to address two basic questions: has the economy really improved? If so, is the improvement sustainable (at least in the mid-term)? It first describes the depth of the crisis. Next it discusses the improving macro picture of the Indonesian economy before exploring whether the recovery will sustain.

The Depth of the Crisis: The 1998 Stories

The Worst in Indonesia's Modern History

At the outset of the crisis, the economy deteriorated faster than expected. Unable to withstand the shock, the financial sector contracted. The real sector was also severely hit and, as a result, the financial sector destabilized even further. In 1998, Indonesia's gross domestic product (GDP) growth dropped by 18 percentage points to –13.1 per cent. The massive cost of the bail-out (more than half of GDP), the amount of output being squeezed (Indonesia's 1998 real GDP equal that of 1995), the number of people being sent back to below the poverty line (as at December 1998, based on a BPS estimate, some 15 million people moved back into poverty), and the systemic nature of the crisis across the financial and the real sectors have plunged Indonesia into the worst economic crisis in its modern history.

The free fall of the rupiah and the rapid deterioration in domestic political and security conditions have led to a collapse in confidence in the economy. Some US$40 billion of capital are believed to have fled the country during late 1997 and 1998. Two additional indicators may be used to detect the loss of confidence in the domestic front.

First, people shifted their deposits to foreign-denominated currencies. Rupiah time deposits, which during the pre-crisis period typically constituted some 77 per cent of the total time deposits (the remaining 23 per cent being foreign exchange-denominated deposits), fell to only 55 per cent in June 1998 — and stayed at or below 70 per cent until end-1998. This was a reflection of a loss of confidence over the rupiah.

Secondly, people shifted their deposit holdings to shorter tenures — an indication of uncertainty faced by households and businesses in the economic environment. The proportion of six-month and twelve-month deposits to total deposits, for example, fell to 10 per cent in September 1998 from the pre-crisis norm of around 50 per cent. One-month time deposits, which during the pre-crisis period typically constituted about 23 per cent of the total time deposits in the commercial banks, shot up to 73 per cent in September 1998, and reached its peak of 77 per cent in April 1999.

The Soaring Inflation Rate

In 1998, year-end inflation was 77.6 per cent year-on-year (which translated into an average figure of 58.4 per cent year-on-year), against the 1997 average figure of 6.2 per cent year-on-year. There were four contributing factors to such a high rate of inflation.

Firstly, higher input prices. Despite Indonesia's export-oriented strategy, manufacturing industries were heavily dependent on imported inputs. The import of raw materials and capital goods consisted of more than 90 per cent of the total imports. The rupiah's free-fall contributed to the soaring price of imports and other production inputs. This significantly burdened the production sector, and the burden was passed on to consumers in the form of higher selling prices.

Secondly, the elimination of subsidies and acts of vandalism. The reduction of various government subsidies on essential items, such as fuel and electricity, led to even higher production costs and higher prices. For example, fuel prices were increased by between 20 per cent and 70 per cent, though it was later lowered by about 10 per cent. Increased electricity prices and water charges were swiftly passed on to the consumers in the form of higher prices. The result was increasing public dissatisfaction with the higher cost of living. This was especially so when the government curtailed energy subsidies without addressing chronic management deficiencies. Such dissatisfaction culminated in demonstrations on the streets and other acts of violence and vandalism that led to a break-down in marketing distribution channels, which in turn jacked up prices even further (via higher transaction and transport costs).

Thirdly, the monetary policy. The systemic banking crisis and the need to bail-out the banking system led the government to inject trillions of rupiah in liquidity support. Such rapid growth in money supply put enormous inflationary pressure on the economy. Interest rates rose to defend the currency and to keep up with inflation. As a result, the production sector shouldered additional burdens that came from higher costs related to meeting interest obligations. On the one hand, liquidity support to deal with the runs on the banks had made goods become relatively more scarce compared to money. On the other hand, along with increased risks, businesses found it safer and more profitable to hold their money in the form of foreign exchange-denominated deposits. Hence, lower utilization occurred in the production sector, with management spreading higher overhead costs over less outputs. This supply contraction resulted in even higher prices.

Fourthly, a higher velocity of money. The collapse of confidence in the banking system had forced people to withdraw their rupiah deposits (and some converted them into foreign currencies). The rupiah lost its function as a store of value. As a result, the velocity of money increased. Panic buying increased the rupiah's velocity even further. This contributed significantly to inflationary pressures.

The Rising Interest Rate

The instrument being used by Bank Indonesia in their attempts to bolster the weak rupiah and deal with rising inflation rates was the prime rate (SBI). As a result, the inter-bank rate shot up to 80 per cent year-on-year in August 1998. However, the total loss of confidence in the banking system made the policy of raising interest rates ineffective. The rupiah failed to strengthen and the bank run continued. With customers unable to service their debt, bank lending turned into bad debts, which in turn squeezed the profits of the banking sector.

In a bid to rescue failing banks, Bank Indonesia was forced to inject them with fresh liquidity (BLBI). The Indonesian Bank Restructuring Agency (IBRA) was set up to deal with ailing banks and to recoup the costs incurred by the government through BLBI. By end-1999 company claims on the IBRA had reached about Rp450 trillion, or some 50 per cent of GDP. It is worth noting that with the establishment of the IBRA, the central bank's function of "the lender of the last resort" was effectively transferred to the Department of Finance. In other words, the financial obligation for these banks was moved to the state budget (APBN). This has made the APBN very sensitive to interest rate fluctuations.

The Squeezing Liquidity

In the external front, Indonesia's foreign exchange reserves, which stood at US$27.6 billion in September 1997, dropped to US$16.3 billion in February 1998, after a number of unsuccessful attempts by Bank Indonesia to stabilize the rupiah. By end-1998, foreign exchange reserves had recovered to US$23.6 billion — as a result of the IMF (International Monetary Fund) bail-out package. However, that amount was only one-eighth of the total foreign debt of about US$150 billion. In 1999, the total international reserves were roughly similar to the total foreign debt repayment due for that year (of about US$25 billion). At that level, the liquidity picture looked over-extended.

On the domestic front, liquidity squeeze was apparent in the stock market, which was devastated, with financial assets losing some 70–80 per cent of their dollar value. According to aggregate figures, more than US$80 billion was lost in the capital market alone, between June 1997 and September 1998, as market capitalization dropped from some US$106 billion to around US$15 billion.

Liquidity was also squeezed from banks. According to the IMF-Government of Indonesia agreement, the central bank has been mandated to implement a tight monetary policy. A number of performance indicators and indicative targets were set by the IMF in order to restore confidence in the financial sector. A fully floated exchange rate regime was adopted. However, the failure to stabilize either the rupiah or inflation made it difficult for businesses to operate. This placed an additional burden on the banking system, which was already heading towards collapse.

Businesses could not find fresh cash to lubricate their operations. Exports came to a halt as companies began to experience acute cash-flow problems. December 1997 saw the beginning of the decline of the economy when manufacturing, including labour-intensive industries, either stopped or significantly reduced production. The stock of raw materials was quickly being depleted, yet new imports were too expensive. As Indonesian exporters failed to meet their export orders, they faced the danger of losing market share. This accentuated the problems faced by Indonesian producers. Already being burdened with debts, they also faced revenue decline because of shrinking markets and weak demand. Many companies were not able to import needed raw materials because overseas banks were not accepting the letters of credit issued by Indonesian banks on their behalf.

Contracting Aggregate Output

There was a rapid slowdown in the real economy. In the first and second quarters of 1997, Indonesia still enjoyed a relatively high rate of growth of 8.5 per cent year-on-year and 6.8 per cent year-on-year, respectively. Following the outbreak of the crisis in July 1997, the growth rate dropped and by the third and fourth quarters of 1997, it was 2.5 per cent year-on-year and 1.4 per cent year-on-year, respectively. Overall, in 1997 Indonesia experienced a 4.9 per cent year-on-year growth rate – significantly lower than the 1996 figure of 7.8 per cent year-on-year and those of the previous four years.

In 1998, the Indonesian economy reached its bottom. Using a seasonally adjusted, quarter-on-quarter, figure, the Indonesian economy reached its bottom in the second quarter of 1998. Overall, in 1998, the economy experienced a contraction of 13.1 per cent year-on-year, with all sectors except agriculture posting negative growth. Data suggest that sectors that were sensitive to currency depreciation and interest rates were the hardest hit. For example, growth in the construction sector declined to minus 36 per cent year-on-year in 1998, from a positive 7 per cent year-on-year in 1997. The manufacturing sector, a primary contributor to Indonesia's GDP, plummeted to minus 12 per cent year-on-year in 1998 from positive 5 per cent year-on-year in 1997. In real rupiah terms, the1998 output level was roughly similar to that in 1995.

As businesses contracted rapidly, notice of termination was served on thousands of construction workers. The liquidation of sixteen banks in early November and another seven in March 1998 led to a large number of lay-offs in the banking sector. Unfortunately, labour market statistics were not able to picture the severity of the crisis in the labour markets. The unemployment rate rose only marginally to 5.5 per cent in 1998 (and then to 6.4 per cent in 1999) from 4.7 per cent in 1997. Similarly, the percentage of people working less than 35 hours a week (that is, the underemployment rate) rose from 30.6 per cent in 1997 to 34.3 per cent in 1998, and the percentage of people working more than 45 hours a week declined from 33.6 per cent in 1997 to 31.5 per cent in 1998.

How can such a marginal increase in unemployment figure be explained? It is worth noting that there was no unemployment insurance/benefit in Indonesia. Therefore, being unemployed was a luxury. Only those who had handsome severance payment, relatively large amounts of savings, or had friends/relatives who could finance them, were able to afford being unemployed after losing their jobs. Those who lost their jobs in the formal sectors might have gone to the informal sectors, for lower income. In other words, the small increase in unemployment rate only indicate that there was an increasing percentage of the labour force who could enjoy the luxury of being unemployed. Similarly, the underemployment data should also be treated with caution. We do not know whether those who worked less than 35 hours a week had done so voluntarily or they were still looking for additional jobs. If they did it voluntarily, then the rising percentage of those working less than 35 hours did not reflect the worsening of the household's financial situation.

As a result of the economic slowdown and high inflation rate, the incidence of absolute poverty — which had actually declined during the past three decades prior to the crisis — rose again to 24 per cent in 1999 (equivalent to about 48 million people) from 12 per cent in 1996 after a decline from 26 per cent in 1990. Thus, one of the hallmarks of the New Order government evaporated as a result of the most serious economic crisis Indonesia has ever faced.

The 2001 Data: An Improving Picture

There is sufficient evidence to suggest that the economy has improved, albeit fragile. However, macroeconomic performance has largely surprised economic analysts. Several critical indicators, covering both the financial and the real sectors, are presented below.

Signs of Stability in the Financial Sector

Mixed Signs of Returning Confidence

If we use the commercial banks' deposit structure as a proxy to confidence, we see a gradual improvement. Time deposits of one-month tenure have gradually migrated to longer tenure (that is, three-month, and to a lesser extent, six-month). The proportion of one-month deposits to total time deposits declined to 57 per cent in April 2001 from 77 per cent in Mach 1999. And it has continued to come down. The proportion of three-month deposits has gone up to 20 per cent (or back to its pre-crisis norm), from 3 per cent in September 1998.

Figure 2.1
Time Deposit Structure by Maturity

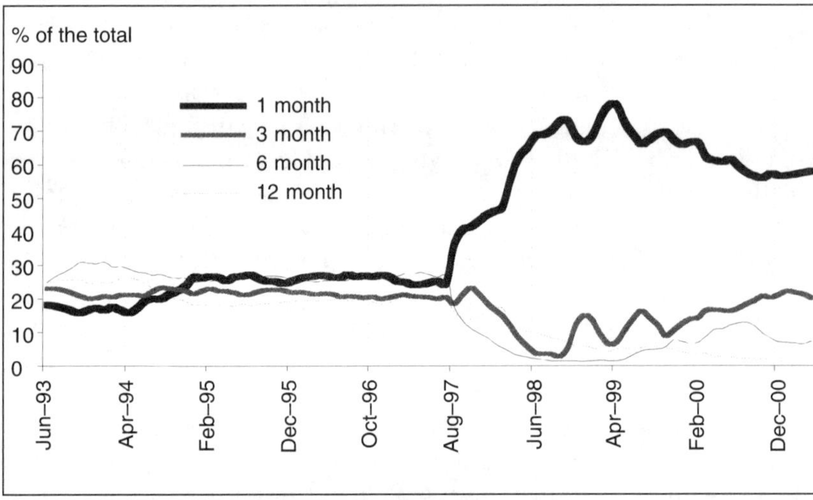

Source: CEIC Data Company Ltd (CEIC), and own calculation.

However, if the rupiah is used as a proxy, the improvement looks patchy. In 1999, the volatility of the rupiah was largely reduced owing to the Frankfurt Agreement, the Paris Club agreements, and Consultative Groups on Indonesia (CGI) loan disbursements. The financial market also stabilized in the lead up to the 1999 general assembly session (SU-MPR) following the first democratic election ever held in the past fifty years. The average value of the rupiah was Rp7800 per US$ in 1999, compared with Rp9900 per US$ in 1998. In 2000, it went down to Rp8500 per US$ owing to political tensions and the huge debt repayment. Currency speculation also depressed the rupiah in the second half of that year. It was only in February 2001 that the speculative element in rupiah trading was removed following the release of Bank Indonesia's Regulation No.3 (PBI No.3/2001) which put a ban on rupiah loans offshore. In 2001, the loss of confidence, largely caused by even more volatile politics, only partly explained the rupiah's weakness. There are two major factors that affect the rupiah. The first is a huge foreign debt repayment (of US$26 billions) amid thin trading. The second is the depreciation in Indonesia's peer currencies. So, while the rupiah weakened in 2001, it was not necessarily due to the fall in confidence. On the back of these three factors, the year-average value of the rupiah was expected to reach Rp9800 per US$ in 2001.

Normalizing General Price Levels

After experiencing two consecutive years of high inflation (58.4 per cent year-on-year in 1998, and 20.5 per cent year-on-year in 1999), the CPI (consumer price index) declined rapidly in 2000 — as a result of a gradual return of confidence, adequate availability of food, and a period of supply expansion. The average inflation rate in 2000 stood at 3.8 per cent year-on-year. In 2001, however, the average inflation rate was expected to normalize to about 9–10 per cent, amid aggressive fuel price increases, rebalancing in various utility tariffs, and stronger domestic aggregate demand.

Figure 2.2
Inflation

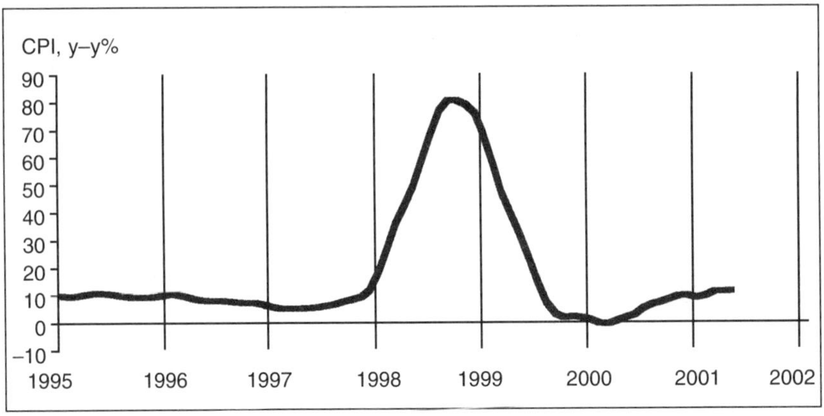

Source: CEIC, and own calculation.

Improving Liquidity Picture

Falling inflation has driven interest rates down sharply and negative spreads have turned positive. After fifteen months in negative territory, real interest rates turned positive in June 1999, and it has normalized to its pre-crisis average of between 4 per cent and 6 per cent. As one would have expected, positive real interest rates (combined with a degree of monetary expansion) have led to output stimulation.

Despite the rupiah's volatility in 2001, interest rates are not likely to go far beyond the existing level of 17 per cent. The plan to phase out Bank Indonesia Certificates (SBI) and to introduce T-Bills should lead banks to liquidate their SBI holdings and invest in T-Bills, and thus remove incentives for a rate hike. Aggressive cutting of the U.S. interest rate throughout 2001 — on the back of a slowdown in the U.S. economy — should help ease pressure on rupiah interest rates.

Figure 2.3
Interest Rate

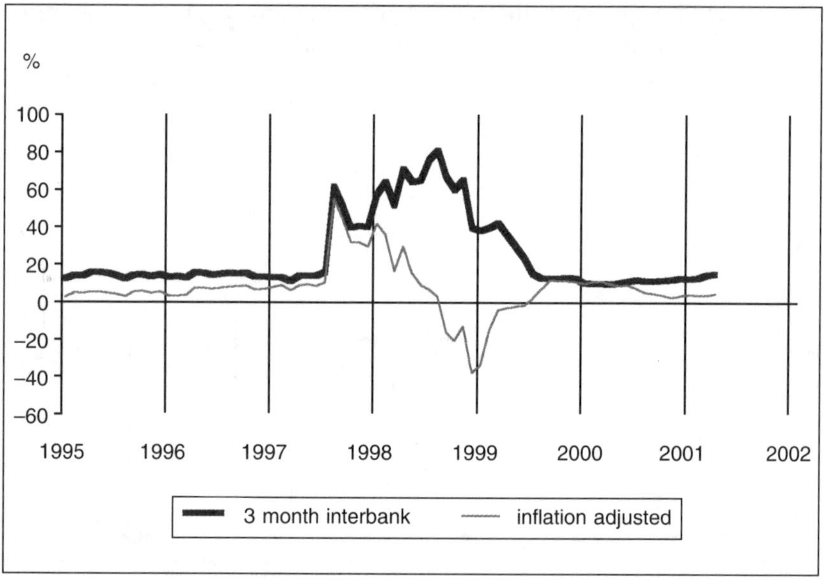

Source: CEIC, and own calculation.

On the external front, balance-of-payment pressure has eased. Since 1998, the Paris Club of official creditors and the London Club of corporate creditors have both agreed to reschedule about US$10 billion of public- and private-sector debts. On top of that, stronger-than-expected oil prices and export performance have boosted the liquidity profile. In 2000, the trade balance was much stronger than expected. Greater non-oil exports and buoyant oil prices combined to lift the trade surplus. The current account showed a surplus at 4.6 per cent of GDP in 2000. The extension of debt maturity has greatly relieved pressures on the balance-of-payment, and provided some breathing space to the economy. At the same time, the wider-than-expected current account surplus has fed into domestic liquidity.

Figure 2.4
Export Values

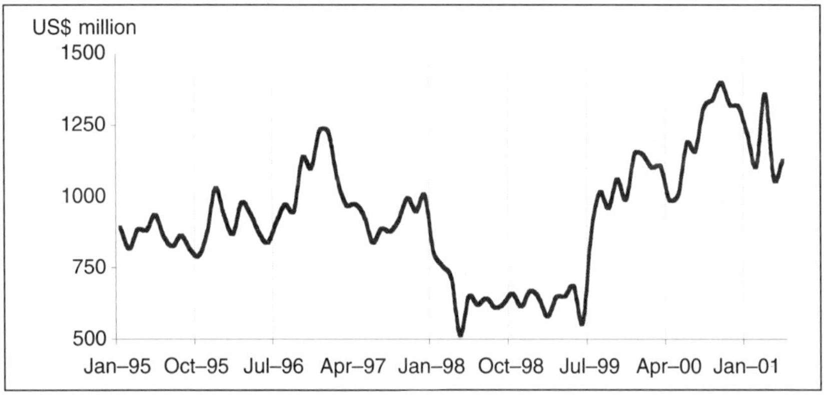

Source: CEIC, and own calculation.

On the domestic front, since August 2000, M2 (broad money supply) growth has picked up. However, real M1 (narrow money supply) balances have grown relatively more strongly. The ratio of M2 to M1 has continued to come down, indicating a stronger preference to hold the currency for transactions — representing a movement in the real economy. Loan-to-deposit ratio that is still in the region of 50 per cent shows that banks are flushed with funds.

Figure 2.5
Current Account and Export Growth

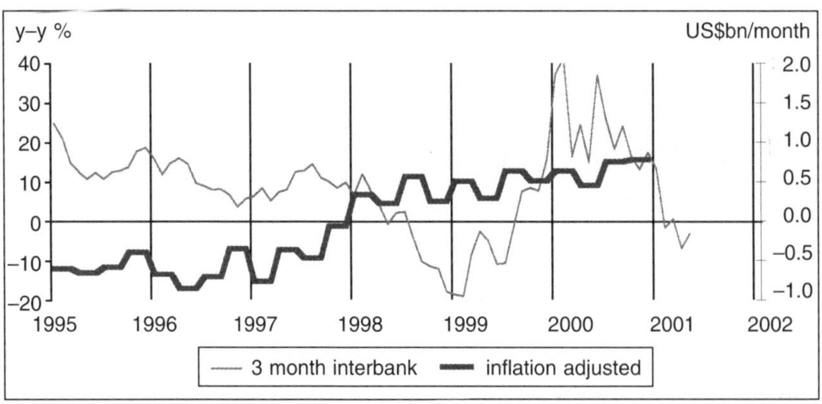

Source: CEIC, and own calculation.

Functioning Banks

Contrary to *a priori* expectations, the distressed picture of Indonesian banks is gradually improving. There are signs that they are starting to supply production sectors with working capital. Credit growth has stabilized since October 1999, and has continued to show an upward trend. This is despite the relatively high real cost of credit of about 17 per cent (as at March 2001).

The amount of loans being channelled through totalled Rp306 trillion in April 2001, compared with Rp223 trillion in March 2000. Credit growth at 33.8 per cent year-on-year in April 2001 constitutes a sharp improvement from negative 60 per cent year-on-year in June 1999. This is another sign of stability in the financial system.

Figure 2.6
Degree of Monetization (M2/M1)

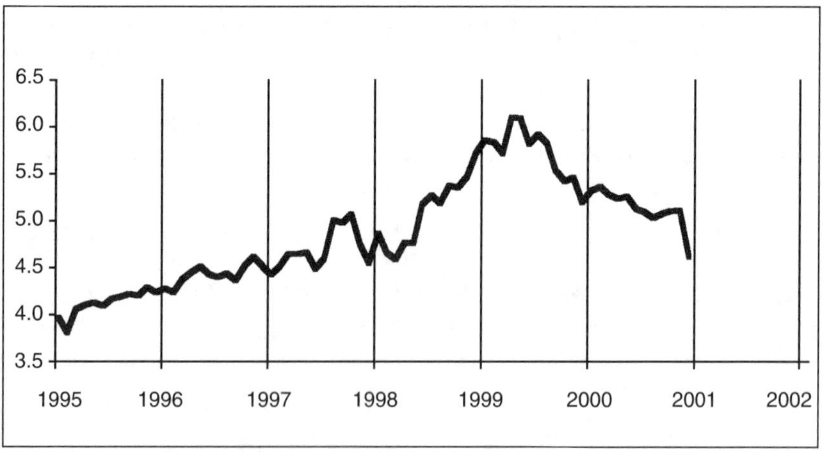

Source: CEIC, and own calculation.

On year-average terms, however, growth of loans still looks depressed. From the supply side, lending constraints still come from capital adequacy ratio (CAR), legal lending limits, net open positions, and risk control. Constraints to lending also come from the demand side. Large corporations, the main drivers for loan demand, are either still tied up with IBRA (Indonesian Banking Restructuring Agency); not able to raise further debt to their debt covenant; or preferring to use their internal cash flow and equity to finance expansion. Meanwhile, SBI holdings by banks declined to Rp72 trillion in April 2001 from Rp92 trillion in March 2000. They provide an indication that the banks have started to function as financial intermediaries.

Figure 2.7
Bank Credit and SBI Holding

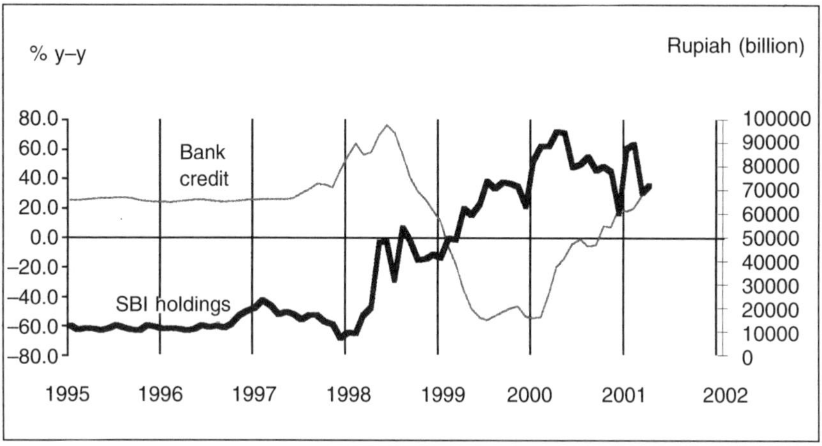

Source: CEIC, and own calculation.

High Financial Risks

Despite these improvements, financial risks are still high. This is the single biggest factor that has made macroeconomic recovery look fragile.

True, external balances have improved as Indonesia managed to reinforce its foreign exchange reserves. As at May 2001, foreign exchange reserves were US$28.7 billion, compared with US$16.3 in February 1998. This was made possible through an accumulation of surpluses in the current account since the first quarter of 1998. The ratio of the current account to nominal GDP expanded to 4.6 per cent in 2000, compared with –2.4 per cent in 1996. More importantly, current account surpluses in 1999 and 2000 were due to strong exports rather than import compression. Since 1999, Indonesia's foreign exchange reserves equivalent to a month's imports has consistently been above six — a comfortable level.

Figure 2.8
External Risks

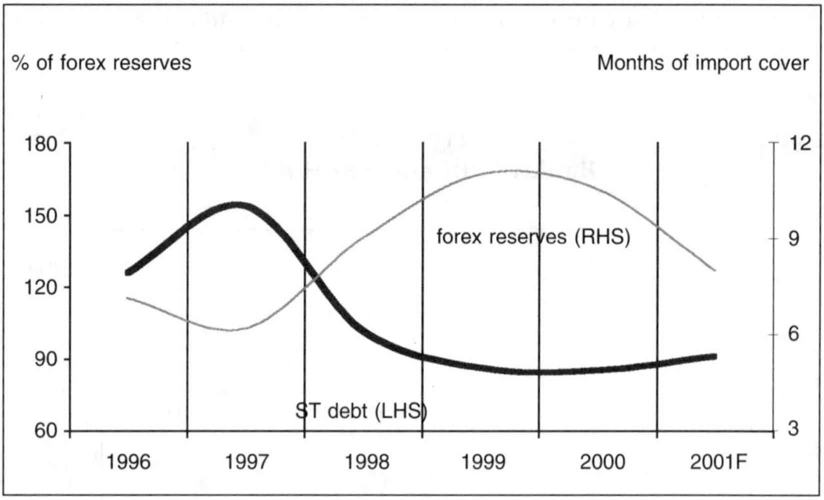

Source: CEIC, and own calculation.

However, the ratio of short-term debt to foreign exchange reserves — a stock measure of external risks — still looks over-extended. The level of short-term external debt has been cut as a result of the Paris Club, Frankfurt Agreement, and the London Club agreement. However, the ratio still stood at 90 per cent by end-2000, against 150 per cent in 1997. To make matters worse, this ratio is expected to sustain until 2005. At this level, financial risks look alarming. In comparison, Korea's ratio was already down to 45 per cent (from 340 per cent in 1997), China's to 12 per cent, Thailand's to 65 per cent (from 140 per cent in 1997), Malaysia's to 25 per cent (from 72 per cent in 1997), and the Philippines' to 56 per cent (from 135 per cent in 1997).

At micro level, high financial risks are also indicated from the low asset quality of Indonesia's financial sector institutions. By end-2000, banks' non-performing loans (NPLs) were still at 23 per cent. Compare this with those of the Philippines (24 per cent), Malaysia (15 per cent), Singapore (10 per cent), and Thailand (19 per cent). If recovery broadens and becomes sustainable, it would be reasonable to expect NPLs to fall, book value at the banks to rise, and financial risks to decline. Although the prospect of deteriorating asset quality (of major corporations) is still seen, the scope is limited.

Figure 2.9
Regional Comparison of NPLs

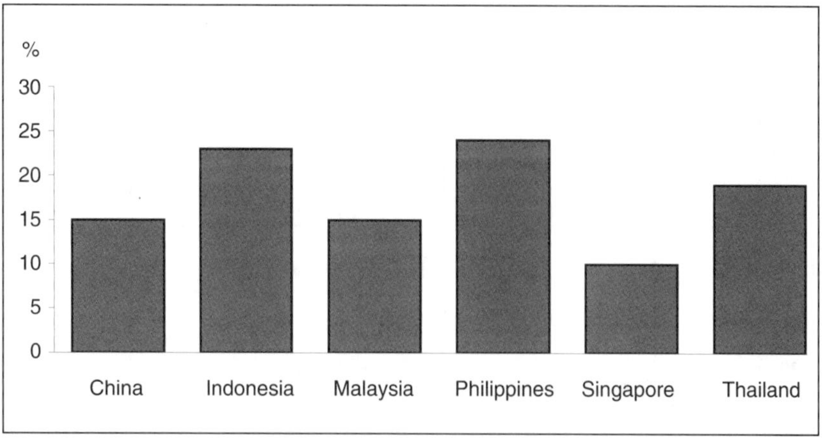

Source: CEIC, and own calculation.

Strengthening of Aggregate Demand and GDP

Based on quarter-on-quarter, seasonally-adjusted data, the Indonesian economy had reached bottom in the second quarter of 1998. In 1999, the economy finally stabilized when it posted a GDP growth of 0.9 per cent year-on-year (a revision from the preliminary figure of 0.3 per cent year-on-year). In 2000, the economy grew stronger, with a 4.8 per cent year-on-year growth. Most importantly, all sectors in 2000 posted growth, with the commerce and manufacturing sectors being the main drivers. The construction sector grew surprisingly strongly at 7.0 per cent year-on-year in 2000. On the demand side, economic growth was driven by private consumption and fixed capital formation. Of note, investment growth was strong despite political uncertainties. In the first quarter of 2001, GDP grew by 4 per cent year-on-year (or 3.6 per cent quarter-on-quarter, seasonally adjusted), with all sectors still posting positive growth. From the quarter-on-quarter trajectory, we see that the economic momentum has actually picked up, not slowed. Indeed, Indonesia ended 2001 with a 3.5 per cent growth amid slowing economic growth elsewhere in the region. Indonesia's 2001 growth was the second fastest in the Asia-Pacific after China. Figure 2.10 shows more indicators that capture the dynamics of this economy.

Figure 2.10
GDP Growth Pattern

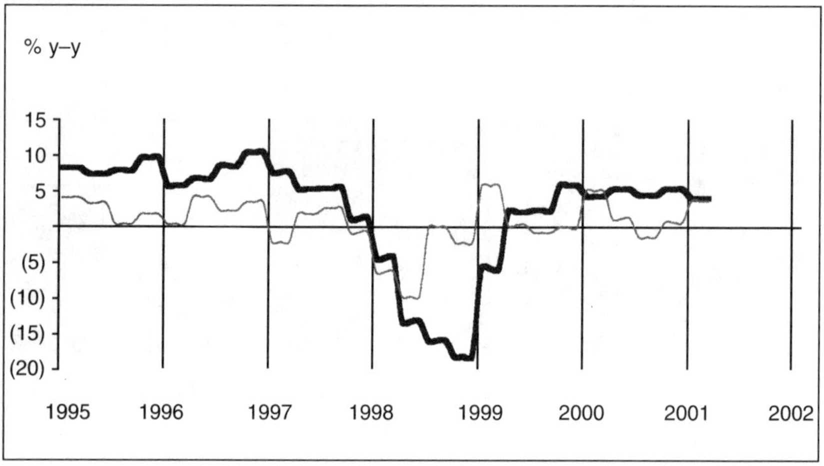

Source: CEIC, and own calculation.

At the macro level, data show that private consumption has strengthened. In 2000, private consumption contributed 2.6 percentage points to GDP growth at 4.8 per cent year-on-year, compared with government consumption (0.5 percentage points) and fixed capital formation (3.4 percentage points). As noted above, there was a sustained momentum in GDP growth in the first quarter of 2001. Private consumption contributed 3.4 percentage points to GDP growth in the first quarter of 2001, at 4 per cent year-on-year (similar to that in the fourth quarter of 2000), suggesting that private consumption had not slowed. At the micro level, anecdotal evidence suggests that the retail sector remains strong. The Bank Indonesia (BI) retail sales index reached 178 in March 2001, compared with 113 in January 2000, confirming the anecdotal evidence. In addition, throughout 2000 international and domestic aircraft passengers, an alternative indicator of economic activity, also increased, both in terms of level and growth.

A more isolated picture of consumption recovery is shown in the pick-up in vehicle sales. Motor vehicle sales grew strongly in 2000, with a sales volume of 348,000 units, compared with the 1998 figure of 69,000 units, and the 1997 figure of 392,000 units. In 2001, vehicle sales volume is likely to reach 275,000 units — the level seen in 1994.

Figure 2.11
Retail Sales Index

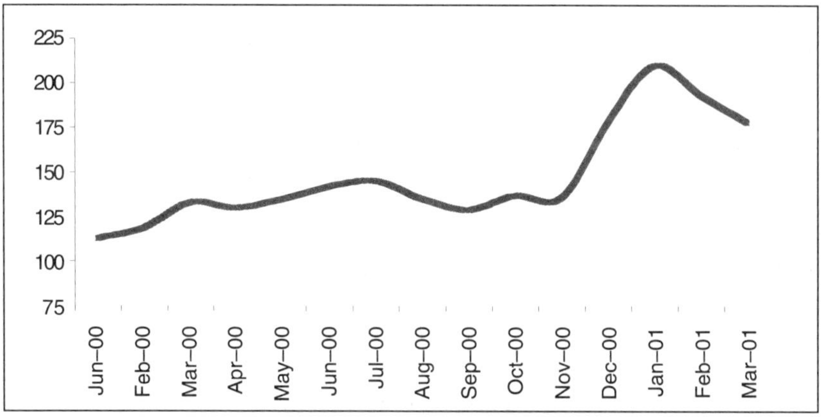

Source: CEIC, and Bank Indonesia.

Most important of all is a broad-based strengthening of household consumption spending. In Indonesia, where the average consumption level is heavily skewed towards the lower income groups, the best gauge of overall consumption strength comes from survey data on poverty and the average household spending level. Indications are that the poverty level (based on the SUSENAS data collected in August 2000) has come down to around 18 per cent in 2000, from 24 per cent in 1999. Mean household consumption in 2000 was 2.30 (1993 PPP US$/person/day), compared with 2.10 in 1998, and 2.85 in 1996. These indicators show a clear improvement over 1998.

Figure 2.12
Vehicle Sales and Production Growth

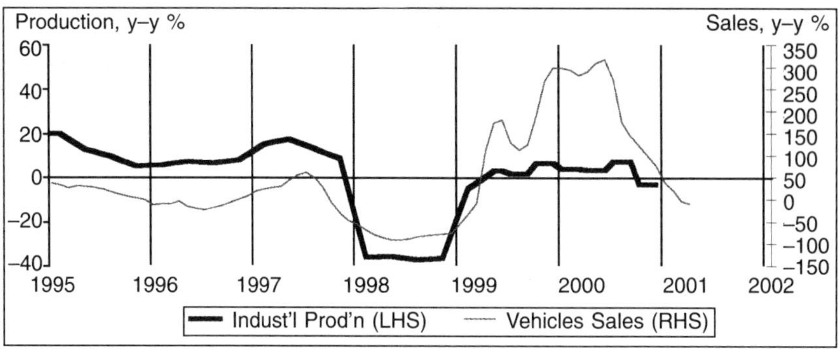

Source: CEIC, and own calculation.

A sizeable shortfall in investment rate, compared with the pre-crisis level (of around 32 per cent) is indeed a concern. However, since the fourth quarter of 1999, the investment rate has shown an upward trend, both in terms of level and growth. The investment rate (that is, investment to GDP ratio) stopped falling in the third quarter of 1999 when it reached 19 per cent and improved to 23 per cent in the first quarter of 2001. To add confirmation, some 1,360 (seven month annualized) investment projects, domestic and foreign, were approved in 2000 (worth about US$14 billion in total), compared with 1,360 investment projects (worth US$24 billion) in 1999. By end-2000, industrial capacity utilization had risen to 75 per cent from 59 per cent in the first half of 1999. There were also signs that the depleted stock of capital was being re-accumulated.

Figure 2.13
Investment Performance

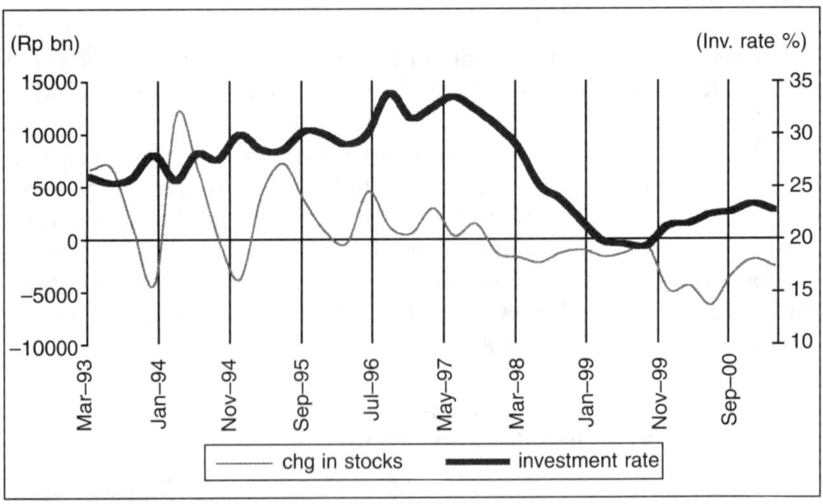

Source: CEIC, and own calculation.

Trade figures were exceptionally strong in 2000, both in terms of value and volume. Export values reached US$62 billion in 2000, of which US$48 billion were contributed by non-oil exports. Non-oil imports picked up both in terms of value and volume, driven by capital goods, confirming that the manufacturing sector had begun to flex its muscles. The cumulative trade surplus reached a new high of US$28.5

billion in the same year. A quarter of it came from oil proceeds, owing to the high prices of crude oil.

Direct confirmation also came from corporate profit growth. Companies (excluding banks) that are listed in the Jakarta Stock Exchange registered sizeable operating profit in 2000. Strong improvement in the corporate earnings of listed companies provides some explanation to the increase in the stock market capitalization of about US$23 billion (monthly average in the first half of 2001), from US$18 billion (monthly average in 1998). This piece of news was lost in the continued flurry of adverse political headlines.

Beyond 2001: Will the Recovery Process Continue?

Key Impediments to a Sustained Recovery

To the question of whether economic recovery is sustainable or not, I reserve my optimism. My optimism is grounded on the fact that key macroeconomic trends continue to signal recovery in the economy. However, improvement on the macroeconomic front has been outweighed by a large dosage of pessimism owing to the structural nature of the problems facing the country. Unending political fights, deeply rooted in the thirty years of Soeharto's administration, are not easy to settle. The complex nature of the economic problems has made it very difficult to design a comprehensive solution.

Political issues form an inherently complicated backdrop to events and has weighed heavily on economic policies. Political battles have manifested in regional tensions, bomb explosions, political scandals, character assassinations, tensions between the President and the Vice-President, and tensions between the President and the DPR. These have made Indonesia a tense, volatile nation and on many occasions politics have clogged the economic pipelines, hampering the productive use of resources. Thus, the recovery process is slower than would have been otherwise largely because of political paralysis. Unless the paralysis is cured, the recovery process may eventually halt.

Politics as the Main Culprit

In politics, the key issue is striking a new balance between economic resources and political power in the post-Soeharto era. The battle between the foot draggers and the reformers covers nearly all ground. On the legal front, there are, for example, battles over the new labour law, amendment of the central bank's law, human rights, and Bank Indonesia's liquidity support. The effort to bring to justice past corruption cases involving big conglomerates and Soeharto's high-ranking officials amid a corrupt and convoluted legal system complicate the picture. Legal uncertainties have provided no floors to business risks.

On the institutional front, Indonesia is confronted with equally complicated problems. The separation of the police force and the military has impacted on security arrangements — raising investment risks. Regional autonomy and fiscal decentralization, as well as the re-organization of the public sector, have tensed the relationship between the central and the local governments. These issues have also injected regulatory uncertainties and have increased business transaction costs.

On the constitutional front, the plan to amend the 1945 Constitution (including the chapter on the power of the President, and Article No. 33 on the economic paradigm) has not been realized because the DPR is busy doing things other than reforming the laws. Higher state institutions (notably the DPR and the President) are fighting with each other over dominance. The supreme justice (MA) is so weak and heavily ridden with past problems that it is just sitting on the fence. The Supreme Audit Body (BPK) is busy investigating old and new corruption cases — but little (if any) of the findings are being followed up. To add to the irony, experts often question the validity of the BPK's findings. These issues, interlinked with one another, weigh down on the capacity to push forward any viable economic policy initiative.

Volatile politics have also led to frequent changes in the Cabinet, which has impacted on the stability and quality of government policies. The sacking of credible ministers and high-ranking officials and the appointment of incompetent ones, as well as the migration of DPR members into the government, have tarnished the image of the state's institutions (most notably the DPR and the President) and political parties (most notably Golkar, PDI-P, PKB, PAN, PPP, Keadilan). They are detrimental to the economy. A cynic might well find a connection between the appointment of certain ministers and the efforts of the faction to which they belong to raise funds and to position themselves ahead of the 2001 special assembly session and the 2004 general election.

From economic perspectives, continued political strife has sustained the distortion of local prices and made it difficult to move away from corruption and cronyism. The gradual elimination of fuel subsidies was not accompanied by the rebalancing of other utility tariffs and public services, leaving relative prices distorted. The result has been a confused market incentive structure. For example, it is still more attractive for smugglers to ship out subsidized diesel than to use it for productive purposes. The element of subsidies that was once embodied in the fuel prices has been transformed into other types of transfers (such as social safety nets) that require a complex administrative arrangement, opening up new areas for corruption and cronyism.

Political fighting has also affected the bank restructuring process. The fact that the IBRA has not been very effective is not new. The pace of progress is slow. The recovery rate of IBRA's assets (of less than 10 per cent) is very low. The way restructuring is being conducted also provides mixed incentives to economic recovery. Some banks have been heavily penalized while others have been bailed out. The acquisition of Bank International Indonesia by Bank Mandiri, and the differential treatment given to the Texmaco group and others are cases in point. Part of IBRA's poor performance lies in the inefficient management. Another part lies in ineffective legal enforcement. Politics also play an important role. The glacial movement in bank restructuring amid turbulent politics has been followed by frequent changes in the top management of IBRA and not by reassigning its middle managers — a critical weakness in IBRA's structure. In order to ensure efficiency, transparency, and accountability, bodies have been established to oversee and monitor IBRA. However, the number of these bodies are just too many, confusing IBRA's management and leaving the problem of transparency and accountability unsolved. To make matters worse, the sale of IBRA's assets has been slowed a great deal by the DPR, slowing down the bank restructuring pace even further. The row between the government and the DPR over the sale of Salim's Plantation to Malaysia's Kelompok Guthrie, and the divestment plan of Bank Central Asia (BCA) and Bank Niaga are cases in point.

Complex Economic Problems

Another critical area of concern is fiscal sustainability. The already tight budget (APBN) has made it very difficult for the government to finance its operations, let alone provide additional funding to speed up the restructuring process. The prolonged economic weakness has overstretched Indonesia's fiscal position, leaving the government with no extra resources. On paper, there are several conditions by which the ability of the budget to finance recovery can be sustained. First, a sustained pick-up in GDP growth over the next four years — of an average of 5 per cent per annum, and within a stable macro environment — is needed. Were this to occur, macro growth can absorb the cost of restructuring. Secondly, interest rates of less than 12 per cent must prevail. This would reduce the interest rate cost of domestic debt. To achieve this, a low-inflation, stable rupiah environment is essential. Finally, effective fiscal consolidation, which includes revenue expansion and spending prioritization is necessary. In our view, there is ample room to increase tax revenues. The current tax revenue over GDP ratio (that is, tax ratio) is only about 11 per cent, very low in comparison with that of other major ASEAN countries (more than 15 per cent). An inefficient tax administration is seen as largely responsible for the low ratio.

These conditions, however, require political stability and a strong government. This brings us back to the issue of political paralysis currently being faced by Indonesia.

The final key risk to a sustainable recovery is external debt, which is mounting. Unless carefully managed, this real and present danger may well bring Indonesia to a second crisis. This time, the trigger will not be currency depreciation, but another mismatch in commercial banks' balance sheet. A renewed confidence crisis over the financial system amid a fragile financial environment could provoke domestic capital flight, which in turn would put the balance-of-payment under heavy pressure, triggering another currency meltdown. A reversal in the ongoing balance-sheet adjustments at companies (that could increase loan defaults) may occur. In combination with a weak currency, more companies may be pushed into insolvency, leading to a collapse in aggregate output. So, if there is one factor that can send the economy to a double dip, it is the high level of external debt.

Summary and Conclusion

One cannot be too bullish about the Indonesian economy. Debt stock is close to 100 per cent of GDP. Tax revenue makes up only 10–11 per cent of GDP, and the economy is at the mercy of debt rescheduling and oil prices. It may be wrong, however, to be overly pessimistic about the economy. Notwithstanding difficulties, the Indonesian economy has shown signs of recovery and stability.

In the financial sector, the rupiah is still under pressure owing to huge debt repayments and volatility from political developments. At the same time, thin trading tends to exaggerate rupiah volatility. However, inflation has normalized compared with 1998 and 1999. Lower inflation has driven interest rates down, and negative spreads in the banking system have turned positive since June 1999. The increased amount of loans being channelled and the declining of SBI holdings signal that they have started to function again as financial intermediaries since the second quarter of 2000.

In the real sector, GDP has shown a clear upward momentum since the third quarter of 1998. The seasonally adjusted, quarter-on-quarter data show that the economy had bottomed out in the third quarter of 1998. Since then, the economy has surprised economic analysts on the upside. In 1999, when the markets expected the economy to still contract, GDP growth turned out to be 0.9 per cent year-on-year (revised from a preliminary figure of 0.3 per cent year-on-year). This represents an upward movement of 14 percentage points from the 1998 GDP growth of 13.1 per cent year-on-year. In 2000, GDP grew by 4.8 per cent year-on-year — higher than the prediction made in early 2000 of about 3 per cent year-on-year. The same was seen in 2001.

On the demand side, the main engines of growth in 2000 were private consumption and gross fixed capital formation — whose growth turned out to be higher than expected. In 2000, private consumption contributed 2.6 percentage points to GDP growth in 2000, of 4.8 per cent year-on-year, compared with government consumption (0.5 percentage points) and fixed capital formation (3.4 percentage points). This shows that the economy started to invest on the back of strengthening consumption. Export values have stayed around US$4.8 billion amid the rapid slowing of the U.S. and regional economies. On the supply side, the commerce and manufacturing sectors have driven the economy. Of note, all sectors showed positive growth in 2000, adding confirmation that the economy has stabilized further.

However, structural risks remain, and they serve as potential impediments to a sustainable recovery. In the mid-term, growth is expected to gain from a low base. Over the longer term, however, serious political and economic issues still need to be addressed to bring the economy to a surer footing. On the economic front, there are three fundamental issues: bank restructuring; budget sustainability; and debt overhang. At present, comprehensive solutions to these economic issues look distant as unstable politics forms an inherently complicated backdrop to economic policy initiatives that are required to resolve the problems. These key risks bring an element of pessimism as to whether economic recovery is sustainable in the longer term.

References

Badan Penyehatan Perbankan Indonesia, Jakarta www.bppn.go.id.
Badan Pusat Statistik, Indonesia. *Indikator Ekonomi*. Jakarta, various issues.
________ . *Statistik Indonesia*. Jakarta, various issues.
________ . *Survey 100 Desa*. Jakarta, various issues.
________ . *Survey Sosial Ekonomi Indonesia*. Jakarta, various issues.
Bank Indonesia. *Statistik Ekonomi Keuangan Indonesia*, various issues.
Bisnis Indonesia, daily newspaper (Jakarta), various issues.
Detikcom news portal, Jakarta, www.detik.com.
Kompas daily newspaper (Jakarta), various issues.
Krugman, P. and L. Taylor. "Contractionary Effects of Devaluation". *Journal of Development Economics* 8 (1979): 445–56.
Lane, T., A. Ghosh, J. Hamann, S. Phillips, M. Schultze-Ghattas and T. Tsikata. "IMF Supported Programs in Indonesia, Korea, and Thailand: A Preliminary Assessment". Occasional Paper 178. International Monetary Fund (IMF), 1999.
MacIntyre, A. "Political Institutions and the Economic Crisis in Thailand and Indonesia". In *The Politics of the Asian Financial Crisis*, edited by T. Pempel. Cornell, Ithaca: Cornell University Press, 1999.
Panggabean, Adrian. "Political Capital Makes the Difference". *Economic Insight*. Hongkong: Nomura Asia, January 2000.
Panggabean, Adrian, and Goei Siauw Hong. "Indonesia: Steady Politics, Wobbly Economy?" *Asia Insight*, pp. 186–20. Hongkong: Nomura Asia, March 2001.
Panggabean, Adrian, et al. *Understanding the Indonesian Crises: The First Step Towards Recovery*. Jakarta: United Nations Development Programme, 1998.
Tempo weekly magazine (Jakarta), various issues.
World Bank. *Global Economic Prospects and the Developing Countries*. New York: Oxford University Press, 1999.
________ . "East Asia's Recovery Gathers Force But Remaining Weaknesses Could Lead To Downturn". Tokyo, 18 September 2000.

~ 3 ~

INDONESIA'S ECONOMIC TRANSFORMATION

Before and During the Economic Crisis

Muhammad Chatib Basri

Introduction

It is a fact that Indonesia's economic performance in the first thirty years of the New Order government had been fairly impressive. In 1969, Indonesia's per capita income was only about US$70. By 1996, the per capita income had increased more than tenfold to US$1080. The continued economic growth in the thirty years of the New Order period had transformed the structure of the economy. Using Chenery and Syrquin's (1975) terms, structural change takes place as per capita income rises.

Booth (1998) has stated that the years from the mid-1960s to the early 1980s were notable ones in Indonesian economic history. The average annual rate of growth of GDP accelerated to more than 7 per cent per annum. This period also coincided with a significant improvement in the country's terms of trade.

However, Indonesia was confronted with a series of problems in the 1980s. The decline in oil prices after 1982 sharply reduced export earnings and budget revenues. At the peak of the oil-boom years, 80 per cent of export earnings and 70 per cent of budget revenue came from oil. As a result, the large decline in oil prices severed Indonesia's balance of payments. The government undertook some adjustment programmes to increase economic efficiency and altered its trade regime to be more outward-looking, making the development of non-oil and gas exports a top priority. During 1983 to 1995, the government introduced no less than twenty-four packages of economic reforms aimed at increasing economic efficiency and encouraging investment as well as non-oil exports. Along with this change of orientation, the government also shifted its investment policy from investment control to investment encouragement.

This adjustment programme commenced in 1983 and was intensified following the dramatic drop of oil prices in 1986. In 1983, the government cut public investment, initiated a major re-phasing of large capital-intensive projects, devalued the rupiah, and undertook financial reforms to remove interest-rate controls and credit ceilings. In 1984-86, tax reforms were introduced to mobilize domestic resources. Finally, various trade reforms were launched to improve the trade and industrial policy regime.

In 1997, however, Indonesia faced the most serious problem in its economic history. The rupiah plummeted to the lowest level in history, and the Indonesian economy experienced negative economic growth, while the banking sector was paralysed. Since 1997, Indonesia has been mired in economic crisis, with fortunes rising or falling in concert with the rupiah. The economic situation at the peak of the crisis can be outlined in the following. The Central Bureau of Statistics estimates that at the end of 1998 nearly 50 million Indonesians were living in poverty. This is an incredible number, and it reached almost the number of poor people twenty years earlier (in 1976, 54 million lived below the poverty line). The situation in the business world was no less grave. At an exchange rate of Rp8000 to the U.S. dollar, 63 per cent of the companies listed on the Jakarta Stock Exchange (JSX) possessed ratios of dollar debt to total assets of 50 per cent or more. At exchange rates of Rp10,000 or greater, more than 70 per cent of the companies were in this position (Soesastro and Basri 1998). In 1998, the per capita income fell significantly to US$640. The total value of exports also experienced negative growth (–8.6 per cent) in 1998. After failing to prevent further depreciation of the rupiah in 1997, the government gave up its managed floating exchange rate to adopt a freely floating one. The declining foreign exchange reserve, together with other deteriorating variables in the domestic economy forced the government to turn to the International Monetary Fund (IMF) with its adjustment policies.

However, in the course of 1998, political disturbances delayed the programme for some time, and the domestic economic condition worsened substantially, amidst the rise of political tension. In addition, the economic crisis eroded capital both in the banking and corporate sectors. As a result, several measures were taken in the financial sector, including bank restructuring carried out by the Indonesian Banking Restructuring Agency (IBRA), corporate restructuring, and settlement of private debt via INDRA, the Indonesian Debt Restructuring Agency. In 1999, the Indonesian economy began to rebound, with a positive growth of 4.8 per cent in 2000.

This phenomenon leads to the question of how structural change has taken place in Indonesia, and how economic transformation was affected by the economic crisis.

In fact, there has been a number of studies on structural change in Indonesia, among others by Anwar (1983 and 1985), Ikhsan, Basri and Saleh (1995), and Aswicahyono (1997). However, all these studies focus on the pre-crisis era. This chapter attempts to fill the gap since then and describes the process of structural transformation before and during the economic crisis. It focuses on the Indonesian economy in general, and the trade and manufacturing sector in particular. The manufacturing sector is chosen because it was one of the sectors that were hit hardest by the crisis, whilst having the potential to gain from the currency depreciation through the expansion of export and import-competing sectors. In particular, three questions are addressed here:

1. How did the economic transformation in Indonesia take place before and during the economic crisis?
2. How did the structural change occur in the manufacturing and trade sectors in particular?
3. As a comparison with the national pattern, this chapter attempts to observe the structural change in some major provinces.

Structural Transformation in the Indonesian Economy

Chenery and Syrquin (1975) have argued that the transformation of economic structure can occur through the interaction of three factors. The first is universal factors which are related to the level of income. Universal factors, such as Engels law, perform an important role. They predict that the pattern of consumption will evolve following a specific pattern in which the share of food in total consumption will decline as the level of per capita income rises. This hypothesis is deduced from the fact that the elasticity of demand for food is less than one while that for non-food items is greater than one. Engels law helps to explain why as income per capita rises agriculture's share of total GDP (gross domestic product) declines, while at the same time manufacturing's share of total GDP increases. Secondly, significant factors specific to individual countries also contribute to structural change, including natural endowments, or market size. Thirdly, economic transformation depends on the country's history, including social and political objectives and government economic policies. Hence, governments can influence and shape the economic structure by influencing the structure of incentives in the economy.

Structural Change in Production

In 1967, the share of the agricultural sector to GDP accounted for 33 per cent, while the manufacturing sector contributed only 6.8 per cent. But in 1996, the share of agriculture to total GDP had declined to 15.4 per cent, whilst the manufacturing sector had risen to 24.7 per cent. It is worth noting that during the structural transformation, the growth of the agricultural sector had remained positive. The shrinking of the share of the agricultural sector took place because of the relatively low growth of the sector compared to GDP. It is clear that the source of growth in the Indonesian economy had shifted from the agricultural sector to the manufacturing sector. During 1983–97 the manufacturing sector grew by 10 per cent per annum.

This fact makes it possible to explore the process of economic transformation in Indonesia. The notable performance of the manufacturing sector, indicated by the steady increase in its share to total GDP, reflects an industrialization process in the Indonesian economy.

Figures 1 to 4 present comparisons between the normal pattern and the actual pattern. The normal pattern is estimated based on the Chenery and Syrquin coefficient of structural change for various countries. It is obtained from an estimation for various countries (Chenery-Syrquin 1983).

The equation is:

$$X = \alpha_1 + \alpha_2 \ln Y + \alpha_3 (\ln Y)^2 + \alpha_4 \ln N + \alpha_5 (\ln N)^2 + \varepsilon$$

Where:

X = share of sector or aggregate macroeconomic components/GDP
Y = GNP/Capita (US$1987)
N = number of population

Chenery and Syrquin's estimates may be misleading because the structural change process can be unique for specific countries. In general, however, there is a consistency between Chenery and Syrquin's normal pattern and the structural change in the Indonesian economy. Nonetheless, there are some significant differences in the level of share between the normal pattern and the actual share of economic transformation in Indonesia.

Figure 3.1 shows the structural change in the agricultural sector. Before the crisis, the pattern was consistent with the Chenery and Syrquin's stylized facts for various countries. Nevertheless, Indonesia experienced a faster structural change than Chenery and Syrquin's normal pattern. This notable performance during the pre-crisis period was attributed to capital accumulation and rapid technical change rather than by relative price effects (Martin and Warr 1993). In other words, it was supply-side rather than demand-side driven.

Figure 3.1
Structural Change in the Agricultural Sector

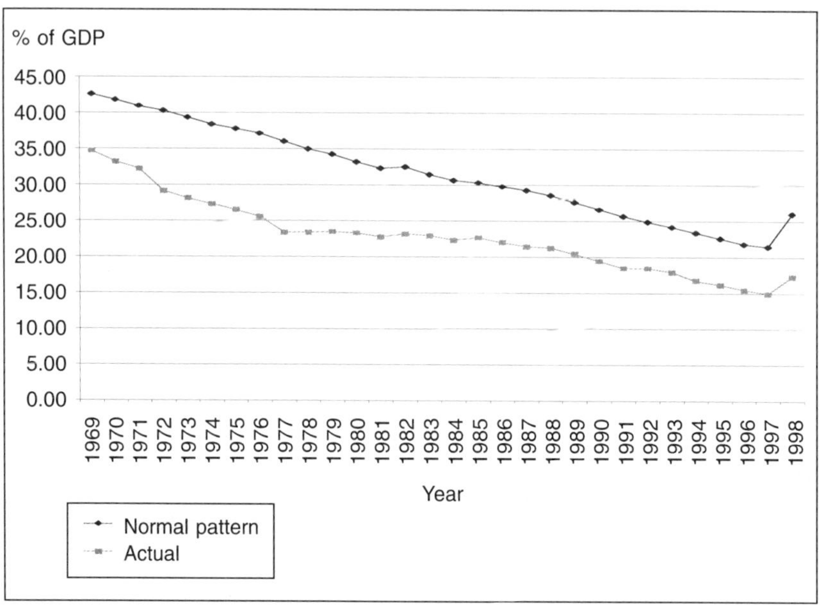

The pattern was reversed after 1997, when agriculture's share of total GDP increased instead of decreased. Thus, during the economic crisis, the agricultural sector grew faster than the overall economy. In other words, throughout the crisis, the economy moved backwards towards the primary base. This finding is consistent with the rapid expansion of agricultural export during the crisis. In 1998, agricultural export grew by 11.6 per cent, which was better than all other sectors such as industry and mining, which grew by –0.7 per cent and –13 per cent respectively.

Figure 3.2 depicts the structural change in the manufacturing sector. The actual trend tended to converge towards the normal pattern, particularly after 1983, and surpassed the normal pattern after 1992. The Indonesian manufacturing sector showed outstanding performance after 1983. This rapid expansion could be credited to some factors, such as devaluation of the rupiah in 1983 and 1986, high savings, high investment rates, and economic liberalization since 1984 (Hill 1996). Moreover, Hill has pointed out that credible macroeconomic management and predisposition towards moderate inflation also contributed to this remarkable performance. One of the important factors which may have contributed to the notable performance of the manufacturing sector after the mid-1980s was trade liberalization. There are a number of surveys on this issue available, such as those by Azis (1994), Hill (1996), Simandjuntak (1989), and Pangestu (1987).

Figure 3.2
Structural Change in the Manufacturing Sector

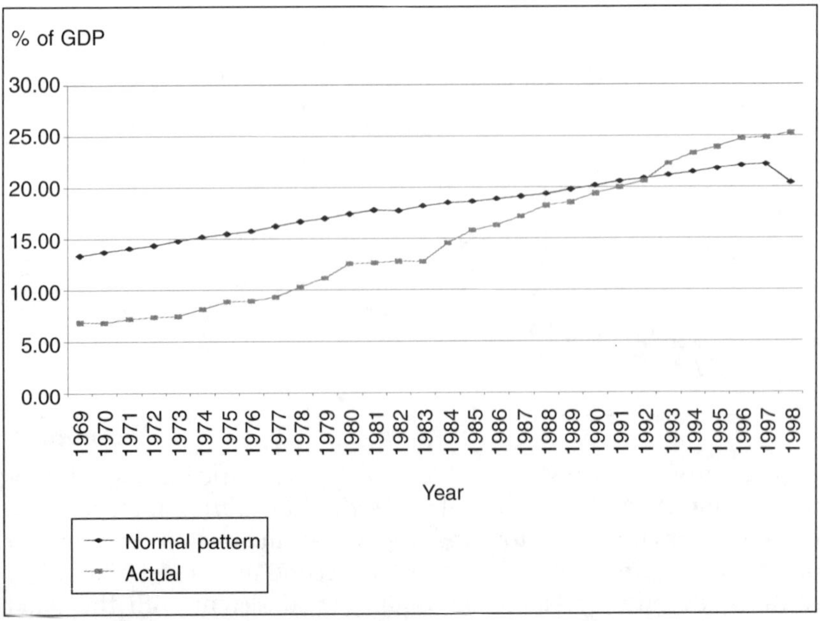

The relationship between trade liberalization and productivity in the manufacturing sector is also supported by Aswicahyono (1998). Aswicahyono has found that the effective rate of protection discourages TFP (total factor productivity) growth. Or, put in another way, trade liberalization encouraged TFP growth and thus drove the structural change in the manufacturing sector.

The share of manufacturing in total exports rose from 3 per cent in 1980 to more than 50 per cent in 1996. This share declined slightly to 42 per cent in 1997 because of the economic crisis. The 1997 economic crisis, undoubtedly, had a major impact on the overall performance of the manufacturing sector and manufacturing exports. In 1998, for example, the manufacturing sector experienced negative growth of –11.8 per cent, while the overall economy grew by –13.2 per cent. The overall economy improved slightly in 1999, experiencing growth of 0.2 per cent whilst the manufacturing sector grew by 2.2 per cent. The share of manufacturing to total GDP was relatively stable during 1999, implying a stagnation of structural change in this sector. This phenomenon leads us to question why the manufacturing sector, which was propelled by manufacturing exports, failed to perform well during the crisis? Other things being equal, currency depreciation had

Figure 3.3
Structural Change in the Utilities Sector

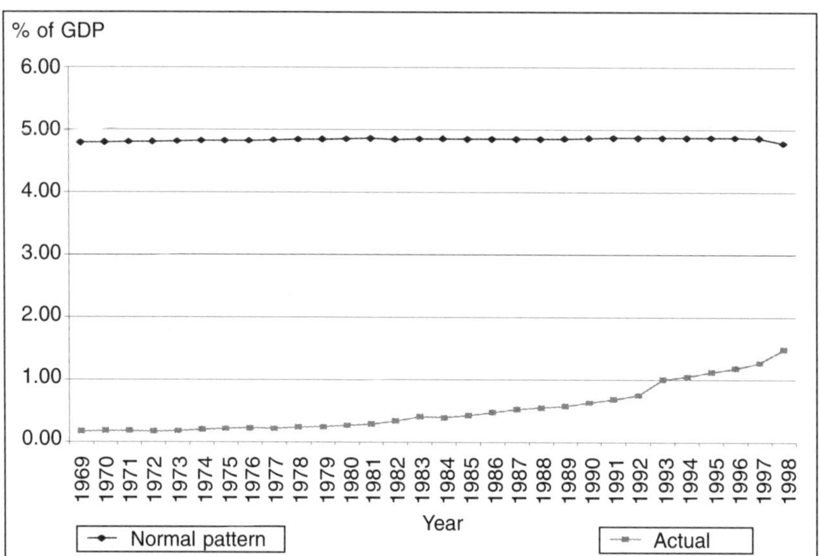

enabled the export and import competing sectors to expand. Perhaps the problem of trade financing and working capital had kept the manufacturing export and import competing sectors from reaping the benefits from the rupiah's fall.[1]

Another sector which is important to observe is infrastructure. Although much of the oil revenue had been recycled into physical infrastructure (Hill 1996), the structural change in the utilities sector was slower than the normal pattern (see Figure 3.3). The utilities sector, in particular, lagged behind the normal pattern. This indicates that the notable performance in the manufacturing and agricultural sectors was not followed by an equivalent growth in infrastructure development. This helps to explain why Indonesia has a big problem in infrastructure development to support the economy.

Structural Change in Employment

Similar to the production side, the structural change in employment was consistent with Chenery and Syrquin's stylized facts. Nevertheless, labour allocation in agriculture was consistently below the normal pattern (Figure 3.4). This reflects a lower absorption rate of employment in

Figure 3.4
Structural Change in Agriculture Employment

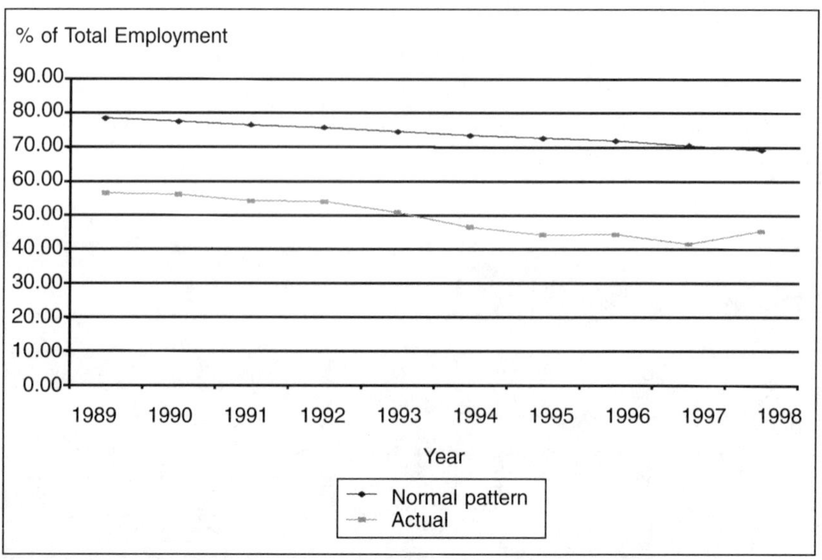

Figure 3.5
Structural Change of Employment in the Manufacturing Sector

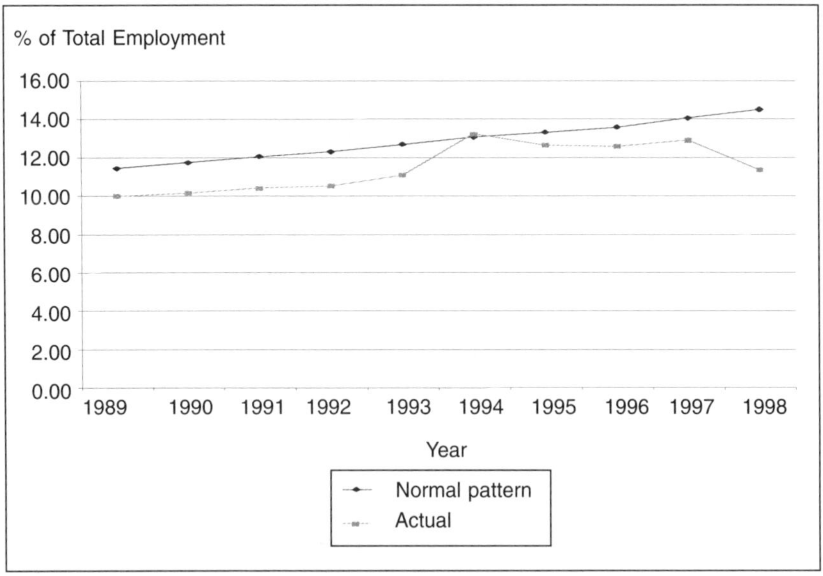

Figure 3.6
Structural Change of Employment in the Services Sector

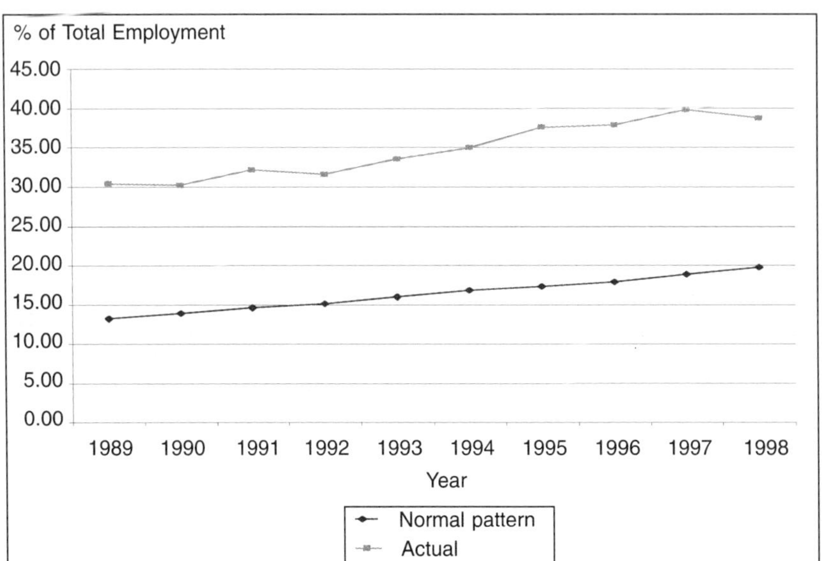

agriculture compared to the normal pattern. This finding is important especially when we relate it to the structural change of employment in the manufacturing sector. Following Lewis' argument, the agricultural sector would release its labour into the manufacturing sector. Thus, we can expect that the lower absorption of labour in the agricultural sector would be compensated by the high absorption rate in the manufacturing sector. However, it was not so, since the actual labour allocation in the manufacturing sector was consistently below the normal pattern (Figure 3.5). So, where did the labour go? The answer is the services sector. Figure 3.6 demonstrates that labour allocation in the services sector was consistently far above the normal pattern. This reflects the role of the informal sector in the economy.

Employment under status 1 (self-employed) consistently increased from 1985 to 1995. Most people under status 1 worked in the agricultural sector. At the same time, employment under status 4 (employer/employee), particularly those in the manufacturing sector, increased steadily during 1985–95. Its share grew from 59.3 per cent in 1985 to 65.9 per cent in 1995. This data support the stylized fact that the rise in employment under status 4 parallels the progress of the economy and is concentrated in the formal sector (LPEM 1999). During the economic crisis in 1997–98, employment under status 1 (self-employed) in the urban areas grew by 25 per cent, whilst that of employer/employee (status 4) experienced negative growth of –4.9 per cent. A similar status was observed in the rural areas. In other words, employment tended to move back to the primary or informal sector during the crisis.

Previous discussion has pointed out that Chenery and Syrquin's pattern was consistent with that in Indonesia prior to the 1997 economic crisis. However, the crisis reversed the structural transformation pattern. The share of employment in the agricultural sector increased while the share of employment in the manufacturing sector significantly decreased. The notable growth of employment in the agricultural sector (15 per cent in 1998) led its employment share in total employment to rise from 44.5 per cent to 48.6 per cent. This finding is consistent with the pattern of agriculture's value-added share in total GDP.

In the manufacturing sector, its employment share in total employment dropped significantly because of the negative growth in employment absorption (–13 per cent). This hypothesis is confirmed by Figure 3.5. Figures 3.3 and 3.4 show a picture which explains that the economic crisis led to a reversed trend in structural change in both production and labour allocation.

Structural Change in the Manufacturing and Trade Sectors

The Manufacturing Sector

Subsequent to the broad picture of structural change in the Indonesian economy, this section focuses on non-oil manufacturing. Considering that non-oil manufacturing is closely related to manufacturing trade, we need to elaborate on the trade sector as well.

As discussed earlier, the manufacturing sector experienced a remarkable growth particularly during the post-deregulation era. Aswicahyono (1998) has demonstrated that TFP growth in the non-oil manufacturing sector in 1976–93 was determined by trade regimes and domestic competition. Other variables, such as foreign and government ownership, provide little evidence in determining the total factor productivity growth (TFPG). Aswicahyono has pointed out that sectors which rely more on export expansion show a superior performance in terms of TPFG, compared with those which are more domestic and import-substitution-oriented. Furthermore, Aswicahyono has found a negative relationship between the change of the effective rate of protection and TFPG. This finding supports the hypothesis that trade liberalization undertaken by the government since 1984 propelled the growth of the non-oil manufacturing sector. This remarkable performance should also be attributed to external factors such the world economic situation, exchange-rate management, and commitment to moderate inflation. In this case, the structural change in the non-oil manufacturing sector was more a supply and policy factor rather than a demand factor, as shown by Engel's law.

In 1975, food production (ISIC 31) accounted for 47 per cent of total manufacturing. This share continued to decline to 16 per cent of total manufacturing in 1996. The figure supports Chenery and Syrquin's stylized facts that the share of food production shrinks as the per capita income rises. On the other hand, the share of footloose and labour-intensive industries (ISIC 32+39) in total manufacturing continued to rise from 11 per cent in 1975 to 21 per cent of total manufacturing in 1996.

The wood and paper product sector (ISIC 32+34) has a strong comparative advantage. It relies heavily on natural resources. The share of this sector continued to rise until 1990. Nevertheless, the share declined slightly in 1995 because of unfavourable conditions in the international market (Aswicahyono 1998).

Heavy processing (ISIC 35+36) is another sector which poses a potential comparative advantage, since wood and paper products rely heavily on natural resources. Nevertheless, heavy processing needs heavy capital investment. Therefore, the ups and downs of this sector are closely related to the ability of the sector to handle the problem of capital. In 1975, the share of the heavy processing sector accounted for 22 per cent of total manufacturing. This share continued to decline until 1995, particularly after 1985. This could be explained as an impact of the decline in oil revenue after 1985. High government revenue during the oil boom period enabled the government to expand this sector, but the collapse of oil revenues made the government postpone or cancel projects in this sector.

Other sectors such as metal goods (ISIC 37+38) actually do not have a comparative advantage. Nevertheless, this sector continued to expand because of high government investments and trade protection. Hence, when the oil price plunged and trade liberalization took place in the mid-1980s, the rate of growth continued to decline (Aswicahyono 1998).

In 1975 agriculture resources intensive (ARI) dominated the non-oil manufacturing products. However, its share in total non-oil manufacturing continued to decline until 1996. The share of another product, unskilled labour intensive (ULI), in 1975 was only about 18 per cent of total non-oil manufacturing. However, its share gradually rose and by 1996 it had increased more than twofold to 43.5 per cent. This rapid expansion in ULI shows how the non-oil manufacturing sector tended to follow its comparative advantage pattern particularly after trade liberalization in 1985. Technology-intensive products also experienced rapid expansion, although slower than ULI.

Trade Sector

The rise in per capita income will also have an impact on structural change in the trade sector. Theoretically, at the early stage of development, primary exports tend to dominate the export sector, while capital goods and raw materials tend to dominate the import sector. As per capita income rises, the export and import of manufacturing goods will steadily expand. Nevertheless, this pattern could be unique for a particular country for several reasons. The first is factor endowment. The second is trade policy. A resource-rich country tends to export resources-intensive products, while a country with labour abundance tends to export labour-intensive goods. Trade policy, as mentioned before, also plays an important role in determining the structure of trade. A country with an import-substitution strategy tends to experience slower growth in manufacturing exports than one with an export-oriented strategy.

Considering these two factors, we can predict that after trade liberalization takes place, Indonesia will experience rapid expansion in manufacturing exports.

Figure 3.7 depicts the pattern of Indonesian exports from 1970 to 1998. In the 1970s, manufacturing exports contributed less than 3 per cent of total exports, and total Indonesian exports were dominated by primary goods.[2] However, by 1987 manufacturing exports had surpassed primary exports.

Figure 3.7
Composition of Indonesian Exports

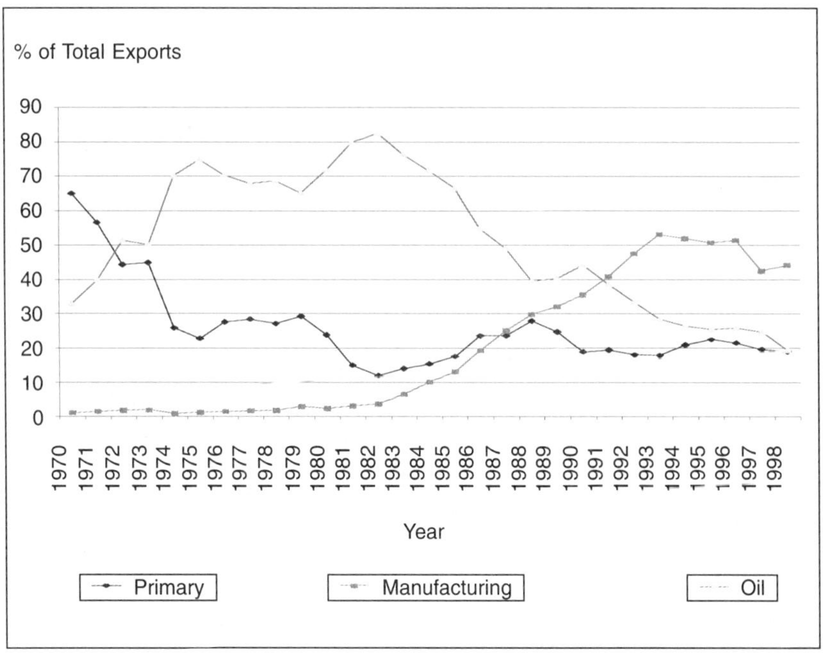

Figure 3.8 shows how manufacturing exports were dominated by capital-intensive goods prior to 1984. Nevertheless, labour-intensive products grew rapidly and surpassed capital-intensive goods in 1987. This notable performance of labour-intensive goods could be attributed to trade liberalization, which had begun in 1985. On the other hand, the share of oil exports to total exports continued to decline from 1983 because of the collapse of oil prices.

Figure 3.8
Composition of Manufacturing Exports

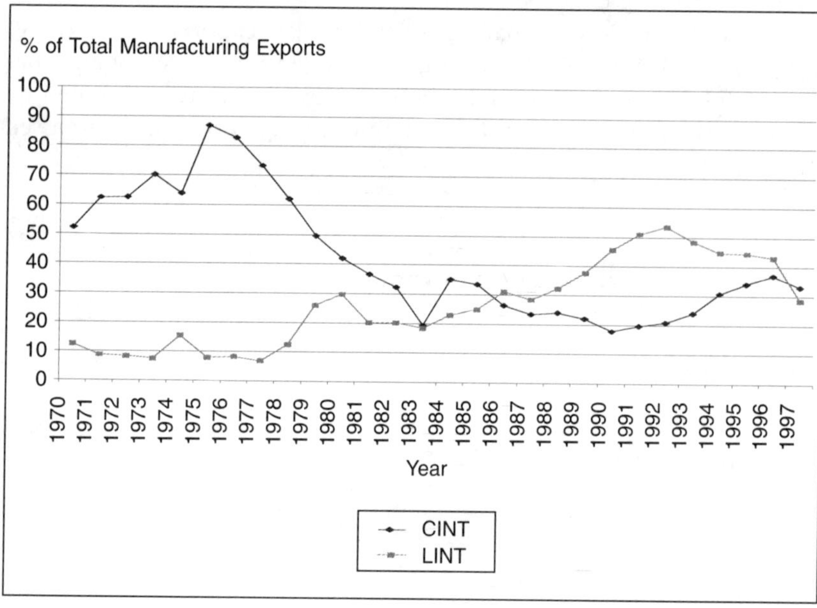

During the 1997 economic crisis, the share of manufacturing to total exports shrank significantly, from more than 50 per cent to 42 per cent. This trend indicated the failure of manufacturing exports to gain from the rupiah's depreciation. This failure could be traced back to several reasons, among others: the problem of acquiring working capital to expand production, the problem of trade financing, and international rejection of Indonesian letters of credit (Pardede 1999). The difficulties in acquiring credit led exporters into difficulties in expanding their production. However, the decline of exports has to be juxtaposed against the argument made by Rosner (2000). Rosner (2000, p. 62) has argued that, while the non-oil export value growth fell from +10 per cent in 1997 to –2 per cent in 1998, and –6 per cent in 1999, the growth of non-oil exports in terms of volume was positive. Moreover, Rosner has also pointed out that the volume of non-oil exports (measured in constant 1994–99 average price) in the second quarter of 1999 was 24 per cent higher than the volume in the second quarter of 1997 (prior to the crisis). Thus, he has argued that the depreciation of exchange rates produced incentives for expanding non-oil exports during the economic crisis in 1998–99.

Figure 3.9 depicts the structural change in the import sector. Since the 1970s, Indonesian imports have been dominated by manufacturing imports. It accounted for more than 70 per cent of total imports. An in-depth observation on manufacturing imports in Figure 3.10 reveals how capital-intensive products continued to dominate manufacturing imports.

Figure 3.9
Composition of Indonesian Imports

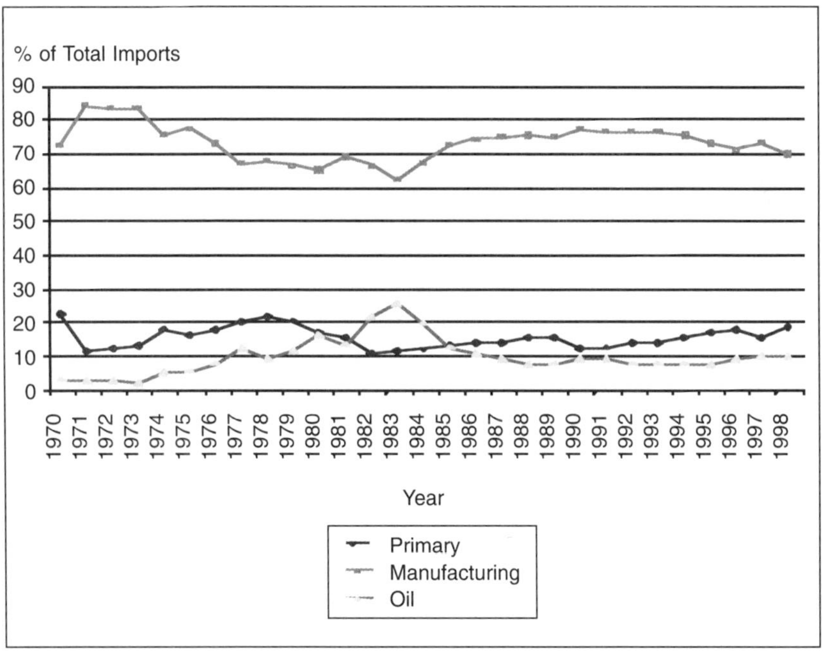

As the rupiah devalued because of the economic crisis, imported goods became even more expensive than domestic goods. Hence, it was expected that the rupiah's plunge would reduce imports. Consequently, in 1997 and 1998 total imports dropped by almost 3 per cent and 34 per cent respectively. The reduction of imports was particularly obvious in manufacturing imports. The other factor which contributed to the decline of imports was the requirement for importers to deposit a fee equivalent to 100 per cent of the imports. This certainly reduced imports significantly because importers could not afford this deposit.

Figure 3.10
Composition of Manufacturing Imports

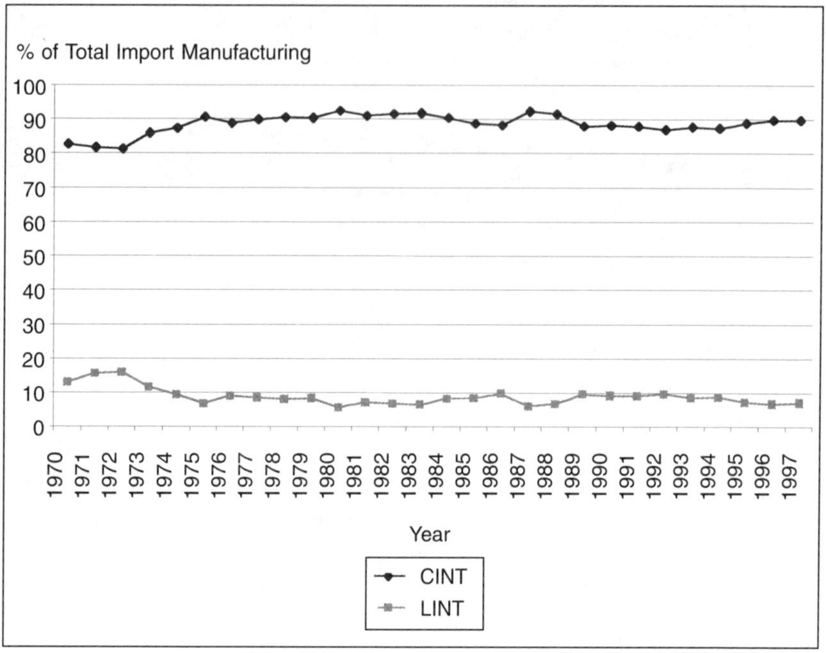

In 1980, natural resource intensive products accounted for 22.2 per cent of total manufacturing exports, while unskilled labour-intensive products contributed 32.8 per cent to exports. The NRI products rose to 46 per cent of total manufacturing whilst the ULI products increased slightly to 35 per cent. However, after the rupiah's devaluation and trade liberalization took place, the ULI products increased to 53 per cent in 1992, whilst the NRI products decreased to 23.8 per cent. Other products, such as technology-intensive (TI) ones, accounted for 29.5 per cent in 1980. Its share continued to decline and accounted for only 9 per cent in 1992. This indicates that trade liberalization gave Indonesian exports its own comparative advantage.

In 1997, the economic crisis came into the picture. This clearly affected the composition of the structure of exports. In 1998, the share of NRI products to total manufacturing exports continued to decline to 13.8 per cent. This was also true for ULI. Thus, the ULI failed to gain from the rupiah's depreciation. Yet, human capital-intensive (HCI) products enjoyed the benefits of the rupiah's fall, particularly for ISIC 64 (paper and paper product) and ISIC 897 (jewellery).

In manufacturing imports, physical capital-intensive (PCI) products continued to dominate manufacturing imports. Its share to total manufacturing imports continued to increase from 49 per cent in 1980 to 53 per cent in 1998. However, the share of HCI consistently decreased from 23 per cent in 1980 to 14 per cent in 1998.

A Regional Perspective on Structural Change in Production

As a comparison with the national pattern, this chapter attempts to observe the structural change in some major provinces and islands. The major provinces are chosen because of their level of GRDP (gross regional domestic product). They are the six largest provinces in terms of the level of GRDP. Since in some provinces, such as Riau and East Kalimantan, the GRDP is dominated by the oil and gas sector, the total GRDP cannot reflect the process of structural change. Therefore, in order to get a more realistic picture of structural change, the non-oil and gas GRDP based on 1993 prices is used. The period of observation chosen is from 1995 to1998, which corresponds to the period before and during the economic crisis. As for the national level, Chennery and Syrquin's (1983) coefficient is applied in this analysis.

Structural Change in Agriculture

The structural change in agriculture in Sumatra demonstrates that the actual pattern was above the normal pattern. This indicates that the process of structural change in agriculture was slower than the normal pattern. During the crisis, as expected at the national level, the share of agriculture in the non-oil 1993 GRDP increased slightly.

It is interesting that the rate of structural change in Sumatra was slower, compared with the normal pattern. In other words, structural change in agriculture should have been faster than the normal pattern in the other regions. The structural change in Java was slightly faster compared with the normal pattern. Java accounted for 46 per cent of the total agricultural sector in Indonesia, while Sumatra accounted for 27.2 per cent in 1995. Therefore, the national pattern has a bias towards the structural change process in Java.

Kalimantan shows a consistent pattern with Chennery and Syrquin's stylized facts. On the other hand, the actual patterns in Sumatra and Sulawesi were slower compared with the normal pattern.

So, what conclusion can we draw from this? First, the structural change process was consistent with Chenery and Syrquin's hypothesis. Secondly, the national pattern was dominated by Java's pattern. Although agriculture in Java experienced faster structural change compared with the normal pattern for national level data, this did not reflect the region's experience. Thus, the national pattern should be interpreted carefully, since it tends to mimic Java's pattern. Thirdly, during the economic crisis, the share of agriculture to the non-oil and gas GRDP tended to increase. This indicates that the economic crisis tended to bring the economy back to the primary base. This trend was seen in Sumatra, Java, and Sulawesi.

Structural Change in the Manufacturing Sector

Like the agricultural sector, the manufacturing sector is also dominated by Java. In 1995, the share of Java's manufacturing in total GDP was 74.6 per cent. We can expect, therefore, that the national pattern would tend to be biased towards Java.

The structural change of manufacturing in North Sumatra was not consistent with Chennery and Syrquin's hypothesis, and this can be seen from a comparison between the actual pattern and the normal pattern. From 1996 to 1998, the share of manufacturing to the total non-oil and gas GRDP in North Sumatra continued to decrease. The 1998 pattern was consistent with the whole of Indonesia, and it can be explained by the economic crisis. Nevertheless, the 1995–97 pattern was inconsistent with Chenery and Syrquin's stylized facts. This indicates that structural change did not take place properly in the manufacturing sector in North Sumatra. Moreover, all the patterns in Sumatra show that the manufacturing sector experienced slower change compared with the normal pattern.

In the case of Java, the process of structural change in the manufacturing sector was consistent with Chenery and Syrquin's stylized facts, except in 1998. The exception can be explained as an impact of the economic crisis, in which the manufacturing sector in Java was badly affected. This result confirms the finding at the national level, in which structural change in the manufacturing sector was faster than the normal pattern. As discussed earlier, the national pattern tended to be biased towards Java's pattern.

It is worth noting that structural change in East Kalimantan was not consistent with Chenery and Syrquin's stylized facts. During 1995–97, the share of manufacturing to total non-oil and gas GRDP tended to decrease, while during the economic crisis the share increased. The increased share of manufacturing to total GRDP indicates that some regions, such as East Kalimantan, benefited from the economic crisis. This finding is consistent with Evans (1998) that the economic crisis had affected Java more substantially than other parts of the country.

In 1998, cement consumption dropped significantly in the major islands of Indonesia. This can be used as one indicator of the economic situation, particularly as a proxy for the development of the construction sector. The drop in cement consumption was consistent with the economic crisis in Indonesia. However, since March 1998, cement consumption has started to increase. The interesting finding is that cement consumption in Java was lower than in other islands. Kalimantan and Sulawesi had the highest consumption. This also supports Evans' findings that the economic crisis had affected Java more substantially than other regions in Indonesia.

For Kalimantan and Sulawesi, structural change in the manufacturing sector was slower compared with the normal pattern. This finding was also consistent with the agricultural sector, in which the actual pattern was slower compared with the normal pattern, particularly outside Java.

Concluding Remarks

The purpose of this chapter is to observe the structural change in the Indonesian economy in general and in the manufacturing and trade sectors in particular. This chapter has shown that most of the patterns of structural change were consistent with Chenery and Syrquin's stylized facts, except for the manufacturing sector in some regions of Indonesia. It has also demonstrated that the economic crisis affected the process of structural change. The economic crisis led to a reversed trend in structural change, both in the structure of production and labour allocation.

Indonesia experienced remarkable growth in the manufacturing and export sectors during the pre-crisis period, and this achievement could be credited to a number of factors, such as devaluation of the rupiah in 1983 and 1986, high savings, high investment rates, and economic liberalization since 1984, as well as credible macroeconomic management and predisposition towards moderate inflation.

In the light of the structural changes in Indonesia, particularly in the manufacturing sector, this study provides a few indications of the early warning signs of the crisis. Although there were some discrepancies to the normal pattern in some sectors, this chapter has found that, in general, the structural changes were consistent with Chenery and Syrquin's stylized facts.

If this is true, then how do we relate this phenomenon, particularly the success story of the pre-crisis manufacturing sector to the economic crisis in 1997–98? The initial debate in the country centred on the link between currency depreciation and economic fundamentals. One view suggested that Indonesia's economy was basically sound as it had been before, while others argued that large depreciations must mean that Indonesia's economic fundamentals were much less sound than were generally believed (Soesastro and Basri 1998). Aswicahyono and Hill (1999) have pointed out that there was no clear link between the Krugman "myth" and the current crisis. They argued that the crisis in 1997–98 was mainly to do with financial markets, exchange rates, the problem of short-term debt, capital mobility, and political disturbances. Furthermore, Rajan and Sugema (1999) have argued that the unique equilibrium Krugman-type model could not be said to have occurred in other East Asian countries besides Thailand. Other economists, such as Corbett and Vines (1999, pp. 167–68) have also stated:

> there does not appear to be a need to appeal to self-fulfilling ideas in order to explain Thailand's original devaluation... (However)... (i)n none of the other economies was overheating or macroeconomic vulnerability nearly as obvious as in the Thai economy... For these economies, there does appear to be a need to appeal to self-fulfilling — currency crisis ideas in order to explain their initial devaluation.

This study has shown that there is little evidence in the relationship between the success in economic structural change prior to the crisis and the current crisis. However, as was mentioned earlier, this is still a subject of debate. Some studies such as that by Cosetti, Pesenti and Roubini (1998) have argued that structural and policy distortions had caused the plunge in exchange rates, asset prices, and economic activity to be more severe than warranted by initial weak economic conditions. Indeed, this question needs to be elaborated on but it is beyond the purpose of this chapter. It is true that the crisis had an impact on structural change in the Indonesian economy, albeit, there is little evidence that the crisis was led by the failure in economic structural change. The answer to why Indonesia was hit by the economic crisis is beyond the simple explanation of economic structural change. Kenward (1999) has correctly pointed out that one cannot take macroeconomic stability for granted. He has pointed out several weaknesses, including weakness in the banking and corporate sectors. This micro weakness eventually magnified when macro shocks came into the picture in July

1997. To make things worse, the corporate sector did not hedge their off-shore borrowing, and as a result when the rupiah plummeted, they faced a financial problem.

Kenward (1999) has also argued that there were structural policy slippages in Indonesia. He said that many of the structural policies had been moving in the wrong direction. He also pointed out that the issue of KKN (corruption, collusion, and nepotism) was drawing international attention. This argument shows that though there were problems in economic fundamentals, one basic question, pointed out by Basri (2000), is why the crisis waited until July 1997. KKN has been pervasive for more than thirty years. In addition, if KKN were the source of the problem, how do we explain the case of China, where corruption has been as bad as in Indonesia? The answer usually put forward is that the crisis itself was triggered by the weakness of the financial sectors. KKN does not lead immediately to crisis, though it hampers the economic recovery process. The practice of corruption and collusion still pervades in many courts, creating difficulties in implementing corporate restructuring. In the case of the bankruptcy law, for instance, during 1998–99, out of 130 cases, only one-fifth of the cases had ended in favour of the creditors. This shows how commercial law has become very commercial in the real sense. It is true that one could set up special courts, or circumvent the use of the courts through arbitration under International Commercial Court (ICC) rules, or revise arbitration procedures with a neutral arbitrator. However, the question is whether ICC rules are applicable to Indonesia. This debate will be long drawn, but meanwhile, corporate restructuring will have to be implemented as soon as possible.

Notes

1. Supported by author interviews with people from the textile, footwear, and automotive industries.
2. The primary sector is defined as SITC 0, 1, 2, 4. The manufacturing sector includes SITC 5–8. The oil sector consists of SITC 3.

References

Anwar, M.A. "Pertumbuhan pertanian dilihat dari pertumuhan produk Domestik Bruto di Indonesia, 1960–1983" [Agricultural Growth examined from Gross Domestic Product in Indonesia, 1960–1983]. Ph.D. dissertation, University of Indonesia, 1983.

———. "Transformasi struktur produksi, pertumbuhan ekonomi dan perencanaan pembangunan" [Transformation of the production sector, economic growth, and development planning]. Speech made at the inauguration of the chair in economics in the Faculty of Economics, University of Indonesia, Jakarta, 1985.

Ariff, M., and H. Hill. *Export-Oriented Industrialisation: The ASEAN Experience*. Sydney: Allen and Unwin, 1985.

Aswicahyono, H.H. "Transformation and structural change in Indonesia's manufacturing sector". In *Waves of Change in Indonesia's Manufacturing Industry*, edited by M. Pangestu. and Y. Sato. Tokyo: Institute of Developing Economies, 1997.

———. "Total factor productivity in Indonesian manufacturing, 1975–1993". Ph.D. dissertation, Australian National University, Canberra, 1998.

Aswicahyono, H.H, and H. Hill. "'Perspiration' v/s 'inspiration' in Asian industrialisation: Indonesia before the crisis". Working Papers in Trade and Development, no. 99/2. Division of Economics, Research School of Pacific and Asian Studies, and Asia-Pacific School of Economics and Management, Australian National University, Canberra, 1999.

Azis, I.J. "Indonesia". In *The Political Economy of Policy Reform*, edited by J. Williamson. Washington: Institute for International Economics, 1994.

Booth, A. *The Indonesian economy in the nineteenth and twentieth centuries: A history of missed opportunity*. New York: St. Martins Press, Inc., 1998.

Chenery, H., and M. Syrquin. *Patterns of development, 1950–1970*. World Bank University Press, 1975.

Corbett, J., and D. Vines. "The Asian currency and financial crises: Lessons from vulnerability, crisis, and collapse". *World Economy* 22 (1999): 155–77.

Cosetti, G., P. Pesenti, and N. Roubini. "What caused the Asian currency and financial crisis? Part I: A Macroeconomic overview". NBER Working Paper No. 6833, 1998.

Evans, K. "Survey of recent development". *Bulletin of Indonesian Economic Studies* 34, no. 3 (April 1998): 5–36.

Hill, Hal. *The Indonesian Economy since 1966: Southeast Asia's Emerging Giant*. Cambridge: Cambridge University Press, 1996.

Ikhsan M., M.C. Basri, and K. Saleh. "Transformasi struktur produksi di Indonesia selama PJP I". In *Sumer daya, teknologi dan pembangunan*, edited by M.A. Anwar, F. Basri and M. Ikhsan. Jakarta: Gramedia, 1995.

Kenward, L.R. "Assessing Vulnerability to Financial Crisis: Evidence from Indonesia". *Bulletin of Indonesian Economic Studies* 35, no. 3 (1999): 71–95.

Martin, W., and P.G. Warr. "Explaining the Relative Decline of Agriculture: A Supply-Side Analysis for Indonesia". *World Bank Economic Review* 7, no. 3 (September 1993): 381–401.

Lembaga Penjelidikan Ekonomi dan Masyarakat (LPEM). "Memo mengenai struktur ketenaga kerjaan di Indonesia". Unpublished, 1999.

Pangestu, M. "Survey of recent developments". *Bulletin of Indonesian Economic Studies* 23, no. 1 (April 1987).

Pardede, R. "Survey of recent developments". *Bulletin of Indonesian Economic Studies* 35, no. 2 (1999).

Rosner, L.P. "Indonesia's Non-oil Export Performance during the Economic Crisis: Distinguishing Price Trends from Quantity Trends". *Bulletin of Indonesian Economic Studies* 35, no. 3 (1999): 71–95.

Simandjuntak, D. "Survey of recent developments". *Bulletin of Indonesian Economic Studies* 25, no. 1 (April 1989).

Rajan, S.R., and I. Sugema. *Government bailouts and monetary disequilibrium: Common fundamentals in the Mexican and East Asian currency crises*. CIES Discussion Paper no 99/2. University of Adelaide, 1999.

Soesastro H., and M.C. Basri. "Survey of recent development". *Bulletin of Indonesian Economic Studies* 34, no. 1 (1998).

Syrquin, M. and H. Chennery. *Patterns of development, 1950–1983*. Discussion papers no. 41. World Bank, 1989.

4

MODELLING THE REPERCUSSIONS OF FINANCIAL SHOCK ON SOCIO-ECONOMIC INDICATORS

Iwan J. Azis

Introduction

Despite the obvious deterioration of some socio-economic variables after the crisis, it is still not clear how the financial shock has transmitted into the social conditions. Almost all analyses on the subject have used socio-economic indicators "before and after", and concluded that any deterioration detected was due to the financial crisis. Such an approach clouds the understanding of the real impact of the financial crisis. More seriously, it is methodologically inaccurate. While attempts to improve social conditions are always necessary, regardless of whether or not there is a crisis, it is equally important to disentangle the real causes of the damages. This is particularly so when policies to counter the crisis-driven damages are to be designed under limited resources, which is the usual condition in a crisis situation.

Moving from a "before and after" approach to a "with and without" one, however, would call for the use of some sort of model. The model should be capable of mapping out the mechanism through which various shocks in the financial variables are translated to selected socio-economic indicators, by taking into account the direct, indirect, and feedback effects.

The primary goal of this chapter is to show how such a model can capture the important events (shocks) during the crisis, and disentangle the impacts of different shocks on some socio-economic indicators. Obviously, the model contains a fairly detailed specification of the financial sector.

First, an economy-wide model of the *structural path analysis* type will be used to measure the total effects of the falling production in selected sectors as a result of the crisis. In the subsequent section, a more comprehensive model featuring endogenous prices is constructed and used to evaluate the sequence of the crisis period in Indonesia. The ultimate purpose of the study is to analyse the impacts of the crisis on selected socio-economic variables.[1]

General Equilibrium Impacts of Production Shocks

The contraction of economic production caused by the crisis could result in severe retrenchment of demand for labour, causing unemployment to increase. In turn, the collapsed demand for a certain type of labour would affect the income and welfare of various household groups differently. Through feedback effects, the resulting income distribution would eventually affect the production structure. Hence, a circular causation between production, factor income, and household income is created.

As the primary interest of this study is to come up with a model that can be used to evaluate the impacts of the crisis on social indicators, this section focuses only on a subset of the problems. More particularly, the question to be raised is: which socio-economic group was hardest hit, and through which path did the transmission of influence take place?

The general equilibrium model adopted in this section falls under the category of *structural path analysis* (SPA), drawing most information from an extensive data system known as *social accounting matrix* (SAM). As SPA has been discussed elsewhere (Azis 2000a; Azis 2000b; Defourny and Thorbecke 1984), the following discussions are devoted only to the results of simulations.

The first task is to determine in what sectors the shock should be introduced. National income data suggest that there are only three sectors which registered positive growth during 1997–98: agriculture, mining, and electricity. Of these three sectors, only agriculture and electricity managed to maintain positive growth in 1998–99. Obviously, there has been a massive contraction in most other sectors, causing a major recession, with a drop of more than 13 per cent in real gross domestic product (GDP) in 1998. The four hardest hit sectors were construction (labelled **Pconst** in Figure 4.1A), trade (**PTrade**), financial (**PBank**), and manufacturing.

The set of simulations in the following analysis is made consistent with such a pattern. For the manufacturing sector, the simulations are done separately, since there are a number of sub-sectors within the industry.

A series of figures (Figures 4.1A–4.1C) display the most relevant paths explaining the transmission of sectoral contraction to different households and other institutions. The latter are listed in descending order based on the size of *global influence* (GI), or SAM multiplier. It should be noted here that these figures are drawn on the basis of SPA results.

According to Figure 4.1A, besides the income of corporate institutions (**Corp**), the hardest hit groups under the scenario of the collapsed construction sector would be the urban household, of both the low and high-income categories (**UrbLow** and **UrbHigh**)

Two relevant paths arrive at **Corp**: the first one travels through various sectors, that is, paper industry (**DPaper** and **Ppaper**), real estate (**DRealEs** and **PRealEs**), and wood manufacturing (**DWood** and **PWood**), and then to private capital (**PrivCap**); the second goes straight to **PrivCap**, before eventually arriving at corporate income (**Corp**).[2]

Figure 4.1

A. SPA Results of a Shock in the Construction Sector

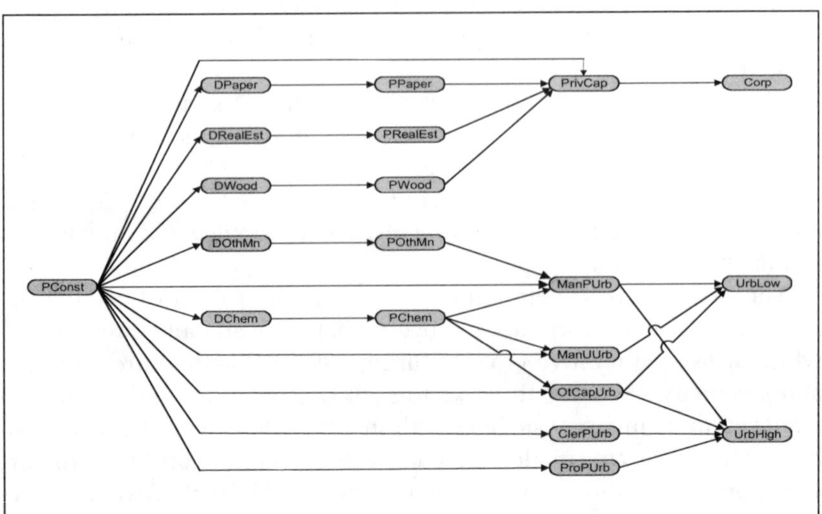

B. SPA Results of a Shock in the Trade Sector

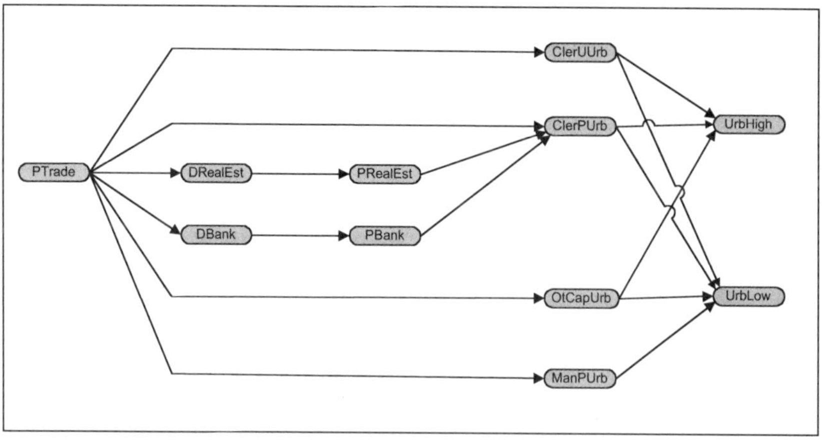

C. SPA Results of a Shock in the Banking Sector

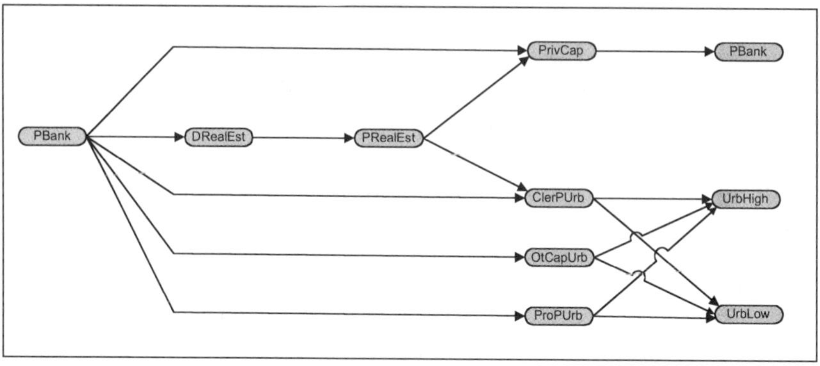

Another important path travels through urban workers, that is, manual workers, both paid and unpaid (**ManPUrb** and **ManUUrb**), and unincorporated urban capital (**OtCapUrb**). There are also two prior paths passing through **ManPUrb**, that is, via domestic and total production of other mining (**DOthMn** and **POthMn**), and chemical industries (**DChem** and **PChem**). Eventually, all of these paths arrive at urban low-income households (**UrbLow**). However, the urban high-income households (**UrbHigh**) also feel the pinch, as shown by the paths travelling through urban clerical (**ClerPUrb**) and urban professional paid workers (**ProPUrb**). Hence, among household categories, clearly those in the urban area are the hardest hit by a severe contraction in the construction sector.

Similar to the above case, the paths linking the trade sector and household income show that urban households are the most severely affected by shrinking trade activities (Figure 4.1B). Although there are actually three relevant paths linking **PTrade** and **ClerPUrb**, the one that goes straight to **ClerPUrb** has the highest ratio between *total influence* and *global influence* (TI/GI equals 67.2 per cent), suggesting that a large part of the trade sector's GI is exercised directly through the reduction in demand for urban clerical paid workers.[3] Nonetheless, the collapse of the trade sector creates a more devastating impact on demand for workers (urban clerical) than on demand for capital.

The next most depressed sector is banking and other financial institutions, labelled **Pbank** (Figure 4.1C). By looking at the size of the **PBank**'s GI, the two most affected sectors are food production and real estate. Most economic activities rely on the operation of the financial sector through savings and investment. The demand for private capital is directly affected by the fluctuation of **PBank** (with TI/GI = 78.2 per cent), and only 3 per cent of the total multiplier is generated through a collapsed demand for the real estate sector. At any rate, in both cases the financial position of the corporate sector (**Corp**) will be eventually damaged.[4]

Which household groups are most seriously affected by the banking sector's depression? Once again, it is the urban household in the high and low-income categories. This occurs primarily because of a significant impact (reduction) of a collapsed banking sector on the demand for urban clerical and professional workers. There are five manufacturing industries to be evaluated. Table 4.1 shows the GIs of those industries. It is not difficult to see from the table that urban households are the most impacted by the shocks in the manufacturing sector.

When one selects the two categories receiving the largest global influence, urban households always appear in the list. If only the top largest is selected, a similar picture is obtained, except in the case of the food processing industry in 1995, when the rural high-income group was the most affected. Judging from the fact that during 1995–98 the largest drop in value-added occured in textiles, wood, and chemical industries, it is unmistakeable that urban households of high and low income types were potentially the hardest hit.[5]

The above analysis is important, particularly for designing social safety net programmes with group targeting in mind. Yet, SPA and

Table 4.1
Largest Global Influence (Multipliers) of Manufacturing on Household Incomes

Year	*Food Proc*	*Textile & Clothing*	*Wood and Product*	*Paper & Transport*	*Chemical & Fert*
1995	Rural High 0.127	Urban Low 0.117	Urban High 0.111	Urban Low 0.098	Urban High 0.124
	Urban High 0.124	Urban High 0.091	Rural Low 0.11	Urban High 0.091	Urban Low 0.099
1998	Urban Low 0.147	Urban High 0.054	Urban Low 0.12	Urban High 0.035	Urban High 0.162
	Rural High 0.147	Urban High 0.048	Rural Low 0.087	Urban Low 0.022	Urban Low 0.118
1999	Urban Low 0.096	Urban Low 0.09	Urban Low 0.14	Urban High 0.079	Urban High 0.143
	Rural High 0.081	Urban High 0.064	Rural Low 0.107	Urban Low 0.077	Urban Low 0.095

Source: Author's calculation based on SPA of SAM 1995, 1998, and 1999.

multiplier analysis suffer from a number of drawbacks. Firstly, there is an assumption of excess capacity in the system. Secondly, it fails to distinguish impacts caused by the crisis from those resulting from some other events unrelated to the crisis. Hence, the collapse of the manufacturing sector is taken exogenously without disentangling the portions that are caused by the financial shock and those caused by other factors. The agriculture-based industries, such as food processing, for example, were clearly dependent on the supply of agricultural products, which in turn were affected by weather conditions in 1997–98, such as the El-Nino-related phenomenon. In such a case, the financial crisis had little to do with the fluctuation. A more important drawback was the absence of price dynamics and substitutions. No non-linear systems are allowed in SPA, yet they are extremely important for the analysis of the financial crisis.

The Mechanism of a Non-Linear Model with Endogenous Prices

In order to incorporate excess capacity, endogenous prices, substitutions, and non-linearity, one needs an alternative model with different specifications. The non-linearity and endogenous price features of the alternative model would allow the system to have some negative and positive multipliers.[6]

Another important feature that should be included in the alternative model is a detailed specification of the financial sector.[7] The financial block reflects a fairly major departure from those previously developed by the author (Azis 2000c).

Beginning with a deteriorating confidence induced by the Thai baht collapse in June 1997, capital began to leave the country. With sizeable corporate sector debts, private domestic investment could not be made, since the corporate balance sheet had severely deteriorated. This was exacerbated by the inability of the banking sector to lend, because of the fast-growing non-performing loans and attenuation of investment activity. Consequently, the economy plunged into recession. This recession itself caused a further loss of confidence. Hence, the circular causality in Figure 4.2 is intensified.

Figure 4.3 displays the detailed mechanism of the CGE model related to the above circular causality (the shaded areas contain the relevant variables in the illustration). With the collapse of confidence, capital began to leave the country, causing foreign equity **EQROW** to decline, leading to rising capital outflows (**PFCAPOUT**). The most direct impact

Figure 4.2
Circular Causality, Multiple Equilibria, and Policy Choices

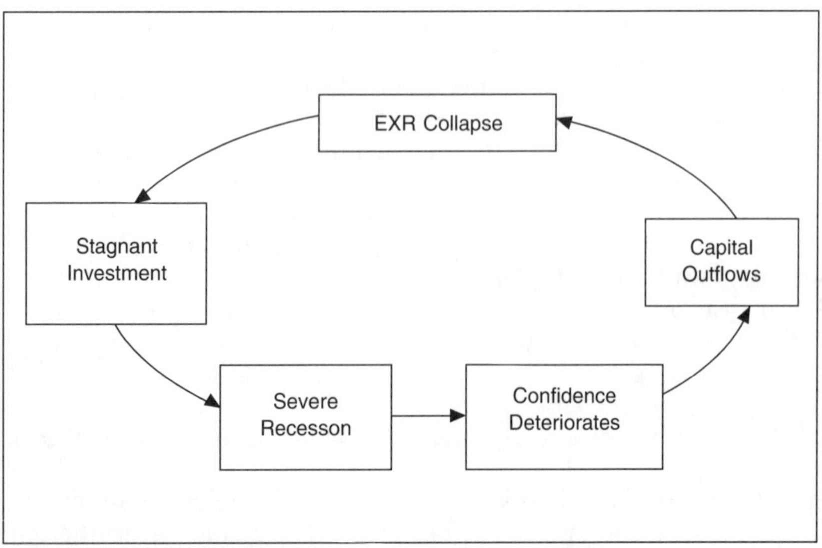

Figure 4.3
Impacts of Capital Outflows on Financial and Real Sectors

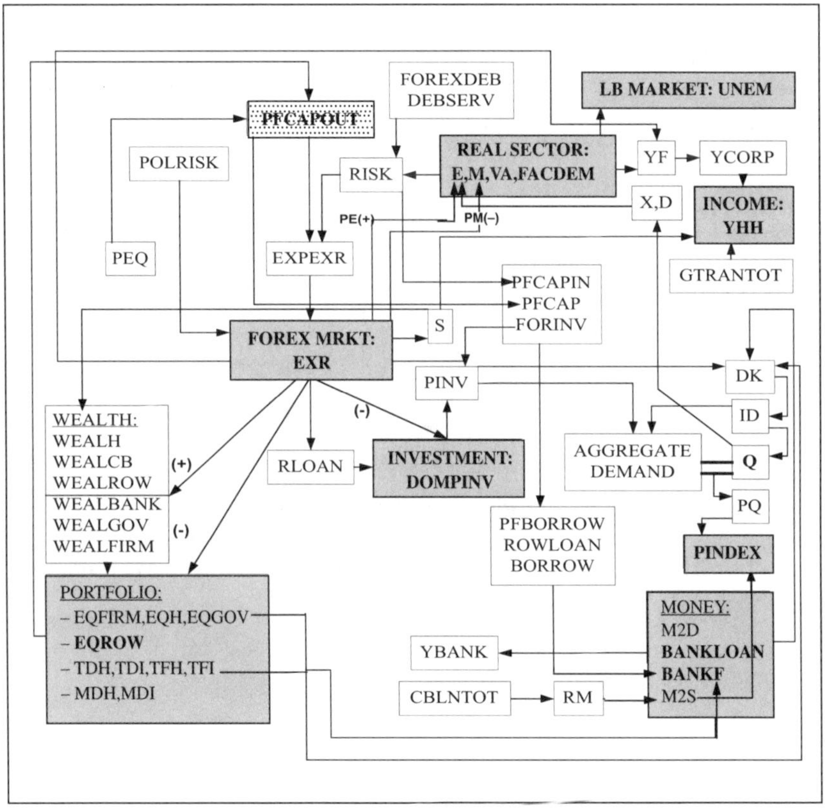

is on the shift in devaluation expectation reflected by the change in **EXPEXR**. With additional pressures from **RISK** factor, the actual (nominal) exchange rate **EXR** collapses.

Four subsequent repercussions are to be expected: (1) standard push on net-exports, **E-M**, via more competitive export prices, **PE**; (2) increased value of foreign savings that will affect household incomes **YHH**, (3) increased domestic value of foreign investment (**FORINV**), and (4) declining domestic investment, **DOMPINV**, via both increased interest rate (**RLOAN**), and direct impact of deteriorated firm balance sheets as a result of rising values of foreign liabilities. Thus, total supply (**Q**) drops and so does the aggregate demand.

The resulting inflation (**PINDEX**) is determined by the interaction between aggregate demand and total supply. In the Indonesian case, however, we need to add several cost-push sources of inflation, one through a drop in food production because of unfavourable weather conditions (El-Nino phenomenon), another through interruptions in the distribution system of some basic commodities (such as rice), especially after the May 1998 riot. This disrupted the effective supply of several commodities, and is captured in the model by adjusting selected parameters in the production function. Finally, import prices soar due to exchange rate depreciation.

Theoretically, pressures on prices can be countered by tight money policy (**MS2**). However, the brakes were not effective, as the central bank began to extend special loans known as BLBI to several commercial banks (increased **CBLNTOT**). This was done in response to the fear of a collapse in the financial system following a major bank run related to the closure of sixteen banks in November 1997. As a result, prices increased significantly throughout 1998.

There are five components of household incomes (**YHH**): (1) factor income; (2) transfers from the rest of the world, inter-household transfers, and government transfers; (3) household income from after-tax corporate dividends; (4) interest income from time deposits; and (5) interest income from foreign currency-denominated time deposits. The disposable income (**YCONS**) is therefore given by equation 2.

$$\begin{aligned} YHH_{ihh} = {} & [\Sigma_f \, factoin_{ihh,f} \cdot TF_f] + [EXR * ROWTRAN_{ihh} \\ & + \Sigma_{ihh} \, transihh_{ihh.ihhh} \cdot YHH_{ihh} \cdot (1 - thh_{ihh}) + gtran_{ihh} \cdot GRANTOT] \\ & + [compdist_{ihh} \cdot (1 - ctax) \cdot YCORP] + [rt \cdot OTDH_{ihh}] \\ & + [rfloan \cdot EXR \cdot OTFH_{ihh}] \qquad \textbf{Eq.1} \end{aligned}$$

$$YCONS_{ihh} = YHH_{ihh} \cdot (1 - th_{ihh}) \cdot (1 - mps_{ihh} - \Sigma_{ihh} \, transih_{ihh,ihhh}) \qquad \textbf{Eq. 2}$$

Notice that if the interest rate **rt** is raised, which is the case under an IMF-sponsored policy response, the **YHH** of households **ihh** which hold savings (**OTDH**) will also increase. Hence, given the interest rate, those holding more time deposits will have higher incomes through interest revenues. The household time deposits **TDH** will be affected by the size of household wealth (**WEALH** in equation 3), the latter being determined by household savings, **HHSAV**, defined as the **mps** (marginal propensity to consume) proportion of **YHH** after tax (equations 4 and 5). Hence, the size of time deposits is determined by incomes. Taken all together, therefore, with a certain time lag, incomes and time deposits are actually interdependent:

$$TDH_{ihh} = gh_{ihh} \cdot (WEALH_{ihh} - MDH_{ihh} - EXP \cdot HHFR_{ihh}) \qquad \textbf{Eq. 3}$$

$$HHSAV = \Sigma_{ihh}\, mps_{ihh} \cdot YHH_{ihh} \cdot (1 - th_{ihh}) \qquad \textbf{Eq. 4}$$

$$WEALH_{ihh} = mps_{ihh} \cdot YHH_{ihh} \cdot (1 - th_{ihh}) + OWEALH_{ihh} + (EXR - EXRO) \cdot OTFH_{ihh} + (PEQ - PEQO) \cdot OEQH \qquad \textbf{Eq. 5}$$

Finally, the sequential dynamics of the model are expressed through the following motion equations for the aggregate capital stock $\boldsymbol{K}$:

$$K_{t,p} = K_{t-1,p}(1 - \Delta_p) + \psi DK_{t,p} \qquad \textbf{Eq. 6}$$

where $\boldsymbol{\Delta}$ is the depreciation rate, and ψ is the absorption rate.

Sequential Simulations

As early pressure on the exchange rate became apparent, following the Thai baht depreciation in July 1998, the government responded by widening the exchange rate band to 12 per cent. At the same time, driven by concern among foreign investors, some capital began to leave the country. This outflow, reflected in the model through **EQROW** and **FCAPOUT**, continued in the following month (14 August), despite the fact that the interest rate (on CB certificate SBI) was raised. Unable to defend the exchange rate further, as a last resort the government floated the rupiah that month. In the model simulation, these two events (in July and August) are captured sequentially.

The third and fourth stages of simulation are basically a continuation of the previous two, except that at these stages the central bank tried to intervene in the forex market by releasing some of its foreign reserves, and the SBI rate was reduced. However, the outflow **EQROW** continued, prompting the government to finally invite the International Monetary Fund (IMF) to rescue. With no deep understanding of what caused the crisis, the IMF demanded its standard prescription — that is, raising the interest rate and closing some banks, despite the fact that the country had virtually no deposit insurance system. The resulting outcome was obvious: a bank run.

When the interest rate continued to rise but capital outflows and the rupiah depreciation persisted (partly because of the IMF's neglect to deal with mounting corporate foreign debts), the situation became worse. The country's financial sector went haywire, and the entire economy fell into a deep recession. The stock market plunged and the rupiah hit an "insane" level of over 11,000 per U.S. dollar. Pandemonium set in when on 8 and 9 January 1998 people went on a buying spree to hoard foodstuff.[8]

In the model specification, the collapse of the exchange rate caused the corporate balance sheet to deteriorate with large negative net-worth (related to unpaid foreign debt). Consequently, no investment could be made, prolonging the recession. As shown in Figure 4.3, a deep recession damaged investors' confidence further, causing capital to continue to leave the country (increased **EQROW**). Furthermore, for the first time, political factors (**POL**) began to play a significant role in the system, as Soeharto's government no longer received a vote of confidence. These shocks are applied in simulations 5 and 6.

Even under the Habibie government, various uncertainties could not be removed, causing market confidence to remain lacking. This was shown by, and captured through, the continued outflows of capital and increased political risks. Such a trend is applied in simulations 7 and 8. By selecting the relevant exogenous variables and adjusting the size of the respective changes based on the above stages, a set of sequential simulations (from stage 1 to stage 8) is conducted.

Figure 4.4 displays the collapse of value-added in various sectors. Clearly, the construction, real estate, and banking & financial sectors

Figure 4.4
Sectoral Value-added: Results of Model Simulation

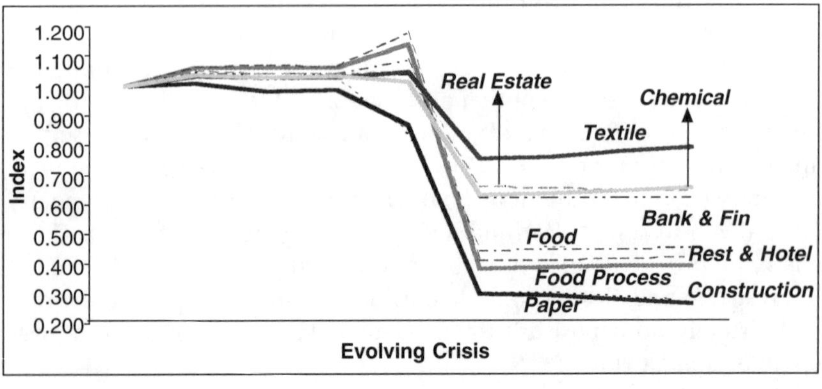

were among the hardest hit during the crisis. Within industries, the largest drop occurred in the food processing and paper-manufacturing sectors. The least affected was textile manufacturing. All categories of manufacturing industries, represented by solid lines, suffered from a significant fall (note that the x-axis represents the eight stages of events described earlier). This is consistent with the national account data that show that all industries declined, and that the largest drop of value-added in nominal terms was in the food processing and paper industries.[9]

The most immediate impact of the economic decline was on the real income of labour. Figure 4.5 shows that the steepest fall of real wages occurred among urban workers of all categories — manual, professional, and clerical types. At the end of the simulation period, real wages of the last two categories are seen to be close to those of agricultural paid and unpaid workers. The difference is that while the real wages of agricultural workers show a slightly upward trend from simulations 6 to 8, real wages of all urban workers decline persistently.

Figure 4.5

Crisis Impact on Labour's Real Income: Results of Model Simulation

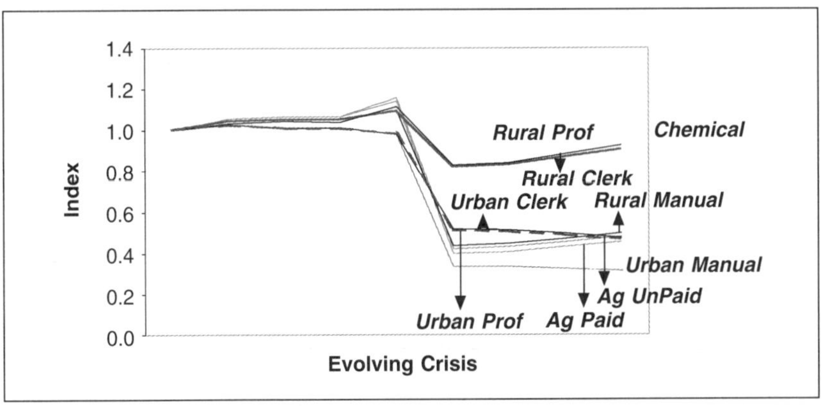

The trend of household real income is even more important to observe, since in reality not all incomes are derived from wage earnings. Furthermore, various forms of transfers have been received by low-income groups during the crisis, either through the government's Social Safety Net and anti-poverty programmes, or prompted by a mutual-help process, which is an important traditional institution existing among rural communities (*gotong royong*). From the perspective of the model specification, however, the most important additional source of income is the interest income received by savers (time-deposit holders), who mostly fall under the category of "urban high" in Figure 4.6. The relatively better position of this group, compared with the "urban low" category, is precisely due to this additional source of income.

Figure 4.6
Crisis Impact on Household Real Income: Results of Model Simulation

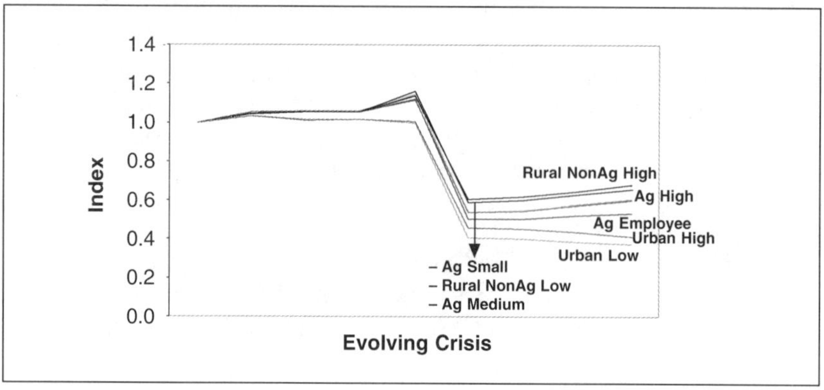

Nonetheless, judging from household incomes, once again the urban areas seem generally to be the hardest hit. Both urban low and high income categories suffer the largest drops in real incomes. Similar to wages, household incomes are moving persistently downwards, while for other categories we observe an increasing trend. Obviously, rising inflation related to a sharp increase in food prices during 1998 contributed significantly to such a decline.

The unemployment result of the simulation clearly indicates that it increased considerably at an annual rate of roughly 10 per cent. This estimate is close to what the CBS data indicated. According to SAKERNAS, based on the official definition of "employment" (that is, those who worked at least 1 hour per week), open unemployment increased from 4.3 to 5.1 million from 1996 to 1998. Of the 5.1 million unemployed, 3.1 million were in the urban (representing 9.3 per cent) and 2.0 million were in the rural (3.3 per cent) areas. Using a different definition of unemployment, the Ministry of Labour predicted that the number of unemployed would reach 36 million in early 2000.

At this stage of the modelling, the unemployment rate was not broken down by sector nor by labour category. Yet, such a breakdown is

Figure 4.7
Gini Index: SAM Data and Model Simulation

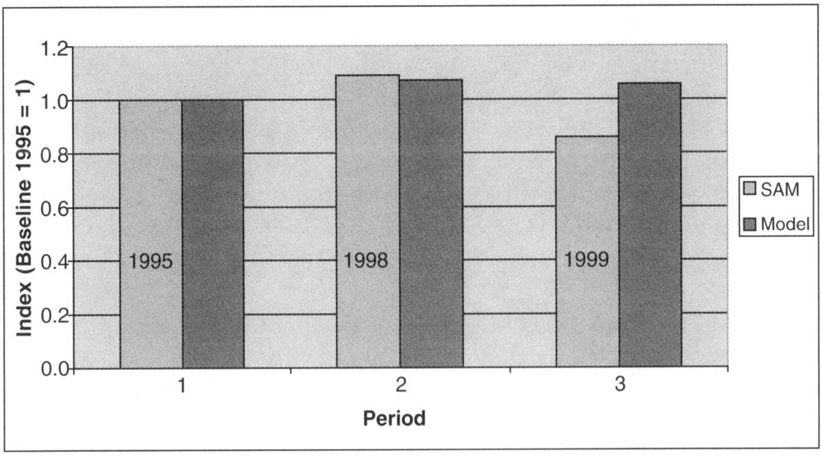

important. For example, while the downturn in the construction sector was likely to hurt male workers more than female workers, within the manufacturing sector different activities would have varying effects on female and male workers. In the machinery sector, for instance, the most affected were male workers, while downsizing in the textile and electronic industries would disproportionately affect female workers.

The combined forces of declining real wages (and incomes) and increasing unemployment could potentially raise poverty levels dramatically. The process could be activated through a decline in consumption levels. If real consumption dropped as much as the rate of price increases, the impact on poverty would be most devastating. Fortunately, there was a process of consumption levelling. Many households either changed their food menu (for example, eating rice only once a day, and eating other less desirable foods the rest of the time), switched to lower priced food (for example, from imported to domestic produce), or used their accumulated savings to purchase food (dis-saving). Moreover, as the price of rice and the consumer price index (CPI) dropped from their 1998 levels, the poverty level went down from 1999, causing the head-count poverty index to decline. However, within the poor group, the conditions may have been more severe, if measured by the FGT index of poverty (not reported here).[10]

There is widespread evidence that a levelling process also took place in non-food consumption. However, the impact on poverty, more particularly on diets, was less serious compared to the levelling in food consumption (especially among the poor). However, the economic crisis was not the only culprit. During 1997/98, Indonesia also suffered from crop failures as a result of the fickle global weather (El-Nino) phenomenon. Subsistence farming areas were the worst affected. Hence, the economic and political crises exacerbated the situation.

Since income can be derived from the model, one can estimate the relative income distribution resulting from the sequential shocks. Figure 4.7 shows the trend of the estimated Gini index, that is, an improvement at the early stage, a worsening in the middle stage, and an improvment again towards the end of the simulation period. Using the income data from SAM 1995, 1996, and 1998, the Gini index shows a fluctuation, with the following trend: 0.31 (1995), 0.34 (1998) and 0.29 (1999).

Two reasons can be posed on why the improved distribution was followed by a worsening situation at the early stage of the crisis. First, as the model suggests, a depreciating exchange rate contributed to rising exports (see again Figure 4.3). This occurred at the early stage largely among the export-oriented primary sector. However, as prices of basic necessities and inputs — including imported inputs — began to rise, the farmers' relative position tended to worsen.[11] Secondly, at the early stage, the hardest hit group comprised the urban households, including the high-income group. However, as specified in equation 8, when the interest rate was persistently high, the middle and higher income groups who held savings in the bank would eventually benefit from their increased interest incomes.

However, the relative income distribution at a certain point in time is highly sensitive to the date of data collection. The results of a survey done during the pre-harvest period tend to differ from data collected during or after the harvest season. The model simulation, on the other hand, does not take into account such seasonal adjustments. This explains why the income distribution index generated by the model is quite different from what the SAM data suggest, although the two produce the same direction of change (see Figure 4.7 again).

Some have argued that the collapse of the formal sectors in the urban areas forced workers either to go back to the rural areas or to accept informal jobs. It turned out that a majority (about 60 per cent) of the laid-off workers remained jobless, even after they had attempted to find jobs once or twice (see Table 4.2).[12] Furthermore, SAKERNAS data also point to a 9.4 per cent and 14.4 per cent increase in urban self-employed and unpaid family workers, respectively, whereas the number of employees dropped from 55 per cent to 52 per cent.

As also argued in Azis (2000a), the urban recession eventually affected the rural non-farm sector. Those in the urban areas who were still fortunate enough to retain their jobs must face the possibility of working fewer hours. Indeed, urban workers who worked less than 15 and 35 hours increased by, respectively, 15.5 per cent and 19.5 per cent (Table 4.3). Obviously, their monetary incomes were also less.

Table 4.2

Percentage of Respondents Ever Experiencing Lay-off and Bankruptcy, by Employment Characteristics, 1997–98

Employment Characteristics/ Problem	*Ever Laid-Off*	*Ever Bankrupt*
Employed	**40.2**	**62.1**
Former Sector	21.7	22.4
Informal Sector	18.5	39.7
Unemployed	**59.8**	**37.9**
Changes in Jobs		
1–2 times	59.8	82.8
>2 times	40.2	17.2

Source: Survey on Crisis Impacts on Cost of Production and Informal Sector, BPS 1998, as quoted in Irawan et al (1999).

Table 4.3

Distribution and Percentage Change of Employment by Region and Working Hours

Region	*1997*		*1998*		
Working Hours	*Number (000)*	*% Distribution*	*Number (000)*	*% Distribution*	*Percentage Change*
Urban					
<15 Hrs	1673.2	5.70	1933.1	6.38	15.53
<35 Hrs	6120.5	20.85	7314.3	24.14	19.50
⩾35 Hrs	23233.3	79.15	22990.2	75.86	–1.05
ALL					
Rural					
<15 Hrs	6497.6	11.59	7260.2	12.66	11.74
<35 Hrs	24444.2	43.61	26987.5	47.04	10.40
⩾35 Hrs	31607.5	56.39	30380.4	52.96	–3.88
ALL	56051.7	100.00	57367.9	100.00	2.35

Source: SAKERNAS 1997 and 1998, BPS.

A CBS survey in 1998 revealed that the average monthly income from the main jobs of people in all income brackets, with the exception of those whose income was greater than Rp400,000, had dropped. The largest percentage drop, by 22.1 per cent, was for the low-income earners (those earning less than Rp200,000), followed by those in the informal sector (20.5 per cent). Combined with the sharp increase in inflation (over 90 per cent during 1996–98), the drop in nominal wages could be translated into collapsed real wages. Indeed, across all sectors real wages had declined (Table 4.4).

Table 4.4
Index of Real Wages, by Type of Industry (1994Q1 = 100)

	1996-II	*1997-II*	*1997-III*	*1997-IV*	*1998-I*	*1998-II*	*% Change*
Hotel	91.4	86.4	86.8	88.9	84.4	72.5	–16.1
Mining	117.8	104.5	100.6	82.1	79.0	85.2	–18.5
Manufacturing Industry	112.9	125.7	121.5	121.5	96.7	92.2	–26.7
Foods	103.3	117.0	113.2	106.2	88.4	84.6	–27.7
Textile	113.5	124.5	118.2	124.6	97.8	89.6	–28.0
Wood/Products	120.4	138.7	140.5	136.7	109.2	107.0	–22.9
Paper/ Printing	128.7	153.9	137.7	129.4	109.7	83.2	–45.9
Chemical	118.2	123.4	118.9	116.8	95.8	95.5	–22.7
Ceramic	111.8	118.2	116.2	117.7	88.8	83.7	–29.2
Basic Metals	95.5	104.7	102.3	98.3	79.5	80.3	–23.3
Metal Products	110.6	131.4	128.4	125.6	97.1	98.8	–24.8
Others	102.5	120.4	115.9	108.8	84.3	75.0	–37.7

Source: BPS, and Bureau for Demographic and Population Statistics, as quoted in Irawan et al (1999).

One estimate reveals that the drop in urban per-capita real income was larger than in the rural areas (30 per cent versus 6.5 per cent), and the sharpest decline in the two areas occurred among the low-income group, that is, 37.1 per cent and 22.7 per cent, respectively (Irawan et al, 1999).

The above arguments do not necessarily mean that there is no urban-rural migration. It is important to note that the selection of the post-crisis year (timing) matters a lot. During 1995–98, the rural and urban populations increased by 4.6 per cent and 3.3 per cent, respectively, but during 1998–99, the urban population declined by 10 per cent, while the rural population increased by 8 per cent (see Table 4.5). Hence, there is an indication that during 1998–99 there might have been considerable urban–rural migration.

Table 4.5
Number of Households and Population, 1995–99

		1995		1998		1999	
	Household Category	*#Household*	*#Pop*	*#Household*	*#Pop*	*#Household*	*#Pop*
1.	Agricultural Workers	5,064,667	20,794,316	5,893,304	24,196,504	7,099,082	30,608,337
2.	Small Farmers (land < 0,5 ha)	8,024,174	32,990,982	8,358,655	34,366,184	10,097,924	40,009,288
3.	Medium Farmers (land 0,501 – 1 ha)	3,076,379	13,796,229	3,204,615	14,371,313	2,915,904	13,694,954
4.	Large Farmers (land > 1 ha)	2,190,677	10,697,076	2,281,994	11,142,975	2,379,946	10,618,552
5.	Rural Low (non-farm)	6,843,656	28,701,887	7,180,472	30,114,475	7,309,818	29,933,080
6.	Non-Labor Force (rural)	2,795,633	9,097,513	2,933,223	9,545,255	3,051,457	9,877,266
7.	Rural High (non-farm)	3,263,466	15,267,947	2,909,464	13,611,768	3,201,555	13,805,324
8.	Low Urban	7,708,983	33,835,022	8,418,047	36,947,134	7,386,730	30,856,354
9.	Non-Labour Force	2,660,015	10,197,213	2,904,680	11,135,142	4,130,884	10,131,141
10.	Urban High	4,025,435	19,376,621	3,623,575	17,442,250	2,930,900	17,902,804
	Total	45,653,084	194,754,80	47,708,029	202,873,000	50,504,200	207,437,100

Source: SAM 1995, 1998, and 1999.

Obviously, there are other social variables of interest, and one of them is the incidence of poverty. What is the mechanism explaining the transmission of a financial shock to poverty? The most direct one is through a decline in nominal incomes or wages, and this is related to the fact that the number of laid-off workers increased during the crisis. Another mechanism is through an increase in prices, especially those of basic commodities, such that the poverty line is also raised.

Endogenous Poverty Estimates

Results from the simulation also indicate that unemployment increased quite considerably. Yet, the allowance of wage decline and mobility of labour (from urban to rural areas, and from the formal to the informal sector) — a prominent sign of a flexible labour market — prevented an even more catastrophic situation from occurring. While during the peak of the crisis the unemployment rate may have increased significantly, towards the end of 1998 and early 1999 the recorded unemployment rate showed only a slight increase from the pre-crisis level. Indeed, from the model simulation the increase in unemployment was surprisingly small (less than 1 percentage point).

Nonetheless, the combined forces of unemployment, declining real wages (incomes), and surging prices have raised the incidence of poverty. There is some evidence of consumption levelling that led to a lower incidence of poverty than originally predicted.[13] Moreover, as prices and the CPI declined at the later stage (Stage 8), the poverty line dropped, and so did the head-count index.

The estimate of poverty incidence is based on a parametric measure of distribution, in which intra-group distribution is directly generated from the SUSENAS-core data, with a 206,597 sample size.[14] It is important to note that the Indonesian Central Bureau of Statistics (CBS) does not produce separate price indices for urban and rural areas. Therefore, price indices had to be generated to produce estimates of urban and rural poverty.

The starting point was the selection of a basket of basic needs (BN) reflecting the consumption pattern of the households around the presumed poverty line and yielding the threshold caloric requirements. Of course, food is by far the most important commodity in this BN basket. In the modelling, this basket was limited to four commodities: food (rice), other food, textiles, and social services. First, the consumption share of each of these goods was estimated in the base year (1996) to derive the BN consumption value for both urban and rural areas (the share of food in the rural BN basket is higher than in the urban BN basket). Next, the weighted average of the BN basket in 1999 was computed, keeping the shares constant but using the prices generated endogenously by the model for the four goods in 1999 .To arrive at the prices of basic needs (prices presumably paid by the poor), these weighted domestic prices were adjusted by the ratio of the consumer price index (PINDEX) to the average domestic price (PD). The above procedure provided rough estimates of poverty line price deflators between 1996 and 1999, distinguishing between the urban and rural areas.

Although the CBS does not compute urban and rural price indices separately, it does compute urban and rural poverty lines based on two extensive baskets of commodities and services (comprising more than fifty items) consumed by the poor. The CBS urban and rural poverty lines for the base year 1996 was multiplied by the above derived price indices to obtain the 1999 (post-crisis) poverty lines that were used in the simulation experiments. The poverty line was taken as $\Sigma_{com} \pi_{com} \cdot P_{com}$, where π_{com} is a basket of quantities of commodities reflecting basic needs. In the calculation, the π_{com} used to obtain the price deflator consisted of four commodities, whereas the π_{com} used to derive the poverty line in 1996 was based on more than fifty items. At any rate, the fluctuations of the monetary poverty lines in the urban and rural areas were commensurate with the movements in the poverty line prices endogenously determined within the model.

Next, the changing poverty incidence in each of the socio-economic household groups in the model was estimated by applying the respective poverty lines. It turned out that, based on SUSENAS-core data in 1996 and 1999, the intra-group distributions in both years for each group (expressed at constant 1996 prices) appeared quite similar, suggesting that the distribution in each of the household categories (at constant prices) can be assumed to be unchanged.[15] Each group distribution was then adjusted by the change in the mean income of that household group generated in the simulation. This means that if the mean income of a specific group were to rise by 100 per cent in nominal terms, for example, each individual's income within this same group would increase, likewise, by 100 per cent. Therefore, both the poverty line and the household income were derived endogenously in the model.

Table 4.6 shows the resulting poverty trend (FGT measures) in the benchmark scenario (the "End of Simulation" column refers to Stage 8 of the simulation). It is clear that the deterioration in poverty conditions was more severe in the urban than in the rural areas. While the head-count poverty among farmers owning land increased from 21 per cent to 26 per cent, and among rural non-farm households the increase was from 11 per cent to 20 per cent (for low income rural) and from 9 to 12 per cent (for high income rural), the poverty incidence within the category of agricultural workers dropped from 18 to 14 per cent. This last result, although surprising, might be explained by the fact that most agricultural workers are employed in the plantation export sector that benefited from the currency depreciation. In contrast, in the two categories of urban households the head-count poverty incidence increased most dramatically among the urban low income, that is, from 16 per cent to 25 per cent. Similar trends were observed for the poverty gap and the severity of poverty indicators. Overall, urban poverty appeared to rise from 12 per cent in 1996 to 19 per cent in 1999, and rural poverty from 16 per cent to 20 per cent.

Table 4.6
Endogenously Derived Poverty Measures

	Baseline			*End of Simulation*		
	alpha = 0	*alpha = 0*	*alpha = 0*	*alpha = 0*	*alpha = 0*	*alpha = 0*
Agemp	0.1783	0.0299	0.0078	0.1417	0.0227	0.0057
Farm	0.2096	0.0421	0.0132	0.2569	0.0541	0.0174
Rurallo	0.1136	0.0183	0.0048	0.1981	0.0362	0.0102
Ruralhi	0.0885	0.0151	0.0042	0.1212	0.0219	0.0063
RURAL	**0.1612**	**0.0300**	**0.0088**	**0.2006**	**0.0392**	**0.0119**
Urbanlo	0.1588	0.0308	0.0091	0.2520	0.0561	0.0183
Urbanhi	0.0803	0.0149	0.0044	0.1156	0.0232	0.0071
URBAN	**0.1222**	**0.0234**	**0.0069**	**0.1863**	**0.0403**	**0.0129**
TOTAL	**0.1485**	**0.0278**	**0.0082**	**0.1965**	**0.0395**	**0.0122**

Conclusion

Numerous factors, including the financial crisis, have caused socio-economic damages in Indonesia. Yet, most analyses do not distinguish between the impact from the financial shock and that caused by other variables, as if all deteriorating conditions were due to the financial crisis. To make such a distinction, a model system needs to be constructed.

The use of such a model to analyse the impact of the financial crisis on socio-economic indicators has been presented in this chapter. The model is of a non-linear general equilibrium type, incorporating detailed specifications of the financial sector and household incomes, allowing under-utilized capacity conditions, and treating prices endogenously. It has been clearly pointed out by model simulations that in the Indonesian case the urban households were generally harder hit by the crisis. These results reflect purely the cause of the crisis, since they are derived from an isolated shock in the financial sector alone (removing the impact of other events). The expected trend of reversed migration, that is, from the urban to the rural areas, appears to have taken place only after a certain time lag — that is, it was not observed in 1998, but was in 1999. It remains to be seen, however, whether such migration is permanent or temporary. The sequential simulations of the model also shed some light on the issues of when and under what conditions the trend of deteriorating social conditions could be reversed.

From the analysis of the poverty trend, it is shown that the crisis has hit the urban households more negatively than the rural households. This result is the outcome of two combined forces: a lower increase in the households' nominal income and a faster increase in the poverty line price indices in the urban areas, compared with the rural areas.

However, the most salient point is the fact that by using the model a set of counterfactual scenarios could be simulated. One of the most interesting counterfactual scenarios pertains to the question "what would be the economy-wide impact if the government had avoided the IMF policy of raising the interest rate to cope with the crisis, and how would the damaging socio-economic conditions be affected?" The analysis of such a question would significantly enhance the quality of policy debates.

Two counterfactual policy scenarios (Azis 2000c; and Azis et al 2001) have been done, one on interest rate (not raising it), and another on the combination of non-high interest rate and partial debt resolution. From such experiments (not reported here), it was found that not only macroeconomic indicators but also social indicators, such as unemployment, income distribution, and poverty conditions would have been better if the country had taken alternative policies.

Notes

1. The endogenous socio-economic variables are limited to unemployment, labour income, household income distribution, and poverty.
2. From the complete results of SPA simulations (not reported here), it has been revealed that a significant part (47.6 per cent) of the GI of the collapsed construction sector is shown *directly* by a contraction in the demand for private capital.

3. By comparing TI/GI of three paths arriving at **UrbHigh**, one will notice that the significant paths are those travelling via reduced demand for urban clerical workers, both paid and unpaid categories. They contribute 29.3 per cent and 27.1 per cent, respectively, compared to only 8.4 per cent for the path that goes through unincorporated urban capital (based on the SPA results not reported here).
4. With the opening up of the economy since the 1980s, the country's banking and other financial sector has also played an instrumental role in channelling foreign capital to the domestic business sector. From a more complete set of simulations, it has been revealed that the collapse of the banking sector also affected the demand for foreign capital (**ForCap**), before finally hitting corporate income.
5. At the outset, it looks as if the path with the highest total influence (TI) will have the lowest path multiplier, as the example of the collapsed construction sector has shown. However, such a pattern is by no means a rule. The case of the impact of the food processing industry on the demand for rural agricultural unpaid workers, for example, indicates a different pattern. While the TI is highest if the path travels through the demand for agricultural food production, its path multiplier is also higher compared to the case in which the path goes through the non-food agricultural sector (1.58 versus 1.57).
6. A drop in the demand for, say, output of the food processing industry during the crisis could have a negative impact on some agricultural products (that is, a positive multiplier). On the other hand, increased demand for agricultural products may create detrimental effects upon (reduced production of) food processing and other light industries, because it drives up prices in this forward industry's input market (negative multiplier). Hence, the corresponding Jacobian multiplier matrix would show a mixture of pluses and minuses, a contrast from the all-positive multipliers in SAM and SPA.
7. The model consists of the following blocks: financial/monetary block, capital flow block, real sector block, price block, trade block, labour market block, and investment-saving block. The financial block plays a pivotal role since the model is designed specifically to capture the financial crisis episode. Given the financial balance sheets of six institutions in the economy, that is, central bank, commercial banks, foreign sector, government sector, households, and production sector, the behaviour of each is specified separately.
8. The author observed the IMF's lack of touch with these chronological events, when in a private conversation with the IMF economists in Jakarta in March 2000 he was told that there was no food hoarding and rioting in January 1998 that caused prices of some basic goods, including rice, to soar. The fact is, there was hoarding and occasional riots, and the inflation rate rose by 13 per cent from December 1997 to January 1998. The IMF remained convinced that the resulting inflation was a demand phenomenon, hence to be solved by aggregate demand management, that is, continue to raise the interest rate.

9. To be comparable with the SAM data used in the model, one needs to do the comparison using nominal — not constant — prices. A different conclusion can be obtained when constant prices are used, for example, the value-added of the two industries increase, not decrease. Moreover, in making the comparison, one needs to take into account the fact that there are some discrepancies in the classification and coverage of the manufacturing sector between those in the national account and in the SAM.
10. FGT stands for Foster-Greer-Thorbecke. See Foster, Greer, and Thorbecke (1984). Note that poverty here is associated with income deprivation. Hence, it does not cover other important poverty dimensions related to Sen's "deprivation of capabilities", which refers to a lack of substantive freedoms necessary for achieving the kind of life that people value. See Sen (1999).
11. Data on farmer's terms-of-trade also indicate an improvement in certain major areas during mid-1997 to mid-1998, then deteriorating during mid-1998 to mid-1999 (CBS, *Buletin Ringkas*).
12. Based on the CBS "Survey on the Crisis Impacts on Cost of Production and Informal Sector", 1998.
13. Many households have either changed their food menu (for example, eating rice once a day, using other less desirable foods the rest of the time), switched to lower price food (such as, from imported to domestic produce), or used their accumulated savings to purchase food (dis-saving). There is widespread evidence showing that a levelling process also takes place in non-food consumption. However, the impact on poverty, more particularly on diets, is less serious compared to the levelling in food consumption (especially among the poor). It is also important to note that the economic crisis was not the only culprit. During 1997/98, Indonesia also suffered from crop failures as a result of the fickle global weather (El-Nino) phenomenon and a massive haze problem. Subsistence farming areas were the worst affected.
14. Note that since the SUSENAS-core does not distinguish between farmers according to different land sizes (small, medium, and large landowners are lumped together), only six, instead of eight, household categories are used in the analysis: four in the rural areas, that is, agricultural employees (Agemp), farmers with land (Farm), non-farm rural low-income household (Rurallo), non-farm rural high income household (Ruralhi); and two in the urban areas, that is, low income urban household (Urbanlo), and high income urban household (Urbanhi). It is important to note also that the SUSENAS survey reflects the conditions around March of the respective years.
15. This is reported in my joint work: Iwan J. Azis, Erina E. Azis, and Erik Thorbecke, "Modeling the Socio-economic Impact of the Financial Crisis: The Case of Indonesia" (Report prepared for the World Bank, May 2001).

References

Armington, P. "A Theory of Demand for Products Distinguished by Place of Production". *International Monetary Fund Staff Papers* 16 (1969): 159–78.

Aghion, P., P. Bacchetta, and A. Banerjee. "A Simple Model of Monetary Policy and Currency Crises". Mimeographed, 1999.

Azis, Iwan J. " Indonesia: The Role of Institutional Weakness in the Crisis". In *The Politics of the Economic Crisis in Asia: Consensus and Controversies,* pp. 49–52. Report published by the Carnegie Endowment for International Peace, 1999.

———. "Simulating Economy-wide Models to Capture the Transition from Financial Crisis to Social Crisis". *The Annals of Regional Science* 34 (Springer-Verlag, 2000a): 1–28.

———. "Non-Linear General Equilibrium Impacts of Financial Crisis and Manufacturing Downfall". *The Developing Economies* 38, no. 4 (December, 2000b).

———. "Modeling the Transition From Financial Crisis to Social Crisis". *Asian Economic Journal* 14, No. 4 (Blackwell, 2000c).

Azis, Iwan J., Erina E. Azis, and Erik Thorbecke. "Modeling the Socio-economic Impact of the Financial Crisis: The Case of Indonesia". Research report for the World Bank, May 2001.

Bernanke, Ben S., and M. Gertler. "Agency Costs, Net Worth, and Economic Fluctuations". *American Economic Review* 79 (1989): 14–31.

Bernanke, Ben S., and Alan S. Blinder. "Is it Money or Credit, or Both, or Neither?" *American Economic Review* 78, No 2 (1988).

Bruner, Karl, and Alan H. Meltzer. "Money, Debt, and Economic Activity". *Journal of Political Economy* 80 (September/October 1972): 951–77.

Central Bureau of Statistics. "Survey on Crisis Impacts on Cost of Production and Informal Sector". Mimeographed. Jakarta: Central Bureau of Statistics, 1998.

———. *SAKERNAS,* various volumes

———. *SUSENAS,* various volumes

———. *Buletin Ringkas,* various volumes.

Defourny, J., and E. Thorbecke. "Structural Path Analysis and Multiplier Decomposition within a Social Accounting Matrix Framework". *Economic Journal* 94 (1984): 111–36.

Foster, James, J. Greer, and Erik Thorbecke. "A Class of Decomposable Poverty Measures". *Econometrica* 52 (1984).

Froot, K.A. "On Efficiency of Foreign Exchange Markets". Mimeographed, 16 November 1990.

Harberger, A. "Monetary Policy in Post-Crisis Period". Report prepared for the USAID, Jakarta, February 2000.

Irawan, P., and H. Romdiati. "The Impact of Crisis on Poverty and Its Implications for Development Strategies". Paper presented at the National Workshop on Food and Nutrition VII. Jakarta, 10–12 May 1999.

Klein, Lawrence R. "The Asian Economic Crisis". Paper delivered to the Second Committee of the UN General Assembly, 7 October 1998.

Krugman, P. "Analytical Afterthoughts on the Asian Crisis". Mimeographed, 1999.

MacDonald, R., and M. P. Taylor. "Exchange Rate Economics: A Survey". *IMF Staff Papers* 39, no. 1 (March 1992): 1–57.

Meredith, G., and Menzie D. Chinn. "Long Horizon Uncovered Interest Parity". NBER Working Paper, No 6797 (November 1998).

Meese, R., and K. Rogoff. "Empirical Exchange Rate Models of the Seventies". *Journal of International Economics* 14 (1983): 3–24.

Mishkin, Frederic S. "International Capital Movements, Financial Volatility and Financial Instability". NBER Working Paper, No. 6390. Cambridge, MA, 1998.

Pradhan, M. and R. Sparrow. "Indonesia Health Sector Analysis — Changes in Health Indicators Collected in the 1995, 1997, 1998 and 1999 SUSENAS Household Surveys". Mimeographed. Cornell University, 9 February 2000.

Pradhan, M. and Sparrow. "Basic Education Outcomes During Crisis: An Analysis Using the 1995, 1997, 1998 and 1999 SUSENAS". Mimeographed. Cornell University, 15 February 2000a.

Sachs, J. D., A. Tornell, and A. Velasco. "Financial Crises in Emerging Markets: The Lessons From 1995". Brookings Papers on Economic Activity, No. 1 (1996).

Sen, Amartya. *Development as Freedom*. New York: Alfred A. Knopf, September 1999.

Tobin, J. "A General Equilibrium Approach to Monetary Theory". *Journal of Money, Credit and Banking* 2 (November 1970): 461–72.

PART II

Human Capital

5

FREEDOM FROM FEAR
Social Disruption and System of Violence in Indonesia

Muhadjir Darwin

> Fear is an important problem in its own right. It makes life miserable for those who fear and prompts citizens to take actions that make their neighborhoods even more dangerous.
>
> — Mark H. Moore and Robert Trojanowicz

> It is not power that corrupts but fear. Fear of losing power corrupts those who wield it and fear of the scourge of power corrupts those who are subject to it.
>
> — Aung San Suu Kyi

This chapter attempts to elaborate "freedom from fear" as an essential social capital needed for Indonesia's economic recovery. First, it argues that fear is an effect, but at the same time a cause of violence. The prolonged and systemic social disorder and violence triggered by the existence of cultural values justify violence and social structures that create inequity in a society. Inequity causes jealousy and distrust, and these are the footsteps of violence. This chapter proposes that to release individuals from fear, violence should not be used, for violence always results in further violence. Rather, the government should focus on two basic factors that can break and resolve the systemic violence, namely, equality and trust.

Years of Violence

Two years before the new millenium, in 1998, the Indonesian people celebrated what was called the most democratic election in the last fifty-three years of Indonesian independence after the 1955 election. The election was the starting point of democratization and the establishment of a civil government. It was, however, not the turning point of prolonged violence and political turmoil. The violence has even escalated since then. When the winning party, the Struggle Indonesian Democratic Party (PDIP), failed to place Megawati Sukarnoputri as the new President in the People's Advisory Assembly plenary session, her fanatic supporters in Jakarta, Solo, Denpasar, and other places raged violently in the streets. Though the leadership of President Abdurrachman Wahid and Vice-President Megawati was widely acknowledged as legitimate, and the *pelangi* (rainbow) Cabinet represented equal power-sharing among the major political parties, violence did not end.

In the first days of Wahid's administration, he visited many countries in East and Southeast Asia, the Middle East, the United States, and Western Europe to assure the world that Indonesia maintained democracy and security, and called on foreign investors to come and invest in Indonesia. However, that call was received coolly by foreign investors. Most of them were wary of investing because of the insecurity and unpredictability that Indonesia still presented. Investments that might fund a recovery remained insignificant. Overall investment shrank by 21 per cent in 1999, according to the World Bank.

It was on Thursday, 4 May 2000, that Jakarta City Police Chief Maj. Gen. Nurfaizi told the security chiefs of dozens of embassies in a meeting in Jakarta that the capital was a safe place to live and was also safe for foreign investment.

> We want to assure the chiefs that the crime rate here is not as high as before, and that the city is a safe place to live in, ...that foreigners are free to come here and invest. ...The total number of crime incidents had declined from a staggering 20,157 incidents in 1997 to 18,503 in 1999. ...We also invited the security chief to ask police for assistance in any matter concerning security, including updates on conditions in the capital (*Jakarta Post*, 6 May 2000).

A few days after that meeting, 13 May 2000, Jakarta was shocked by riots following police raids on pirated video compact disk (VCD) vendors in downtown Glodok. The violence continued in the following months, and there was no indication that it would stop. In August 2000,

Jakarta was shocked by two bomb explosions that took place at the same time as the yearly meeting of the People's Advisory Assembly. The first bomb incident occurred at the Attorney General's office while investigations were being conducted on Tommy Soeharto, one of the sons of the former president, in the same building. No lives were taken on this occasion. The second bombing was at the residence of the Philippine Ambassador for Indonesia by an unindentified man, taking the lives of two local civilians and seriously wounding the Ambassador himself. Many people relate this incident to the action of the Attorney General in bringing Soeharto to court on the allegation of corruption. Another incident happened in September 2000 in Atambua, West Timor, where thousands of armed people attacked the UNHCR (United Nations High Commission for Refugees) office and took the lives of four UNO civilian workers. A more shocking incident, as it affected the exchange rate of the rupiah and also economic stability, was the bombing of the BEJ (Jakarta Stock Exchange) building, just a week after the Atambua incident, on 13 September 2000. The bombing took the lives of fifteen people, and wounded tens of people. All the while, there was pessimism about when the riots would be over.[1] This, in time, affected negatively the interest of foreign investors to invest.[2]

Riots

National Awareness

Riots did not belong exclusively to the reformation order. It has occurred since the day of independence. Hasyim noted that there have been 74 massive riots since 1946 until 1999, apart from serious political turbulence such as the war against the Dutch and the Allies in 1947–49, and some rebellions (by the DI/TII, Permesta, and the Indonesian Communist Party) against the Indonesian Government. Ethnic, race, religion, or economic class jealousy motivated some of the riots (Hasyim 2000).

It seems that the numerous riots indicate that the nation-building project has not yet been completed. Indonesian nationalism, which has been struggling since it was initiated by the founding fathers in the early twentieth century, has been thwarted by the rise of primordial sentiments. The sentiments of ethnicity, race, and religion often became the source of much social conflict in Indonesia. Horizontal conflict involving different ethnic groups, race, and religions occurred when uneven social and economic conditions existed among people of different ethnicity, race, and religions. The policy of the New Order government to de-emphasize primordial identities could not wipe out these sentiments. On the contrary, the primordial sentiments strengthened, especially because of increasing inequality among different social groups. In recent years, the riots have been increasing quantitatively and qualitatively. Some riots were triggered by political disputes, some others by religious, ethnic, or regional fanaticism. The crime rate has also been rising. This increase has not been matched by the capability of law enforcement. In time this problem will give rise to violence by society against the criminals. These riots have not only taken the lives of the people but also caused an enormous loss of belongings that will eventually work against Indonesia's recovery effort from the economic crisis (see Appendix 2).

Riots against the Chinese

Among the most shocking riots were those based on hatred of the ethnic Chinese. The Bagansiapi-api incident, known as *"Serbuan Amat Merah"* (Truly Red Attack) took place just seven months after independence day, in March 1946, and took the life of one Chinese captain. The incident was triggered by the action of the Chinese who did not want to display the Indonesian flag. Five months after the incident, the Tangerang riots happened, at which the masses burned down the homes of Chinese residents who did not take the side of the Indonesian Government. Riots targetting the ethnic Chinese have continued since then. The 30 September 1965 communist rebellion and the Malari riots in 1974, for example, were also coloured by the burning or destruction of homes and belongings of the Chinese, or the slaughter of Chinese residents. The biggest riot targetting the Chinese was probably the May 1998 incident when 1,000 people lost their lives and many more their livelihoods as shops, houses, and offices were burned to the ground by uncontrollable mobs. It was also a riot in which 84 acts of violence against women took place, including rapes, torture, sexual assaults, and sexual harassment, mostly against the ethnic Chinese.

Riots among Native Ethnic Groups

The jealousy of native ethnic groups towards the Chinese residents was not the only potential source of massive riots. Jealousy among the native ethnic groups was also an important factor that could trigger riots. Indonesia is a multi-ethnic country with hundreds of ethnic groups with their own different local languages and cultures. The jealousy between the native ethnic groups was seen, for example, when the people living outside Java showed their unhappiness with the transmigration of mostly Javanese from the densely populated areas to the rural areas and the outlying islands. The facilities provided for the transmigrants (such as land, housing and road facilities), primarily from Java, were criticized as insufficient to support the needs and welfare of the local residents. Apart from the transmigration problem, there were some ethnic groups in Indonesia who were known to have a high level of mobility, such as the Minang (West Sumatra), Maduranese (East Java), and Bugis (South Sulawesi). Their success in their new places of residence sometimes invoked jealousy among the local people and this in turn could trigger conflict between them. One of the most serious incidents was the riot in West Kalimantan when the Dayak and Melayu people slaughtered hundreds of Maduranese.

The conflict between the natives of West Kalimantan, especially the Dayak, against the migrants, particularly the Maduranese, has existed since the 1950s, but the riot in 1996–97 was the most serious. An unofficial source has mentioned that the victims of the riot numbered 1,720 people, while the local government mentioned a smaller number, of about 400 people.

Riots Caused by Religious Sentiments

Some riots during the reformation era were triggered by religious sentiments. One instance of this was the Situbondo incident which happened in East Java on October 1996. The riot started when a civilian named Shaleh insulted Kiai As'ad Syamsul Arifin. The people were furious when they found out that the conviction given by the judge on Shaleh was considered too lenient. Buildings and the courthouse were burned down, twenty-four Christian buildings (churches, schools) were incinerated, a restaurant was also set on fire, and a store, two theatres and four cars were burned. Five people also died during this riot.

A similar riot happened in Tasikmalaya in December 1996. The riot started when an officer of the District Police Station in Tasikmalaya tortured an *ustadz* (Islamic teacher) because he had punished his two *santri*s (students at a traditional Muslim school) who were caught stealing in the *pesantren*, and who happened to be the children of the police officer. This incident triggered a riot which caused three hotels to be damaged, and six private bank buildings, five car dealers, seven supermarkets, three buses, twelve churches, eighteen district police stations, and a *pesantren* to be ruined.

The biggest riot caused by religious sentiments happened in Maluku and Northern Maluku. A massive and prolonged physical war between two religious groups, Moslem and Christian, involving native residents in these provinces, occurred after they had been living side by side under the culture of "*Pela-Gandong*".[3] The truth is that they had kept their suspicions and hatred towards each other for a long time so that when a conflict involving two persons with different religions occurred, it turned into a prolonged and massive conflict. Then, a tragedy, known as "the Idul Fitri tragedy" happened, when the people from Hative Besar (Christian) slaughtered people from Wailete who were praying during the Idul Fitri ritual. Kastor (2000) has identified 127 mosques and 24 churches that were burned or ruined. About 283 Moslems in Ambon died either by being burned, shot, or slaughtered. He did not mention the number of Christians killed during the conflict. The seriousness of the conflict can be observed from the utterance of one of the victims, Muflich M. Yusuf, as mentioned by Kastor (2000, pp. 224–25)

> Wednesday (12/21/99), at 9:00 am East Indonesian time, the Christians from Kampong Kusur Telaga Panca and Kao attacked the Togolihua (inhabited) Moslem village. We, thousands of people, sheltered in the Mosque Al Ikhlas. Those infidels shot the mosque, which was smeared with pork blood with bow and arrows. Some of them threw stones at the mosque. They attacked the mosque. A lot of people escaped. Then the mosque was burned. There were 600 people inside the mosque who were burned to death. I saw a lot of women being stripped their clothes, then raped in groups in front of the mosque. Then trucks carried out women and children. The women who didn't want to go were slaughtered. I saw a woman being hung alive and then burned to death.

Mass Riots and State Violence

Most of the massive riots can be attributed to the role of the state, directly or indirectly. The slaying of sorcerers in East Java, the wars between the Moslems and the Christians in Maluku, the bombing of the Mosque Istiqlal in Jakarta and so forth, were believed to involve military officers as provocateurs, or hidden actors. Under military hegemony, state violence against its people became prominent. The implementation of the Military Operation Area in some provinces such as East Timor, Aceh, and West Papua led to violation of human rights, including kidnapping, killing, and missing people. Military officers often practised coercion to get people to comply with certain government programmes, such as transmigration, farming, and forestry.

Riots Related to Political Processes

Political processes, such as a general election, may result in massive riots, causing death or injury to participants, such as during the campaign. Some of the instances are the Banjarmasin, South Kalimantan, and the Sampang, Madura, riots. The Banjarmasin riot occurred during the general election period in 1997. In the region dominated by the Unity Development Party (UDP), the hatred against the ruling party, Golkar, was strong. During their campaign, the UDP leaders sometimes provoked their followers to hate the "government" party. This analogy, used by a charismatic *ulema* (Islamic religious leader) from Madura in his campaign, is an example:

> New Order government is a corrupt government. Corruption means stealing. Since Golkar is the government party, then Golkar is a thief.

Such words are indeed provocative. Hatred towards Golkar among the Moslem has resulted in violence, as happened in the following case. When Golkar ran a campaign with a car parade, with the noise of tin cans going through the community during Friday prayers at the Mosque Noor, and the parade even crossing the rope divider used to separate those who were praying, the mass of Moslems were infuriated. A riot erupted, resulting in 78 vehicles being burned or damaged, 32 office buildings, stores and churches being ruined, and 151 civilians' homes being burned down. In addition, 123 people were burned to death and 123 people were wounded.

A riot with a comparable setting happened in Sampang. This district is also dominated by the UDP. The incident happened during the general election period in 1997 when the UDP claimed that the vote-counting was not transparent and unfair. An army officer and a sub-district officer shot at the emotional crowd of UDP members. This triggered a riot which caused the death of one person. About 7–11 people were wounded, 10 people went missing, and the residence of the head of the sub-district and some voting areas were also damaged.

The killing of sorcerers in East Java was the result of instigation by a military officer, with the aim of putting the political position of the Nahdlatul Ulama (NU) on edge, especially Abdurrachman Wahid. The 27 July incident was also part of a plot by a government officer to eliminate Megawati and the PDIP (Struggle Indonesian Democratic Party) from the national political arena.

Mass Riots and Civil Militarism

If militarism and state violence characterized the Soeharto regime, then civil militarism seems to characterize the current political system. If independent social organizations or political parties were put on edge by the previous regime, at present, political power is in the hands of the political parties. To demonstrate their strength, political parties have formed a force group with attributes and attitude like those of the military.

The PKB, for example, has the Garda Bangsa (Nation Guard), the members of which overlap with the Banser (Versatile Guard), a force group belonging to the NU with about 400,000 troops. Struggle Indonesian Democratic Party has a force group with 20,000 members. The National Message Party has the Barisan Simpatik with 30,000 members. The members of this force overlap with the Kokam, a force group belonging to the Muhammadiyah organization. Some of them are also members of the Barisan Simpatik, while some members of Kokam have joined the force group belonging to the Unity Development Party under the name of Gerakan Pemuda Ka'bah Pembangunan. Others have joined Brigade Hizbullah belonging to the PBB (Moon and Stars Party), which has 400 members in each district.[4]

During the campaign season, these force groups were often involved in physical contact with the members of different parties. They frequently reacted with violent actions when their leaders were threatened politically. For example, violence was used by the force group of the Struggle Indonesian Democratic Party, the supporters of Megawati, when she was defeated as the President-elect at the Plenary Session of the People's Advisory Assembly in 1999. The Banser of NU also used violence against the *Jawa Post* which released the news of the KKN (corruption, nepotism, and cronyism) case involving their leader, President Abdurrachman Wahid. The show of force was also carried to the annual People's Advisory Assembly (PAA) 2000 meeting when Gus Dur was under the threat of impeachment. This military tendency towards civilians also occurred during the East Timor turmoil, both by the pro-integration (Atarak) and the pro-independence (Falentil) militia. The bloody fight in Ambon and North Maluku was an armed conflict between the militias of Moslem and Christian civilians. The Moslems in Maluku and North Maluku got support from the civilian troops in Java, called *komando jihad* (*jihad* commandos). This tendency of civil militarism has certainly created the fear of threat and violence.

Killing Field against Criminals

The people who distrust the system of justice are often driven to enforce their own rules against incidents that they consider as disturbing the order, such as criminal action. In Jakarta, for example, crime has reached a scale where there is always the fear of violence. Just to snatch a bracelet or a ring, criminals may cut the victim's hand. In the middle of a traffic jam, criminals would calmly take the rear-view mirror of cars, and car owners would be left defenceless. Criminals have also threatened people by pointing a weapon at them and demanding money.

A regular column, called "Rubrik unek-unek", in *Kompas* (5 August 2000, p. 18) featuring "Jakarta bertabur Kriminal" (Jakarta is decorated with criminals), described the people's fears about the lack of safety in Jakarta. It was mentioned (by Toto) in the column that "The criminals in Jakarta are getting more dangerous". It also quoted a complaint from Toto: "Everyday we hear [about] burglaries, plundering, pickpockets, hold-ups, murder, gambling, narcotics, and drug abuse getting worse. Law enforcement, especially the police is getting weaker." Another reader (Erick Wijaya) wrote: "I'm a victim of rearview mirror stealing...the policemen were nearby. They just stood there and didn't do anything. They even gave me a traffic ticket because I didn't have a rearview mirror on my car". Another (Agustina) said, "Nowadays, there is no comfortable feeling travelling at night in any place in Jakarta. The fear is always there. Even the bus passengers are vulnerable to the acts of criminals, especially pickpocketing. These days, they do not hesitate to hurt their victims." *Kompas* conducted a survey via e-mail which showed that 61.5 per cent of the respondents considered the criminal rate in Jakarta to be reaching a dangerous limit, while 34.3 per cent did not care about it, and 4.2 per cent did not answer.

As the law enforcement authorities are somewhat reluctant to handle criminal actions, people often take the matter into their own hands by punishing the criminals ruthlessly, such as killing or burning suspects to death. *Kompas* noted that in 1999–2000, there were 46 serious brutalities against suspects of crime in Big Jakarta, which includes Jakarta, Bogor, Tangerang, and Bekasi (Jabotabek). Thirty-one of them were killed by the masses and fifteen others were burned alive. Not all the victims were proven guilty. One of them was Husen Dalimunte (19 years old), who was called a thief by a group of men (although it was not proven). Husen was attacked and killed by the people (Santoso and Supriadi 2000).

Table 5.1
Some Brutal Cases against Criminal Suspects in Jakarta, Bogor, Tangerang, Bekasi (1999–2000)

	Incident	*Place*	*Cause of death*	*Victim*	*Date*	*Time*
1	Motor-cycle theft	Periok, Jatiuwung, Kodya Tangerang	Killed by overwhelming numbers	1	7 Jan 1999	Night
2	Chicken theft	Pungur, Lengkong Cisoka, Tangerang	Killed by overwhelming numbers	1	9 Jan 1999	Early dawn
3	Vehicle holdup	Da'an Mogot, West Jakarta	Killed by overwhelming numbers	1	25 Jan 1999	Night
4	Robbery against taxi driver	Jl. Sudirman, Cikokol Tangerang	Burned to death	1	8 Feb 1999	Early dawn
5	Robbery against taxi driver	Marunda, Cilincing, North Jakarta	Killed by overwhelming numbers	1	9 Feb 1999	Night
6	Motor-cycle theft	Bintara Jaya, Bekasi	Burned to death	1	10 Feb 1999	Na
7	Motor-cycle theft	Semanan, Kalideres West Jakarta	Burned to death	2	3 March 1999	Night
8	Goat theft	Cijeruk, District Bogor	Killed by overwhelming numbers	1	24 March 1999	Morning
9	Housebreaking	Kampung Melayu, East Jakarta	Killed by overwhelming numbers	1	26 March 1999	Night

Table 5.1 (*continued*)

Some Brutal Cases against Criminal Suspects in Jakarta, Bogor, Tangerang, Bekasi (1999–2000)

	Incident	*Place*	*Cause of death*	*Victim*	*Date*	*Time*
10	Car theft	Bintaro, Pondok Aren, District Tangerang	Killed by overwhelming numbers	1	22 Apr 1999	Early dawn
11	Motor-cycle theft	Tambun, District Bekasi	Killed by overwhelming numbers	1	23 May 1999	Na
12	Suspected as a thief	Sub-district Sukatani, District Bekasi	Burned to death	1	26 May 1999	Night
13	Suspected as a thief	Duri kosambi, Cengkareng, West Jakarta	Burned to death	1	26 Apr 1999	Early dawn
14	Car theft	Rawa buaya, Cengkareng, West Jakarta	Burned to death	1	21 June 1999	Early dawn
15	Housebreaking	Cimanggis, District Depok	Killed by overwhelming numbers	1	21 June 1999	Early dawn
16	Stealing peppers	Purwosari, Darmaga, District Bogor	Killed by overwhelming numbers	1	7 July 1999	Early dawn
17	Sound system theft	Pabuaran, Bojon Gede, District Bogor	Killed by overwhelming numbers	1	12 July 1999	Day time

Table 5.1 (*continued*)

Some Brutal Cases against Criminal Suspects in Jakarta, Bogor, Tangerang, Bekasi (1999–2000)

	Incident	*Place*	*Cause of death*	*Victim*	*Date*	*Time*
18	Motor-cycle theft	Jejalen Jaya, Tambun, District Bekasi	Killed by overwhelming numbers	1	12 July 1999	Night
19	Motor-cycle theft	Semanan, Kalideres, West Jakarta	Burned to death	1	24 Nov 1999	Late afternoon
20	Thievery	East Panunggangan, Cipondoh, District Tangerang	Burned to death	1	25 Nov 1999	Night
21	Motor-cycle theft	Taman Century 2, Pekayon, District Bekasi	Killed by overwhelming numbers	1	16 Dec 1999	Late afternoon
22	Motor-cycle theft	Raya Gandul, Limo, District Depok	Killed by overwhelming numbers	1	31 Dec 1999	Day time
23	Buffalo theft	Wangunharjo, Cibitung, Bekasi	Killed by overwhelming numbers	1	5 Jan 2000	Early dawn
24	Yelled at as a thief	Railway station, Pasar Minggu, South Jakarta	Killed by overwhelming numbers	1	16 Jan 2000	Early dawn
25	Motor-cycle theft	Petukangan, South Jakarta	Killed by overwhelming numbers/burned	2	2 Feb 2000	Day time

Table 5.1 *(continued)*

Some Brutal Cases against Criminal Suspects in Jakarta, Bogor, Tangerang, Bekasi (1999–2000)

	Incident	*Place*	*Cause of death*	*Victim*	*Date*	*Time*
26	Motor-cycle theft	Pondok Gede, Bekasi	Killed by overwhelming numbers	1	4 Feb 2000	Na
27	Walkman theft	Pasir Gadung, Cikupa, District Tangerang	Killed by overwhelming numbers	1	6 March 2000	Night
28	Goat theft	East Panunggangan, Cipondoh, Tangerang	Killed by overwhelming numbers	1	15 March 2000	Day time
29	Goat theft	Ketapang Village, Sub-district Mauk, Tangerang	Killed by overwhelming numbers	1	17 March 2000	Na
30	Car theft	Galur, North Tebet, South Jakarta	Killed by overwhelming numbers	1	20 March 2000	Na
31	Motor-cycle theft	Binong Village, Curuk, District Tangerang	Burned to death	1	25 March 2000	Night
32	Scales theft	Banjarsari, Bekasi	Killed by overwhelming numbers	1	27 March 2000	Na
33	Thievery	Pasar kemis, District Tangerang	Killed by overwhelming numbers	1	29 March 2000	Night

Table 5.1 (*continued*)

Some Brutal Cases against Criminal Suspects in Jakarta, Bogor, Tangerang, Bekasi (1999–2000)

	Incident	*Place*	*Cause of death*	*Victim*	*Date*	*Time*
34	Motor-cycle theft	Porisgaga, Sub-district Batuceper, District Tangerang	Burned to death	1	6 Apr 2000	Night
35	Na	Kampong Sengkol, Sub-district Serpong, Tangerang	Killed by overwhelming numbers	1	6 Apr 2000	Early dawn
36	Motor-cycle theft	Sub-district Cisoka, District Tangerang	Killed by overwhelming numbers	1	6 Apr 2000	Day time
37	Suspected of crime	East Jakarta	Burned to death	2	18 Apr 2000	Night
38	Gas tube theft	East Jakarta	Killed by overwhelming numbers	1	19 Apr 2000	Na
39	Suspicious attitude	Kemang, District Bogor	Burned to death	1	23 Apr 2000	Late afternoon
40	Hold-up in a bus	Pasar baru,Central Jakarta	Killed by overwhelming numbers	1	3 May 2000	Day time
41	Motor-cycle theft	Jatimurni, Jarti Sampurna, Bekasi	Burned to death	4	10 May 2000	Night

Table 5.1 (*continued*)

Some Brutal Cases against Criminal Suspects in Jakarta, Bogor, Tangerang, Bekasi (1999–2000)

	Incident	*Place*	*Cause of death*	*Victim*	*Date*	*Time*
42	Durikosambi	Cengkareng, West Jakarta	Killed by overwhelming numbers	1	11 May 2000	Early dawn
43	Plates theft	Agrabinta, District Bogor	Killed by overwhelming numbers	1	17 May 2000	Na
44	Motor-cycle theft	Complex Cipondoh Makmur, District Tangerang	Killed by overwhelming numbers	1	28 May 2000	Na
45	Suspected of a hold-up	Jl. TB Simatupang, Kampong Rambutan, Central Jakarta	Burned to death	5	10 June 2000	Afternoon
46	Challenging the people	Karikil village, Sub-district Parung, District Bogor	Killed by overwhelming numbers	1	10 June 2000	Na

Note: Na — Not applicable.
Source: *Kompas*, 16 January 2000.

System of Violence

Holistic Approach

It is not sufficient to understand the phenomenon of violence such as that which occurred in Indonesia individually. The phenomenon should be seen holistically, by understanding the violence as a system where different elements affect one another. Therefore, this subsection first discusses the root and culture of violence as well violence as an expression of power. It then examines structural violence, fear, and the spiral of violence, equality, and trust, and the political and economic impact of violence.

The Root of Violence

For a long time, psychologists have recognized the nature of aggressiveness or violence as one of the human instincts. Human beings, according to Sigmund Freud, have two opposite instincts: that for life (Eros) and that for death. The latter instinct is addressed to the organism itself (self-destruction) or to destroy another organism, and the capability for destruction of human beings is as great as the capability for life. According to Fromm (2000, p. 177), modernization and industrialization are not factors that can reduce or eliminate such destructive potentiality, rather it can become more massive and horrible.

The destructive instinct of human beings is even more extreme than that of wild animals, because wild animals only become ferocious towards their prey when they are hungry and need food, or when they are threatened by the presence of other creatures. Wild animals only attack other animals as their prey, while they can get along with the same species socially and peacefully. There is no ethnic cleansing of animals as it happens with human beings. Human beings can be very destructive towards others, and modernization cannot reduce this destructive instinct. It even escalates quantitatively, through increased numbers involved in the destruction, or increased number of victims. Human beings also improve the methods and technology of violence (from using swords or arrows with limited range for hurting/killing the victims to modern weapons such as atomic bombs, hydrogen bombs, chemicals, viruses, and so forth, with enormous killing capability).

There have been 14,000 wars in the last 5,000 years of the history of mankind. The largest number of victims who suffered during a war was in World War II, which took 60 million lives. Human beings also know the different methods of violence against their kind. A few examples are fining, whipping, screwing, tying the body tight, igniting with fire, splashing with acid water, ripping flesh piece by piece using a hot pincer, beating the muscles of the knee, castrating, crossing, releasing a person into the desert, dense forest, or mountains without any supplies, cutting off a hand or leg, slavery, forcing someone to commit suicide, decapitation, throwing someone from a high place, strangling, hanging, drowning, throwing stones at someone, whipping to death, burying alive, cutting the body, pouring hot liquid into the throat, killing children, raping wives in front of their husbands, isolation in a dark and quiet room, illuminating with bright lights, subjecting someone to high levels of noise, striking with electrical rods, hurting the genitals, forcing someone to eat faeces or excrement, killing by slicing the body, and other various methods (Jacob 2000).

Cultural Violence

The instinct of violence is let loose when violence becomes part of the culture of society. It is considered a culture when violent actions are justified by the society as a value. This justification is based on the concepts of religion, traditional values, knowledge, language, or art.

Galtung (1990) has defined cultural violence as aspects of culture, the symbolic sphere of our existence — exemplified by religion and ideology, language and art, empirical science and formal science (logic, mathematics) — that can be used to justify or legitimize direct or structural violence (Singer and Lind 1999, p. 39).

Cultural violence is an aspect of a broader kind of culture. "Cultural violence" may be described as aspect A of culture C, not the whole of C, which in turn has an opposite aspect, that is aspect B. Thus, in any human culture there exists cultural violence and its opposite, which Galtung calls cultural peace — which is defined as aspects of a culture that serve to justify and legitimize direct peace and structural peace.

"Cultural violence makes direct and structural violence look, even feel right, or at least not wrong," Galtung said. This legitimization may arise from language, law, science, or religion. In the English language, there is a term, "killing is self realization." This indicates that even the English language has the capability of expressing violent thoughts. Walter Benjamin (1921), as quoted from Derrida (1999), has pointed out the difference between violence as a means to a "just" end, and violence as a means to an "unjust" end. The constitution of modern law legitimizes institutional violence by the state, for it has a "just" end. Violence against women, including harassment, assault, rape, or killing, is violence that is often legitimized by patriarchal states or societies. Racism and imperialism that dominated the Western world during its colonial history were examples of legitimization by a nation or race to humiliate another. Religion has also often been used to legitimate violence for religious ends, as found in the concept of *jihad fissabilillah* (struggle for the sake of God) in Islam, or mass-suicide practised by orthodox Christians in Uganda. Religion is also a powerful force used to encourage resistance against race domination, as found in Malcom S' famous speech, "The use of violence in the civil right struggle is inevitable. ...Blacks have an obligation to met racist violence with equal force" (Malcom X 1999, pp. 31–35). This was also found in the *Dakwah Bulletin* (003/VII/2000) circulated at Friday prayers in Yogyakarta's mosques, which stated "*jihad* is not a crime, rather a holy obligation of believers to defend Islam from other religion's threats. So the plan of Ahlus Sunnah Wal Jamaah to send 10,000 *jihad* civilian troops to Ambon to defend the Islamic people in Maluku is a *fardhu ain*" (a compulsory duty without exception for all believers).

Violence and the Use of Power

It is not sufficient to explain violence as a cultural trait. Violence is also an expression of power, as "power tends to kill, and absolute power tends to kill absolutely" (Jacob 1999). In the twentieth century, governments all over the world have killed almost 200 million people, not only people of other nations but also their own. Genocide, that is noted in red ink in human history, includes mass killing during the colonial wars and World War II, and people slaughtered by the communist regimes in Russia and Cambodia (Jacob 1999).

Violence is a form of power, for power is defined as the ability to make and enforce decisions. To "enforce" means to coerce since enforcement demands obedience by others arbitrarily. Enforcement is sometimes applied under legitimate authority. Some people tend to exclude such cases as violence. For instance, taxation is not a violence since a government has legitimate authority (based on law) to collect taxes. It becomes violence if the collection of money is made against legitimate laws, or is done by non-legitimate individuals or institutions, as in the case of robbery. Thus, strictly speaking, violence is the illegitimate or unauthorized use of force to effect decisions against the will or desire of others. Thus, murder is an act of violence, while capital punishment by a legitimate state is not (Wolf 1999, pp. 13–15).

However, in a broader definition, legitimacy as a distinguishing factor for an act of violence is questionable. The problem is, firstly, that the meaning of legitimacy differs between a democratic country and an authoritarian one. In an authoritarian state, citizens do not have the right to control the use of power by the regime. The authority of the government is only *de jure* legitimate and never *de facto*. In a democratic state, however, the citizens are in a position to control the use of power by their government. Secondly, the meaning of actions differs between individuals who have different social status and positions in the case of violence. For instance, police action to eradicate slums in urban areas may not be considered as acts of violence. On the other hand, the poor who lose their homes, or the non-governmental organization (NGO) which defends the poor tends to accuse the police of inflicting an act of violence on the poor, because such action is done without a fair deal for the victims. Such acts neglect the sense of equity of the people. Since inequity often signify evidence of violence, then violence should also be understood from a structural perspective.

Structural Violence

The definition of structural violence here differs from Galtung's definition of the same. Galtung (1990) differentiates direct violence (killing, maiming, siege, sanctions, misery, desocialization, resocialization, secondary citizen, repression, detention, and expulsion) from structural violence (exploitation, penetration, segmentation, marginalization, and fragmentation).

Structural violencc is defined here as acts of violence which are related to the differentiation and stratification of a society. This means that in every society there is always horizontal differentiation into social groups, based on gender, education, ethnicity, and spatial identities. At the same time, every society is also diffracted hierarchically, based on social status, ownership, wealth, or degree of power. The vertical differentiation may overlap with the horizontal one, in the sense that social status may have a relationship with gender identity, educational background, ethnicity, religion, or ideology. For instance, men are considered to be superior and women as the subordinate in a patriarchal society.

The vertical and horizontal differentiation may influence the act of violence in a society. This means that an act of violence may occur among individuals because of their different social status (vertical violence) or social identities (horizontal violence). State violence against its citizens and mass violence against the state are instances of vertical violence. Civil war among different religious groups in a society is an example of horizontal violence.

Horizontal violence may coincide with vertical violence. Violence between different ethnic groups, religions, sex, or the residents of two villages or regions are examples of horizontal violence. This kind of violence becomes vertical when there is unbalanced power distribution between groups of society or a resource authority. When native residents conducted violence against the Chinese, it was assumed that the Chinese minority had more control over resources than the natives. The violence conducted by the natives was an expression of jealousy over the resources controlled by the Chinese minority residents. Violence against women involves hierarchies, as the men in a patriarchy are positioned as superior to women in the society.

From the discussion above, it is clear that the key factor that can trigger violence is injustice. Injustice mainly occurs between different social-class hierarchies. An authority situation can drive the authorities to commit exploitation or suppression. At the beginning, this attitude does not encounter direct resistance by the exploited or suppressed. However, the accumulation of disappointment, alliance, and hatred will in time explode into violence by the suppressed against the oppressor. If the explosion of anger in the form of violence is answered also by violence, it will create what is called a spiral of violence (Camara 1971).

Spiral of violence may also occur horizontally between different social groups. When injustice exists between these different social groups, the jealousy, hatred, and intention to cause disappointment will rapidly rise, and such bad feelings may stimulate the act of violence. When violent means are resorted to instead of peaceful negotiation or compromise, the violence of one group will be retaliated by the attacked group in the same way. Violence as a means of retaliation by the attacked group will trigger more severe violence by the first group. A spiral of violence is then created. The horizontal conflict between the Moslem people and the Christians in Maluku and North Maluku is one instance of a spiral of violence.

A spiral of violence can also be the result of a combination of horizontal and vertical violence. For example, a dispute between social groups is handled unfairly by the authority, such as when the government takes the side of one group against the other. If this happens, the neglected group will fight against the unfairness of the government. The riots that occurred in Banjarmasin and Sampang, Madura, are examples of a combination between horizontal and vertical violence. The unfair government treatment was felt when the government committed discriminatory acts against the UDP and gave special protection to Golkar during the election campaign period. Thus, the anger of UDP supporters erupted. This eruption of anger that occurred in Banjarmasin was released not just against government offices but also Chinese stores as the rioters felt jealous and hated the Chinese minority. The incidents that happened in Maluku and North Maluku are other instances. The military, which was supposed to render safety by breaking up the fights, took the side of the fighting groups. There is a military element on both the Moslem side and the Christian side so that the spiral of violence prolonged on a wider scale.

Fear and the Spiral of Violence

Fear and violence are two interconnected emotions. Violence creates fear, but fear may escalate to violence when those who fear violence confront the threat of violence in a violent manner. Fear is an effect but at the same time a cause of violence. The fact that violence creates fear is hard to deny. The flow of refugees from the seething regions (such as Aceh, Ambon, or Timor Lorosae) is an indication of fear of violence among residents in those areas. It is because of fear too that expatriates left Indonesia together with their dollars when riots erupted frequently in Jakarta and many other places in the country after May 1998.

However, the fact that fear is also the cause of violence is widely neglected, or often denied. Yet, this is apparently the key factor that creates a spiral of violence which escalates the violence even more. People are trapped into using violence to protect themselves from the threat of violence. It was the fear of losing certain regions that motivated the army to put DOM (military operation territory) into effect in the tumultous regions such as Aceh, West Papua, and Timor Lorosae. It was also the threat to survival faced by the Christian groups in Maluku that drove them to kill their Moslem brothers. It was also because of the same kind of fear that *jihad* civilian troops were sent to Ambon to help their Moslem brothers in their conflict with their Christian opponents.

As quoted at the beginning of the chapter, Mark H. Moore (1995) and Mark H. Moore and Robert Trojanowicz (1988) have mentioned that "fear is an important problem in its own right". Fear is an unpleasant condition that creates violence. Citing a case of violent crime in the United States, Moore and Trojanowicz have argued that "fear even makes life miserable for those who fear and prompts them to take actions that make their neighbours even more dangerous"(p. 217).

Fear sometimes dictates one's actions. "When citizens stop going out, buy guns, hide behind closed shutters, or fail to confront offenders, a neighborhood can no longer defend itself. Significantly, the police can reduce fear, but not necessarily through the same means they now use to confront violent crime"(p. 217). The writers suggest that this problem can be solved by removing "quality of life" offences that underline the fear and violence. Fear is most commonly triggered by evidence of disorder in a community. In the case of the United States, the disorder was best indicated by social annoyances, such as graffiti, noisy kids, or public drunkenness.

Social disorder then should be a focus in dealing with the problem of fear among people. In the case of Indonesia, what happened was more than just a small-scale social disorder; it was serious social disruption, as indicated by state as well as mass violence on a massive scale. State violence has been prominent in the last thirty years. The state, or army, is estimated to have caused around 16,000 people to be wounded during that period (I.J. 2000). Mass violence is not less threatening. A few examples are robbing timber, embankment of fish by a crowd, or the destruction of public and private properties. Such violence sometimes involves political parties or social organizations. An example is the mob intimidation by the Versatile Guard (Banser) Ansor to force a daily newspaper *Jawa Pos* into suppressing news of its suspicion of corruption and nepotism involving President Gus Dur and his cronies. That news was deemed to bring humiliation on the NU élite leaders and the institution.

Social order, according to Fukuyama (1999, pp. 4–6), is a basic human right for social and economic improvement. Human beings are by nature social creatures, whose most basic drives and instincts lead them to establish moral rules that bind them together into communities. They are also by nature rational, and their rationality allows them to find ways of co-operating with one another spontaneously. To Fukuyama, religion and a strong and expansive state are often helpful in this process, but they are not the *sine qua non* of social order. He rejects Thomas Hobbes' notion that man's natural state is war with "every one against every one." He believes, instead, that civil society can be made orderly by the presence of a host of moral rules. Order arises not as a result of a top-down mandate by hierarchical authority, whether political or religious, but by self-organization on the part of decentralized individuals.

To follow the Fukuyama thesis, social disorder that has presented itself in Indonesia is a consequence of state domination in creating social order, and at the same time, the absence of spontaneous co-operation among different social groups in society. The state was strong and expansive in nature during the Soeharto era, with a high centralized and repressive type of governance that left insignificant space for the development of decentralized individuals. The national slogan, "*Bhineka Tunggal Ika*" (Unity in Diversity), which symbolizes the appreciation of the pluralistic nature of Indonesian society was eroded by anti-pluralist policies. The government restricted the expression of unique identities of ethnicity, religion, and race, and made the issue of SARA (ethnicity, religion, and race) a spectre. Soeharto monopolized power almost without match. The army and civil bureaucracy were totally under his control, and he used the two instruments to control people through what is called the politics of *wadah tunggal* (single container). In this, citizens are compartmentalized into organizations created and controlled vertically by the bureaucracy. This policy in turn made people lose their natural ability to recognize and appreciate diversity and to build co-operation based on mutual trust and honesty.

When the Soeharto regime collapsed, and his successor B.J. Habibie failed to win legitimacy from the people, the society did not have an alternative to keep social order alive. What happened then was anarchy. Religion which has the ability to maintain social order was often used to rouse fanatism and horizontal conflict among different believers.

Equality and Trust

There are two key factors that need to be present to eliminate violence, namely, equity and trust. Violence presents itself when inequality is prominent in a society, either vertically — that is, between the government and its citizens — or horizontally — that is, among social groups that are fragmented by social classes, ethnicity, religion, or gender identities. There must be political, economic or social mechanisms to overcome such inequality. When such mechanisms are absent or found to be ineffective, each of the factions will try to find their own solution. The better-off will protect the benefits they have already gained and the worse-off will seize the benefits that have been robbed by the better-off. Coercion or violence is the easiest, or only way, that they know to rectify the inequality.

Thus, the character of violence is not only individual but also systemic. Under this systemic violence, it will be difficult for society to develop trust among individuals or social groups. On the contrary, distrust will dominate the relationship among them in such a social system. This distrust will escalate when the state falls under an authoritarian regime. In such a system, the rulers tend to perceive citizens or the élite beyond the power circle as a threat to the establishment, and their political privileges in such a government, such as human rights including individuals' freedom of expression, will be neglected. As Suu Kyi has mentioned:

> Within a system which denies the existence of human rights, fear tends to be the order of the day — fear of imprisonment, fear of torture, fear of death, fear of poverty, fear of isolation, fear of failure. A most insidious form of fear is that which masquerades as common sense or even wisdom, condemning as foolish, reckless, insignificant or futile the small, daily acts of courage which help to preserve man's self respect and inherent human dignity (Singer and Lind 1999, p. 315).

This situation was clearly seen during the authoritative regime of Soeharto. Such situation has not changed even when political parties hold political control over the country. There is no public good. The army has never provided security for the citizens, only its superiors, or the political bosses. Its facilities were (and still are) used not to protect the people but the ruler (and now the political parties too).

Political and Economic Impacts of Violence

Altogether, the violence, which has occurred in Indonesia, has been massive, complex, and prolonged. Meanwhile, the restoration of safety in Indonesia is important not only for the recovery of the Indonesian economy, which has been ruined by the economic and political crisis, but also for political stability in Southeast Asia. An unstable Indonesia will affect the political stability of the surrounding countries. Before the reformation, Indonesia had achieved a strategic position in ASEAN co-operation that was an important factor for maintaining the peace and co-operation of the region. This role can no longer be played by Indonesia at present while an alternative leadership has not been raised from other countries.

There has been considerable fear in Southeast Asia about the direction Indonesia will take. The neighbouring countries, such as Malaysia and Singapore, fear a wave of refugees flowing to their countries from Indonesia. Already, these countries have seen large numbers of Acehnese and Indonesian Chinese fleeing from the steadily increasing violence across the archipelago (Dibb2000).

The Political and Economic Risk Consultancy (PERC) conducted a survey of 500 expatriates, asking their opinion on Indonesia's fitness for living. The result of the survey was that living in Indonesia is not safe. Indonesia is ranked ninth of the twelve Asian sample countries for conditions of living. Indonesia's level of insecurity is above that of Vietnam, South Korea, and India, but below eight other countries: Philippines, Singapore, Japan, Hong Kong, Taiwan, Thailand, Malaysia, and the People's Republic of China (PRC) (*Bisnis Indonesia* 1999).

Table 5.2

Ranking of Conditions of Living in Indonesia for Expatriates

Rank	*Country*	*Score*
1	Philippines	3,27
2	Singapore	3,28
3	Japan	3,84
4	Hongkong	4,1
5	Taiwan	4,49
6	Thailand	4,9
7	Malaysia	5,0
8	RRC	5,36
9	Indonesia	5,44
10	India	5,74
11	South Korea	6,27
12	Vietnam	6,32

Note: The data were obtained in a survey of 500 expatriates, especially from Australia, the United States, Europe, and Asia. Grade 10 is the worst ranking and Grade 1 is the best.

Source: *Bisnis Indonesia*, 1999.

Freedom from fear of violence is a public good, and a public necessity, especially for the people of Indonesia who have suffered much from the prolonged turbulence, but it is also important for regional and international communities which used to have Indonesia as a stabilizing factor in the region.

Restoring Freedom From Fear and Social Order

The philosophy of ancient India, as quoted by Aung San Suu Kyi, states, "The greatest gift for an individual or a nation was *abhaya*, fearlessness, not merely bodily courage but absence of fear from the mind." More than just a gift, to Suu Kyi, fearlessness is "the courage acquired through endeavor, courage that could be described as 'grace under pressure' — grace which is renewed repeatedly in the face of harsh, unremitting pressure" (Steger and Lind 1999, p. 315).

To restore freedom from fear of violence, violence should not be used as a way to resolve conflict, for violence will only result in further violence. The first thing of concern here is inequity. As long as inequity remains present, violence will never vanish. To a large extent, it is the orientation of government policy. When the government planned to increase the salaries of high-ranking government officials and parliament members, lower ranking government officials and the public were angered. This shows a lack of policy-makers' sensitivity to equity issues. Inequity often produces jealousy, which is the first step to violence. In the past, the government had often eliminated violence caused by inequity through repressive measures. The army played a dominant role in trying to establish security through a physical approach. A few examples are the way in which the army dealt with labour protests in the Marsinah case, and the way a local government leader (an army colonel) dealt with press news on fraud and nepotism in the Udin case in which he was said to be involved. Such actions produce fear instead of trust in the victims of exploitation or unfair actions.

Under fear, violence may not have a chance to erupt. However, this will accumulate over time, creating a sort of time-bomb that could erupt on a larger scale when the ruler has lost his legitimacy to control citizen behaviour. As distrust can escalate to violence, the restoration of trust in human relations must be the focus of action. Thus, whatever measures the government chooses to eliminate violence, they should be non-violent.

Appendix 1

The Future of Indonesia

Indonesia, which was known as a chain of emeralds on the equator, will be in a mess. The United Indonesian Republic will disintegrate like the Soviet Union, similar to Yugoslavia. The capital can be protected, although more than one army battalion has died in the war on the annihilation of the separatist movement, Free Riau, in Pakanbaru, 3 February 2010. The victims from the Free Riau movement will be more than two armed battalions, while civilian victims have not yet been counted but the hospitals are crowded by war victims up to the aisles.

The effort to keep Riau is a critical problem for Indonesia, after Irian Jaya province gets its freedom in 2008. It is said at the official report of the Ministry of Defence that the Free Papua Movement obtained funding from Freeport to buy weapons and logistics. While Aceh disintegrates in 2005 after an armed conflict that can take the lives of 10,000 soldiers and civilians, Indonesia is now the poorest country in the world, first in corruption as the government implements a closed political policy. Everything the press publishes is under government control; even the officers do not hesitate to censor the news offices in Indonesia. Radio and television, state or private, are only the media of government propaganda. Even the Internet service provider is controlled so that the government can also detect information flow.

Indonesia has become a closed country after the bloody military *coup d'état*. The military has carried out a *coup d'état* against President KH Abdurrachman Wachid, or Gus Dur, for the reason that it is necessary to protect Indonesia from disintegration, because Gus Dur had given the people too much freedom. One of the weaknesses of the Gus Dur government was that his attention was distracted because of the split among the Central Alliance parties, so that part of his attention was on consolidating power against the threat of impeachment by some of the members of the Indonesian Legislative Assembly.

(Author's translation from Rakaryan S., "Upaya Melihat Indonesia Masa Depan," *Kompas*, Tuesday, 9 May 2000).

Appendix 2

A Portrait of Collective Violence in Indonesia, 1995–2000

No	*The Incident*	*Time*	*Source of Motive*	*Conflict Description*	*Number of Victims*
01	The Riot of Liquisa, East Timor	12 January 1995	Political	The armed forces brutally shot the Fretilin gang	• 6 residents of Liquisa killed
02	The Riot of Comoro, East Timor	8–10 September 1995	Matters pertaining to ethnic, religious and racial relations	The prisoners in the Maliana prison, Dili, was offended by the utterance of the local security man, Zakarias Sake, that was assumed to be insulting the Catholics.	• 72 bookstalls and 1 market stall burned down • 1 house ruined • 1 motor-cycle and 1 TV set was burned
03	The Abepura Riot	20 March 1996	Matters pertaining to ethnic, religious and racial relations	Problem of the burial of the Abepura figure in Cipinang prison, Jakarta	• 4 peope killed • 16 others injured • 11 houses ruined • glass windows of stores and offices broken
04	The Tanjunggusta Riot	28 March 1996	Criminal	Jealousy between prisoners over the unequal treatment by an officer	• 6 people died • tens of prisoners injured • some cells burned down
05	The Ujungpandang Riot	24 April 1996	Economic	The students of different universities protested the raising of the common transportation rate.	• 3 people died • 1 car was damaged

Appendix 2 (*continued*)

A Portrait of Collective Violence in Indonesia, 1995–2000

No	*The Incident*	*Time*	*Source of Motive*	*Conflict Description*	*Number of Victims*
06	The incident of 27 July 1996 at Diponegoro Street, Jakarta	27 July 1996	Political	The armed forces took over the office of the Indonesian Democratic Party of Megawati Soekarnoputri. This caused amok among the people	• 5 persons (?) died • 23 persons missing • 149 injured • 56 theatre buildings burned down • 197 motor-cycle burned • total estimation of loss: Rp. 100 billion
07	The Tragedy of Situbondo, East Java	10 October 1996	Matters pertaining to ethnic, religious and racial relations	The trial of a civilian named Shaleh for insulting Kiai As'ad Syamsul Arifin. The people were infuriated as the conviction was considered too lenient.	• 5 people died • 23 church/house for praying were destroyed/burned down • 2 theatre buildings burned down • 1 Christian school was destroyed/burned down • Court house was burned down • 1 restaurant was burned • 1 mini-market was destroyed/burned down • 4 cars were burned

Appendix 2 (*continued*)

A Portrait of Collective Violence in Indonesia, 1995–2000

No	*The Incident*	*Time*	*Source of Motive*	*Conflict Description*	*Number of Victims*
08	The Tasikmalaya Riot	26 December 1996	Matters pertaining to ethnic, religious and racial relations	An officer of the District Police Station Tasikmalaya tortured an *ustadz* (Islamic teacher) and his two *santris* (students at a traditional Muslim school) so that the people were infuriated	• 3 people died • 89 stores pillaged • 43 stores burned down • 60 cars burned down • 12 churches burned/ destroyed • 4 factories burned • 40 cars destroyed • 6 private banks destroyed • 3,340 employees became unemployed
09	The Riot of Sanggau Ledo, West Kalimantan	29 December 1996 – 2 January 1997	Matters pertaining to ethnic, religious and racial relations	Bahari and his Madurese mates asked a Dayak girl to watch the *dangdut* performance just for fun. When the girl refused, Bahari forced her and this triggered the anger of Dayak boys who witnessed the incident. The fight grew into a prolonged combat between ethnic groups.	• 1,720 people died • about 14,000 people evacuated • hundreds of houses destroyed/ burned

Appendix 2 (*continued*)

A Portrait of Collective Violence in Indonesia, 1995–2000

No	*The Incident*	*Time*	*Source of Motive*	*Conflict Description*	*Number of Victims*
10	The Riot of Tanahabang Market, Jakarta	27 January 1997	Economic	The officer in charge of peace and order reprimanded a street vendor fiercely and made the traders angry.	• 3 cars burned • 4 cars seriously damaged • 1 sub-district office burned down
11	The Banjarmasin Riot	23 May 1997	Political	Golkar members riding motor-bikes made a loud noise when going past the mosque Noar during Friday prayers. The people got angry and fighting erupted between the people and Golkar members.	• 133 people burnt to death • 80 injured • 130 houses burned down • tens of offices/hotels burned down • 21 cars burned • 12 cars damaged • 60 motor-bikes burned • 4 motor-bikes damaged • 3 supermarkets burned down • 1 mall burned down
12	The Riot of Sampang, Madura, East Java	29 May 1997	Political	The PPP members felt that they were treated unfairly by the committee during the counting of votes in the general election of 1997, and this aroused their anger.	• 7 people seriously injured • some houses were ruined • the sub-district office and the sub-district police station were burned down • thousands of voting cards and voting boxes were damaged

Appendix 2 (*continued*)

A Portrait of Collective Violence in Indonesia, 1995–2000

No	*The Incident*	*Time*	*Source of Motive*	*Conflict Description*	*Number of Victims*
13	The Riot of Jember, East Java	13 June 1997	Political	The people ran amok because they thought that the government had deceived them in the general election. The government claimed this incident as a purely criminal action.	• 9 people seriously injured • some stores/offices ruined
14	The Makassar Riot	15 September 1997	Matters pertaining to ethnic, religious and racial relations	A mentally ill Chinese killed a small child. This action triggered massive chaos resulting from ethnic, religious, and racial relations	• 5 people died • 1,471 stores ruined • 25 building/stores burned down • 67 cars burned • 10 cars damaged • 100 motor-bikes burned • 50 motor-bikes damaged
15	The Riot of Tanahabang, Jakarta	20 November 1997	Matters pertaining to ethnic, religious and racial relations	The car of a patrol officer brushed against a street vendor. A trader was hit and killed by the car. This incident triggered emotions	• 1 civilian died • some bookstalls were damaged

A Portrait of Collective Violence in Indonesia, 1995–2000

No	*The Incident*	*Time*	*Source of Motive*	*Conflict Description*	*Number of Victims*
16	"Trisakti" tragedy and its sequel (Jakarta Riot)	12–14 May 1997	Political	The student movement kept demanding the resignation of President Soeharto. The Trisakti students marched to the DPR/MPR building. The armed forces started shooting and this triggered a massive riot and also created further political crisis	• 4 students died • 500 people burned to death • 4,939 buildings destroyed • 1,119 private cars burnt • 66 transportation means burnt • 821 motor-bikes burnt down • 64 banks ruined • the total cost of physical losses was Rp2.5 billion
17	Massive Amok in Solo I	15 May 1997	Political	Concern for the shooting of the Trisakti students in Jakarta caused Solo to be totally ruined	• 100 cars burned • 200 motor-bikes burned • 30 houses and stores burned down • two officers injured

Appendix 2 (*continued*)

A Portrait of Collective Violence in Indonesia, 1995–2000

No	*The Incident*	*Time*	*Source of Motive*	*Conflict Description*	*Number of Victims*
18	The case of black magician, Banyuwangi, and the surrounding areas	January–August 1998	Political	The people and a mysterious gang slaughtered hundreds of people suspected of having black magic power. The victims spread out from the isolated areas of Banyuwangi, Jember, Malang, etc. It is still not clear who is the brains behind this incident.	• Banyuwangi: 235D, 3BI, 28SI • Jember: 17D • Pasuruan: 13D, 5BI, 2SI • Probolinggo: 2D, 8SI • Bondowoso: 3D • Situbondo: 2D • Sumenep: 23D, 2SI • Pamekasan: 5D • Bangkalan, Bekasi, Serang (West Java), Demak (Central Java): each 1D Note: D = died BI = seriously injured SI = slightly injured
19	The Kebumen Riot	7–8 September 1998	Matters pertaining to ethnic, religious and racial relations	An employee of a store was beaten by his Chinese employer. When people heard about this incident, they were angry and this triggered a big protest	• 80 stores burned down • 30 vehicles burnt • 1 officer seriously wounded • 1 fireman seriously wounded

Appendix 2 (*continued*)

A Portrait of Collective Violence in Indonesia, 1995–2000

No	*The Incident*	*Time*	*Source of Motive*	*Conflict Description*	*Number of Victims*
20	The Pontianak Plunder	7–8 September 1998	Economic	The price of daily needs was rising so high that the people could not afford them. Without notice, they started plundering big stores.	• 3,000 tons of rice • 1,500 tons of sugar • 500 kg cooking oil • 500 boxes of instant noodles • 100 boxes of drinking water
21	The Riot of Bangkalan, East Java	31 October 1998	Criminal	Police officer arrested a suspect of vehicle stealing. The suspect tried to escape by yelling "Communist, Ninja!" The people came out and started chasing the officers and running amok	• 3 policemen slaughtered by the masses
22	The massive fighting at Mataram, West Nusa Tenggara	31 October 1998	Political	Cemetery land dispute between the people from Kampong Patemon and Karang Genteng, Mataram, started this incident. As the problem was not properly solved, this caused the quarrel between the two kampongs.	• 7 people died • 6 seriously injured • 30 houses ruined

Appendix 2 (*continued*)

A Portrait of Collective Violence in Indonesia, 1995–2000

No	*The Incident*	*Time*	*Source of Motive*	*Conflict Description*	*Number of Victims*
23	The Semanggi Tragedy	3 November 1998	Political	The peaceful students' protest just before the People's Advisory Assembly special meeting was answered by armed officers with violence. This case has not been properly resolved up to now.	• 14 students and civilians died • 195 civilians including officers seriously wounded • 239 civilians including reporters slightly injured
24	The mass protest against the PAA (MPR) special meeting in Jakarta	November 1998	Political	The special meeting of the PAA triggered conflicts between groups. Thousands of students protested, putting pressure on the PAA and causing physical contact with armed officers. People were hurt either by shooting or being beaten.	• 4 students and 1 high school student died • 9 officers wounded • 200 protesters had gun-shot wounds

Appendix 2 *(continued)*

A Portrait of Collective Violence in Indonesia, 1995–2000

No	*The Incident*	*Time*	*Source of Motive*	*Conflict Description*	*Number of Victims*
25	The attack on the military headquarters at the ward level of Alas, Manufahi, East Timor	9 November 1998	Political	The East Timor resistance group demanded an East Timor referendum and the release of Xanana Gusmao from the Cipinang prison. As they received no response, they attacked the military headquarters at the ward level of Manufahi.	• 3 members at the military headquarters died • 13 others were taken hostage by GPK (the resistance group)
26	The Riot of Ambon I	8 November 1998	Matters pertaining to ethnic, religious and racial relations	The students demanded an apology from the commander of the military headquarters at Patimura, Hikayat, who was also a member of PAA, after he had attended the PAA Special Meeting, 10–13 November 1998. The students said that Hikayat did not represent the people's voice. The clash between the students and officers was unavoidable.	• 94 people died • 100 badly wounded • 2,000 houses totally ruined • 31 houses for prayer damaged • the Electric Company office and a discothèque ruined • 1 military vehicle burned • 300 stores burned down

Appendix 2 (*continued*)

A Portrait of Collective Violence in Indonesia, 1995–2000

No	*The Incident*	*Time*	*Source of Motive*	*Conflict Description*	*Number of Victims*
27	The attack on the military headquarters at the ward level of Pontang, Serang, West Java	20 November 1998	Social inequality	Some civilians were injured because they were beaten by head corporal Sulaiman after they collected the leftover of the shrimp harvest at the fish-pond belonging to PT Inmas Salam. This incident triggered a mass attack on the military headquarters of Pontang, Serang	• 17 people wounded • 1 military headquarters office ruined as it was thrown at with stones • 1 office of the fishpond company ruined
28	The massive riot in Jakarta (Ketapang)	22 November 1998	Matters pertaining to ethnic, religious and racial relations	The fight between a group of men gathered in front of the casino and another group from the Gang Pembangunan, West Jakarta, started the riot. The clash spread and involved the residents in matters pertaining to ethnic, religious, and racial relations. Some people believe that the Ketapang incident triggered other actions of violence in Ambon, Kupang, and Mataram	• 6 people died • 3 badly wounded • tens slightly injured • 10 churches damaged/burned • 2 school buildings ruined/burned • 16 cars damaged/burned • 3 motor-bikes damaged/burned • tens of houses ruined

Appendix 2 (*continued*)

A Portrait of Collective Violence in Indonesia, 1995–2000

No	*The Incident*	*Time*	*Source of Motive*	*Conflict Description*	*Number of Victims*
29	The riot of Porsea, Medan	23 November 1998	Economic	This incident was caused by the shooting of an officer at the Sirait Uruk, Porsea, during the protest against PT Inti Indoraya Utama (IIU). The residents got angry and started the riot.	• 5 people shot and wounded • 2 officers injured • 2 patrol cars burned • 3 private cars burned • 23 houses/stores totally damaged/burned
30	Mass riot in Pinrang, South Sulawesi	25 November 1998	Economic	Thousands of people were disappointed, as they could not get their savings back from the illegal banks. They were infuriated and ran amok, targetting the government building, attorney general's office, courthouse and the Golkar party's office.	• 9 government buildings burned down

Appendix 2 (*continued*)

A Portrait of Collective Violence in Indonesia, 1995–2000

No	*The Incident*	*Time*	*Source of Motive*	*Conflict Description*	*Number of Victims*
31	The Kupang riot	30 November 1998	Matters pertaining to ethnic, religious and racial relations	The people of Kupang conducted a mourning ceremony as an act of concern for the violent incidents in Indonesia but the masses became uncontrollable and the ceremony became a chaos, with Moslems being the target.	• 13 people wounded • a number of mosques burned • some houses/stores damaged • 2 restaurants/bookstalls totally destroyed • 1 *hajji* dormitory burned down • some school buildings burned down • 1 wooden factory burned down • 4 trucks and 1 car burned

Appendix 2 (*continued*)

A Portrait of Collective Violence in Indonesia, 1995–2000

No	*The Incident*	*Time*	*Source of Motive*	*Conflict Description*	*Number of Victims*
32	The Solo riot II	13 December 1998	Criminal	Policemen tried to take action against illegal motor-bike racing at night. The participants and the audience refused to co-operate. The clash was unavoidable and ended with rioting.	• 6 people hospitalized • 4 officers wounded • the local police station and the residence of the chief police damaged • 6 bank buildings ruined • 1 supermarket ruined • 1 theatre building damaged • 1 insurance company building damaged • 6 traffic police posts burned down • 7 phone boxes burned • tens of traffic lights damaged
33	The Poso riot I	25–28 December 1998	Matters pertaining to ethnic, religious and racial relations	Roy Runtu (a Christian) was drunk when he cut Ridwan (a Moslem) with a sharp edge in a mosque. Both of them told this to their own group. The clash was unavoidable.	• 100 people wounded • 3 motor-bikes burned • tens of houses damanged

Appendix 2 (*continued*)

A Portrait of Collective Violence in Indonesia, 1995–2000

No	*The Incident*	*Time*	*Source of Motive*	*Conflict Description*	*Number of Victims*
34	The Jakarta riot	17 December 1998	Political	Seven groups joined together to protest at the Indonesian Legislative Assembly building. The armed officers tried to stop them and this led to a bloody clash.	• 144 people wounded
35	The tragedy of Lhokseumawe	January1999	Political	Caused by the endless demands for Aceh's freedom, the government decided to make the area a Military Operation Area. This policy did not cool the anger but strengthened the resistance. Aceh has kept up the fighting to demand the referendum.	• 781 people died (in all of the Aceh area 3,000 persons died) • 163 people missing • 100 women raped • 3,000 women became widows • hundreds of soldiers died

Appendix 2 (*continued*)

A Portrait of Collective Violence in Indonesia, 1995–2000

No	*The Incident*	*Time*	*Source of Motive*	*Conflict Description*	*Number of Victims*
36	The protest in Dili, East Timor	2 February 1999	Political	The demand for freedom by some East Timor residents was unstoppable. Hundreds of young men protested by distributing the Fretilin flag. The clash with the Indonesian soldiers caused some deaths and seriously wounded many.	• 4 people died • 1 seriously wounded • tens of houses ruined • 5,800 Suai residents became refugees
37	The massive clash in East Aceh	3 February 1999	Political	About 3,000 people who were walking home from a big gathering clashed with the armed officers when they continued to yell "Free Aceh".	• 6 civilians died • tens wounded

Appendix 2 (*continued*)

A Portrait of Collective Violence in Indonesia, 1995–2000

No	*The Incident*	*Time*	*Source of Motive*	*Conflict Description*	*Number of Victims*
38	The Ambon riot II	19–25 March, 1999 until July 2000	Matters pertaining to ethnic, religious and racial relations	The prolonged conflict in Ambon began with a very small problem. The first version: a Christian boy named Yopie was forced to give some money by two Moslem Bugis boys, Usman and Salim. The second version: a driver of an urban transportation, Yopie, yelled at his Moslem assistant about the money collected. The resulting combat continued not just for days, but weeks and years without knowing the true version of the incident.	• 4,000 people died (last data) • 2,242 houses and house for prayers ruined and burned • 5,556 families (22,500 persons) became refugees.

Appendix 2 (*continued*)

A Portrait of Collective Violence in Indonesia, 1995–2000

No	*The Incident*	*Time*	*Source of Motive*	*Conflict Description*	*Number of Victims*
39	The riot of Kariatu, Maluku	February 1999	Matters pertaining to ethnic, religious and racial relations	This incident was started by a few people but the heated situation resulted in the riot involving the masses in matters pertaining to ethnic, religious, and racial relations	• 1 person died • 2 badly wounded • 7 slightly injured • 115 houses burned
40	The clash in Haruku Ambon	14 February 1999	Matters pertaining to ethnic, religious and racial relations	The heated situation spread to all the isolated areas of Maluku. Two villages, Palau and Kari, in the Haruku sub-district attacked each other. The armed officers could not control them.	• 7 people died • 19 injured • tens of houses burned down
41	The black magician slaughtering in Ciamis	12 April 1999	Matters pertaining to ethnic, religious and racial relations	The slaughtering of black magicians in Banyuwangi had stopped, but it started again in Ciamis. The issue spread so fast that it took many lives including the civilians who were not black magicians at all.	• 50 people died • 200 people died (data from Commission for Missing Persons and Victims of Violence) • 70 people died (data from PKB Pangandaran)

Appendix 2 (*continued*)

A Portrait of Collective Violence in Indonesia, 1995–2000

No	*The Incident*	*Time*	*Source of Motive*	*Conflict Description*	*Number of Victims*
42	The riot in Dili, East Timor	17 April 1999	Political	The demand for freedom became uncontrollable so that when the activists conducted a provocation, the armed forces fought back	• 12 persons died • 10 injured • a number of offices damaged • 8 houses burned
43	Massive riots in West Kalimantan	6 October 1999	Political	Hundreds of people on three buses attacked the building of the Indonesian Legislative Assembly in West Kalimantan, Pontianak. They protested against the composition of their local representatives at the PAA as they considered it unfair. The head of the local ILA could not prevent chaos although he changed the composition of the local representatives.	• Indonesian Legislative Assembly building of West Kalimantan ruined • Glass windows, desks and office rooms damaged • estimation of total loss, Rp250,000,000

Appendix 2 (*continued*)

A Portrait of Collective Violence in Indonesia, 1995–2000

No	*The Incident*	*Time*	*Source of Motive*	*Conflict Description*	*Number of Victims*
44	The Solo riot III	October 1998	Political	The winning of the Struggle Indonesian Democratic Party in the general election, which was not followed by Megawati Sukarnoputri (the head of the party) becoming President triggered the anger of its members. The provocateurs used this chance to create a riot. The City Hall was burned down. Similar actions also happened in Klaten, Buleleng (Bali), Medan, and other cities	• The City hall complex burned down • ILA building burned down • The Golkar party building burned down • The bank office burned down • The Sriwedari Park burned down • Some bookstalls burned down • Police patrol car burned • The store in Tirtonadi bus station burned/ruined • The Bank of Central Asia building burned down • The residence of the relative of Amien Rais damaged

Appendix 2 (*continued*)

A Portrait of Collective Violence in Indonesia, 1995–2000

No	*The Incident*	*Time*	*Source of Motive*	*Conflict Description*	*Number of Victims*
45	The attacking of the Doulos Foundation in Cipayung	December 1999	Matters pertaining to ethnic, religious and racial relations	The Moslems living around Cipayung, Jakarta, were annoyed as the School of Theologia, Doulos, was founded illegally. The Front of Islamic Defender (FID) took advantage of this situation to spread rumours about it. A week after the FID revealed the threat at City Hall, the School of Doulos was attacked. However, the FID denied their involvement in organizing this incident.	• 3 people died • some buildings burned down

Appendix 2 (*continued*)

A Portrait of Collective Violence in Indonesia, 1995–2000

No	*The Incident*	*Time*	*Source of Motive*	*Conflict Description*	*Number of Victims*
46	Street justice	During the year 1999	Others	Street justice happened everywhere during 1999. Even a little thief would be brought to justice by being killed and burned to death. This is still happening. According to an expert in sociology, this happens because the people can no longer trust the law.	• In Jakarta only, 73 people died and tens wounded
47	The Poso riot II	17–19 April 2000	Matters pertaining to ethnic, religious and racial relations/Politics	The riot was started by a fight between two drunken men at the Kasiwuntu station. One of them cut his own hand then yelled that he was cut by one of the Lambogia residents among the Christian majority. The issue of murder by a Lambogian pushed this incident into a riot from Monday to Thursday. Some say that this riot was triggered by the election of the District Secretary	• 3 people died • 4 wounded • 267 houses burned down • 6 cars burned • 5 motor-bikes burnt • 3 churches totally damaged • 5 police dormitories damaged/burned

Appendix 2 (*continued*)

A Portrait of Collective Violence in Indonesia, 1995–2000

No	*The Incident*	*Time*	*Source of Motive*	*Conflict Description*	*Number of Victims*
48	The Poso riot III	23 May 2000	Matters pertaining to ethnic, religious and racial relations/Politics	Some people dressing like the Ninja suddenly attacked some Moslem territory. The police force could not control the fight and it led to a riot	• 3 people died • hundreds of houses in some villages burned down • thousands of people were evacuated
49	The Poso riot IV	2 June 2000	Matters pertaining to ethnic, religious and racial relations	An act of revenge from the previous incident	• 116 people died • 164 shot • 25 wounded
50	The sinking of the *Cahaya Bahari* ship	28 June 2000	Matters pertaining to ethnic, religious and racial relations	Caused by the panic of several rioters. 500 people from Galela sailed on the *Cahaya Bahari* ship that was in no condition for sailing, headed for Manado. The boat sank and some of the passengers died.	• hundreds of people drowned

Appendix 2 (*continued*)

A Portrait of Collective Violence in Indonesia, 1995–2000

No	*The Incident*	*Time*	*Source of Motive*	*Conflict Description*	*Number of Victims*
51	The riot in Kumai, Central Kalimantan	5 July 2000	Matters pertaining to ethnic, religious and racial relations	Some people dressed like the Ninja suddenly attacked some Moslem territory. The police force could not control the fight so it led to a riot	• 4 people died • 20 slightly injured • 2 houses burnt
52	The Ambon chaos	Since 6 July 2000	Matters pertaining to ethnic, religious and racial relations	Maluku is still on fire. Civil Emergency has been declared since 27 June 2000 but it has not shown any important results. At Waai village, sub-district of Salahatu, Ambon, the Moslem group (white) attacked the Christians. A week before, the Christian territory in Leihitu was totally ruined and 7 people died. The fight between these groups could not be stopped by the armed forces. Some witnesses said that the armed forces were also involved in this fight.	• 22 people died • hundreds of others wounded

Appendix 2 (*continued*)

A Portrait of Collective Violence in Indonesia, 1995–2000

No	*The Incident*	*Time*	*Source of Motive*	*Conflict Description*	*Number of Victims*
53	The conflict between kampongs in Cilacap, Central Java	6 July 2000	Criminal	The fight between criminals and civilians grew into a riot.	• 1 person died • 32 houses burned down • motor-bike burnt
54	Massive riot in Central Java	10 July 2000	Criminal	A fight during a puppet show that took the life of a person from Karang Malang, grew into vengeance between two villages. These villages were involved in a fight that totally ruined their homes.	• 1 died • 368 houses burned down • 126 houses damaged

Data compiled by Hadi Supeno, July 2000.

Notes

1. Advisory board member of the Commission for Missing Persons and Victims of Violence, Munir, made a grim prediction: violence is here to stay. The government is still busy with political affairs and the political elite's attention on how to reduce social tension is low. Violent actions will become a routine feature among people in the coming years (Abdullah 2000). See *Jakarta Post*, 23 May 2000.
2. For a detailed list of violence in the last five years (1995–2000), see Appendix 2.
3. *Pela-Gandong* is a brotherhood oath which is based on a belief that those who took the oath and violate a prohibition they had agreed upon, would be involved in a fatal accident. See Kastor (2000), pp. 15–16.
4. Materials from *Kompas* Information Centre.

References

Abdullah, Rizka. "Rights Activist Predicts Violence to Prevail". *Jakarta Post*, 23 May 2000, p. 1.

Ali, Novel. "Partai, Keteladanan Demokrasi Versus Satgas" [Party, Democratic Model Vs. Squad]. *Kompas*, 5 May 2000.

Camara, Dom Helder. *Spiral of Violence*. London: Sheed & Ward, 1971.

Derrida, Jacques. Excerpts from "Force of Law: The Mystical Foundation of Authority". In *Violence and Its Alternatives: An Interdisciplinary Reader*. New York: St Martin's Press, 1999.

Dibb, Paul. "A Stable Indonesia is Vital for Southeast Asian Security". *Jakarta Post*, 10 May 2000, p. 5

Fibb, Paul, David D. Hale, and Peter Prince. *Asia's Insecurity*. A limited published paper. Jakarta: Information Resource Center, Public Affairs Section, Embassy of the United States of America, 9 May 2000.

Fukuyama, Francis. *The Great Disruption: Human Nature and the Reconstitution of Social Order.* New York, NY: The Free Press, 1999.

Galtung, Johan. "Cultural Violence". *Journal of Peace Research* 27, no. 3 (1990): 291–305.

Hasyim. "Aspek dan problem Pembinaan kesatuan Bangsa, Studi Kasus kekerasan Massal di Indonesia" [Aspects and Problems in Maintaining National Unity. A case study of mass violence in Indonesia]. Master's thesis in Public Administration, Gadjah Mada University, July 2000.

I.J. "Sedikitnya 16000 orang Dihilangkan Negara" [The country has taken away at least 16000 persons]. *Kompas*, 29 April 2000, p. 10.

Jacob, T. "Kekerasan dan Penderitaan" [Violence and Suffering]. Paper presented at the seminar on "Manusia, Kekerasan dan Nirkekerasan" [Human Beings, Violence and Non-Violence], University Center, Gadjah Mada University, Yogyakarta, 25 February 2000.

Jacob, T. "Perjuangan Melawan Rakyat" [Fight Against People]. *Kedaulutan Rakyat*, 29 August 1999, p. 1.

Kastor, Rustam. *Fakta, Data dan Analisa Konspirasi Politik RMS dan Kristen Menghancurkan Umat Islam di Ambon, Maluku* [Facts, Data and Analysis of RMS and Christian Political Conspiration Against Moslem in Ambon, Moluccas]. Yogyakarta: Wihdah Press, 2000.

Kompas. "Di luar Jam Sekolah Kehidupan Ajarkan Kekerasan" [Outside School Hours Life Teaches Violence]. 3 May 2000, p.34.

Kyi, Aung San Suu. "Freedom from fear" . In *Freedom from Fear and Other Writings*. Revised ed. Translated by Michael Aris. London: Penguin, 1991, pp. 180–85.

Malcolm X. Excerpts from "Wretched of the Earth". In *Violence and Its Alternatives: An Interdisciplinary Reader*, edited by Manfred B. Steger and Nancy S. Lind. New York: St Martin's Press, 1999.

Maliki, Zainuddin. *Penaklukan Negara Atas Rakyat* [Subjection of State Toward Its People]. With an Introduction by Muhadjir Darwin. Yogyakarta: Gadjah Mada University Press, 1999.

———— . *Agama Rakyat Agama Penguasa: Konstruksi tentang Relitas Agama dan Demokratisasi* [Religion of People, Religion of Authority: Construction of Religious Reality and Democratization]. With introductions by Komaruddin Hidayat and Muhadjir Darwin. Yogyakarta: Galang Press, 2000.

Moore, Mark. *Creating Public Value: Strategic Management in Government*. Cambridge, MS: Harvard University Press, 1995.

Moore, Mark and Robert Trojanowicz. "Policing and the Fear of Crime". *Perspectives on Policing*, no. 3 (Washington D.C.: National Institute of Justice and Kennedy School of Government, 1988).

Santoso, F. Harianto and M. Supriadi. "Penghakiman Massa" [Killing Field]. *Kompas*, 16 June 2000, p. 6.

Steger, Manfred B., and Nancy S. Lind, eds. *Violence and Its Alternatives: An Interdisciplinary Reader*. New York, NY: St. Martin's Press, 1999.

Snyder, Jack. *From Voting to Violence: Democratization and Nationalist Conflict*. New York & London: W.W. Norton & Co, 2000.

Jakarta Post. "Embassy Security Chiefs Told Jakarta is Now Safer to Live". 6 May 2000, p. 3.

Wolf, Robert Paul. "On Violence". In *Violence and Its Alternatives: An Interdisciplinary Reader*, edited by Manfred B. Steger and Nancy S. Lind. New York: St Martin's Press, 1999.

6

HEALTH STATUS IN INDONESIA DURING THE ECONOMIC CRISIS

Budi Utomo

Introduction

After two decades of sustained economic growth and rapid social development, as indicated by the reduction of poverty from 40 per cent to 11 per cent and the halving of the child mortality rate (GOI and UNICEF 2000, p. 1), Indonesia, in mid-1997, entered a period of sustained economic insecurity. Towards the end of 1997, the rupiah began to lose value. By January 1998, when the monthly inflation rate had reached 6.9 per cent, the Government of Indonesia officially stated that the country had been hit by a severe monetary crisis (Gardner and Amaliah 1999). Since then, inflation has soared. The value of the rupiah to the U.S. dollar had been dramatically falling from 2,470 in July 1997 to 15,000 in February 1998. During that period, the annual inflation rate was 34.2 per cent. Inflation continued to rise to reach 47 per cent in April 1998 and 59 per cent in July 1998. Only after early 1999, the rupiah began to stabilize at around 8,000 to the U.S. dollar. Nevertheless, its value against foreign currency continues to fluctuate.

The monetary crisis soon became an economic crisis, which ballooned into a full social crisis with wide-ranging effects on wages, employment, education, and health services. These, in turn, affected the people's health, particularly the vulnerable and the poor, including children and women. The crisis, among other things, caused the costs of basic commodities, health services, and school tuition fees to rise. It also seriously eroded the already limited resources of the government, the private sector, communities, and families.

The crisis has radically transformed the nature of state governance. Since the start of the crisis, the Soeharto government has crumbled and fallen, the interim government of Habibie has opened doors to democratization but failed to carry the nation through the portals, and the democratically elected government of Abdurahman Wahid has found itself beset by faction fighting and social conflict. Indonesia continues to experience a profound period of wide-ranging transition and great uncertainty. This has led to wider religious and ethnic conflicts in different regions of the country, posing a threat to survival, development, and protection of the vulnerable, especially children and women.

Given the above, this chapter aims to review the health status and health services in the country during the past decades, and to assess the impact of the economic crisis on the health status and health services. The discussion begins with an examination of the Indonesian people's health status during the past decades through available indicators, especially those that measure level, trend, and pattern of mortality, nutritional status, and morbidity. Because of the data availability, the discussion on health status focuses more on women and children than on other groups in the population. Moreover, as the survival and the fate of children and women depend on the capacity of their community to provide health care, the health status of this group would also indicate the health status of the community. At the same time, the discussion also assesses the impact of the economic crisis on their health status, and health services. The chapter then goes on to assess the level and quality of two important factors affecting health status: food security, and health services, especially in the context of the economic crisis.

How does the Economic Crisis Affect Health?

Gani (2000) has systematically described how the economic crisis affected health, in three major areas. Firstly, on the supply side, the crisis reduced the ability of the government to provide health services at an adequate level of quality, and at the same time increased the price of medical care inputs, including drugs, and medical supplies. This led to declining performance of both public and private health providers, which in turn led to lower health status. Secondly, on the demand side, the crisis reduced the ability to pay for health care in the community. This also led to lower health status. Thirdly, the crisis directly affected health status because of reduced food consumption, change in the health environment, and change in lifestyle.

The devastating effects of the crisis on the private sector have endangered not only the survival of the private health-care providers, but also reduced the tax revenue collected by the government. This, in turn, has caused the government to reduce health-care spending. Moreover, the political pressure resulting from the crisis has increased the level of food and fuel subsidies, which could lower the government budget for health-care. All these would decrease the availability of government resources for health-care provision (Johnson et al. 1999). For fiscal year 1999, a budget increase, from 5 per cent to 63 per cent, was applied across all divisions of the Ministry of Health (MOH). The Directorate of Community Health received an increase of 10 per cent, a percentage increase that was far below the inflation rate triggered by the devaluation of the rupiah, which meant that the MOH budget actually declined in real terms (JHPIEGO-MNH 1999).

The crisis also adversely affected the capacity of organizations responsible for managing health-care and insurance schemes, because of the decline in premiums, increased payments to health-care providers, and decreased training programmes in management skills (Johnson et al. 1999).

The price of drugs and medical supplies has also sky-rocketed as a result of the economic crisis. Studies have indicated that until April 1998 — less than a year after the crisis began — the price of most pharmaceutical, medical supplies, and infuse sets had increased three to four times (cited in Gani 2000, pp. 287–88). Such an increase also occurred among the generic drugs as most of their raw materials were still imported. With the price increases, government health facilities experienced a shortage of drugs and supplies and, consequently, faced difficulties in sustaining their quality of services. In addition, the already low operational and maintenance budget, which included personnel salaries, drugs and supplies, electricity, water, communication, etc., suffered even more. It was estimated that even before the crisis the allocated budget had covered no more than 60 per cent of real requirements (Gani 2000). For health centres, the budget insufficiency affected their capacity to render curative medical care as well as community health programmes.

The significant reduction in income and increase in the cost of living as well as the substantial increase in the number of persons living in poverty during the crisis have resulted in a sharp decline in the purchasing power of households. This decline in purchasing power in turn has had a serious impact on the family's ability to pay for health-care (ATP) — the amount of money that presumably would have been used to pay for the needed health-care. Such an impact has varied between regions and areas. In his analysis of data for Indramayu and Bandung, Gani (2000) has estimated that the percentage of households with ATP of Rp2000, or more, declined from 79 per cent to 64 per cent in Indramayu, while in Bandung it decreased from 81 per cent to 74 per cent. Thus, at least 36 per cent of households in Indramayu and 26 per cent in Bandung would require subsidies in order to enable them to utilize health centre services.

The reduction in ATP also affects the health-seeking behaviour of the population. Because of this reduced ATP, people tended to shift from private providers of health-care to public health providers. In western Jakarta, the number of visits to government health centres increased by 40 per cent (Gani 2000). This shift has put a heavier burden on government subsidies. Based on 1995 prices, the government should provide subsidies of Rp2,500 to Rp3,000 per visit. On the other hand, a number of private facilities have reported a reduction in utilization rates. Practising doctors in Bandung and Jakarta have also reported that the number of patients they see has declined by 50 per cent. Another change in health-seeking behaviour is the tendency to self-treatment. Sales of antibiotics without prescriptions from drugstores have also been reported to have increased by 200 per cent (Gani 2000).

Health Status

Together, measures of mortality, nutritional status, and morbidity, especially among children and women, are commonly used to indicate the status of community health.

Infant and Child Mortality

In Indonesia, child mortality has declined during the past two decades, but the under-fives mortality rate is still higher than that of neighbouring countries: 4.6 times higher than Malaysia, 1.3 times higher than the Philippines, and 1.8 times higher than Thailand (UNICEF 1998). The infant mortality rate (IMR) declined from 71 deaths per 1,000 live births in 1986 to 52 deaths per 1,000 live births in 1996. During the same period, the under-fives mortality rate declined from 103 to 71 deaths per 1,000 live births. These mortality statistics imply that from approximately 4 million children born each year, 300,000 would have died before age five. Five of every seven deaths of under-fives occurred during the first year of life. Moreover, the data also indicated that of the deaths during the first year of life, about one-third occurred during the first month of life (UNICEF 1998).

The infant and child mortality rate in Indonesia is not only relatively high, but it also varies widely between provinces, between urban and rural areas, and between social aggregations, reflecting the gaps between the rich and the poor. According to the 1997 SUSENAS data, the five worst provinces in terms of infant mortality rate were West Nusa Tenggara (111 per 1000), Central Sulawesi (95 per 1000), Southeast Sulawesi (78 per 1000), Bengkulu (72 per 1000), and South Kalimantan (71 per 1000) (GOI-UNICEF 2000). As expected, the infant mortality rate was higher in the rural than urban areas.

According to the 1995 Household Health Survey (HHS), most of the infant deaths were associated with three causes: acute respiratory infections (32 per cent), diarrhoea (27 per cent), and perinatal complications (16 per cent) (MOH 1997). These three causes accounted for 75 per cent, or approximately 150,000 infant deaths per year. On the perinatal deaths, the main causes were neonatal tetanus, low birth weight, and asphyxia. Neonatal tetanus accounted for 2 to 4.5 per cent of the infant deaths.

Lack of assistance and care from a trained person at the time of birth is often cited as related to the high rate of perinatal deaths. The percentage of birth deliveries attended by trained personnel ranges from only 20 per cent in West Nusa Tenggara to 70 per cent in Bali and Jakarta (MOH 1997). In 20 out of the 26 provinces, including West, Central, and East Java which house 60 per cent of the Indonesian population, less than half of births were attended by a trained midwife.

On the deaths of under-five children, the main causes were acute respiratory infections (ARI) and diarrhoea. The percentage of child deaths attributed to diarrhoea declined from 37 per cent in 1980 to 14 per cent in Java/Bali, and 21 per cent outside Java/Bali in 1995. Diarrhoea has apparently become relatively less important as a cause of child deaths but continues to affect millions of children who survive and suffer from diarrhoea consequences. The percentage of child deaths caused by ARI has increased from 29 per cent in 1980 to 39 per cent in Java/Bali, and 33 per cent outside Java/Bali in 1995.

Stemming from unsafe water, poor sanitation and hygiene, parasite infections emerge as a major cause of death of under-fives, contributing to approximately 11,000 deaths, or 14 per cent of the total child deaths (MOH 1997). Immunizable diseases, such as measles, diphtheria, and pertussis still account for an estimated 4 per cent of child deaths. Neonatal tetanus has decreased to about one-third of the 1990 level of 1,590 per year. In 1995, there were only 409 reported cases of neonatal tetanus.

Tuberculosis (TB) remains a significant cause of infant and child deaths. The number of reported TB cases decreased from 114,489 in 1997 to 73,462 cases in 1997. Nonetheless, Indonesia is currently ranked as the fourth worst country in the world in terms of TB cases. With the threat of HIV/AIDS epidemic, there is concern that TB will become an even more common cause of child deaths.

Dengue haemorrhagic fever (DHF) is increasingly recognized as a factor in the causes of death among children. Currently, more than 200 districts are considered as dengue-endemic. The highest incidence of reported dengue is in Jakarta, followed by Yogyakarta and Central Kalimantan. Malaria is also an important cause of death, particularly in the Outer Islands (GOI-UNICEF 2000).

Child Malnutrition

Even before the economic crisis, about 40 per cent of Indonesian children were malnourished, as measured by the prevalence of underweight (Gillespie et al. 1996, p. 20). Despite an overall decrease of 5 per cent in the prevalence of malnutrition since 1992, regional as well as urban–rural variations seem to have widened. Anthropemetric data from the 1998 SUSENAS reported that in some of the remote rural districts in Sulawesi, Kalimantan, and East Nusa Tenggara, the child malnutrition prevalence was up to 50 per cent (Jahari et al. 1999). In the rural areas, 32 per cent of under-fives were underweight, while the percentage in the urban areas was 27 per cent.

There is no national representative data on stunting and wasting children as their height is generally not measured in any of the routine surveys. However, the complementary feeding study conducted in 1997 in six districts of five provinces indicated that less than 5 per cent of infants 0–6 months of age were stunted, but by two years this percentage had increased eightfold to more than 40 per cent. That study found that the prevalence of stunting among children under 24 months of age ranged from 9 per cent in Purworedjo to 28 per cent in Belu, and an average of 16 per cent across all the six study sites (Sharma et al. 1998a). Data representative of all ecological zones in Central Java suggest that 47 per cent of children aged 12 to 23 months are stunted (HKI 1999). These data suggest that Indonesian children are not born stunted but many become so because of environmental factors and deficiencies in care and nurture during the early years of life, particularly in the first two years.

On the prevalence of wasting children, the 1997 Complementary Feeding Survey found that 6 per cent of under-twos were wasted; this percentage ranged from 3 per cent in Bogor to 11 per cent in Belu (Sharma et al. 1998a). The HKI Nutrition Surveillance found alarmingly high rates of wasting in under-twos in poor urban areas of major Indonesian cities, from 13 per cent in Semarang up to 29 per cent in Jakarta (HKI 1999).

A recent analysis of 1989, 1992, 1995, and 1998 SUSENAS data suggests an improvement in the prevalence of underweight from 36 per cent in 1989 to 30 per cent in 1998 (Jahari et al. 1999). However, when the data are analysed more closely, specifically for children under two — the most vulnerable — the percentage was higher in 1998 than in 1995. Among urban children, the percentage was higher in 1995 than in 1992. Moreover, the percentage of severely underweight children appears to have been increasing since as far back as 1992, and had reached alarming levels even at the time of the recent SUSENAS in early 1998, before the impact of the crisis had been fully felt.

Concerning the growth of Indonesian children, studies consistently show that the growth is acceptable during the first six months,[1] but begins to falter at 4–6 months of age. The progressive growth faltering continues until 24 months of age, and after that there is steady growth, parallel to reference curves but at a lower level (Jus'at 1991; Soekirman et al. 1992; Utomo 1996; and Jahari et al. 1999).

Indonesian children do not grow well. They suffer from stunted growth by an average of 5–7 cm, and underweight by an average of 2 kg at two years of age. After two years of age, the prevalence of malnutrition plateaus and remains at about 30 per cent from age 2 to 5 (GOI-UNICEF 2000). According to the 1989 SUSENAS data, the prevalence of underweight (WAZ<-2SD) by age of children was reported at about 40 per cent for 6–11 months, and 60 per cent for 12–36 months (Jus'at 1991). Of these undernourished children, the majority (78 per cent) suffered from mild, and the rest, 19 per cent and 3 per cent, suffered from moderate and severe underweight respectively (Soekirman et al. 1992).

With regard to sex differential of child nutritional status, the World Bank analysis of the SUSENAS data show that the prevalence of malnutrition is 6 per cent higher in boys than girls (Saadah et al. 1999). This may be explained by the fact that boys have slightly higher nutritional requirements related to their slightly higher average height and weight. If boys and girls were fed equally, more boys than girls would become underweight because of their higher nutritional requirement.

Micro-nutrient Deficiencies

Beyond obvious malnutrition, as seen in underweight, shortness, and wasting, Indonesian children suffer from "hidden hunger" malnutrition because of micro-nutrient deficiencies, notably with respect to Vitamin A, iron, and iodine. Deficiencies in these micro-nutrients contribute to poor growth and also debilitate children's immunity and cognitive development and predispose them to lower productivity and higher risk of degenerative diseases later in life.

Vitamin A Deficiency. Before the crisis, the prevalence of Vitamin A deficiency had been substantially reduced during the 1980s, as shown by the fall in xeropthalmia of children from 1.20 per cent in 1977 to 0.34 per cent in 1992 (DepKes 1997). Nevertheless, in terms of sub-clinical deficiency, the prevalence of Vitamin A deficiency among under-fives at the pre-crisis period, as indicated by the 1995 National Vitamin A Survey, remained high at 50 per cent (DepKes 1997).

Iron Deficiency. In the two decades preceding the crisis, the prevalence of iron deficiency among pregnant women had decreased, as indicated by a drop from 70 per cent in 1983 to 50 per cent in 1995 (Thaha 1998). Iron deficiency remains a widespread problem affecting an estimated 9 million (40 per cent) of under-fives and 50 per cent of pregnant women (Latief et al. 1999). Even as young as six months of age, already half of Indonesian infants suffer from iron deficiency in areas such as Indramayu (Utomo and Hidayat 1999), Lombok (Fahmida 1999), and Central Java (HKI 1999). A similar situation would also happen in other areas with similar socio-economic and environmental conditions.

Iron deficiency in pregnancy would result in low iron stores in the infant and young child. The Ministry of Health has a policy that every pregnant woman should take 90 iron tablets during pregnancy. However, the availability of iron tablets and compliance are known to have limited the programme's effectiveness (Achadi et al. 1999). Low intake of dietary iron is likely exacerbated by environmental factors, including parasite infestations and carbon monoxide contamination. In Purworejo, the University of Gadjah Mada found that 70 per cent of pregnant women had parasites: 61 per cent were infected with *Trichuris*, 29 per cent with *Ascaris*, and 27 per cent with *Nector americanus* (Nurdiati et al. 1999a). The last infestation is particularly devastating for those with iron deficiency because of bleeding caused by this type of worm.

Iodine Deficiency. Iodine Deficiency Disorder (IDD) causes brain damage and impairs intellectual potential. IDD threatens an estimated 142 million of Indonesia's 200 million people (Latief 1995). The Nutrition Research Centre has estimated that in Indonesia there are 295,000 cretins, 8.8 million Indonesians with severe IDD, 8.2 million with moderate IDD, and 35.8 million with mild IDD (cited in Latief 1995).

The current strategy to control IDD is salt iodization and the distribution of iodine capsules in areas of persistently low iodine concentration in salt. This strategy has reduced the prevalence of IDD by 65 per cent in less than ten years. The goitre prevalence rate in school children has decreased from 28 per cent in 1990 to 9.8 per cent in 1998 (Latief et al. 1999). Two provinces, West Sumatra and West Nusa Tenggara (NTB), are classified as having a problem of IDD, which is moderate in severity as indicated by a total goitre prevalence of between 20 per cent and 30 per cent. East Nusa Tenggara (NTT) and Maluku are classified as provinces with a severe IDD problem as in these two provinces, almost one in three children have some degree of goitre due to IDD.

Impact of the Economic Crisis on Child Nutritional Status. Estimates on the increase in poverty related to the crisis vary, but the most conservative estimate is that over 40 million people, or one in five, are currently living in poverty. Data from the 100-village survey have showed that the average household spending per person fell by 24 per cent between 1996 and 1998, while in the urban areas it declined by 34 per cent (GOI-UNICEF 2000). Java was the hardest hit. The total household expenditures declined as a result of the crisis, but the share of expenditures on food as a percentage of the total increased by 10–12 per cent. This suggests that household spending on education and health had declined (BPS-UNICEF 1999).

The crisis has worsened the already poor nutritional status of Indonesian children. By September 1999, more than 23,000 cases of severe malnutrition had been reported to the Directorate of Community Nutrition (GOI-UNICEF 2000). In East Java, severe malnutrition cases among infants and young children have been increasingly reported since 1997.[2] Obviously, these reported cases represent only the "tip of the iceberg". The analysis of the 1998 SUSENAS data found that 10.5 per cent of under-fives were severely underweight (WAZ <-3SD) (Jahari et al. 1999). This implies that 2.3 million under-five children were severely malnourished.

Independently, the HKI nutrition survey also showed that nutritious food consumption had significantly decreased and the micro-nutrient deficiency incidence had increased because of the crisis (HKI 1999). In areas worst affected by the crisis, such as the urban poor, the prevalence and severity of Vitamin A deficiency has increased since the crisis. The percentage of women who reported night blindness in poor areas of Jakarta and Ujung Pandang in 1998 was 2.5 per cent and 3.3 per cent respectively (HKI 1998). A longitudinal survey of 5,000 pregnant women in Purworejo between 1996 and 1998 showed 6.8 per cent with night blindness (Nurdiati et al. 1999b).

Child Morbidity

Indonesian children are often sick. The 1997 multi-site complementary feeding study showed that at any given time, 20 per cent of young children have a cough or cold, 11 per cent have fever, 4 per cent have diarrhoea and 8 per cent have a poor appetite (Sharma et al. 1998b). On top of this, many children have intestinal worms on a year-round basis. Representative surveys have not been done, but small-scale studies suggest that about 80 per cent of children have at least one parasite, with *Ascaris* being the most common. Hadju et al. (forthcoming) found that 80 per cent of schoolboys had *Ascaris* and 100 per cent had *T. trichiura* in Ujung Pandang. Hookworm may also be endemic in the rural areas, such as Purworejo where 37 per cent of women had hookworm (Nurdiati et al. 1999b).

The 1997 Demographic and Health Survey (DHS) data indicate that the prevalence of morbidity among children varies across provinces, from 5 per cent to 20 per cent for all types of diarrhoea, and from 15 per cent to 40 per cent for cough and respiratory symptoms (CBS, NFPCB, MOH, and Macro International 1998). The later period of infancy and the second year of life are times of greatly increased risk of diarrhoea and acute respiratory infections. The prevalence of these symptoms doubles from age 0–6 to 6–12 months of age, coinciding with the onset of growth faltering.

Illnesses have been responsible for more than half of all malnourished children. The remainder of malnourished children is associated with inadequate food intake because of, among other things, poverty, ignorance, and limited food access. On the other hand, malnourished children are prone to infections, so that these children are trapped in a perpetual cycle of malnutrition-infections. Thus, malnutrition-infection syndrome would remain and continue to be a major child health problem.

Health Problems Among Adolescents

Nutrition and health problems during infancy and childhood often continue into adolescence and adulthood. The 1995 Household Health Survey showed that 52 per cent of adolescent girls suffered from anaemia (DepKes 1997). Adolescents between the ages of 15 to19 years had the highest percentage of chronic malnutrition — about 36 per cent (BPS, DepKes, and UNICEF 1995). Parasitic diseases, such as chronic hookworm parasitosis and malaria, cause iron deficiency anaemia because of chronic blood loss (Santosa 1997). When anaemia occurs in a mother, the foetus is affected, with possible intrauterine growth retardation and reduced ability to absorb iron from the mother.

Indonesian adolescents are increasingly at risk of contracting HIV infections. The data showed that 88 out of 1,235 persons living with HIV are between the ages of 15 and 19 years (MOH 2000). The earlier the adolescents become sexually active, the more likely they are to change their sexual partners, which means greater risk of sexually transmitted infections.

Health Status of Reproductive-Age Women

Health issues for reproductive-age women (15 to 49 years) include considerable problems of sexuality and reproduction. Sexuality is not only about sex, but also about the right of women to make choices and decisions related to sexual behaviour and practices, relationships, breastfeeding, contraception, and abortion. Reproductive health problems are affected by women's access to the means to protect themselves from unwanted pregnancies and sexually transmitted infections, including HIV.

Despite the dramatic reduction of the fertility rate from 5.6 to 2.8 births per woman during the past thirty years, many aspects of women's reproductive health remain largely unmet (CBS, NFPCB, MOH and MI 1998). The 1997 DHS data showed that every year, 8.3 per cent of women aged 15–49, or 4.6 million, experienced unwanted pregnancies; this did not change from the 1994 DHS findings of 8.2 per cent (CBS, NFPCB, MOH and MI 1995). At the same time, however, the number of pregnant women whose pregnancies were mistimed ("wanted later") declined from 16 per cent in 1991 to 8.8 per cent in 1997.

Estimates of unmet need for contraception in the DHS data showed a decline from 13 per cent in 1991 to 9 per cent in 1997.[3] Data from the 1997 DHS also showed that 9.5 per cent of women aged 15–19 had had their first child ("too young"), about 22 per cent of women had four children or more ("too many"), and 15.4 per cent had birth intervals of less than two years ("too close").

Maternal Mortality. Maternal mortality rates in Indonesia are unacceptably high. Although different studies have reported a wide range of estimates from a couple of hundreds to four times that level, an estimate of 400 maternal deaths per 100,000 live births has been generally accepted as the prevailing level (CBS, NFCB, MOH, and MI 1995; and Iskandar et al. 1996). In contrast, maternal mortality ratios in developed countries are very low — 7 to 15 maternal deaths per 100,000 live births (Lettenmaier et al. 1988, p. 2). Thus, compared with developed countries, the risk of maternal death in Indonesia is very high, about 45 times higher (McCarthy and Maine 1992, p. 23). For one maternal death, many more suffer from chronic, even serious maternal morbidity complications (McCarthy and Maine 1992, p. 23). Studies suggested 17 to 70 episodes of serious maternal illnesses for every maternal death (cited in Goodburn, Gazi, and Chowdury 1995, p. 22).

Maternal death is not only a tragedy for the victim, but also has a devastating effect on the remaining members of her family, especially the children. The survival and fate of young children depend on their mothers. The death of a mother is often followed by the death of her infant. Studies have reported that 90 to 95 per cent of newborn infants whose mothers died in childbirth also died within one year after birth (cited in Winikoff and Sullivan 1987). It is estimated that for every dead mother two children would be left motherless (Winikoff and Sullivan 1987).

In Indonesia, 75–85 per cent of maternal deaths are related to one or a combination of the three maternal complications: haemorrhage, infection, and eclampsia (GOI-UNICEF 1988). One study in Bali showed that 67 per cent of maternal deaths were related to maternal haemorrhage (bleeding) (Fortney 1985). Most cases of maternal haemorrhage are post-partum haemorrhage, especially found in women with high parity. Data from the 1995 Household Health Survey show that the principal causes of maternal deaths are haemorrhage (46.7 per cent), eclampsia (14.5 per cent), and infection (8 per cent). These complications occur during or shortly after child-birth. The underlying causes of these complications may differ from one community to another. In communities where many young women are pregnant, long labour or obstructed labour could be the main underlying factor. On the other hand, in communities where family planning services are not available or under-utilized, illegal abortion could be the main underlying factor.

Causes of high maternal mortality are complex but include poorly trained health staff and midwives, late referral, and lack of emergency facilities and transport. In Indonesia, only one in two pregnant women use a trained midwife for her delivery (BPS 1998). This substandard of maternal care has been aggravated by the present crisis. The 100-village survey showed that from 1997 to 1998, up to 10 per cent fewer women used a trained midwife during delivery (BPS-UNICEF 1999). Women are also working longer hours. The same survey showed an 11 per cent increase from 1997 to 1998 in the number of women working more than 35 hours a week. The long hours of work for women can seriously affect their health.

Induced Abortion. It is estimated that 750,000 to one million induced abortions occur each year in Indonesia (Hull et al. 1993). This implies a rate of 18 abortions per 100 conceptions, assuming there were 4.5 million live births in 1989. Studies indicate that legal prohibitions do not deter women from having abortions (Utomo et al. 1982). Women attempt abortion using a variety of means, or consult illegal practitioners, or trained doctors and other medical personnel. Abortion is not limited to adolescents and unmarried women, but is also a recourse of many married women who are sexually active and do not want more children but have not used regular contraception or have experienced contraception failure (Affandi et al. 1986).

Women Malnutrition and Low Birth Weight. Reproductive-age women are at high risk of chronic energy deficiency. The 1994 DHS showed that 8.4 per cent of the women surveyed had body height of less than 145 cm, while nearly a third had upper arm circumference of less than 23.5 cm (CBS, NFPCB, MOH and MI 1995). On the other hand, the 1995 HHS showed that 14.5 per cent of married women in five provinces — West Java, Central Java, East Nusa Tenggara, Maluku, and Irian Jaya — had chronic under-nutrition, as indicated by a body mass index of less than 18.5 kg/m^2 (Setyowati and Utomo 1999). Similar levels of chronic energy deficiency were also reported by other independent sources: the Crisis Surveillance Program (HKI 1999), the 1997 Multi-Site Complementary Feeding Study (Sharma 1998a), and the Indonesia Family Life Survey (IFLS) (Frakenberg et al. 1999). Chronic energy deficiency with multiple micro-nutrient deficiencies would have negative carry-over effects on the developing foetus. Malnourished mothers would have a higher risk of having low-birth-weight (LBW) babies.[4]

National representative data on the prevalence of low-birth-weight babies[4] are not available, given that most children are not weighed at birth. A study conducted in seven different sites in 1990 showed variation in LBW prevalence, with an average of 10 per cent (Alisyahbana 1991). Recent community-based studies showed LBW prevalence of 12–14 per cent (Hakimi et al. 1999; and Kusharisupeni 1999). Most LBW babies in Indonesia are associated with foetal growth retardation. The babies are "small" not because of prematurity but because of intrauterine growth retardation.

LBW is an indicator of malnutrition in pregnant women and their unborn children, and also a predictor of child growth and survival. Studies have indicated that the growth of LBW children is hampered right from the start (Utomo 1996; and Kusharisupeni 1999). The studies also showed that LBW children have a higher risk of mortality than normal-birth-weight children (Utomo 1996).

Maternal Morbidity. According to the 1995 HHS, the prevalence of maternal morbidity was 23 per cent. The highest prevalence was found in NTT (40 per cent) and the lowest was Central Java (16 per cent). The prevalence was particularly high during pregnancy and delivery, 15.5 per cent and 14.3 per cent respectively. The prevalence during post-partum was reported at 3.3 per cent. On the other hand, another study by Fortney and Smith (1996) reported a morbidity prevalence of 17.9 per cent during pregnancy, 18.3 per cent during delivery, and as high as 11.3 per cent during post-partum.

The 1995 HHD data showed that the common morbidity during pregnancy included paleness, dizziness, and fatigue (9.8 per cent), high fever (5.4 per cent), oedema (2.5 per cent), and haemorrhage (2.5 per cent). The prevalence of hypertension, jaundice, dysuria, or convulsion was below one per cent. The most frequent morbidity during delivery was prolonged labour, followed by haemorrhage (4.4 per cent), high fever (2.4 per cent), and convulsion (0.2 per cent), while the most frequent morbidity during post-partum was fever or high fever (7.5 per cent), followed by haemorrhage (0.9 per cent) (Setyowati and Utomo 1999).

Food Security and Health Services

Food security and health services are among the key factors associated with community health status. Other associated factors include care for children and women and the household and community environment.

Food Security

During the two decades prior to the crisis, food security had been steadily improving, as indicated by the increase in energy intake, from an average of 1,824 calories per day in 1970 to 2,732 calories per day in 1995. These aggregated statistics, however, are the average and hide the low-income families, who subsist on only two or even one meal a day.

The drought of 1997/98 and the economic crisis have worsened an already fragile food security situation. Rice imports in 1998 (3.1 million metric tonnes) were five times higher than in 1995, and ten times higher than in 1985 (Esrey et al. 1999). The price of rice increased sharply from Rp1,250 per kg in November 1997 to Rp3,000 in September 1998. The rice price fell in 1999, but remained almost triple the price prior to the economic crisis.

Many families could not accommodate the increase in food prices to maintain the same quality of diet as before. According to the IFLS data, households have increased the percentage of total expenditures allocated to food from 65 per cent to 74 per cent, but still, families cannot afford the same quality of diet as before (Frakenberg et al. 1999).

The 100-village survey and the HKI Nutrition Surveillance data indicate that the consumption of micro-nutrient rich food from animal sources has substantially declined since the crisis. Because of the crisis, most families have managed to maintain rice consumption at pre-crisis levels, but have compromised and reduced their consumption of meat, eggs, cooking oil, and other substances (HKI 1999). Before the crisis, households in the poorest sub-group consumed 0.7 to 1.0 eggs per person per week, but since the crisis the mean egg consumption per week was zero. Since egg is the least expensive source of animal food, and if people cannot afford to consume eggs, this implies that they can no longer afford other types of animal foods.

Health Services

In Indonesia, health-care services are highly subsidized by the government and funded through taxes, international grants, and contributions from the private sector, but resources are shrinking because of the economic crisis.

The IFLS data suggest that more and more of both public and private facilities are experiencing stock-outs of contraceptives. The data also suggest that the costs of services, including public services have increased between 1997 and 1998 (Frakenberg et al. 1999). For example, the cost of IUD insertion doubled from Rp1,000 to Rp2000.

Prices were found to be higher in public than private facilities, but even then, absolute prices were still several fold lower in public facilities. Because of the economic crisis, the number of people who used the government subsidized public health facilities had increased (Johnson et al. 1999).

The quality of health services has remained a problem, even before the crisis. Many examples can be given to indicate the inadequacy in terms of quality of health services in Indonesia. According to the 1997 DHS, 22 per cent of children taken to a health centre for acute respiratory infection apparently did not receive adequate treatment. Stock outages undermine the quality of services, and appear to have worsened since the crisis. The crisis seems to have aggravated the already poor utilization and quality of primary health services. IFLS data suggest that the percentage of families who use Puskesmas services fell from 46 per cent in 1997 to 35 per cent in 1998 (Frakenberg et al. 1999). Of great concern is the coverage of the Expanded Programme for Immunization (EPI), which decreased from 91 per cent in 1993/94 to only 82 per cent in 1997/98.[5]

The quality of services offered by the village nutrition and health posts, known as *posyandu*, greatly diminished over the 1990s, especially after the withdrawal of UNICEF funding. SUSENAS data suggest that in 1992, more than two-thirds of under-five children were taken to *posyandu* for growth monitoring on a monthly basis. Since the early 1990s, however, *posyandu* attendance appears to have declined. The IFLS found a further drop in participation at *posyandu*, from 57 per cent in 1997 to 41 per cent in 1998 (Frakenberg et al. 1999).

In the secondary obstetric services, for example, the majority of district hospitals could not function effectively as referral sites because of the lack of facilities and professional competence. By 1995, it was estimated that only 30 per cent of hospitals had the capacity to provide surgical intervention for obstetric services (GOI and UNICEF 1995). As of 1997, the total number of obstetricians at general hospitals throughout the entire country was only 704, and less than half (42 per cent) worked in district-level hospitals (Types C and D) (DepKes 1998).

Efforts for Crisis Recovery

The degree of impact of the crisis and what responses should be implemented have been much debated. With substantial support from international donors, including the World Bank, the Asian

Development Bank, and the International Monetary Fund (IMF), the Government of Indonesia (GOI) introduced a broad Social Safety Net (SSN) programme. Those implementing the SSN programme are the Government of Indonesia, an NGO consortium, and the UN group of development organizations.

The SSN programme has four major interventions: food security; employment creation and sustainable income generation; social protection for access to public health and education services; and support for small and medium-sized enterprise development. The government adopts a four-stage strategy for crisis response: (a) a rescue stage in the first and second years (1998/99), (b) a two-year recovery stage following rescue, (c) a stabilization phase, and (d) a development phase that bridges the crisis period and regular development programming. Provisions for implementing the SSN programme emphasize community development, and the mobilization of self-help organizations. The programme is supposed to be managed in a way that ensures quick disbursement of the fund; transparency in allocation and expenditure; accountability at local as well as national levels; effective targetting of the poorest and most vulnerable groups; sustainability of interventions beyond the crisis response period; going to scale with successful interventions; and government facilitation and co-ordination.

In the 1998/99 fiscal year, SSN funds totalled Rp18 trillion (approximately US$2 billion) for seventeen implementing sectors (Hidayat 1999a). The implementing sectors plan SSN activities with the National Development Planning Board (Bappenas), the IMF, the World Bank, and bilateral and multilateral donors. Overall co-ordination is managed by an independent steering committee affiliated with Bappenas and established by the President (Hidayat 1999b). At the same time, a consortium of NGOs and community groups established a Community Recovery Programme (CRP) aimed at empowering local communities to assist the poorest and most vulnerable segments of the population affected by the crisis. In addition, several UN development organizations have realigned their programmes to help address the emergency and recovery needs in Indonesia.

In its management and implementation, however, the SSN programme faces frequent criticisms and questions. Lack of socialization, inaccurate information regarding the groups that need to be targetted by the programme, and lack of professionalism among the implementing organizations were among the problems constraining the achievement of the SSN programme objectives. An evaluation study by the University of Indonesia (2000) has indicated that there has been confusion in the field regarding the criteria and validation of the poor families targetted by the SSN programme. In many cases, the categorized families are not really poor, while those categorized not poor were in fact the poor families. This confusion has led to incorrect programme targetting.

The study has also identified problems of fund allocation and distribution. While the fund was disbursed directly to the health providers at sub-district and village levels, these health providers were generally not ready to professionally manage and administer the fund to the needy individuals. Many sub-district and village health providers, in particular the Puskesmas doctors and village midwives, did not know what to do with the funds. Lack of co-ordination between the related sectors and the implementing organizations add more problems to the SSN programme.

Conclusion

After gaining economic growth for two decades, Indonesia, in mid-1997, entered a period of sustained economic insecurity and social uncertainty. The economic crisis soon ballooned into a full crisis, with wide-ranging effects on social aspects, including health. Food security and access to and quality of health services, which are among the essential factors associated with health status, have been eroded by the crisis. The crisis has aggravated the already relatively low level of health-care among the Indonesian people, especially those from the poor families. In fact, the data indicate that health-care in Indonesia seems to have worsened since the early 1990s, long before the onset of the economic crisis. Even before the crisis, for example, one in every three under-five children were underweight and stunted by an average 2 kg, and 5–7 cm at two years of age. "Hidden hunger" deficiencies of micro-nutrients, including Vitamin A, iron, iodine and zinc, affect about half of Indonesian children under five.

The government of Indonesia, with support from international donors, has developed and implemented various emergency programmes, such as the Social Safety Net programme, to help the poor families and the most vulnerable in the population. Criticisms and questions, however, have repeatedly been raised with regard to the management and implementation of the SSN programme. Studies have also indicated many problems in fund-targetting and distribution. Thus, there remain unresolved issues regarding how to alleviate the impacts of the crisis on the lives of the people.

Notes

1. This relatively acceptable growth during the first six months of age is because of the near universality of breast-feeding practice.
2. Summary of Findings and Recommendations: Intersectoral Meeting on the Identification and Response to the Emergence and Spread of Severe Malnutrition in Indonesia, Dr. Soetomo Regional Hospital, Surabaya, East Java, 25 August 1998.
3. "Unmet need" is defined as the percentage of currently married women who do not want any more children or want to wait before having their next birth, but are not using any method of family planning.
4. Low birth weight is below 2,500 grams.
5. Coverage of Immunization, *Annual Report*, Ministry of Health.

References

Achadi, E. L., I. Jus'at, A. Zazri, T. Marshall, and R. Galloway. "Determining the prevalence and risk factors of maternal anaemia in South Kalimantan". *Indonesia*. MotherCare/JSI Project, 1999.

Affandi, B., S. Suharto, and W. Dharmabrata. "Psychosocial aspects of pregnancy termination in Yayasan Kusuma Buana and NFPCB". *Inventory of Biomedical Contraceptive Studies in Indonesia*. Jakarta: National Family Planning Coordinating Board, 1986.

Alisyahbana, Anna. "Birthweight distribution, low birthweight, and perinatal mortality in seven selected rural areas in Indonesia: A multi-center study". Project report. Bandung: School of Medicine, University of Padjadjaran, 1991.

Atinc, T. M., and M. Walton. "Social Consequences of the East Asian Financial Crisis". In *Responding to the Global Financial Crisis. A Report to the World Bank*. Washington D.C.: World Bank, September 1988.

Badan Pusat Statistik (BPS). *Statistik Kesejahteraan Rakyat*. Jakarta, 1998.

BPS, DepKes, and UNICEF. *Laporan Hasil Survei Kesehatan Ibu dan Anak 1995*. Jakarta: Badan Pusat Statistik, 1995.

BPS-UNICEF. "Draft Results of the 100 Villages Sentinel Survey (Round 2)". Jakarta: BPS, 1999.

Central Bureau of Statistics (CBS), Indonesia, National Family Planning Coordinating Board (NFPCB), Ministry of Health (MOH), and Macro International Inc. (MI). *Indonesia Demographic Health Survey 1994*. Calverton, Maryland, 1995.

———. *Indonesia Demographic Health Survey 1997*. Calverton, Maryland, 1998.

DepKes (Departemen Kesehatan). "Analisis Status Kesehatan, Disusun dalam Rangka Penyusunan REPELITA VII Kesehatan". Working Group I, Jakarta, 1997.

———. *Profil Kesehatan Indonesia 1998*. Jakarta: Pusat Data Kesehatan, Jakarta, 1998.

Esrey, S., Soekirman, and V. Krause. *Critical Analysis of the Impact of the Economic Crisis on Nutrition of Women and Children in Indonesia towards Charting the Course for Programme to Overcome Indonesia's Nutrition Crisis*. Jakarta: UNICEF, 1999.

Fahmida, Umi. "Preliminary report on the iron/zinc, supplementation trial in East Lombok". Jakarta: SEAMEO, 1999.

Fortney, J. A., and J. B. Smith. *The Base of Iceberg: Prevalence and Perceptions of Maternal Morbidity in Four Developing Countries*. North Carolina, USA: Family Health International, 1996.

Fortney, J. A., et al. *Maternal Mortality in Indonesia and Egypt*. Geneva: World Health Organization, 1985.

Frakenberg, E., D. Thomas, K. Beegle. *The Real Cost of Indonesia's Economic Crisis: Preliminary Findings from the Indonesia Family Life Surveys*. Jakarta: The Demographic Institute, University of Indonesia, and RAND Corporation, 1999.

Gani, Ascobat. "Effects of Economic Crisis on Health". In *Health Social Science Action and Partnership: Retrospective and Perspective Discourse*, edited by Muhadjir Darwin et al. Proceedings, Part 2, of the fourth Asia-Pacific Social Science and Medicine Conference (APSAM), 7–11 December 1998. Yogyakarta: Population Studies Center, Gadjah Mada University, 2000.

Gardner, M., and L. Amaliah. "An Analysis of Conflicting Crisis-related Research Results, Frontiers in Reproductive Health Cooperative Agreement". Jakarta: The Population Council, 1999.

Gillespie, S., J. Mason, and R. Martorell. *How Nutrition Improves, Administrative Committee on Coordination Sub-Committee on Nutrition*. World Health Organization, Geneva, 1996.

Goodburn, E. A., R. Gazi, and M. Chowdury. "Beliefs and practices regarding delivery and postpartum maternal morbidity in rural Bangladesh". *Studies in Family Planning* 26, no. 1 (1995): 22–32.

Government of Indonesia (GOI)–UNICEF. *Situation Analysis of Children and Women in Indonesia*. Jakarta: UNICEF, December 1988.

________ . *Challenges for a New Generation: The Situation of Children and Women in Indonesia, 2000*. Jakarta: Government of Indonesia and UNICEF, 2000.

________ . "Maternal and Child Survival Development and Protection 1995–2000: Master Plan of Operations". Jakarta: Government of Indonesia and UNICEF, 1995.

Hadju, V., Satriono, K. Abadi, L. S. Stephenson. "Relationship between soil-transmitted helminthes and growth in urban slum school children in Ujung Pandang". *International Journal of Food Sciences and Nutrition*. Forthcoming.

Hakimi, M., A. Surjono, D. Nurdiati, M. J. Dibley, and S. H. Ninuk. "Impact of Vitamin A and zinc supplementation on maternal postpartum infections, neonatal infections, low birth weight and prematurity in rural Central Java, Indonesia". Paper presented to the Ministry of Health, Community Nutrition Directorate. Jakarta: Gadjah Mada University and Ministry of Health, Republic of Indonesia, 29 August 1999.

Helen Keller International (HKI). "Re-emergence of the threat of Vitamin A deficiency". *Indonesia Crisis Bulletin*, 12 October 1998.

________. "Indonesia's crisis: A comparison of its impact on nutrition and health in urban and rural populations". Report based on the results of the HKI/ GOI Nutrition Surveillance System, August 1999.

Hidayat, S. "Jaring Pengaman Sosial: Konsep dan Aplikasinya untuk Mengamankan Kualitas SDM". Paper presented at the Workshop on "Jaring Pengaman Sosial dalam Perspektif Kesejahteraan Sosial", Bappenas, Jakarta, March 1999a.

________. "Jaring Pengaman Sosial: Hakikat, Pendekatan, Arah, Tujuan, dan Sasaran". Paper presented at the Workshop on "Jaring Pengaman Sosial dalam Perspektif Kesejahteraan Sosial'. Jakarta: Bappenas, March 1999b.

Hull, T. H., S. W. Sarwono, and N. Widyantoro. "Induced abortion in Indonesia". *Studies in Family Planning* 24, no. 4 (1993): 241–51.

Iskandar, Meiwita, B. Utomo, T. Hull, N. G. Dharmaputra, and Y. Azwar. *Unravelling the mysteries of maternal deaths in West Java: Re-examining the witnesses*. Depok, Indonesia: Center for Health Research, University of Indonesia, 1996.

Jahari, A. B., Sandjaja, S. Herman, I. Jus'at, and F. Jalal. "The hidden problem: Nutritional status of under-fives in Indonesia during the period of 1989 to 1998. An analysis of anthropometric indicators of protein energy malnutrition based on SUSENAS data". Bogor: Pusat Penelitian dan Pengembangan,1999.

JHPIEGO-MNH. *Maternal and Neonatal Review with Recommendations to USAID/ Indonesia*. Jakarta: JHPIEGO-MNH, 1999.

Johnson, C. N., et al. "Assessment and Lessons Learned from the Klaten Integrated Health Care Reform". Jakarta: USAID, 1999.

Jus'at, Idrus. "Determinant of Nutritional Status of Pre-school Children in Indonesia: An Analysis of National Socio-Economy Survey (Susenas), 1987". Ph.D dissertation, Cornell University, Ithaca, N.Y., 1991.

Kristiadi, J. "Pengantar". In *Masa Depan Ekonomi Politik Indonesia, di Indonesia yang berubah*, edited by P. Haryono and G. A. Prayitno. Jakarta: Pusat Data Indikator, 1990.

Kusharisupeni. "Peran berat lahir dan masa gestasi terhadap pertumbuhan linear bayi di Kecamatan Sliyeg dan Gabus Wetan, Kabupaten Indramayu, Jawa Barat 1995–1997". Ph.D. dissertation, University of Indonesia, 1999.

Latief, D. "Recent progress in IDD elimination in Indonesia". A report to the Ministry of Health, Nutrition Directorate. Jakarta: Ministry of Health, 1995.

Latief, D., A. Kurniawan, E. Schoffelen and V. Krause. "Indonesian experience on research and program development to overcome micro-nutrient deficiencies". Paper presented at the Joint Symposium between Sebelas Maret University and the University of Sheffield on micro-nutrient issues in Indonesia. Surakarta: Sebelas Maret University and University of Sheffield, 2–3 March, 1999.

Lettenmaier, C., L. Liskin, C. A. Church, and J. A. Hariss. "Mother's lives matter: Maternal health in the community". *Population Report*, edited by W. Rinehart, Series L, 7 (1988): 1–31.

Maine, D., and Allman. "The demography of maternal and child health in developing countries". In *Health Care of Women and Children in Developing Countries*, edited by H. M. Wallace and K. Giri, pp. 26–35. Oakland: Third Party Publishing Company, 1990.

McCarthy, J., and D. Maine. "A framework for analyzing the determinants of maternal mortality". *Studies in Family Planning* 23, no. 1 (1992): 23–33.

Ministry of Health (MOH). *Household Health Survey 1995*. Jakarta: Research and Development Institute, Ministry of Health, 1997.

________. "Data on reported number of HIV and AIDS cases until 30 April 2000". A report. Jakarta: Directorate General of Communicable Disease Control, Ministry of Health, 2000.

Nurdiati, D. S., M. Hakimi, A. Surjono, and M. J. Dibley. '"The effect of Vitamin A and zinc supplementation during pregnancy on maternal iron status and night blindness". Paper presented to the MOH Community Nutrition Directorate. Newcastle, Australia: Gadjah Mada University and University of Newcastle, 29 August 1999a.

Nurdiati, D. S., S. Sumarni, Suyoko, M. Hakimi, and A. Winkvist. "Intestinal helminthic infection, haemoglobin and ferritin status during pregnancy". Paper presented to the MOH Community Nutrition Directorate. Newcastle, Australia: Gadjah Mada University and University of Newcastle, 29 August 1999b.

Rosenfield, Allan, and Deborah Maine. "Maternal mortality — a neglected tragedy: Where is the M in MCH?". *Lancet* 2, no. 8 (1985): 83–85.

Saadah, F., H. Waters, P. Heywood. "Indonesia: Underweight in young children". World Bank East Asia and the Pacific Region Watching Brief, 1999.

Santosa, R. "Effects of chronic parasitosis on women's health". *International Journal of Gynaecology and Obstetrics* 58 (1997): 129–36.

Setyowati, T., and B. Utomo. "Relationship of maternal nutrition status and morbidity". In *Maternal Morbidity and Mortality Study: CHN-III/ Household Health Survey 1995*, edited by Soemantri et al. Jakarta: MOH and National Institute of Health Research and Development, 1999.

Sharma, S., S. Bunch, J. M. Peerson, S. Murphy, K. H. Brown, H. Hermana, M. Karmini, B. Utomo, M. Hakimi, A. Suyono, S. Kardjati, R. Thaha, V. Hadju. "Complementary feeding practices of young children: Results of a multi-site study". Report 2 on Analysis of anthropometric data, August 1998a.

________. "Complementary feeding practices of young children: Results of a multi-site study". Report 4 on Prelacteal feeding, breastfeeding and other feeding practices, December 1998b.

Soekirman et al. *Economic Growth, Equity and Nutritional Improvement in Indonesia, UN ACC/SCN Country Case Study*. Supported by UNICEF. Jakarta: United Nations, 1992.

Thaha, R. "Reduction in malnutrition in Indonesia in the 1990s: Unresolved issues". Draft, 1998.

UNICEF. *The State of the World's Children 1998*. New York: Oxford University Press, 1998.

University of Indonesia. "Manajemen Pemecahan Masalah Program Jaring Pengaman Sosial". Final draft. Depok, Indonesia: Research Institute, University of Indonesia, 2000.

Utomo, B., S. Jatiputra, and A. Tjokronegoro. "Abortion in Indonesia: A Review of Literature". Faculty of Public Health, University of Indonesia, Jakarta, 1982.

Utomo, Budi. "Health and social dimension of infant feeding: Lessons from Indramayu, West Java". Ph.D. dissertation, Australian National University, 1996.

Utomo, Budi, and Adi Hidayat. "Field trial of the efficacy of iron and zinc supplementation to reduce anaemia and growth faltering in infants in Indramayu, Indonesia". Report of September 1999.

Winikoff, B., and M. Sullivan. "Assessing the role of family planning in reducing maternal mortality". *Studies in Family Planning* 18, no. 3 (1987): 128–43.

7

THE INDONESIAN ECONOMIC CRISIS
Impacts on School Enrolment and Funding

Djoko Hartono and David Ehrmann

Introduction

The impacts of the economic crisis in Indonesia on education enrolments and drop-out rates have not been as devastating as initially feared. School incomes, however, have been hit hard by the crisis.

This chapter examines how the crisis has affected key educational indicators since the 1997/98 academic year. The findings of the study reflect the authors' analysis of several previously published sources of data from the Central Independent Monitoring Unit (CIMU), which independently monitors and evaluates the Scholarships and Grants Programme (SGP), one component of the Indonesian Social Safety Net programme. The CIMU has published a number of reports on the economic crisis, education, and the Scholarships and Grants Programme.

The analysis begins with a description of the education system, summarizing the policy focus at the time when the crisis first struck Indonesia. Detailed findings from the CIMU national survey data are used to describe the varying effects of the crisis on education. Other data sources are also examined to determine the consistency of findings from the CIMU data with those from other sources. The chapter concludes with an analysis of the impact of the Scholarships and Grants Programme, a major donor-supported government intervention to mitigate the effects of the crisis on the school system.

The Indonesian Educational System and Development

The Indonesian education system consists of several levels, including pre-school, primary school, junior secondary school, senior secondary school, and a range of post-secondary education programmes. According to Indonesian law No. 2/1989, basic education lasts for nine years, consisting of six years of primary school plus three years of junior secondary school.

Management responsibility for education falls on several different government ministries. The Ministry of National Education manages the general primary schools, junior secondary schools, and senior secondary schools. However, the general primary schools are not only managed by the Ministry of National Education but also by the Ministry of Home Affairs. The Ministry of Religious Affairs administers some primary schools known as Madrasah Ibtidaiyah (MI), some junior secondary schools known as Madrasah Tsanawiyah (MTs), and some senior secondary schools known as Madrasah Aliyah (MA). In addition to the distinction between general and Islamic education, there is also a distinction between general and vocational secondary education (Sekolah Menengah Kejuruan or SMK). Vocational secondary education emphasizes specific occupational skills and preparing students to enter the world of work. This vocational secondary education is also managed by the Ministry of National Education.

In 1984, the Government of Indonesia declared six years of compulsory education for primary school-age children (7–12 years). This policy has increased participation rates in primary schools from 79.3 per cent in 1983 to 92.2 per cent in 1993. In 1994, compulsory education was extended to nine years (*Wajib Belajar Pendidikan Dasar 9 Tahun*) commonly referred to as Nine Year Universal Basic Education (NYUBE) so that it would encompass both six years of primary education and three years of junior secondary education.

Educational indicators showed improvements before the crisis, particularly during the 1990s. The percentage of school-age children who had never attended school declined, school attendance rose, and there was a decline in drop-outs. These indicators varied slightly across different age groups.[1]

The trend of enrolment rates in Indonesia from 1980 until the current crisis showed general increases although there was a marked decline in junior secondary enrolment between 1988 and 1994 (see Figure 7.1 on "Gross Enrolment Rates"). At the same time, there was a significant rise in drop-outs at the junior secondary level. This figure reached 12.4 per cent during the 1988/89 school year. It has been widely accepted that

Figure 7.1
Gross Enrolment Rates (%)

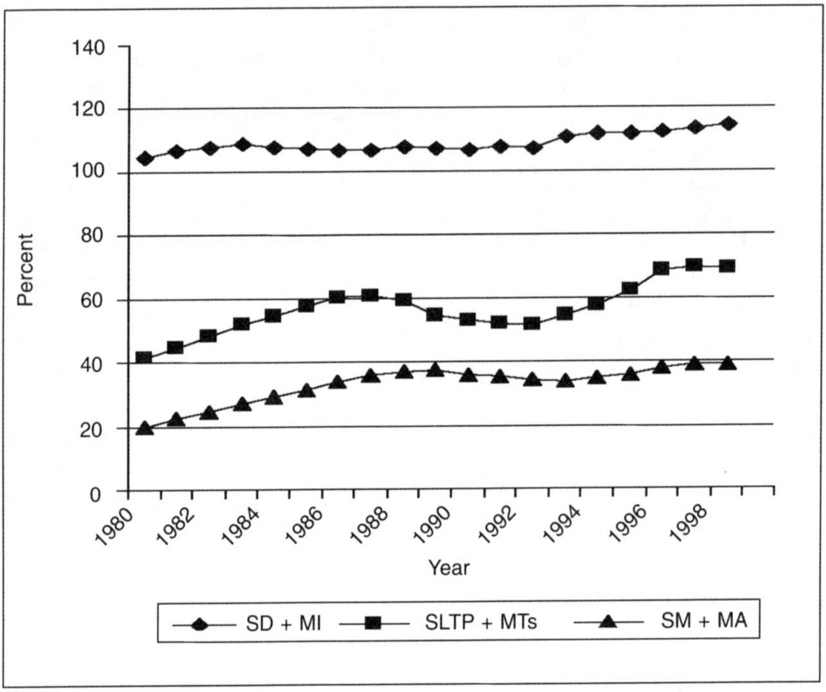

Note: SD + MI (general and Islamic primary school)
SLTP + MTs (general and Islamic junior secondary school)
SM + MA (general and Islamic senior secondary school)
Source: The World Bank (1998).

these trends resulted from the economic crisis that occurred in 1986/87.

Enrolment rates have remained at a generally constant level since the attainment of "universal" primary school enrolment in the early 1980s. The most likely reason for this trend is that the numbers of primary school-aged students have not grown. This may have been the result of a very successful national planning programme which has reduced fertility. The result is that over time, schools have had reduced numbers of new entrants, particularly among primary school-age students.

As mentioned, during the ten to fifteen years preceding the 1997 crisis, Indonesia had achieved a high primary school participation rate.

Table 7.1
Status of School Enrolment by Age Groups, Indonesia 1993–98
(In percentages)

	1993	*1994*	*1995*	*1996*	*1997*	*1998*
5–6 years:	100.0	100.0	100.0	100.0	100.0	100.0
Never attended school	84.8	82.5	82.5	80.7	77.3	77.4
Attending school	14.9	17.3	17.3	19.1	22.5	22.3
No longer attending school	0.3	0.2	0.2	0.2	0.2	0.3
7–12 years:	100.0	100.0	100.0	100.0	100.0	100.0
Never attended school	4.5	3.8	3.8	3.5	2.9	3.0
Attending school	92.8	94.1	93.9	94.4	95.4	95.1
No longer attending school	2.7	2.1	2.2	2.1	1.7	1.9
13–15 years:	100.0	100.0	100.0	100.0	100.0	100.0
Never attended school	1.3	1.3	1.2	1.2	1.0	1.0
Attending school	68.9	72.4	73.2	75.8	77.5	77.2
No longer attending school	29.8	26.3	25.6	22.9	21.5	21.9
16–18 years:	100.0	100.0	100.0	100.0	100.0	100.0
Never attended school	1.6	1.4	1.4	1.5	1.3	1.3
Attending school	42.6	45.3	44.6	47.6	48.6	49.3
No longer attending school	55.8	53.3	53.9	50.9	50.1	49.4

Note: Each year of the SUSENAS data pertain to one school year. The 1993 SUSENAS data pertain to the 1992/93 school year, while the 1994 SUSENAS data pertain to the 1993/94 school year, etc.

Source: BPS, special tabulations from SUSENAS 1993–98. This table is taken from Oey-Gardiner (2000).

The education policy was therefore focused on achieving the nine-year universal basic education (NYUBE) by expanding participation through junior secondary schools. Efforts to achieve NYUBE focused on the junior secondary level and on the transition from primary to junior secondary schools, a critical juncture that can determine further educational continuation. The government then pledged to achieve NYUBE by 2020. The number of junior secondary students would be increased by nearly two million students, in order to raise crude participation rates to 87 per cent by 2004. The move would require a major investment, including about 45,000 new classrooms and tens of thousands of new teachers. Achieving NYUBE was still the focus of the educational policy when the crisis broke out in 1997.

Figure 7.2
Proportion of Physical School Buildings by the Level and Type of School during the 1999/2000 School Year

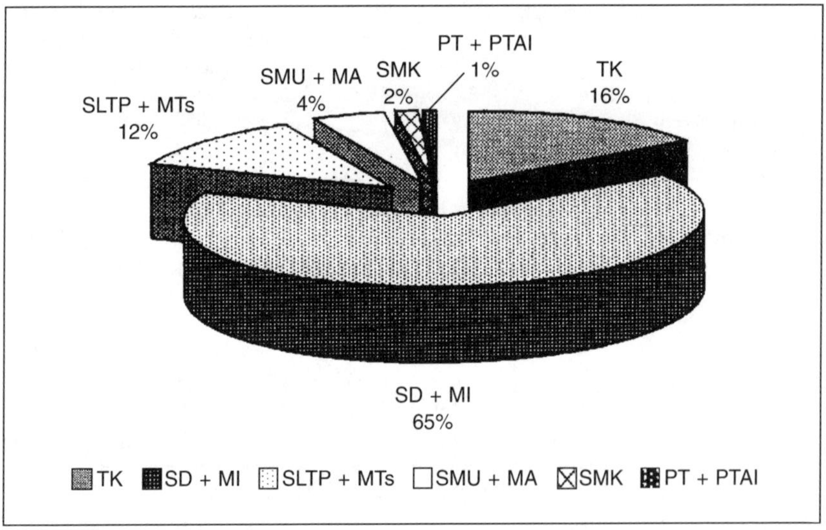

Note: SD + MI (general and Islamic primary school)
SLTP + MTs (general and Islamic junior secondary school)
SM + MA (general and Islamic senior secondary school)
Source: Departemen Pendidikan Nasional (Ministry of National Education) (2000).

The number of school buildings also rose during this same period. Data from Depdiknas (Indonesian Ministry of National Education) show an increase in school infrastructure since 1994. This increase combined with the increased demand for schooling may be related to enrolment gains. Figure 7.2 depicts the proportion of physical school buildings by the level and type of school during the 1999/2000 school year.

During 1997/98, the World Bank conducted a review of the sector, which showed the overall context of the education policy to be favourable. The review described several positive features: the system was expanding, there was a solid commitment to universal basic education, several pro-poor policies were being implemented, there was a narrowing in gender differentials, and there were positive economic returns. The review also recognized the progressive introduction of policies aimed at decentralization. These policies hoped to address existing institutional rigidities and fragmented responsibilities which were apparent throughout the system, particularly at the district level.

In spite of these, several underlying deficiencies remained. The system was inefficient, rigid, and non-responsive to the labour market. Many teachers lacked sufficient training and were not provided with adequate salaries or incentives. The curriculum was criticized as being overloaded and poorly integrated. Class time was extremely low in the lower grades. The quality and quantity of materials and textbooks were wanting, particularly in the remote or rural areas. Many primary school buildings were in very poor condition (World Bank, cited in Jones et al. 2001, p. 215). Administrative arrangements were extremely complex, particularly at the lower levels. Three major agencies were then and remain responsible for different aspects of education. The Education Ministry is responsible for the curriculum and teacher training at all school levels, for running public secondary schools, and for inspecting private secondary schools. The Ministry of Religion manages Islamic (Madrasah) schools. The Ministry of Home Affairs manages financing and human resources (including teacher employment) for public primary education. Many of the poorest students attend private schools, particularly at the secondary level.

Studies funded by the World Bank and the Asian Development Bank (ADB) have criticized education funding as being fragmented: routine and development budgets have been drawn up in isolation and with little regard for actual needs. According to an ADB study in 1998, the net effect was particularly stark at the primary level: 88 per cent of government funds supported in-school spending, mostly on teachers' salaries. Only 70 per cent of the remaining non-salary funding actually trickled through the administrative superstructure to the schools. There have also been significant and persistent concerns about educational quality. Teachers tend to demand rote learning, learning materials are in short supply, and there is need for curriculum reform.

Anticipated Consequences of the Crisis on Education

Analysts predicted that the crisis would result in rising unemployment, decreased purchasing power, and reductions in education spending. There were concerns that worsening household economic conditions might eventually affect the ability of poor households to pay for goods and services, including education for their children.[2]

Many of the predictions related to the current economic crisis were based on experiences with the educational setbacks that had occurred as a result of the 1986/87 crisis. Three immediate risks were identified that might have resulted from the current crisis on education. Firstly, enrolment in basic education might decline as needy families kept their children out of school. Poor parents might withdraw older children from school so that they can contribute to family income. Parents might also withdraw younger children from school to reduce education-related costs. Secondly, the quality of education might be affected by the crisis as the government, schools, and parents struggle to minimize educational costs during this period of economic hardship. It was also feared that poorer communities might not have sufficient funds for the operation and maintenance of schools. Even before the crisis, many schools had lacked books, supplies, and substantial maintenance. Thirdly, inefficiencies and corruption in the government might exacerbate the worsening conditions and funds shortages.[3]

When the 1997 crisis struck, the leadership in the Ministry of National Education (MONE) and the lending agencies immediately thought of the economic crisis of 1986/87. That downturn was caused by a decline in oil prices and a prolonged drought. It hit the education sector particularly hard, causing sharp declines in enrolment, particularly among the poor. At the junior secondary level, the gross enrolment rates fell for four years, from 62 per cent to 52 per cent between 1988 and 1992, and this decline did not recover to its previous level until 1995. Primary enrolment rates also saw some declines even though these were much smaller than those at the junior secondary level (World Bank 1998, p.13).[4]

One characteristic of the 1986/87 crisis was that the worst effects on enrolment did not occur until nearly two years after the crisis broke. That crisis caused a shortage of government funds for routine and development expenditures. These reductions in public expenditures on education, compounded by increases in the price of schooling and a drop in family incomes, might have been responsible for the declines in enrolment.

Everyone in the Indonesian Government and in the lending agencies thought that the 1997/98 crisis would be much more serious than that of 1986/87. Various government agencies produced differing projections of the effects that the crisis would have on education, and all held one common belief: the impact would be severe. In early 1998, both the MONE and BAPPENAS (National Planning Board) produced estimates of the impact that the crisis would have had on enrolment. The MONE predicted that junior secondary enrolment rates would drop from 72 per cent in 1997/98 to 57 per cent in 2001/02, and from 40 per cent to 23 per cent at the senior secondary level. BAPPENAS anticipated that at least 10 per cent of primary and junior secondary students would require immediate financial assistance to stay in school.

A variety of plans were drafted during the period preceding the May 1998 riots. Each of these reflected the differing goals of the government and the lending agencies, which did not always focus on the same priorities. This early planning period lacked effective co-ordination, and the organizations involved frequently moved in differing directions.

Moving each of the partners involved in the planning phase to a single shared vision required a substantial effort. Strong leadership from BAPPENAS played a key role in developing the kind of co-operation that was necessary between all of the partners involved. This ultimately resulted in agreement and in the production of a final plan for what would eventually become the SGP (Scholarship and Grant Programme).

Early government plans called for a broad-based intervention rather than a focused approach aimed at a single target. The government wanted to include a range of both short-term financial support structures and longer-term "infrastructural" assistance. Included in these early strategies were components that would counteract the perceived threat to enrolment rates, particularly among students that came from the poorest families. These measures would include scholarships for students in primary and junior secondary level education, and vouchers that would allow Grade 6 students (in their last year of primary school) to continuc to junior secondary school. The plan also included grants for schools that served poor communities and it would fund improvements to poor primary schools. Components that were targeted for long-term support were directed towards improving relations between communities and schools and on supporting school-based resource management. As valuable and as appropriate as each of these priorities might have been, government funding was not sufficient to support them. Similarly, none of the detailed planning had been developed to describe how any improvement efforts would be implemented.

On 5 May 1998, the Indonesian Government released a circular that outlined an extensive list of measures that were created to mitigate the financial burden that parents might have to bear in sending their children to school. This marked the first significant policy shift in response to the growing crisis. The circular listed exemptions from a variety of payments, including BP3 (monthly fees for school operating costs), SPP (school fees at private schools), and payments for national examination fees (EBTANAS). It also listed exemptions from costs for school trips, extra-curricular activities, and other extra costs. The government lifted the requirement that students wear uniforms or shoes if they were unable to afford them. Finally, students were exempted from paying school entry fees during the upcoming school year 1998/1999. Head teachers who continued to require these payments or who required students to pay for supplementary school books were to be disciplined by the Provincial Education Offices. What the circular failed to explain was how schools could compensate for the income that they could lose by implementing its provisions.

The Government of Indonesia and the lending agencies were able to agree on a few defining issues. Both the World Bank and the Asian Development Bank firmly requested the government to maintain basic education development budgets in real terms. This principle later became one of the components of the Asian Development Bank's Social Protection Sector Development Programme (SPSDP). It also became a condition of the World Bank's Social Safety Net Adjustment Loan. The government formally stated that its education development expenditures would remain at 1997/98 levels (in real terms) until the end of 1999/2000.

Effects of the 1997–2000 Crisis on Education

Introduction

The primary data used in the analysis comes from two national surveys conducted by CIMU in November and December 1999, and again in late June and early July 2000 in 77 districts (*kabupaten* and *kotamadya*) and in 197 sub-districts (*kecamatan*) throughout 26 provinces. A total of 1,027 schools were surveyed, 95 per cent of which were included in CIMU's first national survey held in November–December 1999. Trained independent monitors collected data for the two surveys using questionnaires.

The sample was chosen to achieve a spread of geographical locations. On average, a total of 40 schools were surveyed from each province. These were stratified to reflect each school level, public or private status, and general or Islamic affiliation. Every school in the sample had received a block grant (DBO) under the Scholarships and Grants

Programme (SGP) in the 1999/2000 school year. In effect, the survey population included those poorer schools that had received DBO under the SGP.

This analysis also compared data collected by CIMU to data from other sources, the most comprehensive of which were the educational data produced by the Ministry of National Education (Depdiknas), and the Annual Socio-Economic Survey (SUSENAS) implemented by the Central Statistical Board (BPS). The Social Safety Net Survey conducted by the BPS in 1999 is another important data source that supplements the 1999 SUSENAS data.

The chronology of the economic crisis in Indonesia is an important factor to keep in mind when assessing the utility of these data. Dating the start of the crisis is difficult. Although the Asian financial crisis began in mid-1997, the financial and banking crisis began to have a severe impact only in November 1997. This impact rapidly worsened in the early months of 1998. On the other hand, some financial institutions in Indonesia had been in trouble even before the fall of the Thai baht, and some provinces had been suffering severely from prolonged drought and forest fires.

Enrolment data for the 1997/98 academic year relate to the period before the financial crisis affected enrolments or other aspects of education. This is because the reference point for the enrolment data was early in the school year — 31 August 1997. Education data for 1998/99 and 1999/2000 reflect the impact of the crisis.

Data from Other Sources

It is worthwhile to summarize the findings from other data sources that can be used to examine the impact of the crisis on enrolment. This allows a comparison between the CIMU findings and findings from other sources. The following is the summary of findings by individual data sources.[5]

SUSENAS. SUSENAS data from 1997 through 1999 show no significant enrolment declines. They do show that previous gains in the proportion of 5–6 year-olds and the 7–12 year-olds in school were halted. However, at the junior secondary ages (13–15 years old) enrolments began to rise again in 1999 after a brief stall. At the senior secondary level (ages 16–18) enrolments have continued to rise.

SUSENAS data also show a variation in enrolment by income group. Using trends by expenditure quintile as a proxy for income groups,

SUSENAS data show that if anything, enrolment rates have shown greater rises within the poorer parts of the population.

At the primary level, SUSENAS data show no major differences in enrolment ratios between the various expenditure quintiles from 1993 to 1999. At the junior secondary level, however, enrolment ratios have risen overall for the lowest three quintiles, while they have changed little for the highest two quintiles. Senior secondary enrolment ratios rose for all quintiles except the richest, with the sharpest rises in the poorest two quintiles (Table 7.2).

Table 7.2
Age-Specific Enrolment Ratios in Junior and Senior Secondary Age Group by Quintile Expenditures

	1992/93	*1993/94*	*1994/95*	*1995/96*	*1996/97*	*1997/98*	*1998/99*
7–12 years (Primary School Age Group)	*92.8*	*94.1*	*93.9*	*94.9*	*95.4*	*95.1*	*95.2*
Poorest quintile	88.3	89.9	90.1	90.3	91.8	91.4	91.8
Richest quintile	98.1	98.6	98.3	98.5	98.8	98.9	99.1
13–15 years (Junior Secondary Age Group)	*68.9*	*72.4*	*73.2*	*75.8*	*77.5*	*77.2*	*79.1*
Poorest quintile	51.6	55.8	57.4	60.3	62.7	63.3	66.3
Richest quintile	89.3	89.3	91.0	91.9	92.3	92.9	92.8
16–18 years (Senior Secondary Age Group)	*42.6*	*45.3*	*44.6*	*47.6*	*48.6*	*49.3*	*51.2*
Poorest quintile	18.2	20.8	20.7	22.5	25.6	25.6	29.1
Richest quintile	69.5	71.3	70.3	74.2	72.9	75.4	75.0

Source: BPS, special tabulations from SUSENAS 1993–99. For the years 1993–98, data taken from Oey-Gardiner (2000).

Depdiknas. At the primary level, Depdiknas data do not show significant change in either net enrolment repetition or drop-out rates between 1997/98 and 1998/99. The junior secondary enrolment rates fell from 54.4 per cent to 53.2 per cent between 1997/98 and 1998/99, and then recovered in 1999/2000. The junior secondary dropout rate rose from 3.2 per cent in 1996/97 to 6.0 per cent in 1998/99, causing the proportion of 13–15 year-old children in school (including children in primary school who were over-age) to fall from 73.4 per cent to 72.3 per cent during this period. Depdiknas data indicate that there were about 255,000 fewer children in school as a result of the crisis. Depdiknas data do not show a significant change in the proportion of students who attended private schools at each level or the proportion of all schools that were private during the years of the crisis.

100 Village Survey. The 100 Village Survey showed a rise in primary school enrolment rates. At the junior secondary level, enrolments fell in Java from 65.9 per cent to 59.6 per cent by August 1998, but returned to 63.2 per cent by December 1998. This recovery may have resulted from a new provision allowing late enrolment. The enrolment rate in the eastern region of Indonesia also fell from 73.2 per cent in 1997 to 70.6 per cent in December 1998.

Special Surveys. The Ministry of National Education conducted two special surveys in 1999 that showed enrolment trends. The first survey showed little change in enrolments; however, the second and larger survey showed enrolment declines at all school levels. Declines were largest in the urban areas, and were larger among students attending private schools than those attending public schools. However, this decline appeared to have begun during the year before the crisis broke and may have been related to a prolonged drought in 1997.

Other Data Sources. The SMERU (Social Monitoring and Early Response Unit) also conducted a study in four provinces that showed a rise in continuation rates at the primary school level during the 1999/2000 school year.

From this summary, it can be concluded that these sources of data show no indication of marked declines in enrolment at either the primary or junior secondary school level during the 1999/2000 school year.

Findings from the CIMU Data

Enrolment, Transition, and Drop-out. The second CIMU national survey found no discernable drop in primary and junior secondary enrolment during the first three academic years of the economic crisis (academic years 1997/98, 1998/99 and 1999/2000). It is also apparent that enrolment generally increased in senior secondary schools.

Within the overall picture, however, some general trends are evident. During the crisis, total enrolments in primary schools did not fall but actually rose slightly less than 1 per cent between 1997 and 1999. Total junior secondary enrolment was unaffected in the first year of the crisis, then rose slightly less than 1 per cent by the 1999/2000 academic year, Total enrolment for senior secondary schools increased substantially during the crisis. By the 1999/2000 academic year, total senior secondary enrolment had risen 5.2 per cent from its 1997/98 level (Figure 7.3).

Figure 7.3
Gross Enrolment Rates (%)

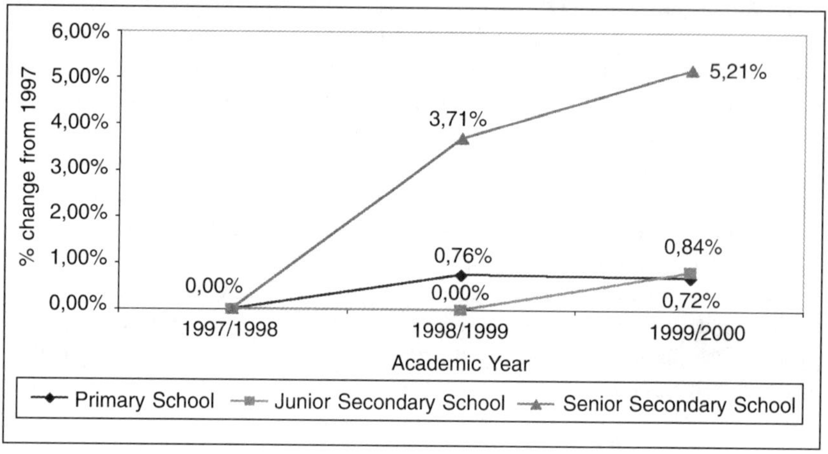

Enrolments in the more developed areas of Java and Bali suffered somewhat while slight enrolment increases occurred outside that region. Within these broad groupings, the crisis seems to have affected school attendance in the urban areas more than in the rural areas. These findings seem to confirm that the effects of the economic crisis were uneven throughout different parts of Indonesia. The more developed areas, which included the Java-Bali region and urban areas, were hit harder by the crisis than the less developed areas (agriculture-dominated areas located outside Java and in the rural areas).

The impact of the crisis on enrolment in primary schools (grades 1–6) did not differ markedly between the more developed region of Java-Bali and the rest of Indonesia. However, within Java-Bali, despite a continuous positive trend, it was found that during the crisis the trend for grades 1–6 took a slight dip during the 1998/99 school year (Figure 7.4).

There was a regional difference between junior secondary enrolments within Java-Bali and those outside. In Java-Bali, the enrolment dropped substantially during the crisis, while that within the rest of Indonesia rose significantly (Figure 7.5).

Figure 7.4
Percentage Change in Total Enrolment of Primary School Students, Grades 1 to 6, by Region and Academic Year (N = 450)

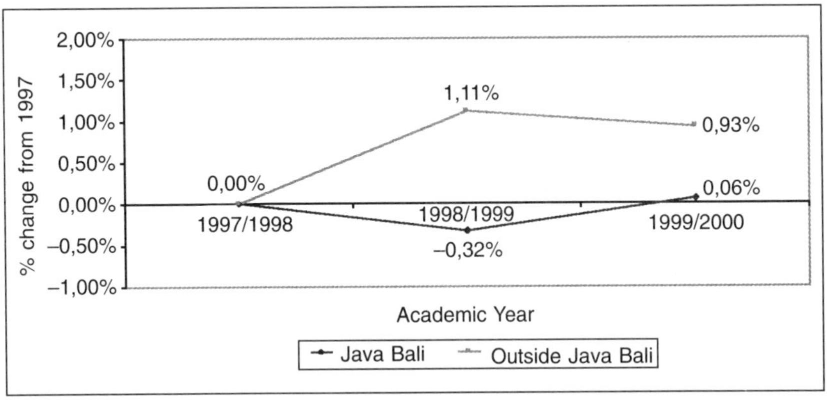

Figure 7.5
Percentage Change in Total Enrolment of Junior Secondary School Students, Grades 1 to 3, by Region and Academic Year (N = 286)

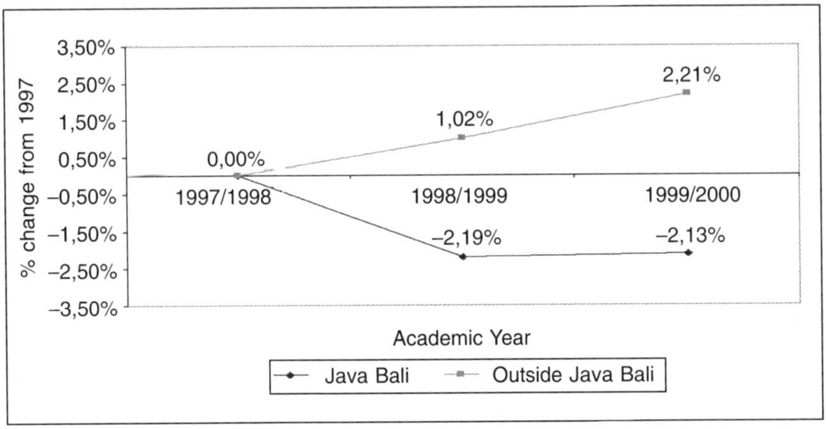

At the senior secondary level, enrolments within Java-Bali remained virtually the same while they increased substantially outside the region. During the first year of the crisis, enrolment in Java-Bali rose by almost 2.0 per cent but in 1999, that figure fell to 0.5 per cent above its 1997 level. By comparison, total enrolment outside Java-Bali continued to rise during the crisis to end 7.1 per cent higher in 1999 than its 1997 level (Figure 7.6).

Figure 7.6
Percentage Change in Total Enrolment of Senior Secondary School Students, Grades 1 to 3, by Region and Academic Year (N = 191)

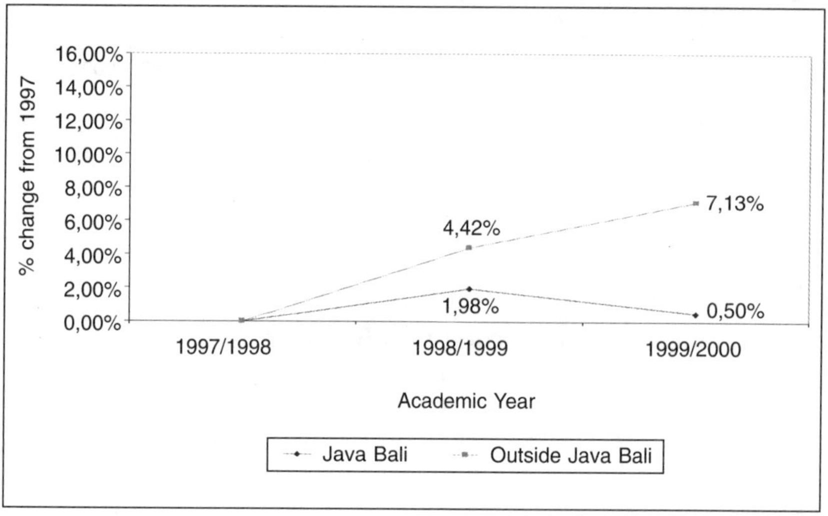

Enrolments at private schools appear to have dropped while the number of students enrolled in public schools rose. This is particularly true at the junior secondary level in the urban areas. Private junior secondary enrolment in the urban areas fell each year after the beginning of the crisis — 8.0 per cent in 1998, then another 1.3 per cent in 1999. Two years after the crisis began, private junior secondary enrolments in urban areas declined 9.3 per cent below the level of 1997. Meanwhile, public enrolments in the urban areas rose 2.2 per cent in 1998, and again 0.7 per cent in 1999, finishing some 2.9 per cent above the level of 1997 (Figure 7.7). Loss of income during the crisis may have caused parents to withdraw their children from expensive private schools and send them to public schools.

The survey data also suggest an increase in junior secondary enrolments in Islamic schools, particularly in the rural areas. As can be

Figure 7.7
Percentage Change in Total Enrolment of Junior Secondary School Students, Grades 1 to 3, by General School in Urban Areas (N = 84)

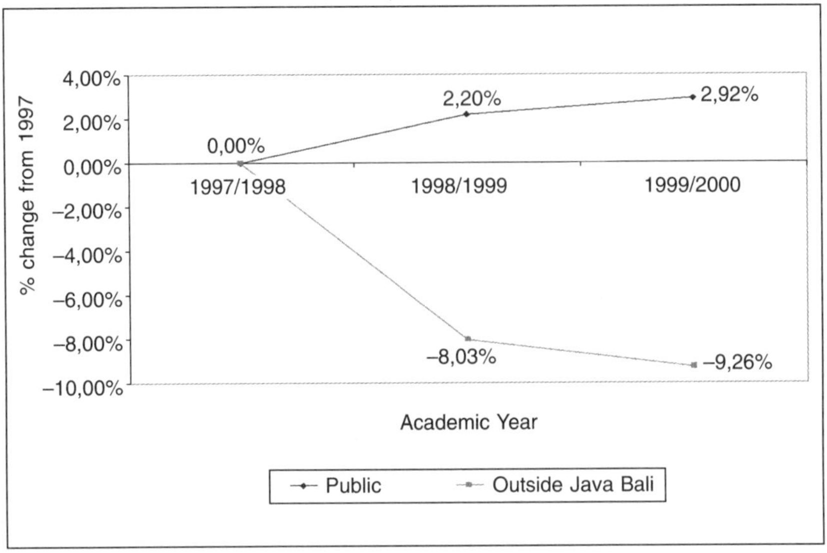

seen in Figure 7.8 (urban area), and Figure 7.9 (non-urban area), the trend of enrolment between the general and Islamic schools at the junior secondary level was the same, but the magnitude of the trend was different. The percentage increase in enrolment in Islamic junior secondary schools located in the non-urban areas was greater than the percentage increase in enrolment in Islamic junior secondary schools located in the urban areas.

Migration from urban to rural areas may be one possible explanation for the apparent increase in enrolment in Islamic schools (particularly in non-urban areas). Declining employment opportunities in the urban areas may have caused people who had previously resided in the urban areas and worked in sectors that were hardest hit by unemployment (construction, manufacturing), to migrate to the rural areas to seek informal agricultural jobs. Hugo (2000), in his study on population mobility during the crisis, observed that population mobility turned out to be an important coping mechanism for people confronting the effects of the crisis. In order to enable families to survive the loss of income resulting from the crisis, a range of permanent and non-permanent

Figure 7.8
Percentage Change in Total Enrolment of Junior Secondary School Students, Grades 1 to 3, by Type of School in Urban Areas (N = 145)

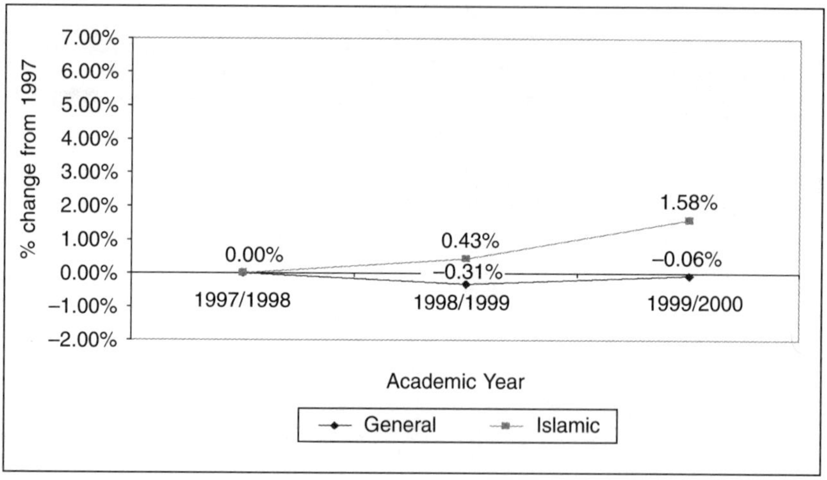

Figure 7.9
Percentage Change in Total Enrolment of Junior Secondary School Students, Grades 1 to 3, by Type of School in Non-Urban Areas (N = 141)

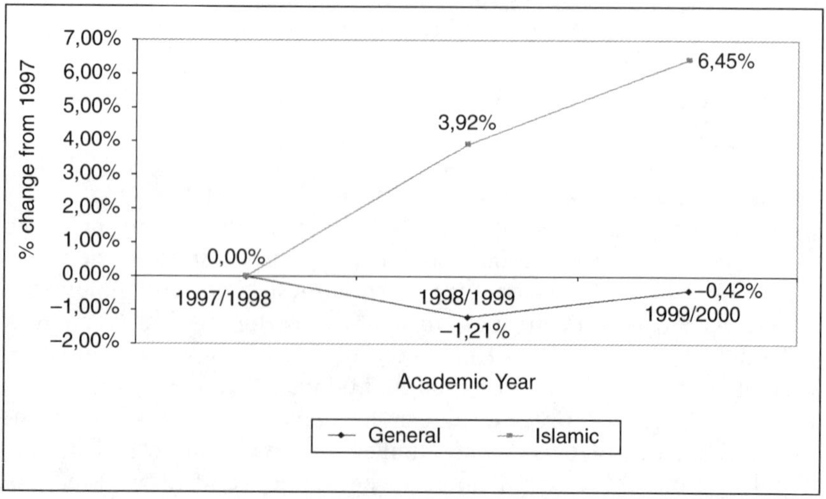

mobility modes have been adopted.[6] The migrants who returned to the non-urban areas may have sent their children to Islamic schools in order to reduce their educational expenditures.

Transition Rates. The transition from primary to secondary education is also assessed in order to appreciate whether the crisis affected first-year secondary enrolment. The transition from primary school to junior secondary school, and from the latter to senior secondary school is calculated by using first-year enrolment data from a panel of junior and senior secondary schools as a proxy. First-year enrolments are compared between 1997 and 1998, and between 1998 and 1999. Since the survey could not cover all schools feeding into a higher level, this is only approximate.

The transition from primary to junior secondary school and from junior to senior secondary school appears to have increased slightly during the economic crisis. Within this overall picture, there was some regional variation.

Taking the first-year enrolments at both junior and senior secondary school levels as a proxy for transition, the rates at both key points fell in Java-Bali and rose in other parts of Indonesia.

As can be seen in Figure 7.10, the transition from primary school to junior secondary school in Java-Bali first fell substantially in 1998, then rebounded almost to its pre-crisis level. This trend, however, did not

Figure 7.10
Percentage Change in Transition to Junior Secondary School from Primary School by Region, 1997 to 1999

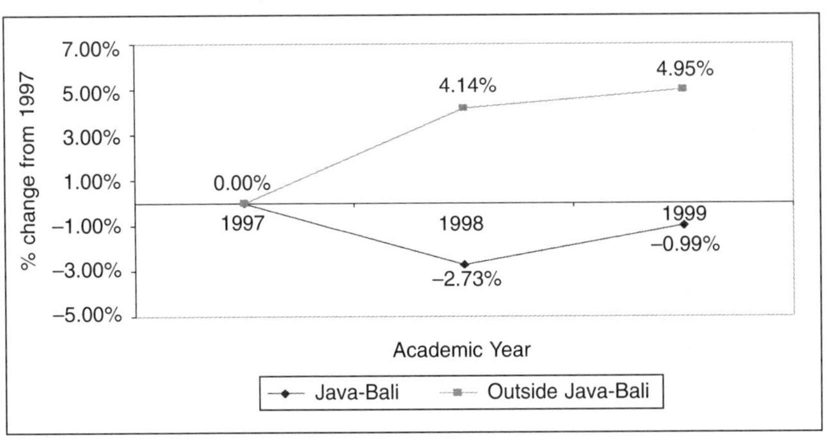

occur for the transition from junior secondary school to senior secondary school (Figure 7.11), with a tendency to further decrease during the three years of crisis.

The transition rates to both junior and senior secondary schools were higher for Islamic schools than for general schools. This trend seemed to follow the shift from general to Islamic schools (Figure 7.12).

Figure 7.11
Percentage Change in Transition to Senior Secondary School from Junior Secondary School by Region, 1997 to 1999

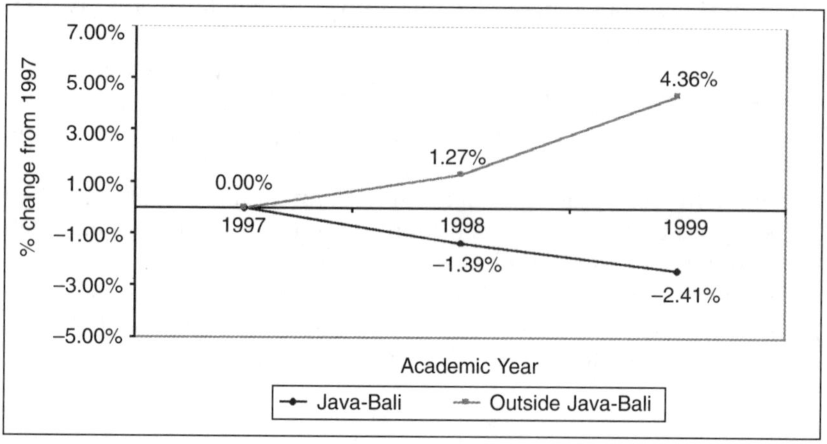

Figure 7.12
Percentage Change in Transition to Senior Secondary School from Junior Secondary School by Region, 1997 to 1999

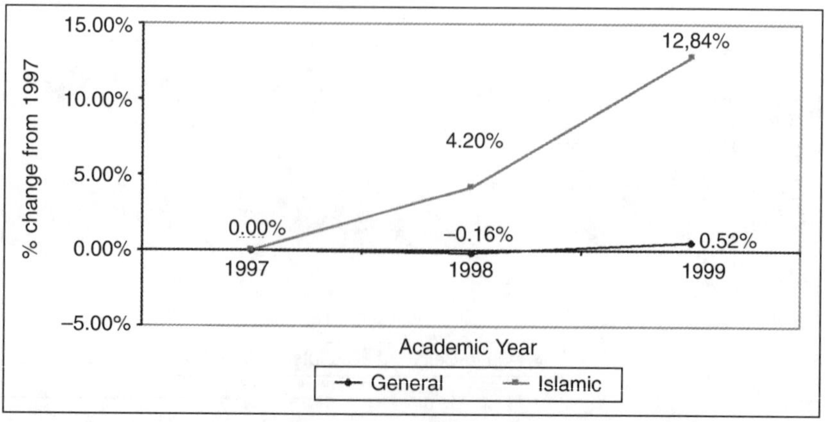

The survey also found that the transition from primary to junior secondary school for boys in 1999 was 1.9 per cent higher than in 1997, while for the girls it was 4.4 per cent higher than two years earlier. Thus, the discrepancy of the transition between boys and girls in 1999 was 2.5 percentage points. This discrepancy was narrower for the transition from junior secondary to senior secondary school, which varied by only 0.60 percentage points (Figure 7.13).

Figure 7.13
Percentage Change in Transition to Senior Secondary School from Junior Secondary School by Sex, 1997 to 1999

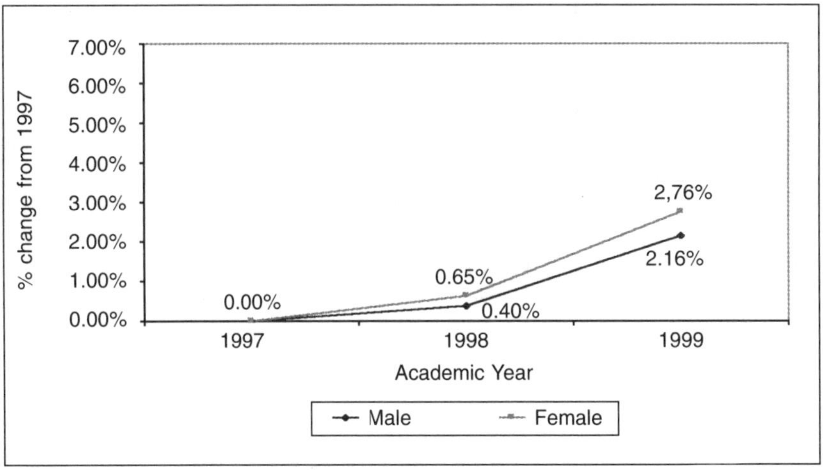

Drop-out. The CIMU surveys found no evidence of increased drop-outs from the 1996/97 to the 1998/99 school year. Data on drop-outs were obtained from head teachers within the sampled schools. This figure is difficult to acquire with any certainty, as the definition of a drop-out can vary between head teachers. For example, in one school, a student who has left a sample school and moved to another town may be counted as a drop-out even though the student may continue his schooling in another school in the new town of residence. Head teachers are often reluctant to admit that students have dropped out from their school. This chapter will therefore not provide an analysis of drop-outs based on data originating from the CIMU national surveys. Qualitative research conducted by CIMU in some schools suggests that school drop-outs do not appear to have been a significant factor in the first year of the economic crisis.

The Contribution of SGP. The introduction of the Indonesian Scholarships and Grants Programme (SGP) should also be taken into account when assessing the impact of the crisis on education. The SGP that was started in June 1998 has distributed scholarships to roughly four million students, and grants (known as Dana Bantuan Operational or DBO) to approximately 132,000 schools per year. The SGP now forms the basis of the education safety net, providing scholarships and grants to the poorest schoolchildren and schools.

Every district in Indonesia has received an allocation of both scholarships and block grants, the amount of which varies according to the "*Kabupaten* (district) poverty index." While district committees decide the allocations of SGP scholarship and grant recipients at the *kabupaten* and *kecamatan* (subdistrict) levels, subdistrict committees decide the allocations of recipients at the *kecamatan* level. District committees select recipient junior and senior secondary schools, while the selection of recipient primary schools is made by subdistrict committees. Within each school, it is the school committee, led by the head teacher that determines individual scholarship recipients.

In addition to scholarship funds, part of the DBO can also be used to pay for the school fees of needy students who do not receive scholarships. When the SGP was conceived, planners intended that schools would use DBO funds to maintain educational quality throughout the crisis. This would be achieved by spending funds on areas that would benefit the teaching and learning process, or by using the funds to support poor students who might otherwise drop out from school. A study on DBO usage conducted by CIMU found that at almost all school levels, the largest proportion of DBO funds (ranging from 31 per cent in primary schools to 41 per cent in junior secondary schools) was used to purchase consumable materials (stationary). However, some of the DBO funds were also used to waive formal and informal school charges for needy students, ranging from 12 per cent in senior secondary schools to 26 per cent in junior secondary schools.

The provision of scholarships certainly helps poor students to pay school fees, transportation, and books. However, the extent to which the SGP has contributed to sustain enrolments through the economic crisis is difficult to assess precisely, since it is only one of several factors that may have influenced enrolments. By supporting school incomes, all students would likely benefit from the funding that schools receive from student scholarships. By enabling parents to pay fees which had previously been delayed or simply remained unpaid, the scholarships channelled much needed funds back to the schools.

It is difficult to isolate the effects of the SGP as several other factors may have exerted an independent influence on enrolments. These other influences should be taken into account when assessing the impact of SGP on enrolment. Other factors that may have influenced enrolments include:

- Students were not forced out of school for not paying fees or for late payment of school fees. This phenomenon may have been due to teachers helping poor students who faced financial hardship during the crisis. It may also have been influenced by whether the school retained the non-paying, or late-paying students because the school's survival depended on maintaining student numbers in the hope that with economic recovery the number of students who were able to pay school fees would improve.
- There was a wide-scale campaign throughout the country (the *"Aku Anak Sekolah"* campaign) which emphasized the importance of keeping students in school. This may have raised parents' awareness of the need to keep their children in school.
- School fees were not increased as dramatically as other costs of living.
- Traditional coping strategies, such as family networks and efforts to reduce unnecessary expenditures, may also have helped poor parents to keep their children in school.
- The increase in enrolment, particularly at the senior secondary level in both 1998 and 1999, may also have resulted from a loss of employment opportunities. Students who might normally have dropped out at this level in order to start working may have postponed the move either to wait out the crisis or to improve their marketability by continuing in school.
- The availability of scholarships from other sources, such as from GNOTA, *beasiswa prestasi* (scholarships given on the basis of academic achievement), and from private companies or other sources, may also have had some impact.

There was an indication of the occurrence of mistargetted scholarships. This might mean that some scholarships went to children who were actually at lower risks of dropping out. Although some mistargetting simply resulted from poor selection by committees, there were several structural reasons why scholarships may not have reached many of the most needy. Students who had already dropped out of school were not eligible to receive scholarships. Many of these drop-outs were among the poorest and really in need of financial assistance. The number of scholarships allocated to the primary level covered a smaller percentage of the needy student population than at the junior and senior secondary levels. Fewer students at the senior secondary level come from poor families. Primary schools, however, tend to have a higher percentage of needy students than junior or senior secondary schools. The poorest students at the senior secondary level are generally better off than the poorest students at the primary and junior secondary levels. The proportion of scholarships allocated to each school level meant that some junior and senior secondary recipients were not as needy as some primary school students who did not receive scholarships.

The SGP has made an important contribution of much-needed resources at a time of economic hardship. Without this additional support, schools might have faced the possibility of raising fees higher than they did, enforcing payment of school fees, and possibly even closing. As will be discussed in the next section, SGP funds have certainly played some part in mitigating the impact of the economic crisis on school incomes. The CIMU studies have also revealed that SGP funds together with other sources of government funds have made a significant contribution to school incomes. The question of what will happen when these funds are no longer available to the schools that now rely on them for support in their day-to-day operations is very relevant. Recent visits by independent monitors to several schools have revealed that few head teachers were aware that the SGP will end in June 2002.

School Income. Most comparisons of school income have been made for non-wage income, since individual schools control little or none of the salaries paid to regular teachers. This non-wage income is termed *disposable income,* meaning that the school can use it for its overall operations.

For public schools, non-wage income is derived from both government funds and payments made by students' parents. Student payments include monthly school fees known as BP3, fees for extra-curricular activities, and entrance fees (although entrance fees have been officially waived by the government, in practice, many schools still charge entrance fees for new students). Government sources of non-wage income include routine operational funds and project-based funds, including DBO (SGP block grant), deductions from SGP scholarships, OPF and DOP (non-routine operational funds).

For private schools, the non-wage income is derived from the foundation (or *yayasan*) and from school fees (known as SPP). In some cases, private schools rely solely on students' monthly school fees and entrance fees. This is particularly true for smaller private schools. Private schools also derive non-wage income from government sources, including DOP, DBO, and deductions from SGP scholarships.

This section compares school income during the 1999/2000 school year with the situation two years earlier in 1997/98. School income in 1999/2000 is adjusted to compensate for the high inflation from a pre-crisis base in July 1997 to July 2000.

Data from the CIMU's Second National Survey reveal that school incomes have fallen significantly in real terms since the start of the economic crisis. While nominal school incomes appeared to have risen during the crisis, in terms of the total amount of rupiah, this increase has not been large enough to compensate for the losses caused by high inflation which has eroded the rupiah's purchasing power. Overall, schools' real incomes have declined by as much as one-third from 1997 to 2000. Adjusting for inflation in the education sector (a figure provided by the Indonesian Central Statistical Board, BPS, which differs from overall inflation) reveals that school incomes from both government and parental sources have declined significantly in real terms. Income derived from BP3/SPP fees and from routine operating funds, together constituting nearly half of school incomes, fell in real terms by about 27 per cent between 1997 and 2000.

The survey found that wages and fringe benefits for teachers and non-teaching personnel in 1999-2000 constituted 55.2 per cent of all school income for all schools combined. In 1997–98, wages and other benefits comprised a slightly smaller percentage of 52.9 per cent of income of schools. BP3 fees (or SPP in private schools) were the major source of school income derived from students and were equal to 21.3 per cent of non-wage income (or 9.6 per cent of all income) in 1999–2000. In the first year of the crisis (1997–98), BP3/SPP represented 22.9 per cent of non-wage income (or 10.8 per cent of income including wages).

Although BP3/SPP fees rose in nominal terms between 1997 and 2000, their real value fell from one-fifth to one-quarter. For example, average monthly BP3 fees in senior secondary schools rose in nominal terms from Rp9,001 in 1997–98, to Rp10,055 in 1998–99, to Rp11,242 in 1999–00. From the 1997/98 to 1999/2000 academic years this constituted a nominal rise of 24.9 per cent. In real terms, however, when adjusted for inflation in the education sector, there has been a fall in monthly BP3 fees of 24.2 per cent (Figure 7.14).

The proportion of students paying BP3/SPP fees at all school levels did not vary significantly during the three school years from 1997 to

Figure 7.14
Nominal and Real Average BP3 Fees,
Senior Secondary School
(Real Income = value in 1997 Rupiah)

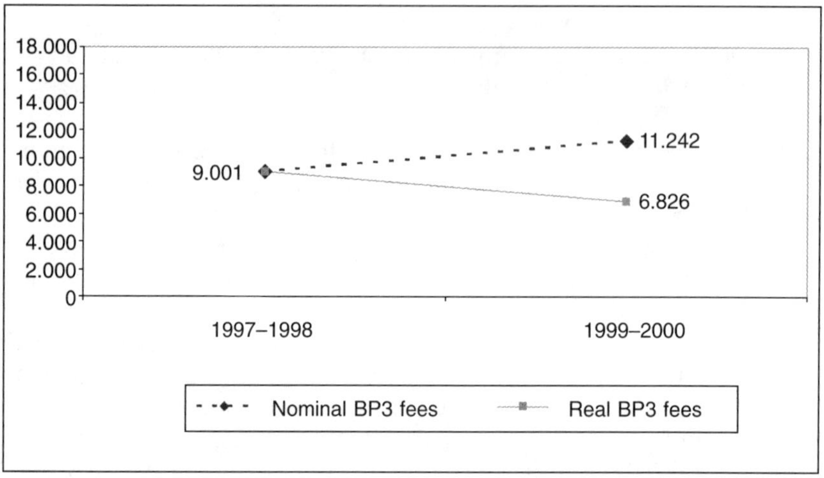

2000. The proportion remained at a steady 84 per cent for primary school, 92 per cent for junior secondary school, and 93 per cent for senior secondary school students. Although it is not known to what degree payment rates would have fallen without the SGP, it is reasonable to assume that the SGP was compensating the fall in the number and proportion of students paying BP3/SPP. However, it is worth mentioning that, in addition to the SGP, another possible source of funds to enable students (especially those coming from poor families who were unable to obtain SGP scholarships) to pay fees included scholarships from other sources and traditional coping mechanisms.

In short, though the SGP did not fully mitigate the impacts of inflation following the crisis, to some extent the SGP made up the loss of school income caused by the inflation (Figure 7.15).

As can be seen in Figure 7.15, without the DBO and scholarship deductions, primary schools at the end of the 1999–2000 school year would have suffered a loss of 12.5 per cent of their disposable (non-wage) income compared with the previous three years. SGP funds, together with the assistance that schools receive from DOP (a special government allotment to primary schools that was introduced in 1999), have brought real primary incomes nearly back to their pre-crisis levels. The situation, however, would have been far worse at the junior and

Figure 7.15
Real School Income by School Level, during the 1997 and 1999 School Years

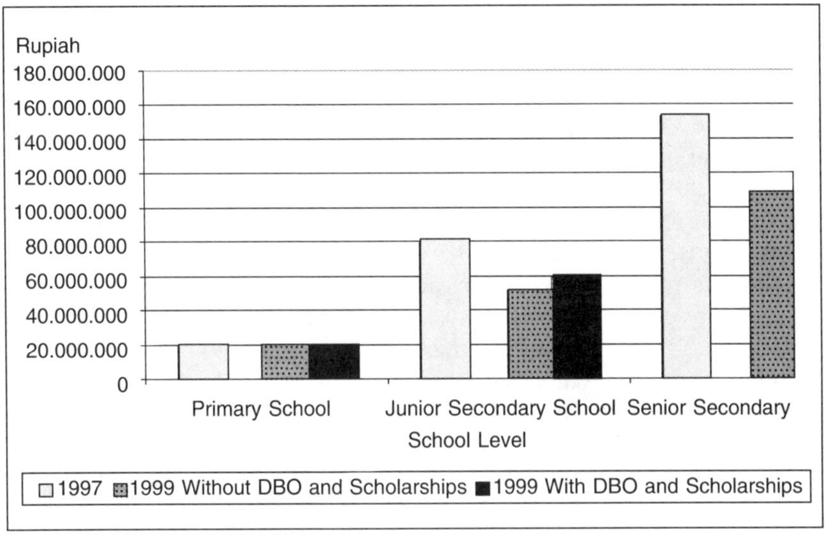

senior secondary levels. Without the contribution from the SGP, these junior and senior secondary schools would have lost 34.9 per cent and 29.5 per cent of the value of their 1997–98 incomes, respectively. Even with SGP assistance, junior and senior secondary schools have suffered a significant loss of income from 1997 to 2000. In order to compensate fully for the effects of inflation on real incomes, in 1999/2000 the contribution of DBO and scholarships to school incomes should have been three to four times higher at the junior and senior secondary levels.

These findings have implications for the future of school funding. If parental contributions remain at their present level and grants alone are used to fund school incomes, grant funding levels would need to be significantly higher than current DBO levels to restore school incomes to pre-crisis levels. If in the future school funding is to be provided by grants only, such grants will need to be seven times larger than the current level of DBO assistance per senior secondary school and eleven times higher than the current level of DBO per junior secondary school. An alternative solution would be to increase parental contributions significantly. Such a move may have severe social and political implications.

Maintaining the Quality of Education

It is difficult to identify information that can help measure the quality of education in Indonesia (Jones et al. 2001, pp. 220–21) There is a lack of useful data on educational outputs in Indonesia. Test scores (from Cawu and EBTANAS test scores) provide unreliable indicators of student attainment, which makes it necessary to rely on input measures for research into the impact of the crisis on educational quality. For this reason, the CIMU used school income and expenditure as a proxy for educational quality.

Since school incomes are a critical component of school quality, falling incomes raise fears that school quality might also decline. Although there is little consensus on the measures of educational quality, continued reductions of financial resources caused by inflation will almost certainly have an adverse effect. The physical condition of schools, particularly classrooms, is certainly one element of school quality. The number and variety of extracurricular activities offered by schools can also be used as a school quality indicator.

Spending on classroom repairs climbed in real terms between 1997 and 2000 at the primary level, while it fell substantially at the secondary level. This parallels the pattern of school income losses where junior and senior secondary schools suffered the most.

Reductions and cancellations of extracurricular activities between 1997 and 2000 do not appear significant at the primary level, but there are indications of the beginning of a decline at the higher levels. While still too early to tell, this may be related to a sustained real income loss at these levels.

Teacher quality and morale also play a very important role in educational quality. The crisis has adversely impacted on teachers' income, which has reduced teacher enthusiasm. Reductions in extracurricular activities and private lessons have been documented as students can no longer afford to pay for these extra expenditures. This has forced many teachers to seek supplemental sources of income (Jones et al. 2001, p. 221).

Even though there have been significant and successful efforts to build new schools and increase student enrolments, these have not always been accompanied by improvements in educational quality. For example, despite the widespread implementation of the *SD Inpres* programme throughout the country, gaps in educational quality persist between the urban and rural areas, and also between Java and the regions outside Java.

Other studies attempting to determine some measure of educational quality have shown indications that the compulsory education programme seems to focus only on increasing the numbers of students and not on improving educational performance or on raising standards. An estimated 0.23 per cent of all public and private primary schools meet the criteria for category A classification (the highest of five categories), while only 2.89 per cent of junior secondary schools meet the criteria for category B.[7]

Other studies have found that more children are going to school without eating a proper breakfast, and parents can less afford to provide their children with money to buy snacks during the day. This has in some cases caused health and nutritional problems and affected pupils' ability to concentrate while at school (Jones et al. 2001, p. 221).

Other studies look at the quality of basic education as an important issue that will influence the capacity of students to continue with further education and to enter the labour market. These studies have revealed that graduates are leaving the basic education system with low levels of competency in achieving basic standards and are therefore not adequately prepared for post-basic education and for a lifetime of learning and employment.[8]

Maintaining the quality of education is a costly endeavour that requires expenditures on good textbooks, equipment, teaching materials, and on teacher training and compensation. Based on estimated levels of public spending on education in Indonesia, the poor quality of education appears to be linked to inadequate spending on education.[9] A sustained improvement in quality can only be achieved with a much greater commitment of government funding.

Conclusions

The economic crisis has had different impacts on education from those expected. On the whole, schools have remained open and enrolments have been maintained, although there have been regional variations, reflecting the severity of the crisis in different parts of the country. The anticipated increase in drop-outs has not happened. School incomes, however, have suffered from the cumulative effects of price inflation during the period. This was not anticipated or at least was not at the top of the government's list of concerns when the economic crisis broke out.

Attempts made to maintain spending on education, principally through the Scholarships and Grants Program and other interventions, such as DOP, have contributed to the closing of the funding gap. A large number of schools have benefited. Some have been able to cover as much as 40 per cent of their non-salary expenditure from the Dana Bantuan Operasional (DBO) and money recovered from scholarships. They have not been forced to raise school fees to levels that might result in high levels of drop-out. Operational expenditure has been subsidized. This form of funding is, however, temporary. The SGP is set to decline from 2001 and will be phased out completely in 2003. Other sources of funding such as the DOP will also disappear. The question may arise as to how the schools can maintain their income once the SGP and other funds are stopped.

The situation is further complicated by uncertainties over the levels of future school funding and channelling mechanisms as a consequence of the decentralization of education governance. The true effects of the economic crisis on education may well have been muted by the measures taken by the government. They may have simply stored up problems for the future.

Glossary

ADB	Asian Development Bank
Aku Anak Sekolah	'Back to School' campaign related to the Social Safety Net in Education Programme
AusAid	Australian Agency for International Development
BAPPENAS	National Development and Planning Board
BP3	Parent-Teachers' Association
BP3 fee	School fee in state schools
BPS	Badan Pusat Statistik, or Central Statistical Board
CIMU	Central Independent Monitoring Unit
DBO	Dana Bantuan Operasional, or School Block Grant from the SGP which began in June 1998
DOP	Dana Operasional Pendidikan, a primary school block grant for operation and maintenance, which has been established since 1999. This grant was previously known as BOP.
Depdiknas	Departemen Pendidikan Nasional, or Ministry of National Education

EBTANAS	National Educational Attainment Test
GNOTA	Gerakan Nasional Orang Tua Asuh, a National Foster Parent Movement.
IDT	Inpres Desa Tertinggal, or Governmental Grants Programme for "under-developed" villages
JPS	Jaring Pengaman Sosial, or Social Safety Net Programme
JPS Pendidikan	Social Safety Net Programme in Education
kabupaten	non-urban district
kota	urban district
kecamatan	subdistrict
MHA	Ministry of Home Affairs
MONE	Ministry of National Education
MORA	Ministry of Religious Affairs
OPF	Operasi dan Perawatan Fasilitas, or Project-Based Fund for the Maintenance and Operation of Secondary Schools Facilities
SGP	Scholarship and Grant Programme, which has been established since 1998
SPP	Sumbangan Pembinaan Pendidikan, or school fees for private schools
SUSENAS	Survey Sosial Ekonomi Nasional, or Yearly National Socio-Economic Survey
Wajib Belajar Pendidikan Dasar 9 Tahun	nine years universal basic education, or NYUBE

Notes

1. Mayling Oey-Gardiner (2000), p. 145.
2. Abimanyu (2001), pp. 101–2.
3. World Bank (1998), p. 15.
4. Ibid., p. 13.
5. The data summarization is taken from Gavin Jones et al. (2000), pp. 10–20.
6. Hugo (2000), p. 136.
7. Prijono (1999), p. 163.
8. World Bank (1998), p. 23.
9. Prijono, op. cit., p. 164.

References

Abimanyu, Anggito. "The Socio-Economic Impacts of the Crisis". In *Gus Dur and the Indonesian Economy*, edited by Anthony L. Smith, pp. 101–9. Singapore: ISEAS, 2001.

Booth, Anne. "The Impact of the Indonesian Crisis on Welfare: What Do We Know Two Years On?". In *Indonesia in Transition: Social Aspects of Reformasi and Crisis*, edited by Chris Manning and Peter Van Diermen, pp. 145–62. Singapore: ISEAS, 2000.

Departemen Pendidikan Nasional. Badan Penelitian dan Pengembangan. *Data Pokok Pendidikan 1999/2000 Dan Perkembangan Sejak 1994/1995 (Termasuk Madrasah)*. Jakarta: Balitbang Depdiknas, 2000.

Hugo, Graeme. "The Impact of the Crisis on Internal Population Movement in Indonesia". *Bulletin of Indonesian Economic Studies* 36, no. 2 (2000): 115–38.

Jones, Gavin W., Peter Hagul, and Damayanti. "The Impacts of the Scholarships and Grants Program". Mimeographed. Jakarta: CIMU, The British Council, 2000.

Jones, Gavin W., and Peter Hagul. "Schooling in Indonesia: Crisis-Related and Longer-Term Issues". *Bulletin of Indonesian Economic Studies* 37, no. 2 (2001): 207–31.

Oey-Gardiner, Mayling. "The Value of Education and the Indonesian Economic Crisis". *Ekonomi dan Keuangan Indonesia* 48, no. 2 (2000): 143–73.

Prijono, Onny S. "Education: Access, Quality, and Relevance". In *Indonesia: The Challenge of Change*, edited by Richard W. Baker, M. Hadi Soesastro, J. Kristiadi, and Douglas E. Ramage, pp. 159–78. Singapore: ISEAS,1999.

World Bank. *Education in Indonesia: From Crisis to Recovery*. Report No. 16369-IND, Education Sector Unit. East Asia and Pacific Regional Office, World Bank, 1998.

8

POPULATION MOBILITY AND SOCIAL CONFLICT
The Aftermath of the Economic Crisis in Indonesia

Riwanto Tirtosudarmo

> Migration is a dream gone sour in Indonesia, with scenes of weary refugees dominating nightly news broadcast.
>
> (*Far Eastern Economic Review*, 8 April 1999, p. 26)

Introduction

An unprecedented reversed stream of population movement characterizes the pattern of Indonesia's demographic configuration today. Thousands of migrant families were forced to leave their homes as rampant conflict erupted in several provinces that were previously major destination areas of the state's transmigration policy. Social conflicts, among others, were manifested in the form of violence between migrants and the local population, apparently marking the shattering of the New Order's political order. Soeharto himself, the New Order's main pillar, was hesitantly pushed down, after more than three decades at the apex of power. The interconnection of population and conflict is not a new phenomenon, as Choucri (1984) has argued, "...conflict is a central feature of all political behavior, at all levels of human interaction, and the prominence of population variables in shaping political behavior places population issues and conflict in close proximity". The incidence of social conflicts in Indonesia in 1999 and

2000 shows that, given the archipelagic nature of the country and its ethnic and religious plurality, the most serious population variable that has a strong link with social conflict has been geographical population mobility. As the conflict is often strongly loaded with an ethnic tone, the lack of information on the ethnic background of the migrants has resulted in difficulties for social demographers and social scientists in general to comprehend the conflict.

The demography of Indonesia has long been the object of the ruling élite's engineering schemes that have resulted in the establishment of current political-demographic construction. Besides its explicit social and economic objectives, strategic and political goals have always been at the centre of the state's demographic engineering practices.[1] Populating the empty areas in the outer islands through colonial emigration policy and post-colonial transmigration policy has been a major demographic engineering initiative for almost a century. After independence, national integration was the ultimate goal perceived by the national leaders as the major justification to continue engineering the country's demographic configuration. Ethnicity was apparently manifested in disguise within the state demographic engineering process as the national government suppressed the expression of ethnicity to avoid the danger of national disintegration. Magdalena (1996) has defined ethnic groups as people who express a distinctive and enduring collective identity based on shared experiences and cultural traits, fortified by a myth or history. People define themselves, and may be defined by others, in terms of some of the following traits: religious beliefs, language, physical appearance, region of residence, and a history of conquest and repression by other people.

Yet, given that the majority of transmigrants are Javanese, it is only logical that Javanization is, by and large, implanted within the transmigration policy. It therefore came as a turning point in the history of the state's migration policy in Indonesia when a reversed migration stream occurred following social conflicts in the outer islands in the aftermath of the economic crisis and the collapse of the New Order regime.

This chapter, consisting of four major parts, is an attempt to analyse the current demographic situation in Indonesia from the perspective of political demography. The first part is a brief historical review of the nexus of politics and demography since the colonial era up to the present period. The chronological evidence show that the notion of political dichotomy between the centre (Java) and the region (outer islands) had been socially constructed since the colonial period and fostered after independence. In this context, the state's demographic engineering process that had been conducted for almost a century has played an important role in emphasizing the existing dichotomy. The second part is devoted to the study of the process of economic and political development after independence, particularly during the New Order period. A deepening process of unequal development between Java and the other islands is presented to contextualize the dynamics of geographical population mobility. The third part of this chapter focuses on the linkages between demography and politics in the second half of the 1990s, particularly the emergence of ethnic mobility and the increasing tensions and conflicts between migrants and the local population. In this part, the likely ramifications of economic crisis to social conflicts will be discussed. The fourth part concludes the chapter.

The Nexus of Demography and Politics: A Colonial Legacy

Java's rapid population growth after the mid-nineteenth century was one of the dominant facts of the late colonial era. Java, especially in its central and eastern parts, was becoming seriously overpopulated, while there were still vast areas of unpopulated or under-populated land in the outer islands. Java's growing population was considered by the colonial government to be the underlying cause of the decline of its people's welfare. The Dutch colonial government, however, had no idea of developing policies that could directly solve the problem of population growth. The only answer they offered was emigration from Java to the "outer islands". As a result, the nation's wealth was used for the interests of foreign enterprises, hindering the development of indigenous industries. The main economic development took place on the "outer islands", while the main welfare problems grew in Java. The Ethical Policy, introduced at the dawn of the twentieth century, was almost entirely concerned with raising agricultural productivity, and the colonial government apparently had no serious intention to introduce drastic changes in the colonial economic structure by such means as large-scale industrialization.

Legge (1964) has argued that the measures taken by "ethical" colonial governments to improve the living standards of the indigenous population were in the nature of mere palliatives; they provided some alleviation of particular areas of hardship, but they did not achieve — and they did not attempt to achieve — any thoroughgoing technological changes. The importance of large-scale industrialization was actually stressed by a number of ethical reformers, but until the worldwide economic depression of the 1930s, the various plans suggested were not implemented. Van Oorchot (one of the Dutch ethical reformers) mentioned three reasons why the Dutch colonial government was not interested in proposing industrialization (Penders 1969). First, internal freight rates were too high; secondly, a widespread distribution apparatus was missing, and thirdly, import duties on industrial goods were too low to afford sufficient protection.

Penders (1969, pp. 29–30) argued, however, that van Oorchot did not mention — or at least did not spell out fully — the fundamental reason why the attempts at industrialization failed. Indeed, industrialization would have been a strong opposition to the politically powerful plantation companies. Large-scale industrialization would have tended to increase the demand for labour and its price. This would have been damaging to the plantations, which were largely dependent on low wages for their profits. Furthermore, Dutch industrialists, as well as Dutch labour, were unwilling to be priced out of the Indonesian market. In the final analysis, then, the industrialization of Indonesia militated against the interests of the imperial economy as a whole. In serving the interests of the plantation companies, the Netherlands Indies' government issued the first Coolie Ordinance in 1880 to regulate labour relations, particularly in East Sumatra. This Ordinance was later extended to other regions on the "outer islands". It protected the interests of plantation companies by retaining workers for the duration of the contract period, and sanctions were imposed on workers who violated their labour contracts. The first Coolie Ordinance was followed in 1884 and 1855 by other ordinances, which provided employers with effective legal control over their indentured workers. In addition to the penal sanctions, employers resorted to other means to keep their workers. One favourite way was to provide gambling opportunities for the workers on pay day. Often, workers became so deeply indebted that they had no other choice but to sign a new contract with their employers (Thee 1969, pp. 7–9).

Until 1909, the recruitment of Javanese estate labour remained in the hands of professional agents, but in that year, planters were encouraged by law to appoint their own agents, who were often aided by worker-recruiters. The Deli Planter's Association, for example, led the way by setting up its own agency in Semarang, Central Java. Then, direct recruitment of labour became gradually widespread. In 1930, it was found that 84 per cent of the labour employed on plantations on the outer islands were Javanese. Of the remaining, 13 per cent were Chinese and three per cent local (Thompson 1947, pp. 134).

From a different perspective, Kartodirdjo (1973) perceived that the rural history of Java in the nineteenth and early twentieth centuries was marked by sporadic movements of peasant unrest. Many of these erupted in more or less violent clashes with the colonial authorities. Protest movements and social unrest occurred between 1900 and 1920 in various places in rural Java, such as in Tanggerang, Pamanukan, Sukabumi, Ciasem, Kuningan (West Java), Pekalongan, Gombong, Semarang (Central Java), Mojokerto, Sidoardjo, Kediri, and Jember (East Java).[2] Although a direct link between social unrest in rural Java and the initiation of the emigration policy cannot be established, it is not implausible to posit a cause-effect relationship. A major complicating feature of agrarian unrest in Java has been its correlation with social change in general, and with the colonial impact in particular. Kartodirdjo strongly argued that the social movements had their background in the rapid penetration of a colonial economy whose impact on rural Java reached a climax during the course of the nineteenth century. The colonial rulers introduced a new legal and social relationship covering agrarian and labour matters. Excessive demands for compulsory services and the levying of new taxes exacerbated popular discontent. Turning over some land to sugar cultivation and the exaction of a compulsory contribution of paddy rice had a direct bearing on some of the instances of social unrest.

Emigration as an attempt by the colonial government to move people from Java to the other islands is considered to be the least successful measure of the Ethical Policy, since the number of families to move was actually small. The first organized attempt in this direction was made in 1905, when an agricultural colony of 155 families, called Gedong Tataan, was set up in Lampung, South Sumatra, as an experiment. By 1930, it had 30,000 colonists. Efforts to settle Javanese farmers in the southeast of Kalimantan and Sulawesi met with failure. As a result of more skilful propaganda, better selection methods, and more extensive preparatory work in the settlement areas, the situation improved somewhat during the 1930s when more farmers could be induced to leave. From 1933 to 1941, 222,586 migrants were resettled in Lampung and South Sumatra,[3] and almost 2,500 migrants in Kalimantan.[4] During the Japanese Occupation (1942–45), the government's migration policy practically halted, and the economic situation in Indonesia deteriorated. The population continued to increase, but the growth in economic productivity fell seriously behind that of the population, owing to the destruction of the economic apparatus during the Japanese Occupation and the revolution.

As one of the three Ethical Policy objectives, Dutch colonial migration policy (*emigratie*) was essentially formulated and maintained as a result of a combination of three main factors. The first was the political changes in the Netherlands that allowed the Calvinist-Catholic Coalition to come to power in 1901. The outstanding feature of the policy outcomes from this new coalition was the official abandonment of the goal of economic exploitation and the introduction of direct intervention in the economic sphere to improve the conditions of the indigenous population. The second factor was economic opportunity, particularly as seen by the Dutch capitalists after the whole archipelago was successfully brought under effective colonial control. The vast land areas on the outer islands attracted private companies looking to open plantations. Given the scarcity of labour, the Javanese were recruited as cheap labour for new economic activities. The third factor was social and political unrest in many parts of rural Java, resulting from simultaneous economic exploitation and population pressures. These, in turn, encouraged the colonial government to deal with social unrest by moving people to the "outer islands".

Emigration policy, as developed by the Dutch, therefore, can be summarized as a useful instrument to serve the many goals and interests of the state and its ruling élite. The relocation of people to ease the social and political tensions is a form of demographic engineering to serve the state's strategic and security purposes.

Demographic Engineering After Independence

After independence, the government formulated for the first time its Five-Year Development Plan from 1956 to 1960, in which transmigration was described as an instrument to reduce population pressure in Java; to provide labour in sparsely-populated provinces; to support military strategy; and to accelerate the process of assimilation (Hardjosudarmo 1965, pp. 128–29). The Plan's most significant change in its transmigration policy was its explicit reference to strategic military purposes and assimilation, and industrialization was no longer the goal. This was apparently due to increased political unrest in some regions resulting from disappointment with the central government leadership. The important role of transmigration was further emphasized in 1962 as a result of a change in the national constitution whereby President Soekarno proclaimed the so-called Guided Democracy system of government to replace the Parliamentary Democracy system that he considered to be a failure. The establishment of autocratic Guided Democracy took place with the support of the central military leadership (Kuntjorojakti 1978, pp. 138–39). The political role of the military had increased considerably after they had successfully put down the regional rebellions in West Sumatra, North and South Sulawesi, which had occurred between 1956 and 1958.

As Feith and Lev (1963, p. 37) have argued, the end of the rebellion removed regionalists from the political and military scenes, clearing the way for the emergence of a new set of power relationships. From the three main political forces of 1957 (the president, the central army leadership, and the regionalists) only the first two remained by mid-1958, and these two were markedly distinct and, in many ways, competitive with one another. Furthermore, the course of the regional rebellions had caused the government to adopt more centre-oriented policy attitudes. As noted by Kuntjorojakti (1978, p. 139), several presidential edicts on regional matters were issued at the national level, treating the regions as simple administrative units within the framework of a highly centralized national bureaucracy. Undoubtedly, feelings of resentment grew as the central government paid little attention to local concerns.

The resentment of the local populations towards the central government's implementation of the transmigration policy in the 1950s and 1960s was not a new phenomenon. The sources of resentment and dissatisfaction were mostly related to land disputes. Problems arose partly because the concept of land ownership on the outer islands was generally based on customary (*adat*) law, in which all land belonged to the *marga* or clan. The reluctance of the local people in Lampung, where population resettlement was implemented to a large extent, to allow colonization of their lands in the Dutch period had resulted in the formation of Javanese enclaves separate from the indigenous settlements (Heeren 1979, p. 47). When the local people refused to give up their homelands for colonization, the Dutch used *perintah halus* (gentle command) to gain permission to use land outside *marga* jurisdiction. The colonized areas, therefore, were usually located outside the local settlements.

Nitisastro, from a somewhat nationalist stance, criticized the Dutch assumptions that had led to enclave politics (Heeren 1979, p. 17). According to Nitisastro, the typical Dutchman's conservative politics had hampered the assimilation process among ethnic communities in the resettlement areas. Furthermore, Nitisastro argued that enclave politics were obviously in contradiction with the primary goal of Indonesian independence — to build one Indonesian nation. Assimilating the Javanese with the local population was expected to bolster unification. However, this goal proved to be more difficult than the government or nationalists such as Nitisastro had anticipated.

Wertheim (1959, p. 196), for example, noted from his observations in Lampung in 1956 that the assimilation of Javanese migrants resulted in neither a Sumatran nor a general Indonesian society, but rather a Javanese society modified by a Sumatran environment. This situation, according to Wertheim, led to an increasing resistance by Sumatrans to resettlement policies. Such resistance could seriously hamper further transmigration efforts, Wertheim argued, since the absorptive capacity of the outer islands was not only restricted by spatial and technical factors, but also by social ones.[5]

The change in national political structures since the declaration of the Guided Democracy system significantly affected the subsequent course of the transmigration policy. The goals of transmigration were now stated to be increased national security and improved social welfare through the attainment of three intermediate goals: first, the opening-up of new areas of natural resources and land; secondly, by moving the population from densely-populated areas to empty ones; and thirdly, by developing strategic regions in order to achieve greater national resilience (Hardjosudarmo 1965, pp. 129–30). In conjunction with the declaration of Guided Democracy, the central government introduced a change in local administration in 1959. Under the new system, the *marga* and *negeri* were abolished. Regional authority was transferred to the *Bupati* (District Head), who was assisted by the *Camat* (Sub-district Head). The higher authorities appointed both the *Bupati* and *Camat*. Such structural arrangements, in turn, contributed to circumstances in which neither the local people nor the migrants had the opportunity to influence the course of regional development.

The local populations strongly criticized government budgets that allocated more funds to transmigration settlements than to other areas. Road construction, schools, agricultural offices, health and many other facilities were usually concentrated in transmigration areas, with smaller allocations to other places. However, regional disappointment with the central government had a much broader base. As Paauw (1963, p. 156) has argued, resistance among the peoples of the outlying islands to the President's new development reflected a fear of the centralization of authority, as well as more moderate attitudes on their part towards capitalism and foreign enterprise. Behind these attitudes we find both ethnic considerations and significant differences in historical experience. In such circumstances, a transmigration policy that was basically aimed at resettling the population from Java to the other islands further exacerbated discontent towards the central government among the local people. Local discontent with the transmigration policy, for example, was clearly articulated at an *Adat* Congress, first in Palembang, South Sumatra, in January 1957, and later in Bukittinggi, West Sumatra, in March of the same year.[6]

While the Dutch colonial government used emigration policy only implicitly as an instrument of demographic engineering for security purposes, after independence, the government of the Republic of Indonesia explicitly relocated the population to fulfill political and strategic goals. Demographic engineering became an important part of the state's strategic policy to reduce the increasing possibility of social and political tensions, particularly in areas surrounding the national capital city of Jakarta. Transmigration policy, among other military strategies, was also explicitly utilized to support the state's foreign policy during the confrontation with Malaysia, by populating the border areas such Riau, and West and East Kalimantan provinces. After independence, several ideological leaders, such as Yamin and Soekarno, also perceived transmigration as a tool for assimilating different ethnic groups to construct a homogenized cultural identity and national integration.

At the beginning of the New Order period, the conventional view among the economist-technocrats was that the rate of population growth is a significant determinant of the success of a country's economic development efforts. Compared with the problem of rapid population growth, which at the beginning of the New Order was accorded high priority, the economist-technocrats had not generally regarded the problem of uneven population distribution between Java and other islands as an issue of urgency. Nitisastro (1970, p. 238), widely known as the architect of the New Order's economic development policies, strongly argued that what was needed to overcome the population problem in Indonesia was a massive development effort to create expanding employment opportunities, accompanied by a rapid spread of fertility control. Yet, curiously enough, the problem of uneven population distribution and the role of transmigration as a means to overcome it had long been a focus of government thinking, and became a very important policy within the national development plans during the New Order.

From the beginning of the New Order, the real motive of President Soeharto for the continuation of transmigration, however, was not difficult to identify. The explanation lies in the idea of harmony among the Javanese, which in the Indonesian political context can be translated into the concept of cultural homogeneity and national integration, as suggested by Koentjaraningrat, strongly endorsed by the President and the military.[7] In this context, transmigration was perceived as an instrument to accelerate the process of national integration and ultimately to achieve cultural homogeneity. Government policies to relocate people from overcrowded Java to other islands were also considered as an alternative to land reform.[8] Despite this, the legacy of colonial policies, as well as the population policies of the Old Order (which were basically pro-natalist and viewed uneven distribution of population as the main population problem), could not be easily eliminated from the thinking of the ruling élite.[9]

National Integration: Centralized State and Uneven Economic Development

At the declaration of independence on 17 August 1945, Indonesia's founding fathers stated that Indonesia was to be a unitary state. Yet, the struggle to materialize a genuinely integrated nation-state proved to be a long and complicated political process. The war against the Dutch continued until 1949, when *de facto* independence was finally achieved. The period 1950–57 was one of parliamentary democracy, marked by constant political conflict both among the political parties and between the central and provincial governments. Two major regional conflicts occurred during this time: the PRRI/PERMESTA in West Sumatra, South and North Sulawesi, and the DI/TII in West Java. The Guided Democracy period of 1957–65 followed, firmly establishing a strong central government *vis-à-vis* a weak regional government. The outcome of the political crisis in 1965 that toppled Soekarno and at the same time elevated General Soeharto as the President, further established the domination of the state *vis-à-vis* civil society. From 1967, under Soeharto's presidency, the political system, called Pancasila Democracy, was engineered in such a way as to establish him as the sole authority in the country. During the New Order period, separatist movements raged in Irian Jaya and East Timor (Eastern Indonesia), and in Aceh (Western Indonesia). However, not until the collapse of the New Order in May 1998, did these separatist political movements pose a challenge to the political stability and national integration of a unitary state in Indonesia.

According to Mackie (1986), since about 1970, several important development changes in Indonesia had greatly strengthened the central government's capacity to control the regions. First, the tightening of central authority within the military had significantly reduced the power of the regional commanders over their territories. Secondly, the process of depolitization totally eliminated the possibility of a political party being able to stir up mass grievances against the central government. Thirdly, the improvement in inter-island shipping and airline services, as well as telecommunications, commercial and banking networks, played an important role in integrating the regions into a single economy. In addition to the three important centrifugal factors indicated by Mackie, the use of Bahasa Indonesia as a national language also played an integrating role as a tool of communication among peoples of such a plural ethno-linguistic society.

The national political system, which was highly centralistic and tightly controlled by President Soeharto and the military, directly influenced the structural relationship of the central and provincial level governments. Furthermore, such an unequal relationship also affected regional development planning formulation and implementation. In 1974, the government promulgated Law No.5, which designated the legal framework for the role and authority of the provincial governments. According to this Law, the provincial government authorities would exercise only those powers that were granted to them by the central government. The national government, primarily represented by the Department of Home Affairs, which acted through the Governors, had the responsibility to supervise and to support all development activities carried out in the provinces.

Development activities at the provincial level, based on Law No.5 (1974), were classified into three broad categories. The first category included the development activities and programmes which were implemented by the sectoral-line agencies in the regions. In this category, the central government was responsible for all activities related to development, such as planning, implementation, control, and financial support. The second category included development activities that were funded and implemented by the district-level Government Technical Offices (*Dinas*). In the third category were development activities that were supposed to be controlled by the provincial governments but which, because of their limited financial capacity, were handed over to the central government to control. An example of such activities is the so-called Inpres (Presidential Instruction) project, which was implemented by provincial governments under the control and supervision of the Ministry of Home Affairs.

In 1976, the central government created Regional Development Planning Boards (BAPPEDA) to strengthen the provincial governments' ability to plan and co-ordinate the development programmes. In theory, the BAPPEDA should have performed a number of functions, such as formulating basic regional development plans, co-ordinating planning among the sectoral line agencies at the provincial level, drafting regional development budgets, and monitoring as well as evaluating development. In practice, however, what seemed to be neatly described as bottom-up planning, did not really take place. The actual planning was still largely a top-down process. The development programmes and projects at the provincial level were mostly designed and planned by the National Planning Board (BAPPENAS) and various ministerial offices in Jakarta.[10]

The central government procedure in allocating provincial budgets was also criticized as not considering the potential ability of the regions. Pangestu and Azis (1994), for example, have argued that the central government's planners did not consider incentives for local resource mobilization as each region received the same amount per head of population, especially in the case of package development grants (such as the Inpres project). The primacy of population size as the major criteria in allocating provincial budgets therefore, not surprisingly, ensured that the largest proportion of the budget still poured into Java. Furthermore, this imbalance was reinforced by the lack of an incentive criterion, such as tax efforts, and the failure to consider regional potential in fund allocations. Thus, the financial transfer from the centre to the regions played no significant role in reducing the existing regional disparity, particularly between western and eastern Indonesia.

The President in a parliamentary meeting in January 1990 formally stated the government's recognition that the eastern Indonesian provinces had been economically left behind by the western provinces. In his speech, the President argued that the pace of development in the eastern Indonesian provinces had to be accelerated in order to narrow the development gap between eastern and western provinces. The policy to develop eastern Indonesia was formally stated in the Broad Outlines of State Policy (GBHN) as the basis for the Sixth Five-Year Development Plan (1994–88). It was stated explicitly in the Sixth Plan that priority should be given to the expansion of transport systems in eastern Indonesia. An explicit policy statement on transmigration, for example, clearly showed the trend towards eastern Indonesia:

> The policy to direct transmigration to Eastern Indonesia is intended to develop a better economic and socio-cultural infrastructure; to accelerate communication and transportation; to develop social institutions, such as co-operation, financial institutions, and market facilities to enhance the bargaining power to the society...[11]

After the 1990 presidential speech, a great deal of discussion on development in eastern Indonesia flourished among economists and development experts. Although the presidential statement on eastern Indonesia's development successfully attracted wide academic debate, real moves were surprisingly slow to emerge. The slowness of the decision-making process in the central government, for example, was indicated by the creation of the National Advisory Council on Development of Eastern Indonesia (Dewan Nasional Pembangunan KTI) in 1993. The Council, which was headed by President Soeharto himself, consisted of no less than twelve ministers, and clearly reflected the consensual nature of the policy on eastern Indonesia. In addition, the appointment of Professor B. J. Habibie, the State Minister for Research and Technology, who was originally from eastern Indonesia, and three former governors also from those provinces as advisors, showed the heavily symbolic approach of the central government in dealing with development in eastern Indonesia. Furthermore, the central government's decision on the provinces designated as eastern Indonesia, which eventually also included all the provinces on Kalimantan Island, raised the question of the effectiveness of the policy.[12] The nature of both the organizational structure and the wide area designated as eastern Indonesia clearly reflected the usual consensual practices adopted by the central government to solve the classic problem of co–ordination between departments which was crucial in tackling the complex task of uplifting development in eastern Indonesia.[13]

At a parliamentary session on 16 August 1990, President Soeharto stated his intention to give more autonomy to the regions. The regions concerned here were the second-level regional governments (district) that, according to National Law No. 5 (1974), were considered as autonomous. Yet, as many observers had noted, the intention to give greater opportunity to the regions by the Soeharto government was merely a political gimmick with no substantial effect on the existing unequal central–regional government relationship. The second-level regional governments, though legally designated as autonomous, in practice were economically dependent on both the provincial and central governments.[14] The implications of the New Order's bureaucratic arrangement, particularly the suppression of the local people's political participation, were obvious. As shown by the findings of a study conducted in 1992 by the Centre for Regional and Political Studies, Indonesian Institute of Sciences, the political sphere of society at the regional level was very limited, and the local people were therefore marginalized. A 1997 study conducted by another research team of the Indonesian Institute of Sciences indicated that the central government's regional autonomy project mainly dealt with the technical administrative aspects of regional autonomy, and clearly did not have a significant effect on the existing centre-regional relationship.[15]

At the provincial level, the resentful feeling of being "economically squeezed" by the central government was also prevalent among people in the provinces rich with natural resources, such as Aceh, Riau, Kalimantan, North Sulawesi, and Irian Jaya. The flourishing primordial sentiments, originating from ethnic and religious self-identifications, were perhaps also natural human responses in a climate of political uncertainty. In the early 1990s, the emergence of many quasi-intellectual associations based on religious affiliation significantly supported the parochial and sectarian political tendencies among the educated urban–based population.[16] A more anthropological observation on the local society and culture during the New Order period suggested that the imposition of the Village Law of 1979 significantly transformed the remaining local social institutions based on customary (*adat*) laws. The social processes that had been tremendously remoulded by economic and political changes during the New Order period had led to a situation where the conflict between segments of the population became increasingly unavoidable.[17]

From State Engineering to Spontaneous Migration: A Mobility Shift

Based on the results of the 1971 population census, Titus (1978), using Samir Amin's (1974) centre–periphery approach, tried to show that development strategy and foreign economic activities played an important role in affecting interregional population movement in Indonesia. The most favoured foreign company investments were in the extractive industries, such as timber and oil, as well as the assembling and construction industries, followed by commerce and services. These activities had attracted a great deal of foreign capital. The development of extractive industries was almost exclusively limited to the "outer islands", the other activities being mainly in the urban centres of Java. Titus classified a province as centre or periphery based on the presence of such economic activities. In addition, every region was assessed on the existence of "attraction factors" (that is, employment opportunities, regional per capita income, urban attraction) or "expulsion factors" (that is, rural population pressure, ecosystem instability, lack of education facilities, political upheavals).

According to Titus, the greatest mobility together with net in-migration was to be found in the economic "boom" provinces of both the centre type (Jakarta, North Sumatra) and the relatively developed periphery type (South Sumatra, Riau, East Kalimantan). The lowest mobility and a zero migration balance were to be found in the isolated and still largely self-sufficient periphery type of provinces (that is, East and West Nusa Tenggara). The highest mobility, together with net out-migration, appeared in the highly integrated but stagnating peripheral provinces close to centre groups (that is, West Sumatra, Central Java, and Yogyakarta). Criticizing the work of Titus, which ignored short-term and non-permanent movements, Forbes (1981), using the same approach, conducted a study in South Sulawesi, mainly in Ujung Pandang. He focused attention on the circulation of petty traders between Ujung Pandang and the hinterland and showed that the majority of migrant, petty producers kept in contact with their villages with regular trips home. There was an important circulation between Ujung Pandang (now Makassar) and the hinterland not only of labour, but also of cash and goods. The main theme of Forbes' study is the importance of viewing population mobility as a reflection of the structure and processes of Indonesian society.

The general pattern of migration trends between Java and other islands showed an interesting shift after the mid-1980s. The net out-migration from Java to the other islands, between the periods 1970–80 and 1980–90, markedly declined from 137 to only 15.7 per cent.[18] This change reflected the increasing pull factors in Java and the decreasing role of the transmigration policy as the major push factor for out-migration from Java, particularly after the mid-1980s. Eastern Indonesia, as part of the other islands, also showed a similar pattern and trends. In more recent developments, based on the 1995 Intercensal Population Survey (*SUPAS*), Raharto and Romdiati (1998) have shown that in-migration to the eastern Indonesian provinces also significantly declined between 1990 and 1995. In 1990, in-migration to eastern Indonesia accounted for 54 per cent, whereas out-migration to western Indonesia was only 36 per cent. In 1995, in-migration to eastern Indonesia dropped to 49 per cent, while out-migration significantly increased to 49 per cent.[19]

The changes in the volume and pattern of migration between eastern and western Indonesia strongly indicated that the regional disparity between eastern and western Indonesia was increasing. The general pattern of the migration phenomena apparently reflected that the New Order's regional development had basically failed to achieve more equally distributed economic benefits between Java and the "outer islands", as well as between western and eastern Indonesia.[20] In terms of population size, according to the 1995 Intercensal Population Survey, eastern Indonesia comprised only 13.3 per cent of Indonesia's total population. From a national demographic perspective, eastern Indonesia comprised of nine provinces, located in Sulawesi, Maluku Islands, Irian Jaya and Nusa Tenggara islands (excluding Bali), and therefore, could not be simply put into one distinctive demographic system.[21] The population density, for example, varied, with Maluku and Irian Jaya together showing the least densely populated areas in Indonesia.[22] The Javanese-dominated bureaucrats in Jakarta therefore easily perceived eastern Indonesia as empty land. Such a perception was apparently behind the development policy decision in the 1980s to redirect the transmigration programme to the eastern Indonesian provinces.[23]

In the view of the military, geographic integration, in which transmigration policy played an important role by providing human resources, was a necessary condition for the attainment of national integration. Another important element of this military thinking was the concept of "basic defence". The basic defence of the Indonesian armed forces, according to Crouch (1986), was essentially based on the doctrine of territorial warfare. This doctrine required that the defence forces, especially the army, be organized principally along territorial rather than functional lines. The whole nation, under this doctrine, was divided into territorial commands more or less parallel to the civilian administration. In terms of the defence doctrine, a major function of the territorial commands was to maintain contact with the local people so that they could be mobilized quickly to support guerrilla operations whenever necessary. It may be added, of course, that this territorial structure had also been very convenient for the purpose of domestic political control. The role of transmigration in the concept of basic defence was to populate the empty regions in order to support the territorial military commands. Tanter (1991, quoted from Sebastian 1996, pp. 88–89) has described three elements that influenced the territorial strategic concept of the military in Indonesia. According to Tanter, *geography* is the framework, within which *demography* is the content, and *social conditions* (*IPOLEKSOSBUDMIL*) is the factor of social life that results from the synthesis of the other two elements.

The important role of transmigration for national defence and security was explicitly stated in 1985 by the Chief of Armed Forces, General Moerdani, who said that transmigration was the only policy within the economic development framework which had a direct linkage with national security and defence. Moerdani argued that it was necessary for the military to be involved in site selection primarily because transmigration location had a strong relation with the concept of territorial management.[24] There is a strong indication that the decision to resettle transmigrants to Irian Jaya was motivated by security and military reasons. The perceived increasing separatist movement under the Free Papua Movement (OPM) in several places in Irian Jaya obviously worried the military élite in Jakarta as it could provoke greater political instability in Irian Jaya.[25] The selection of transmigration sites along the border with Papua New Guinea (PNG) clearly indicated military intervention in the planning of resettlement areas. It was during the early 1980s that the transmigration programme was designed to serve the military's strategic goals, particularly in the troubled provinces, such as Aceh, Irian Jaya, and East Timor.

In the case of Irian Jaya, the transmigration policy by the central government has contributed to an increase in ethnic tensions. In the mid-1980s, as Irian Jaya became the main destination of the transmigration policy, strong resentment from the local population was aroused. Their resentment towards the transmigrants, who mostly originated from Java, was partly due to their perception that the government was treating them unfairly. They felt that the transmigrants received more help than the locals. Controversial issues, such as "Javanization", "internal colonization" and "Islamization" were also strongly voiced towards the Indonesian Government by many foreign non-governmental organizations (NGOs). The World Bank, the main financial supporter of the transmigration programme, was also criticized by both foreign and Indonesian NGOs as supporting the destruction of indigenous peoples and tropical forests in Indonesia.[26]

The impact of the central government's decision to bolster the transmigration programme in eastern Indonesia was clearly shown by the positive net migration trends from 1980 in the designated destination provinces, such as Irian Jaya, Maluku, and Southeast and Central Sulawesi. In-migrations apparently also played an important role in the relatively high annual rate of population growth in those provinces. On the other hand, in provinces such as North and South Sulawesi, as well as in West and East Nusa Tenggara, negative net-migration contributed to the low level of annual population growth in those provinces.[27]

As a result of the collapse of world oil prices in the mid-1980s, the national budget for the transmigration programme was drastically cut back, which, in turn, substantially reduced the number of transmigrant families that had originally been planned for resettlement.[28] The decision to move transmigrants to eastern Indonesia significantly contributed to the increased transmigration budget as transportation costs rose.

Data on population mobility and employment during the last two decades indicate that the mode of population mobility was strongly associated with the broader socio-economic processes instigated by government policies. The increase in the volume of population mobility, as mentioned earlier, was essentially the logical consequence of three factors: first, the surplus labour; second, the improvement of transportation means and networks; and third, the opening up of economic activities, particularly in the urban areas where the informal sector provided many different job choices for migrants.[29] In the eastern Indonesian provinces, the most prominent migrants, besides the Javanese, who were almost everywhere, were the three ethnic groups from the southern parts of Sulawesi, namely, the Bugis, the Makassarese, and the Butonese.[30] These migrants are well known as seafarers and traders and have successfully developed their social and economic networks in major urban areas in eastern Indonesia, where these three ethnic groups are pejoratively labelled as the BBM, an acronym for Bugis-Buton-Makassar.

Even though transmigration achievements have been scaled down since the mid-1980s, the net in-migration to eastern Indonesia is positive, particularly to urban destination areas. As shown by Raharto and Romdiati (1998) in their analysis on inter-provincial migration in eastern Indonesia, the shift of migration to the urban areas was strongly identified in provinces such as Irian Jaya, Maluku, and East Timor. The shift from the rural to the urban areas, as a result of the decline of the transmigration programme, also reflected the elasticity of the urban economy, most notably in the informal sectors, in eastern Indonesia. The labour surplus, particularly as the proportion of new working-age cohorts was increasing in western Indonesia, and in Java in particular, could be a significant determinant for the young to search for economic opportunities by migrating to eastern Indonesia. It is likely that the majority of the migrants to urban areas would be engaged in many kinds of informal sector activities. In this regard, migrants tended to be more enterprising than the locals as a result of their previous experience in their place of origin. The migrants generally also had higher educational attainment compared with the locals.[31]

Ethnic Mobility and Its Socio-Political Repercussions

About 30 per cent of the population of eastern Indonesia reside in South Sulawesi. Given its large population and central location, South Sulawesi is very important within the migration system operating in eastern Indonesia. The central location of South Sulawesi, of which the harbour of Ujung Pandang is the third largest seaport after Jakarta and Surabaya, and the prominent migrating behaviour of its people, provide this province with a dominant role in the development of the eastern Indonesian provinces, both economically and politically.[32] South Sulawesi is also the home of the three ethnic groups — the BBM. The notorious BBM migration behaviour and its social and economic implications in eastern Indonesia are very well depicted in various studies. Lineton (1975), Peluso (1987), Pelras (1994) and Acciaioli (1998) provide very rich descriptions of the behaviour of the Bugis migrants and their adaptive strategy in different social and economic environments in the archipelago. Aditjondro also gives a lively portrayal on how the BBM migrants conquered, socially and economically, the local peoples in Irian Jaya.[33] In Maluku, and most notably in Ambon, the Butonese migrants comprise the major population group who engage in unskilled jobs and the informal sector economy.[34]

After the annexation of East Timor by Indonesia in 1976, the BBM migrants apparently were the group most prepared to go to the new territory to fill the business sectors presumably left by the Chinese-Portuguese after Indonesia occupied the territory. In East Timor, the migrants mostly originated from Java, Bali, and East Nusa Tenggara. On the other hand, transmigrants, apparently because of social and political reasons, were mostly recruited from Bali. Up to 1994, there were 1,634 transmigrants from Bali, who were Hindu, and 1,212 transmigrants from Java, the majority of them being Catholic. The government also relocated the local population under the so-called local transmigration scheme.[35] The concentration of migrants in Irian Jaya occurred, among others, in Timika where the copper-mining industry by an American company, Freeport Inc., was located. Since the 1980s, the population of Timika has increased dramatically in conjunction with the increase in economic activities in the area. The population is currently estimated to be about 20,000, and about half are migrants.[36]

Since the beginning, the indigenous population has been against mining exploration, as they perceive the area to be sacred. The first conflict occurred in 1967 when the exploration started. Resentment against Freeport began for the second time in 1973, and in 1977 a larger conflict occurred which involved the rebellious group of OPM. After the second conflict, the military was deployed to Timika and this further inflamed resistance from the local population. The perception that Freeport only benefits the foreign investors and the central government has been the major source of resentment. Furthermore, the atrocities committed by the military on the local people and various human rights violations increased the potential for conflict in Timika. The local resentment towards Freeport and the military culminated in several riots in 1995 that become national and international issues.[37]

During January and February 1997, a series of ethnic conflicts occurred in West Kalimantan. The conflicts were between the Madurese migrants and the indigenous Dayak people. Hundreds of people, mostly Madurese migrants, were reported to have been killed during the clashes. Thousands of Madurese families abandoned their villages and were evacuated by the government. The latent conflict between the Madurese and the Dayak, partly resulting from cultural gaps and stereotyping perceptions, was easily triggered by small incidents. The recent conflict, for example, was instigated by a quarrel between a Madurese youth and a Dayak youth in the Sanggau-Ledo district, and rapidly spread to the surrounding districts, resulting in mass ethnic violence. Conflicts between Madurese migrants (well-known as strong Muslims from the island of Madura, east of Java) and Dayaks (mostly Catholics) have occurred many times, but the latest incident seems to have been the worst during the New Order.[38]

A close observation of the lives of the indigenous Dayak people under rapid external pressures induced by the central government's development strategy basically confirmed that the very resources upon which they had depended for centuries — the land, forests, and rivers — were no longer able to sustain them.[39] The ongoing exploitation of natural resources in Kalimantan in the last two decades has forcefully transformed the local people into marginal peasants, estate workers, and urban wage labourers. In West Kalimantan, population pressures further exacerbated the process of marginalization of the Dayak people as Madurese migrants as well as transmigrants increasingly settled the region. The Madurese, like the Buginese, Makassarese, and Butonese, are prominent in their migrating behaviour; and they are also well known as seafarers and traders.[40]

In eastern Indonesia, most specifically in Irian Jaya and East Timor, the division of labour by ethnic groups is somewhat different in comparison with other places.[41] The upper level economic sectors are usually in the hands of the Chinese whereas the middle and the lower levels are dominated by the Makassarese, the Buginese, and the Butonese. The Javanese, including other migrant-ethnic groups usually occupy the limited government jobs, such as public servants and the military. The Javanese domination of various governmental occupations is a by-product of the process of employment recruitment, which is conducted by the central government in Java. In Irian Jaya and East Timor, because of their political histories, the appointment of officials by the central government is also dictated by security and military considerations. The feelings of resentment among the local population towards the domination of migrants in both governmental and private occupations are obvious, and easily perceived even by a casual observer.[42] Given their distinct socio-political circumstances, conflict between migrants and the local populations in Irian Jaya and East Timor cannot be related to demographic and economic issues only. In assessing the events, the political histories of the provinces in their relation to the nation-state building processes should be given special consideration.

Irian Jaya province, formerly West Papua — a Dutch colony — was integrated into the Indonesian state in 1963, after long diplomatic negotiations and incidences of armed conflict between Indonesia and the Dutch. Irian Jaya was incorporated into Indonesia after the state won a referendum under United Nations supervision. A group of West Papuans, however, rejected the outcome of the referendum and proclaimed their organization (OPM) as the legitimate owner of the province and took up armed struggle against Indonesia. East Timor was annexed by Indonesia in 1976 in the midst of an internal conflict between political parties competing for their legitimacy to rule the former Portuguese colony. Despite Indonesia's strong claim to the territory, the United Nations still recognized the Portuguese as the administering power of East Timor. The rise of the underground movement, organized by young people, received more international attention after the so-called Dili Incident on 12 November 1991, in which an estimated one hundred people were murdered by Indonesian soldiers while holding a protest rally.

In spite of the continuing volatile political climate, the central government provided the province with substantial budget allocations, most notably to develop various physical infrastructures. The construction of asphalt roads linking West and East Timor, the beginning of regular flights and shipping to and from Dili, the East Timor capital, significantly contributed to the increase of in-migration to East Timor. An underpinning demographic factor in the building up of tensions between migrants and the local people was the burgeoning unemployment, particularly among the educated youth in the urban areas. In 1990, for example, in Dili, the capital of East Timor, more than 20 per cent of the labour force between the ages of 15 to 30 were unemployed (Tirtosudarmo 1996a). In most cases, the involvement of local youth in various forms of protest against the migrants was very prominent. Furthermore, the role of the underground resistance movement within East Timor against Indonesia's occupation should not be underestimated in assessing the conflicts between in-migrants and the local population. Migrants often decided to leave the province in order to avoid the harsh treatment by the East Timorese. The exodus of migrants, many of them belonging to the BBM, from East Timor occurred in September 1996 and July 1998, following large anti-integration protests.

From Economic Crisis to Social Conflict?

Indeed, it is not an easy task to find evidence to explain direct causal-effect relationships between the worsening economic situation resulting from the monetary crises started in August 1997 and the increasing incidence of conflicts between different ethnic and religious groups, more particularly between migrants and the local population, in several places in Indonesia. Yet, at the same time, it is also difficult not to notice the increasing violence and conflicts between different groups of the population in many regions during the economic crises. The most obvious one occurred in May 1998 in Jakarta, as well as in several other cities in Java, in which riots against the Chinese ethnic group were blown up to a scale never experienced before. As mentioned earlier, ethnic conflicts had already occurred at the beginning of 1997, just before the economic crises began, between the local Dayaks and the Madurese migrant ethnic group, in Sambas district, West Kalimantan. In early 1999, two fresh violent conflicts occurred between the migrants and the local population in Sambas, West Kalimantan, and in Ambon, Maluku. To everyone's surprise, for the first time a brutal conflict between the local Malays and Madurese migrants occurred in the sub-district of Salamantan in Sambas, West Kalimantan. This conflict further pushed out the Madurese from this area. In February 2000, Sambas was divided into two districts (Sambas and Bengkayang), apparently as a consequence of the intensifying ethnic politics between the Malays and the Dayaks in West Kalimantan.[43]

In the case of Ambon, the conflict which began with a quarrel between two youths from different ethnic backgrounds, also identified as between the local people and the migrants, escalated into widespread and brutal ethnic and religious conflicts that have not been resolved until today. The Ambon conflicts instigated a widespread communal conflict in the adjacent island of Haruku and Seram, as well as in Halmahera, in North Maluku.[44] Violent ethnic conflicts in West Kalimantan and Maluku resulted in the exodus of thousands of Madurese from Sambas to Pontianak and East Java, and migrants from Ambon, Central Maluku, to South Sulawesi (mostly BBM) and from Halmahera islands, North Maluku, to Bitung, North Sulawesi. The transmigrants, mostly from Java and Bali, although not directly involved in the conflicts, obviously became the targets of local resentments in many places in Indonesia. From Aceh to Papua, the Javanese migrants felt threatened as the local populations strongly demanded that "everything" in the regions should be first given to the indigenous or local population before the migrants.[45] The number of returning migrants — some of them were transmigrants — rapidly increased as the locals took strong actions against many things that they perceived as representing exploitation by the central government.[46]

One of the possible explanations that can be proposed in relating the economic crisis with the increasing ethnic conflicts is that the state's inability to control the declining economy, followed by the weakening of the state's repressive apparatus, undermined its strong grip on the society. In other words, the New Order's hegemonic power that had successfully integrated the aspirations of the different ethnic groups had suddenly collapsed, as their basic economic foundation could not be sustained. In such a situation, which opened a Pandora's box, many latent conflicts that had been forcefully covered up before immediately sprang to the surface. The previously suppressed tensions resulting from a long and often subtle economic and political contestation that had generally disadvantaged the local population in the regions were now beyond the state's control.[47] The demand for more autonomy was most clearly articulated by the East Timorese and Irianese.[48] The new government under President B. J. Habibie responded positively to the demand for more autonomy in East Timor. The mass out-migration from East Timor occurred prior to and after the vote ballot on 30 August 1999, when the majority of East Timorese voted for independence from Indonesia. At the same time, the demand for autonomy also increased in Irian Jaya, which led, for example, to the formation of the Reconciliation Forum of the People of Irian Jaya (Foreri), comprising three groups, which respectively called for "an autonomous state", "an independent state", and "a federal state".[49] In the westernmost province, Aceh, which had long experienced political repression by the central government, under the banner of the Free Aceh Movement (Gerakan Aceh Merdeka or GAM) secessionist movement, revived its call for independence from the republic.[50] After East Timor declared its independence from Indonesia, Aceh and West Papua, which were unofficially declared as Military Operations Areas (Daerah Operasi Militer or DOM) during the New Order, became the most problematic provinces with regard to the sustainability of the republic as a unitary state.

The power equation between the centre and the regions was shattered after the downfall of Soeharto on 21 May 1998, as various groups protesting against the central government's domination began to flourish. The further cracking-up of the New Order regime and its political order apparently resulted in a semi power vacuum within the state institutions in the region. It easily provoked and aroused latent and potential tensions into the open, resulting in violent conflicts among various groups in the society. The return of migrants from places such as Aceh, West Kalimantan, Maluku, and Irian Jaya, to Java and Bali is presently under way. This phenomenon again shows that the idea of cultural homogeneity, strongly advocated by the ruling élites during both the Old and New Orders, simply did not materialize. Moreover, the idea of pluralism and social cohesion is in danger in today's Indonesia. In this regard, although President Abdurrahman Wahid was democratically elected, he was confronted with problems of social and political conflicts resulting from the political suppression under the previous regimes. The incidents of ethnic and religious conflicts in Maluku, besides the problem of secessionist movements in Aceh and West Papua, have to be resolved as the political repercussions could be very detrimetral to the peaceful political transition which is necessary before consolidated democracy can be achieved.

Concluding Remarks

Cliffort Geertz, a noted anthropologist, has argued that "...archipelagic in geography, eclectic in civilization, and heterogeneous in culture, Indonesia flourishes when its accepts and capitalizes on its diversity and disintegrates when it denies and suppresses it".[51] What is happening now evidently confirms what was predicted by Clifford Geertz. The demographic engineering policies, which had been implemented for almost a century — in the beginning through emigration, and after independence through transmigration — essentially point to the state's ultimate goals to integrate the diverse social and cultural configuration of Indonesia's population. Such an ambitious design culminated during the New Order period, in which the regime was sustained primarily by two important technocratic pillars: strong military control, and the obsession with economic development. Yet, the New Order's hegemonic control was apparently vulnerable to external shocks, as shown by the almost non-resisting monetary crisis that hit the country in August 1997. The following events have demonstrated that the seemingly strong homogeneous state was merely a façade, and it was left almost in ruins as social conflicts became the order of the day.

As the crisis is still looming large, it is obviously too early to predict the outcome of the current national political saga. In the current heated political climate, issues of regional economic development, for example, can clearly no longer be isolated from the debate surrounding regional political autonomy and the demand to rebuild the nation-state. The emergence of various ethnic-based organizations, demanding for recognition of their indigenous customary rights are closely interconnected with the demand for more autonomy and independence of the regions from the central government.[52] A strong indication of the increasing politics of identity, that actually began in the early 1990s, can be found in several provinces in Indonesia. The recent agreement by the Parliament to give way to the demands of the people residing in Banten and the Gorontalo Kabupaten (district) areas by giving them provincial status — which is likely to be followed by other regions — can also be seen as the formalization of ethnic-geographical territories into definite regional administrative boundaries. This decision could enhance the establishment of ethno-territorial identity politics. Furthermore, the ability of the central government to contain the strong pressure from separatist groups in Aceh and West Papua for independence will be crucial to the future nation-state political format.

Notes

1. Demographic engineering is a term borrowed from Bookman (1997), which is broadly defined as the state's attempt to reconfigure the ethno-demographic composition of the population for various strategic purposes.
2. These movements were comprehensively documented by the National Archives of the Republic of Indonesia (Arsip Nasional Republik Indonesia) in 1981.
3. Heeren (1979), p. 14.
4. Pelzer (1945), pp. 223–25.
5. Wertheim's prediction about the probability of social conflict in Lampung as consequences of rapid population growth and social tensions between migrants and local people occurred in February 1989 in the so-called "Lampung Affairs" (Peristiwa Lampung). See an interesting personal account by Wertheim on this affair in *Inside Indonesia*, July 1989, pp. 20–21)
6. In 1964, an evaluation of the government transmigration programmes led to a new policy in January 1965 called New Transmigration Model (*Transmigrasi Gaya Baru*). In one of his speeches, President Soekarno stated that "Indonesia does not need birth control, Indonesia can feed at least 250 million people... if they are properly distributed, if their energies are utilized adequately...". Under the new plan, the government aimed to resettle 100,000 families every year. The records show that in the first half of 1965, the government successfully moved almost 25,000 transmigrants. However, as a result of the political turmoil after the abortive coup of October 1965, the implementation of transmigration was significantly impeded.
7. See "An Interview with Koentjaraningrat", in Visser (1988).
8. The New Order government identified the programme on land reform as a communist strategy, which was aggressively promoted by the Indonesian Communist Party (PKI) prior to the 1965 abortive coup.
9. An illustration of how the élite, particularly the military, have persistently regarded transmigration as an important undertaking is shown by a request

from General Soeharto to the U.S. Ambassador in Indonesia, Marshall Green, at their first meeting on 29 May 1966. In the meeting, Soeharto asked for US$500 million in grants or soft loans to assist the transmigration programme. This information is based on personal communication with Dr. Terrence Hull (Australian National University), who received a letter from Marshall Green, dated 19 March 1988.

10. Many sources note that the personal lobbying of the provincial bureaucratic leaders, particularly the governors, was very important in determining project and budget allocations for their respective provinces.
11. The Sixth Five-Year Development Plan, Book I, p. 55.
12. In a seminar on eastern Indonesia's development at LIPI in 1996, former governor of South Sulawesi, and advisor to B. J. Habibie, Amirrudin acknowledged that the reasons for incorporating Kalimantan into eastern Indonesia was merely because the bureaucratic élite in Kalimantan provinces would complain of being neglected by the central government if it was not included in the eastern Indonesia development plan.
13. It was not surprising that such a high-level organization would face problems in their decision-making process. For example, it took more than one year after its designation for this organization to hold its first plenary meeting.
14. A study conducted by the Centre for Regional and Political Studies, Indonesian Institute of Sciences, in 1992, showed that in reality the district level government cannot be called autonomous as it has only quasi-autonomous governmental control (Sulistyo 1995).
15. See PEP-LIPI (1997).
16. All the formal religions have created their own intellectual associations, such as the ICMI (Muslim), PIKI (Protestant), ICKI (Catholic), PCHI (Hindu), and ICBI (Buddhist).
17. In response to the experience of disintegration among Eastern European countries, Anne Booth (1991) has perceptively argued that Indonesia could have a similar disintegration problem if the unequal centre-regional economic relationship persists.
18. For a detailed analysis of the changing patterns and processes of migration in Indonesia during the New Order, see Hugo (1997).
19. See Raharto and Romdiati (1998).
20. The shift in macroeconomic policies from import substitution into export orientation policies, after the collapse of the world oil prices in the mid-1980s, was among the major factors that resulted in the further concentration of manufacturing industries in Java rather than decentralizing to the regional economic growth centres in the outer islands.
21. The official definition of eastern Indonesia includes all provinces on Kalimantan Island.
22. In 1995, the density of both Maluku Islands and Irian Jaya was only eight people per square kilometre, while for Java it was 850 people, and for the whole of Indonesia it was 95.

23. The surge in the transmigration target to eastern Indonesia in the early 1980s was supported by the fact that the central government was very confident of its financial ability, as the World Bank had fully committed to back up the programme. The government also declared that traditional transmigration destination areas such as Lampung and South Kalimantan were closed for new transmigrants.
24. Moerdani's statement was part of his keynote address at the National Defence Institute's seminar (*Kompas* daily, 8 March 1985).
25. In the early 1980s, OPM was very active in the border areas. The military conducted harsh operations in an attempt to curtail OPM insurgencies. In 1984, thousands of Irianese were reported to have taken refuge in PNG. On the Irian Jaya-PNG border issues, see studies by Bhakti (1991) and by the Center for Population and Manpower Studies (PPT-LIPI), (1997).
26. For a useful reference on the regional development in Irian Jaya under the New Order, see Manning and Rumbiak (1987).
27. East Nusa Tenggara, and more recently followed by West Nusa Tenggara, is becoming the major sending area of overseas migrant workers to Malaysia and Saudi Arabia.
28. The polemics on the place and roles of the transmigration programme in the discourse on regional development in Indonesia briefly surfaced among Australian academics, in *Bulletin of Indonesian Economic Studies* in the late 1970s and early 1980s. The views debated in this polemic, unfortunately, were mainly confined to the realms of demographic and economic issues, undermining the critical political aspects of the programme.
29. Since the 1980s, large numbers of migrant workers have also moved across the national boundaries, particularly to Malaysia. On the politics of Indonesian migrant workers in Malaysia, see Tirtosudarmo (1996b).
30. See Raharto and Romdiati (1998).
31. On the role of Ujung Pandang as the centre of the maritime industry in Indonesia, see Dick's articles on Prahu shipping in eastern Indonesia (1975).
32. Aditjondro's monograph is a useful source on voluntary migration of the Buginese, the Makassarese and the Butonese in eastern Indonesia, particularly in Irian Jaya (see Aditjondro 1986).
33. For details of the population composition in Ambon, see Djohan (1997).
34. On migration to East Timor, see Aditjondro (1997) and Soewartoyo (1994).
35. See Widjojo (1997).
36. For a detailed account of the conflict between the indigenous people (Amungme and Kamoro) and Freeport Inc., see Part 4 of a book on human rights violations in the mining industries in Indonesia (Bachriadi 1998).
37. The actual number of people who were killed in the incident was difficult to obtain. The local army commander estimated that about 300 people were killed, but non-government sources believed that the actual number of deaths was much larger than the government estimation.

38. King (1995) provides a comprehensive account of the historical and social development in Kalimantan. The last chapter on modernization and development is particularly relevant.
39. Reference to Madurese migration is unfortunately lacking in the literature.
40. Information on the division of labour by ethnicity was observed on the author's intermittent visits to eastern Indonesia between 1991 and 1993; see also Tirtosudarmo (1997). Statistics on the composition of the population according to ethnicity are lacking in Indonesia as the national government had decided not to ask the ethnic background in the population census.
41. The migrants are pejoratively called by the locals, the "straight-haired", while the migrants call the locals the "curly-haired".
42. For a detailed account of ethnic conflict in West Kalimantan, see Davidson (1998).
43. See the unpublished interim report on the root and solution of the conflict in Ambon and North Maluku by a POLWIL-LIPI research team (2000). On ethnic and religious conflict in North Maluku, see a detailed account by Tamagola (2000).
44. The local demands, loudly voiced, mirrored the popular regional appeals of the 1950s.
45. The number of returned migrants, according to the Ministry of Transmigration, as of December 2000 was 1,003,924 persons.
46. An empirical study should be conducted to provide rigorous evidence that support the direct causal-effect relationships between the economic crisis and ethnic conflicts in Indonesia.
47. Most notably, the anti-integration student and youth organizations were now loudly calling for a referendum that had been suppressed during the Soeharto regime.
48. *Jakarta Post,* 3 August 1998. In this chapter, I use Irian Jaya and West Papua interchangeably.
49. For a detailed account of the impact of the military operation in Aceh, see ELSAM (1995), pp. 13–31.
50. Quoted from Mackie (1986).
51. This new form of cultural movement is termed "politics of recognition" by Taylor (1992). See Kahn (1999).

References

Acciaioli, Gregory L. "Bugis Entrepreneurialism and Resource Use: Structure and Practice". *Anthropologi Indonesia* 57 (1998): 81–89.

Aditjondro, G. J. *Datang dengan Kapal, Tidur di Pasar, Buang Air di Kali, Pulang Naik Pesawat* [Coming by Ship, Sleeping in Market Place, Toileting at River]. Jayapura: YPMD, 1986.

———. *In the Shadow of Mount Ramelau: The Impact of the Occupation of East Timor.* Netherlands: Indonesian Documentation and Information Center (INDOC), 1997.

Amin, Samir. "Modern Migration in Western Africa". In *Modern Migration in Western Africa*, edited by Samir Amin, pp. 65–124. London: Oxford University Press, 1974.

Arsip Nasional Republik Indonesia [National Archive of Republic of Indonesia]. *Laporan-Laporan tentang Gerakan Protes di Jawa pada abad XX* [Reports on Protest Movements in Java in the 20th Century]. Jakarta, 1981.

Bachriadi, Dianto. *Merana di Tengah Kelimpahan* [Misery Amidst Plenty]. Jakarta: Lembaga Studi dan Advokasi Masyarakat (ELSAM), 1998.

Bhakti, Ikrar Nusa. "The Dynamics of Indonesia-Papa New Guinea Relations: From Conflict to a Better Understanding". Ph.D. thesis, Division of Asian and International Studies, Griffith University, Brisbane, Australia, 1991.

Bookman, Milica Zarkovic. *The Demographic Struggle for Power: The Political Economy of Demographic Engineering in the Modern World*. London: Frank Cass, 1997.

Booth, Anne. "Can Indonesia Survive as a Unitary State?". Indonesia Circle Annual Lecture, School of Oriental and African Studies, 19 March 1991.

Choucri, Nazli. "Perspectives on Population and Conflict". In *Multidisciplinary Perspectives on Population and Conflict*, edited by Nazli Choucri, pp. 1–25. New York: Syracuse University Press, 1984.

Crouch, Harold. "Security Concerns Posed by Indonesia's Armed Forces". *Indonesian Issues*, No. 3 (November, 1986).

Davidson, Jamie. "Ethnic Violence and Electoral Politics on the Periphery: The Case of West Kalimantan". A draft report, 1998.

Department of Information, Republic of Indonesia. *Soal Transmigrasi adalah Soal Mati Hidup Bangsa Indonesia* [Transmigration is a matter of Life and Death for Indonesia]. Speech by President Soekarno at the General Meeting of National Movement of Transmigration on 28 December 1964, Jakarta.

Dick, H. W. "Prahu Shipping in Eastern Indonesia, Part I". *Bulletin of Indonesian Economic Studies* 11, no. 2 (July 1975): 69–107.

Djohan, Erniati. "Gambaran Umum Daerah Penelitian" [General Description of the Research Field]. In *Pemuda, Pendidikan dan Ketenagakerjaan di Kotamadya Ambon Propinsi Maluku* [Youth, Education, and Employment in Ambon Municipality, Maluku Province], edited by Roosmalawati, pp. 50–73. Jakarta: Puslitbang Kependudukan dan Ketenagakerjaan LIPI, 1997.

ELSAM. *Ke Arah Ratifikasi Konvensi Anti Penyiksaan: Kajian Kasus-kasus Penyiksaan Belum-Terselesaikan* [Towards a Ratification of Convention on Anti Torture: Study on the Unfinished Cases of Torture]. Jakarta: Lembaga Studi dan Advokasi Masyarakat (ELSAM), 1995.

Feith, H. and Lev, D. "The End of the Indonesian Rebellion". *Pacific Affairs* 36, no. 1 (Spring 1963): 32–46.

Forbes, D. "Mobility and Uneven Development in Indonesia: A Critique of Explanations on Migration and Circular Migration". In *Population Mobility and Development: Southeast Asia and the Pacific*, edited by G. W. Jones and H. Richter, pp. 51–70. Development Studies Centre no. 27. Canberra: Australian National University, 1981.

Hardjosudarmo, S. *Kebijaksanaan Transmigrasi dalam rangka Pembangunan Masyarakat Desa di Indonesia* [Transmigration Policy in the Context of Rural Development in Indonesia]. Jakarta: Bhratara, 1965.

Heeren, H. J. *Transmigrasi di Indonesia* [Transmigration in Indonesia]. Yogyakarta: Gadjah Mada University Press, 1979.

Hugo, Graeme. "Changing Patterns and Processes in Population Mobility". In *Indonesia Assessment: Population and Human Resources*, edited by Gavin W. Jones and Terrence H. Hull, pp. 68–100. Canberra: Research School of Pacific and Asian Studies, 1997.

Kahn, Joel, ed. *Southeast Asian Identities: Culture and the Politics of Representation in Indonesia, Malaysia, Singapore, and Thailand.* Singapore: Institute of Southeast Asian Studies, 1999.

Kartodirdjo, Sartono. *Protest Movements in Rural Java: A Study of Agrarian Unrest in the Nineteenth and Early Twentieth Centuries.* Singapore: Oxford University Press, 1973.

King, Victor T. *The Peoples of Borneo.* Oxford, UK: Blackwell, 1975.

Kuntjorojakti, Dorodjatun. "The Political Economy of Development: The Case Study of Indonesia under the New Order Government". Ph.D dissertation, University of California, Berkeley, 1978.

Legge, J. D. *Indonesia.* Englewood Cliff, New York: Prentice Hall, 1964.

Lineton, Jacquiline E. "An Indonesian Society and Its Universe: A Study of the Bugis of South Sulawesi (Celebes) and their Role within a Wider Social and Economic System". Ph.D. dissertation, School of Oriental and African Studies, University of London, 1975.

Mackie, J. A. C. "Integrating and Centrifugal Factors in Indonesia's Politics since 1945". In *Indonesia: The Making of a Nation*, vol. 2 of *Indonesia: Australian Perspectives*, pp. 669–84. Canberra: Research School of Pacific Studies, Australian National University, 1986.

Magdalena, Federico V. "Ethnicity, Identity, and Conflict: The Case of the Philippine Moros". ISEAS Working Papers, Social and Cultural Issues, No. 1. Singapore: Institute of Southeast Asian Studies, 1996.

Magenda, Burhan D. "Ethnicity and State-Building in Indonesia: The Cultural Base of the New Order". In *Ethnicities and Nations: Processes of Interethnic Relations in Latin America, Southeast Asia, and the Pacific*, edited by Remo Guideri, et al. Austin: A Rothko Chapel Book, University of Texas, 1997.

Manning, C. and M. Rumbiak. "Irian Jaya: Economic Change, Migrant Labor and Indigenous Welfare". Paper presented at the Indonesian Regional Economic Surveys Workshop, ANU, Canberra, 2–6 February 1987.

Nitisastro, Widjojo. *Population Trends in Indonesia.* New York: Cornell University Press, 1970.

Paauw, D. S. "From Colonial to Guided Economy", In *Indonesia*, edited by Ruth McVey. Southeast Asian Studies, Yale University. New Haven, Conn: Human Relation Area Files Press, 1963.

Pangestu, Mari and Iwan J. Azis. "Survey of Recent Development". *Bulletin of Indonesian Economic Studies* 30, no. 2 (1994): 3–47.

Pelras, Christian. *The Bugis.* Oxford: Blackwell, 1994.

Peluso, Nancy Lee. "Merchant, manipulation, and minor forest product on the Mahakam: Bugis political economic strategies in pre-colonial Kutai". Paper presented at the International Workshop on Indonesian Studies No. 2, Royal Institute of Linguistics and Anthropology, Leiden, 2–6 November 1987.

Pelzer, K. J. *Pioneer Settlement in the Asiatic Tropics.* New York: Institute of Pacific Relations, 1945.

Penders, C. L. M. "Java's Population Problem during the Colonial Period". *World Review* 8, no. 1 (March 1969): 24–34.

________ . *Indonesia: Selected Documents on Colonialism and Nationalism, 1930–1942.* Brisbane: University of Queensland Press, 1977.

PEP-LIPI. *Otonomi Daerah: Laporan Kegiatan Pengembangan Ilmu-Ilmu Sosial.* [Regional Autonomy: Report on Social Sciences Development Activities]. Jakarta: Puslitbang Ekonomi dan Pembangunan, Lembaga Ilmu Pengetahuan Indonesia (LIPI), 1997.

________ . *Mobilitas Penduduk Perbatasan Di Irian Jaya* [Population Mobility in the Border Area of Irian Jaya]. Jakarta: Puslitbang Kependudukan dan Ketenagakerjaan, LIPI, 1997.

Raharto, Aswatini and Haning Romdiati. "Mobilitas Penduduk dan Pembangunan di KTI" [Population Mobility and Development in Eastern Indonesia]. Paper presented at the LIPI Seminar, Menado, 18–19 February 1998.

Sebastian, Leonard C. "Indonesian National Security and Defense Planning". Ph.D. dissertation, Australian National University, 1996.

Soetrisno, Loekman, et al. *Éast Timor: The Impact of Integration. An Indonesian Socio-Anthropological Study.* Australia: Northcote, 1995.

Soewartoyo. "Migrasi Internal di Timor Timur: Kajian di daerah Tujuan Pasca-Integrasi" [Internal Migration in East Timor: A Study on Destination Area — Post Integration). *Analisis* 26, no. 3 (May–June 1997): 265–75.

Sugardo. "Pengaruh Distribusi Penduduk terhadap Geo-Politik dan Geo-Strategi Indonesia" [The Impact of Population Distribution on Geo-politics and Geostrategy]. Jakarta: Kantor Menteri Negara Kependudukan dan Lingkungan Hidup, 1986.

Sulistyo, Hermawan. "Kapasitas Masyarakat Lokal" [State and Local Society: Study on Regional Autonomy, Local Government, and the Capacity of Local Society]. In *Negara dan Kemiskinan di Daerah* [State and Poverty in the Regions], edited by Didik J. Rachbini dkk. Jakarta: Pustaka Sinar Harapan, 1995.

Tamagola, Thamrin Amal. "Krisis dan Solusi Tragedi Maluku Utara" [Crisis and Solution of the Tragedy in North Maluku]. Paper delivered at a public meeting, organized by LBH, 14 January 2000.

Tanter, Richard. "Intelligence Agencies and Third World Militerization: A Case Study of Indonesia, 1969–1989". Ph.D. dissertation, Department of Politics, Monash University, Australia, 1991.

Taylor, Charles. *Multiculturalism and the "Politics of Recognition".* Princeton: Princeton University Press, 1991.

Thompson, V. *Labor Problems in Southeast Asia.* New Haven: Yale University Press, 1947.

Thee, Kian Wie. "Plantation Agriculture and Export Growth: An Economic History of East Sumatra, 1863–1942". Ph.D. dissertation, University of Wisconsin, 1969.

Tirtosudarmo, Riwanto. *The Political Demography of Development in Indonesia: From Riau to East Timor* (in Indonesian). Jakarta: Pustaka Sinar Harapan, 1996a.

———. "The Politics of Population Mobility in Southeast Asia: The Case of Indonesian Migrant Workers in Malaysia". Paper presented at the conference on Movement of Peoples Within and From the East and Southeast Asian Region: Trends, Causes, Consequences, and Policy Measures, Jakarta, 5–6 June 1996b.

———. "Economic Development, Migration and Ethnic Conflict in Indonesia: A Preliminary Observation". *SOJOURN* 12, no. 2 (October 1997): 293–329.

Titus, M. J. "Inter-regional Migration in Indonesia as a Reflection of Social and Economic Activities". *Tijdschrift voor Economische en Sociale Geografie* 62, no. 4 (1978): 194–204.

Visser, L. "An Interview with Koentjaraningrat". *Current Anthropology* 29, no. 5 (December 1988): 749–53.

Wertheim, W. F. "Sociological Aspects of Inter-Islands in Indonesia". *Population Studies* 7, no. 3 (March 1959): 184–201.

Widjojo, Muridan S. "Pemberdayaan Masyarakat 'Lain-Lain' di Timika Irian Jaya" [Empowering 'The Others' in Timika, Irian Jaya]. *Analisis* 26, no.3 (May–June 1997): 296–320.

PART III

Purchasing Power

∞ 9 ∞

CHANGE IN CONSUMER PRICES
Indonesian Cities, 1997–99

Aris Ananta, Daksini Kartowibowo, and Nurhadi Wiyono

Price Change and Welfare

When price levels increase but incomes do not increase proportionately, purchasing power will decline, as well as welfare. However, when the increase does not occur for all goods and services, but only for a particular group of goods and services, people may not have to suffer. The rising prices may force society to reduce the consumption of those particular goods/services, and substitute with cheaper goods and services. For example, if the increase in the price of meat and fish is higher than the increase in the price of eggs, people may reduce the consumption of meat and fish and increase the consumption of eggs. However, it is unlikely that the increase in the price of rice will be followed by a reduction in the consumption of rice if the people view rice consumption as a must. For these people (the majority of Indonesians may still be categorized in this group) a rapid increase in the price of rice will hurt them severely.

When the prices of many goods/services increase but not at the same rate, the relative prices of those goods/services will change. If the price of one simple lunch in the canteen of the University of Indonesia was Rp1,000 in June 1997 and Rp2,500 in June 2000, the price of that good has risen by 150 per cent. If the price of the Kijang (a car) was 60 million rupiah in June 1997 and 120 million rupiah in June 2000, the price of the Kijang has risen by only 100 per cent. Therefore, the price of the simple food in the University of Indonesia has risen faster than the price of the Kijang. The relative price has changed. To buy one Kijang in June 1997 people had to sacrifice 60 thousand simple lunches in the University of Indonesia; in June 2000 people had to sacrifice only 48 thousand simple lunches. In other words, the Kijang had become cheaper relative to the simple lunch, or that simple lunch had become relatively more expensive compared with the Kijang.

The above example may illustrate that those whose budget for a simple lunch is relatively large in their overall budget may suffer more than those whose simple lunch does not comprise a big portion of their overall budget. An administrative staff in a state university who did not think of buying a Kijang because of their budget limitations may have experienced a relatively larger drop in welfare, compared with those who had considered the Kijang as a relatively more important item in their budget.

This chapter aims to examine the change in relative prices from January 1997, before the crisis started, to December 1999, in an attempt to know whether there are any patterns of changes in relative consumer prices during the three years in twenty-six provincial capital cities and one at the national level.

This analysis aims to contribute to a better understanding of the welfare of consumers during the period January 1997 to December 1999, by examining the trend in the CPI (consumer price index) at the national and provincial capital city level, for various kinds of commodities. It should be cautioned from the outset that CPI has many limitations and that the analysis contributes to only one of the many aspects of consumer welfare during the crisis. The analysis is limited to the big cities because of the scarcity of data although as mentioned in Chapter 1 of this volume, the crisis is more an urban phenomenon.

The chapter starts with some illustrations on the situation in Indonesia during the crisis, especially relating to how the people coped with the crisis. The concept, limitation, and strength of a CPI analysis are elaborated in the third section, followed by the empirical results and the conclusion.

Some Ways of Coping with the Crisis

Indonesia is a big and diverse country. It is becoming clearer that it is difficult to talk about "Indonesia". The autonomization of the government and its emerging local authorities necessitates separate analyses for different regions. So does the discussion on welfare during 1997–99.

Sumarto, Wetterberg, and Prichet (1999) have attempted to examine which province (urban and rural) had been the worst and which one had been the least affected by the crisis in 1998. They measured five aspects: food security, coping strategy, employment, education, and health as well as the overall impact which combines the five aspects.

Table 9.1 presents the ranking of the severity of the crisis in each province, with number 1 as the most severely affected region and

Table 9.1
Comparison of Sumarto et al. and CPI: Food Security by Province, 1998.

No.	*Sumarto et al.*	*CPI*
1	Bengkulu	DKI Jakarta
2	Maluku	East Kalimantan
3	Central Sulawesi	Lampung
4	South Sulawesi	Central Kalimantan
5	Central Kalimantan	East Java
6	Riau	East Nusa Tenggara
7	Jambi	DI Yogyakarta
8	North Sulawesi	West Kalimantan
9	Bali	North Sulawesi
10	West Sumatra	Bali
11	Southeast Sulawesi	South Sulawesi
12	DKI Jakarta	West Java
13	North Sumatra	South Kalimantan
14	South Sulawesi	Jambi
15	Lampung	Riau
16	West Java	Bengkulu
17	Central Java	DI Aceh
18	South Kalimantan	Central Java
19	East Java	South Sumatra
20	West Kalimantan	Southeast Sulawesi
21	East Kalimantan	West Sumatra
22	DI Aceh	North Sumatra
23	DI Yogyakarta	West Nusa Tenggara
24	West Nusa Tenggara	Maluku
25	East Nusa Tenggara	Central Sulawesi

Note: Papua and East Timor are excluded.
No. 1 is the best and no. 25 is the worst in the ranking.

number 51 as the least severely affected region. They found a lack of association between pre-crisis poverty and the magnitude of the impact of the crisis.

Conversations with people in Banyumas, Central Java, in early 2000 revealed interesting observations. People in the rice field (*sawah*) area said that rice was the most important commodity for them. They also had plenty of vegetables. If they did not have any vegetables, they could simply ask their neighbours. They said that during the crisis they did not really have any problem, because the availability of rice was not a problem for them.

The hardest time for them was the *lebaran*, marked with a feast after completing a one-month fasting. At the 1998 and 1999 *lebaran* they could not buy new clothes, especially in 1998 which was the hardest time. (It is customary to buy new clothes during *lebaran*). The *lebaran* in 2000 was much better than the two previous ones. They also mentioned that books were expensive, but their burden was reduced because of the Social Safety Net programme in education.[1]

The most important thing for people working in the forest area was the availability of rice. However, they felt that rice was the most expensive need they had. Thus, they were most affected when the price of rice rose to Rp3000 per kg. Fortunately, they were used to being poor, and hence, the crisis did not really shock them.

As in the forest and rice field areas, people in the urban areas also regarded rice as the most important need in their lives. They were afraid of any increases in the price of rice. When prices rose, they would always make sure that they could afford to buy rice. However, the poor could not buy as much rice as the rich. They said that the price of rice then declined to Rp2300, from Rp3000, which was good for them. They could not buy new clothes in the 1999 *lebaran*, but they were able to buy new clothes in the 2000 *lebaran*.

With data collected in several areas in Indonesia in mid-1998, Ananta et al. (1999) showed how people had adjusted their consumption patterns to maintain their welfare level. The welfare seemed to have declined and they changed their consumption pattern to reduce the decline in their welfare. They could satisfy their basic needs (especially rice) by reducing secondary goods consumption, or by borrowing.

They also found that the respondents did not give much attention to education. Absence or dropping out from school was tolerated because the opportunity cost of going to school might be too high. The children could earn money if they did not go to school. Education was a low priority in their consumption pattern.

On the other hand, they valued health highly. They maintained their health expenditure although medical costs had been rising rapidly. (This was before the Social Safety Net programme which started in the second half of 1998.) For example, although the price of contraceptives increased, they still tried to practise contraception. Interestingly, they also maintained the level of consumption for transportation. On the other hand, demand for recreation declined.

There was a change in the buying habit. As an illustration, they bought rice more frequently but smaller amounts at each purchase. This seemed to be an attempt to distribute their smaller purchasing power. They also bought sugar at shorter intervals. Consumers in Java bought sugar at longer intervals, which may indicate that households in Java had better purchasing power. The respondents outside Java reduced their consumption of eggs greatly.

As expected, households also reduced the consumption of meat, fish, eggs and the like, but they maintained the consumption of vegetables and processed soybean, such as *tahu* and *tempe*. Interestingly, the consumption of cigarrettes did not change.

They also reported a decline in the consumption of durable goods or assets. Yet, a different pattern was found in Java compared with non-Java. Households in Java preferred land to cattle and cars; households outside Java preferred cattle to cars and land.

An office worker in Jakarta, with a *sarjana* degree (equivalent to a Bachelor's degree), reported in 2000 that the crisis had not caused him to suffer from hunger, but it had reduced the fulfilment of his higher needs. He said that he used to buy *Kompas* daily before the crisis to keep himself abreast with current developments in Indonesia. It cost only 500 rupiah. The price then rose rapidly to 1,500 rupiah, an increase of 200 per cent, so he stopped buying it. He also used to buy *TEMPO*, one of the leading weekly news magazines in Indonesia, but during the crisis he stopped buying it because the price rose from 5,000 rupiah to 10,000 rupiah — an increase of 100 per cent.

He also changed his pattern of consumption. He used to spend only about 2,500 rupiah for his simple lunch (rice, vegetable, chicken or fish, and *tempe*), but during the crisis he had to spend about 4,500 rupiah for the same menu. On average, he might have suffered an increase in the price of his lunch by almost 100 per cent. He therefore changed his "lunch pattern"; he brought his own lunch from home. However, he was still fortunate. He had a small baby, but his wife breastfed the baby. He knew that his neighbour suffered much because the wife did not breastfeed their baby.

Another office worker mentioned that he used to budget 50,000 rupiah a month to buy books. With that money, he could buy two or three books. Unfortunately, during the crisis, the same amount of money could buy only one book. He used to go for "fitness" exercise and paid 100,000 rupiah a month, but he stopped this activity.

Kuntanegara (1998) found that people in Srihardjo, a village in Yogyakarta, tried to cut down their expenditure, especially on non-food items during the crisis. They spent more on food, which became a major part of their total expenditure. They even tried to reduce the consumption of rice and substitute it with *gaplek/tiwul*, or combine rice with *gaplek/tiwul*. They reduced the *lauk-pauk* (other food besides rice). They did not eat meat but limited their consumption to vegetables, even without *tempe* or *tahu*. *Tempe* and *tahu* had become luxury food items because of the imported soybean. They ate less fried food, to save on oil. They did not buy new clothes. They also cut down expenditures on health and education.[2]

Consumer Price Index

Concept

"The CPI (Consumer Price Index) is designed and constructed as a measure of the changes in prices of a fixed basket of goods and services that a designated group of consumers purchased during some past period" (Cagan and Moore 1981). OECD (1994) mentions that the scope of the CPI includes goods and services for household consumption. It excludes the purchase of dwelling, life insurance, social security contribution, and direct taxes. Change in consumer preference is not included. Indeed, the purpose of the CPI is purely to measure the change in the price of goods and services which supposedly represent the consumption habits of households.

The CPI includes the consumption of imported goods as well as domestically produced goods and services — that is, it includes all goods and services consumed by domestic consumers.

The CPI has several shortcomings in measuring the escalation of income needed to maintain a constant standard of living. First, it only computes consumption expenditure. It excludes government services to the public. Secondly, it does not consider the substitution of goods and services. It assumes a fixed basket of goods and services. Indeed, consumers often, as mentioned above, substitute the goods and services to maintain their standard. Thirdly, it does not allow for quality change, especially in health services.

That is why the CPI is not examined as a whole here, but as part of groups of goods and services, and some particular goods and services, in order to know the change in the relative prices of the respective groups and particular goods and services.

The CPI is conceptually different from the cost of living (COL) index. COL includes items that are not in the CPI — for example, government expenditures. Security is another example of a service that is not included in the CPI, but it should be part of the COL. Singapore has a relatively low crime rate, especially compared with Jakarta. The relatively higher rate of crime in Jakarta should contribute to a higher COL. The relatively greener and cleaner air and water in Singapore would make the COL in Singapore lower than in Jakarta, especially with regard to the cost of being healthy.

Bresnahan and Gordon (1997) have mentioned that the contribution of new goods to consumer welfare cannot be separated from the measurement of the true COL index. The standard definition of a COL index is the ratio of the minimum expenditure required to have the same level of welfare in two different periods of time. If the CPI is linked meaningfully to consumer welfare, then the CPI should approximate the COL. However, it has been difficult to translate the theoretical concept of COL into empirical CPI. What does "the same level of well-being" mean when products are replaced by new versions embodying different quality attributes? Or what does "the same level of well-being" mean when entirely new products are introduced that were unavailable in the first time period?

The Sears Catalogue Experiment

Bresnahan and Gordon (1997) have conducted a "Sears Catalogue Experiment" (Sears, Roebuck & Co is a famous department store in USA), with the Sears Catalogues of 1993 and 1893 — a century apart. People were asked to imagine living a century ago, in 1893, by looking at the catalogue of the Sears Department Store in 1893. Things were extraordinarily cheaper in 1893 than in 1993. Yet, with the money people had in 1993, would they prefer to return to 1893 to shop in the Sears of that time?

People may spend the first two or three hundreds dollars at 1893 Sears, to buy steak at $0.50 per pound, on four-course restaurant meals at $1.29 a piece, or on men's work pants at $2.29 a pair. Yet, they would not spend all their income in the 1893 Sears. The rest of the money would be spent on video-cassettes, compact-disc players, and other wonders of life which were not present in the 1893 Sears.

The 1993 Sears sold much more expensive goods than the 1893 Sears, but the 1993 Sears also sold many "modern wonders" that did not exist in 1893. These "modern wonders" had added to the welfare of the society. Hence, change in consumer prices may not necessarily reflect change in the cost of living, and hence the welfare, of the society.

Complementarities of consumption on goods and services may also lower the cost of living. The relatively much lower crime rate in Singapore, compared with Jakarta, tends to lower the cost of feeling secure to live and work in Singapore. People can walk or move around in Singapore without feeling afraid of being robbed or stolen. Thus, seen from this angle, people in Singapore have a lower cost of living than people in Jakarta. The relatively cheap telephone cost in the United States, compared with that in Indonesia, also tends to make the cost of many aspects of life using the telephone service in the United States much cheaper than in Indonesia. The existence of many, and good, facilities such as public, free libraries in the United States has lowered the cost of education for the American people more than in Indonesia.

Unfortunately, this phenomenon is not captured by the consumer price index. Thus, this weakness should be borne in mind when interpreting changes in CPI.

Why CPI?

The CPI certainly has many limitations. Over time, many new goods and services are introduced and hence it is difficult to compare the welfare of the people. However, in this chapter, the time horizon taken is only three years, January 1997 until December 1999. Yet, there is still some risk of not capturing the consumption of new goods and services.

With all these limitations, the purpose of the chapter is simply to examine the relative change of prices of some groups of commodities. It certainly excludes new commodities. The purpose of the analysis is not to examine the change in welfare but simply attempts to show what happened to the relative prices of several goods during the three-year period. From this examination, inference can be made on which groups suffered relatively more. The data are based on Statistics Indonesia (1998, 1999, and 2000) and the study is limited to the provincial capital city. It therefore may not reflect the situation in the lower administrative areas, and the rural areas. To examine the relative change of prices each year, the graphs are drawn with a CPI equal to 100 in January each year.

Empirical Results

Nine Selected Cities

It is not easy to make detailed comparisons of the twenty-six capital cities, especially when the comparison is across the years (1997, 1998, and 1999). Hence, for convenience (though some "representativeness" may be sacrificed) the cities are categorized into four groups, according to whether in 1998 the increase in the price of food was less than 100 per cent (group 1), between 100 per cent and 120 per cent (group 2), between 120 per cent and 140 per cent (group 3), and between 140 per cent and 160 per cent (group 4). For representation in the figure, certain cities are further selected from each group. The cities are: Jakarta from group 1, Makassar from group 2, Palembang from group 3, and Ambon from group 4.

The 1997 Pattern

There were no big changes or increases in price during 1997 although the crisis started in July that year, relative to the changes in 1998. Compared with January 1997, with the exception of Manado and Palembang, the prices in December 1997 increased by less than 20 per cent.

In Pontianak, the price of clothing had risen the most, with more than 20 per cent in December 1997 compared with January 1997. Clothing was relatively more expensive than food and even other groups of commodities in December 1997, relative to January 1997.

Food experienced the highest increase in price, while clothing had the smallest increase although the difference between food and the non-food group was not large. In other words, compared with January 1997, food was relatively more expensive in December 1997 *vis-á-vis* other groups of commodities. The differences in price rises began to widen in October or November 1997.

An exception was found in Samarinda, Padang, and Makassar. In these two cities, the relative price of food tended to converge with those of other groups of commodities. Furthermore, Makassar showed an interesting pattern. The price of food declined during the whole of 1997 except at the end of the year.

In general, by the end of 1997, the impact of the crisis on increase in prices was not great although people might have felt the creeping prices, especially that of food. Those whose budgets were mostly spent on food might have suffered the most.

The 1998 Pattern

The 1998 pattern was strikingly different from that of 1997. Prices rose rapidly. Assuming that food was the most important commodity for the people, we classified the pattern of increase in the price of food into four general groups. The first group included those places where prices rose less than 100 per cent, or almost doubled in December 1998 compared with January 1998; the second, less than 120 per cent; the third, less than 140 per cent, and the fourth, less than 160 per cent.

The first group (<100 per cent) included: Lampung, Jakarta, Surabaya, Yogya, Samarinda, Pontianak, Palangkaraya, Kupang, and Jayapura. The increase in the price of prepared food was lower than that of other foods in Lampung, Jakarta, Yogya, and Surabaya, but the increase was higher for other foods in the rest of the cities. The "Java" cities seemed to show a pattern of higher increase in prepared foods than in other foods. In general, the increase in food or prepared food was often the highest. However, the increase in the price of clothing was the highest in Jakarta, which was followed by prepared food and other food. In Lampung, Kupang, and Jayapura, the increase in health costs was the second highest after prepared food or other food.

The second group (<120 per cent) included: Manado, Makassar, Denpasar, Bandung, Banjarmasin, Aceh, Pekanbaru, Bengkulu, and Jambi. The general pattern was that the price of food had risen the most, followed by prepared food. Bandung, which is in Java, was no exception. In Denpasar, the second highest increase was shown by health costs.

The third group (<140 per cent) consisted of Semarang, Mataram, Kendari, Palembang, Padang, and Medan. Here, the price of food rose the most. However, there are some different patterns. In Medan and Mataram, the increase in the cost of health was the second highest after the price of food. Prepared food ranked second in Palembang, Bengkulu, and Padang, but clothing was second in Kendari and Semarang.

Ambon and Palu belonged to the last group, with an increase of almost 160 per cent in the price of food in December 1998, compared with January 1998. The change in the relative price of food compared with others was most striking in Ambon, where other prices rose by at most only 60 per cent. Hence, in December 1998, compared with January 1998, the price of food in Ambon was relatively more expensive than other commodities. In Palu, the price of prepared food rose almost 100 per cent, more than in Ambon.

It is interesting to observe that in the cities where the price of food had more than doubled (that is, had increased by more than 100 per cent), the increase was always the highest compared with other commodities.

From each group, some cities have been selected for discussion on the items of food consumed. In the first group, Jakarta, Palangkaraya, and Kupang have been selected. In the second group are Denpasar and Makassar. In the third group, Medan, Palembang, and Semarang have been chosen, and in the fourth group, Ambon. This is to represent the heterogeneity of the groups.

In the chosen cities, the increase in rice was always relatively high, usually more than double. In Palembang, it rose by almost 170 per cent in September 1998, although it later declined to a little more than 150 per cent by the end of 1998. The price of meat rose by more than 230 per cent in November 1998, and dried fish by almost 230 per cent in August 1998.

In Ambon, the increase in the price of rice was also high, at about 100 per cent. However, the prices of other foods rose much more. The price of fresh fish rose by almost 330 per cent in October 1998, although it later declined to about 230 per cent in December 1998.

The price of vegetables also rose much. Jakarta and Kupang were the only chosen cities with increases of less than 100 per cent. The price of vegetables only rose by almost 60 per cent in Jakarta and Kupang. However, in other cities the increase was more than double. It even rose by almost 170 per cent in Medan in September 1998.

In Jakarta and Kupang, initially the price of vegetables rose more than that of rice; but later in 1998, the rise in the price of rice was larger than that of vegetables. In some cities such as Semarang, Ambon, and Denpasar, by the end of 1998, the price of vegetables and fruits had risen more than the price of rice; in other cities, the increase in the price of rice was larger than the increase in the price of vegetables. In Palangkaraya, the price of vegetables rose more than the price of rice, but the increase in the price of fruit was less than the increase in the price of rice.

In other words, in some cities the price of vegetables and fruit had become relatively more expensive than that of rice. In these cities, the consumers would tend to reduce the consumption of vegetables and fruits if they felt that these were not so important for their diet. For those who considered vegetables and fruits very important, including the vegetarians, in cities such as Semarang their welfare might have suffered more than those who did not put a high priority on vegetables and fruit. In cities such as Jakarta, the increase in the price of vegetables and fruit was also lower than that of other foods. The "fruit and vegetable eaters" might have fared better because the increase in the prices of these commodities were relatively lower.

In terms of protein, we compared the increase in the prices of meat, fresh fish, dried fish, egg, and nuts. Here we could not find a strong pattern of price increases among the selected nine cities. In seven out of the nine cities, the increase in the price of nuts was the highest, except Jakarta which was the second highest, and Medan which was the third highest. The rise was the least only in Makassar, next to which was Ambon. In other words, the "non-meat and egg eaters" might have suffered more because they might have reduced the consumption of nuts, including *tempe* and *tahu*.

The increase in the price of dried fish was the highest in Jakarta, Makassar, and Medan, while the increase in the price of fresh fish was the highest in Semarang and Ambon. Interestingly, the increase in the price of meat was never the highest — in Semarang, the increase in the price of meat was almost the same as that of fresh fish. In all selected cities, the increase in the price of egg was relatively moderate, not the lowest nor the highest.

In Yogyakarta (outside the nine selected cities), the increase in the price of nuts was very high, about 242 per cent in December 1998 compared with that in January 1998. It was only lower than the increase in the price of oil (245 per cent). Meanwhile, the increase in the prices of "egg and milk" was only 152 per cent; and those of meat, only 118 per cent; of fresh fish, 144 per cent; and of dried fish, 160 per cent. It is no wonder that Kuntanegara (1998) found that the society in Srihardjo limited their consumption to vegetables and fruits and reduced or stopped the consumption of meat, fish, eggs, and even *tempe* and *tahu*.[3]

In general, however, the increase in the price of rice did not seem to be the highest compared with other food items. Usually, it ranked second and third highest.

In one city, Medan (group 3), the cost of health-care more than doubled. Six cities — Mataram and Kendari in group 3, Denpasar in group 2, and Lampung, Surabaya, and Kupang in group 1 — experienced an increase of 80 per cent to 100 per cent. The remaining cities experienced an increase of less than 80 per cent or even 60 per cent. The relatively low increase in the cost of health-care may reflect the impact of the Social Safety Net programme in the health sector.

Health can be classified into two categories: health services and drugs; and physical treatment and cosmetics. The data do not reject the thesis that the Social Safety Net programme for health-care may have prevented the price of health services and drugs from soaring dramatically. The price of health services and drugs rose generally by 40 per cent, but to almost 60 per cent in Medan. However, the cost of physical treatment and cosmetics rose to almost 140 per cent. Denpasar was an exception where both prices rose at almost the same rate of about 100 per cent.

The price of education increased even less, never more than 60 per cent. There were only eight cities with an increase close to 60 per cent: Yogyakarta in group 1; Aceh, Bengkulu, Banjarmasin, and Manado in group 2; Palembang, Mataram, and Kendari in group 3. The rest experienced increases of no more than 40 per cent. Jambi (group 2), Padang (group 3), and Palu (group 4) experienced increases of less than 20 per cent.

The price of education was even lower when "education" was broken down into "education", "educational equipment", and "recreation and sport". The price of education experienced almost no change. The increase was at most 20 per cent. This result does not reject the hypothesis that the Social Safety Net programme for education prevented the cost of education from rising drastically. Yet, the cost of educational equipment rose much more. In Jakarta, it rose by about 120 per cent; and in Semarang, almost 140 per cent. In other cities, the increase was about 40 per cent to 60 per cent. The increase in the cost of recreation and sport was sometimes lower, and sometimes higher, compared with the increase in the price of educational equipment.

From this information, the price of human capital (as seen from the perspective of education and health only) does not seem to have increased as much as that of food. Unfortunately, the price of obtaining freedom from fear — another element in human capital — is not measured here as data are not available.

It is interesting to compare the results of the 1998 pattern with the study by Sumarto et al (1999), which ranked provinces according to indexes of the impact of the crisis. Because the analysis here is limited to the provincial capital cities, the results here can only be compared with those for the urban areas in the study by Sumarto et al. It should also be pointed out that our analysis is limited to the provincial capital cities, not the whole urban area. Furthermore, change in prices is only one, though important, element, in the food security of the people.

In Table 9.1 we compare the index of food security in the study by Sumarto et al. with our ranking of CPI for food. Our result is almost the opposite of that of Sumarto et al. East Nusa Tenggara is the worst case in Sumarto et al., but it is ranked sixth in terms of CPI. Bengkulu is the best case in Sumarto et al., but ranked sixteenth in terms of CPI. Maluku is second in Sumarto et al., but number twenty-four in terms of CPI. In some provinces, however, the ranking is similar. West Nusa Tenggara, for instance, is number twenty-four in Sumarto et al. and number twenty-three in CPI; but North Sulawesi is number eight in Sumarto et al. and number nine in CPI.

From this comparison, we do not say that the ranking according to the CPI contradicts with the results of Sumarto et al.; the two studies may have seen the same problem from different angles.

We also compare their index of education with our analysis of education in the CPI. See Table 9.2. As with food, the results seem to show opposite rankings, with Maluku, which is the best according to Sumarto et al., as number eleven in the CPI analysis; but West Kalimantan, which is the worst according to Sumarto et al., is number ten in the CPI analysis. Bengkulu, which is the second best according to Sumarto et al., is number twenty-three in the CPI analysis.

Table 9.2
Comparison of Sumarto et al. and CPI: Education by Province, 1998.

No.	*Sumarto et al.*	*CPI*
1	Maluku	West Sumatra
2	Bengkulu	East Nusa Tenggara
3	Bali	North Sumatra
4	East Kalimantan	Central Sulawesi
5	West Nusa Tenggara	DKI Jakarta
6	South Sulawesi	Bali
7	Southeast Sulawesi	Jambi
8	Central Kalimantan	West Java
9	Central Sulawesi	Central Java
10	Lampung	West Kalimantan
11	DI Yogyakarta	Maluku
12	South Kalimantan	East Kalimantan
13	North Sulawesi	Central Kalimantan
14	East Java	South Sulawesi
15	South Sumatra	Riau
16	Jambi	Lampung
17	Central Java	East Java
18	West Sumatra	DI Aceh
19	West Java	West Nusa Tenggara
20	DKI Jakarta	North Sulawesi
21	Riau	South Sumatra
22	DI Aceh	Southeast Sulawesi
23	North Sumatra	Bengkulu
24	East Nusa Tenggara	DI Yogyakarta
25	West Kalimantan	South Kalimantan

Note: Papua and East Timor are excluded.
No. 1 is the best and no. 25 is the worst in the ranking.

A slightly different result is shown in Table 9.3, a comparison in the area of health. Central Kalimantan is ranked first in the study by Sumarto et al., but number twelve in the CPI analysis; Yogyakarta is the worst in Sumarto et al., but number seventeen in the CPI analysis. North Sumatra is number seventeen in Sumarto et al. but the worst in CPI. Bali is number twenty-four in Sumarto et al. and number twenty-three in CPI; West Nusa Tenggara is number twenty in Sumarto et al., and number nineteen in CPI. However, West Kalimantan is number twenty-three in Sumarto et al., but number two in CPI; East Nusa Tenggara is number four in Sumarto et al., but number twenty in CPI. The rankings are still

Table 9.3
Comparison of Sumarto et al. and CPI: Health by Province, 1998

No.	*Sumarto et al.*	*CPI*
1	Central Kalimantan	West Kalimantan
2	South Kalimantan	Bengkulu
3	South Sumatra	Riau
4	East Nusa Tenggara	South Kalimantan
5	West Sumatra	Jambi
6	Bengkulu	East Kalimantan
7	Maluku	South Sulawesi
8	Central Java	South Sumatra
9	South Sulawesi	Central Java
10	DI Aceh	Maluku
11	Central Sulawesi	West Java
12	DKI Jakarta	Central Kalimantan
13	North Sulawesi	Central Sulawesi
14	Riau	West Sumatra
15	East Java	DI Aceh
16	West Java	North Sulawesi
17	North Sumatra	DI Yogyakarta
18	East Kalimantan	DKI Jakarta
19	Southeast Sulawesi	West Nusa Tenggara
20	West Nusa Tenggara	East Nusa Tenggara
21	Jambi	Southeast Sulawesi
22	Lampung	East Java
23	West Kalimantan	Bali
24	Bali	Lampung
25	DI Yogyakarta	North Sumatra

Note: Papua and East Timor are excluded.
No. 1 is the best and no. 25 is the worst in the ranking.

the opposite, but they are not as different as in the case of food and education.

Again, the comparison is not meant to show "which one" is right or wrong. The survey done by Sumarto et al. is limited in sample and may not be "representative" of the population. On the other hand, neither is the CPI ranking meant to represent the welfare of society. The CPI analysis has many limitations, and the presentation represents only one view of consumer welfare — prices. The CPI analysis has not captured the income side of consumer welfare, or even the substitution effect of consumer behaviour. In other words, the analyses of Sumarto et al. and the CPI may not be comparable, but they both provide more information to better understand the socio-economic situation during the Indonesian crisis.

The 1999 Pattern

Prices of goods were relatively stable in 1999. The increase in prices ranged from 35 per cent to minus 20 per cent. They were much lower increases compared with those in 1998, with the maximum increase being 160 per cent. There was no decline in prices. Indeed, the national economy underwent deflation during March to September 1999. Inflation started again at the end of 1999, especially in December. The regional economies seemed to follow approximately similar patterns.

Though deflation occurred in the second half of 1999, prices in December 1999 were still higher than those in January 1998. Nationally, the prices in December 1999 were 68.95 per cent higher than in January 1998, just a little higher than the increase of 65.54 per cent in December 1998 compared with January 1998. The price of food in December 1999 was 168 per cent (Ambon) higher than in January 1998; and 71 per cent (Jakarta) higher in December 1999 than in January 1998. The increase in the price of prepared food ranged from 70 per cent (South Kalimantan) to 127 per cent (Aceh). The cost of education rose within a range of 48 per cent (Jambi) to 112 per cent (Lampung and Bali), and from 27 per cent (West Sumatra and Central Kalimantan) to 70 per cent (Yogyakarta).

The highest increase in prices was seen in August 1999 in Ambon, where the price of food had increased by 35 per cent compared with the price in January 1999. This is a striking contrast to the increase of almost 160 per cent for the whole of 1998. The price of food declined after August 1999 in Ambon. By the end of 1999, the increase in the price of food in Ambon was less than 5 per cent, compared with the price in January 1999. The price was even lower in November than in January 1999. Although the price of food had increased, it was not as much as that in 1998.

Some cities even experienced a decline in the price of food compared with that in January 1999, with an initial increase of no more than 5 per cent. Jayapura, for example, experienced a decline in the price of food, prepared food, and education by the end of 1999, compared with January 1999. Kendari and Makassar experienced a 10 per cent decline in the price of food in the second half of 1999, compared with January 1999. Pontianak even experienced an almost 20 per cent decline in the price of food in October 1999, compared with January 1999. Kupang was an exception. The price of food in Kupang increased by almost 10 per cent in September–October 1999, compared with January 1999.

Is the deflation good or bad? Some say that it is bad because deflation indicates a smaller demand for goods and services in the economy, and hence the economy will slow down. Others say that deflation is good because it reduces the pain of the consumers, as they have higher purchasing power. Thus, from the welfare point of view, deflation or the relatively much slower increase in prices might have at least maintained the welfare of the people during 1999, though they would still be worse off than in January 1998, or July 1997. Some groups of people who might have gained more income might have enjoyed better prosperity in 1999.

Compared with January 1998, the price of food was relatively more expensive than prepared food (the price of food increased more) in North Sumatra, West Sumatra, Riau, Jambi, South Sumatra, West Java, Central Java, Bali, West Nusa Tenggara, East Nusa Tenggara, South Kalimantan, Central Sulawesi, and Maluku. In these provinces, those who relied more on food and less on prepared food might have suffered more. People who were "on the go" might have been relatively better off than those who mostly consumed food at home.

In general, the increase in the cost of health and education was small. This may mean that during the crisis, the price of acquiring human capital (in terms of education and health only) was relatively cheaper than acquiring food and prepared food. We cannot say, however, whether the relatively cheap way of acquiring human capital was good or bad for the society. The answer may depend on which one — food and prepared food on one hand and human capital on the other hand — is more important for the society. For the relatively better off people, human capital might be more important because they could still afford the food. Thus, for these people, the development in 1998–99 had made them relatively better off compared with the poorer people who still relied mostly on food and prepared food.

Conclusion

It seems that finding patterns or regularities in the changes of CPI in the twenty-five provincial capital cities during 1997–99 was difficult. Probably, they will never exist. At least, it appears from the discussion that the situation in Indonesia has been heterogenous. It is almost impossible to say, for example, that those who consumed mostly rice had suffered relatively more than those who consumed mostly "meat, fish, egg", or those who consumed more "nuts, vegetables, and fruits". The pattern varied from city to city.

The ranking according to the CPI analysis also did not match with the ranking from other analyses, in particular that of the World Bank. However, because of the limitations in both approaches, the two analyses may not be compared; instead, they should be seen as contributing to a better understanding of the socio-economic situation during the crisis from two different perspectives.

The general conclusion might be that which is consistent with the traditional macroeconomic indicators: that 1998 was the worst year of the crisis in Indonesia, while 1999 might have been a time to "breathe", or to try to catch up with what they had lost previously. The price of human capital (measured by education and health only) had not risen as much as the increase in the prices of food and prepared food. Therefore, people who still considered food and prepared food as more important elements in their budget might have suffered more than those who had considered human capital as a more important element in their budget.

Finally, it should be noted that the discussion does not really reveal the "truth" of the relative cost of human capital and food. First, the discussion on human capital only included education and health, and excluded freedom from fear and labour mobility. Secondly, even the discussion on health and education was limited because many other aspects were not measured. For example, the low-income people in Jakarta needed much higher expenditure to enjoy a better quality of air compared with the low-income people in Singapore. The cost of enjoying good quality air was not included in the analysis. Therefore, the analysis might not show that the price of human capital had risen relatively slowly compared with the increase in the price of food.

Notes

1. For more discussions on the Social Safety Net programme, refer to Chapters 10 and 11 of this volume.

2. Pande Made Kuntanegara does not mention when the survey was conducted. We guess, however, that the survey was conducted in 1998.
3. The comparison may not be valid, because our CPI analysis was based on urban, provincial cities, while that of Pande Made Kuntanegara was done for one of the villages in Yogyakarta special district.

References

Ananta, Aris, Martin Panggabean, Bambang Brodjonegoro, and Benedictus R. Mahi. "Coping with the Economic Crisis. Analysis based on the Data Generated by the On-the-Ground Monitoring Survey". Report to the UNDP, BPS, and BAPPENAS. Jakarta, 1999.

Abdullah, Irwan, et al. "Dampak Krisis Ekonomi terhadap Kehidupan Masyarakat Kecamatan Jatinom [skala usaha dan rumah tangga]". Yogyakarta: Pusat Penelitian Kependudukan Universitas Gadjah Mada, 1998.

Bresnahan, Timothy F., and Robert J. Gordon. "Introduction". In *The Economics of New Goods*, edited by Timothy F. Bresnahan and Robert J. Gordon. Chicago, USA: The University of Chicago Press, 1997.

Cagan, Phillip, and Geoffrey H. Moore. *The Consumer Price Index. Issues and Alternatives*. Washington, D.C.: American Institute for Public Policy Research, 1981.

Liegey, Paul R. Jr. "Adjusting Apparel Indexes in the Consumer Price Index for Quality Differences". *Price Measurements and Their Uses*, edited by Murray F. Foss, Marilyn E. Manser, and Allan H. Young, pp. 209–226. Chicago: The University of Chicago Press, 1993.

Kutanegara, Pande Made. "Dinamika Kesejahteraan: Sriharjo dalam Masa Krisis". Paper presented at the seminar on "Social Security and Social Policy". Yogyakarta: Pusat Penelitian Kependudukan Universitas Gadjah Mada, 28–29 November 1998.

OECD. *Sources and Methods. Consumer Price Indices*. Paris: OECD, 1994.

Statistics Indonesia. *Consumer Price Indices in Provincial Capital Cities in Indonesia (April 1988–March 1989 = 100) 1997*. Jakarta: Statistics Indonesia, 1998.

———. *Consumer Price Indices in Provincial Capital Cities in Indonesia (1996 = 100) 1998*. Jakarta: Statistics Indonesia, 1999.

———. *Consumer Price Indices in 44 Cities in Indonesia (1996 = 100) 1999*. Jakarta: Statistics Indonesia, 2000.

Sudarmo Sumarto, Anna Wetterberg, and Lant Pritchett. "The Social Impact of the Crisis in Indonesia: Results from a Nationwide Kecamatan Survey". www.worldbank.org, 1999.

10

SOCIAL SAFETY NET PROGRAMMES IN INDONESIA
Some Efforts to Survive

SRI HARIJATI HATMADJI
AND
TIRTA NUGRAHA MURSITAMA

Introduction

To overcome the impact of the crisis, the Government of Indonesia (GOI) has implemented a number of policies under the Social Safety Net (SSN) programmes. Managing a large and heterogeneous country in the midst of far-reaching political and economic transition, the GOI has stressed the importance of reaching as much of the affected population as possible.[1]

As mentioned in the presidential speech in front of the DPR (House of Representatives) on 15 August 1998, the Social Safety Net programmes are aimed at integrating special development programmes to overcome the impact of the crisis (crash programmes), including those dealing with disparity, poverty, and backwardness.

The SSN programmes were the result of negotiations in early 1998 between the GOI and the World Bank, representing donor countries. A rescue package for the GOI was recommended as part of the implementation of the Letter of Intent from the International Monetary Fund (IMF). In addition to helping people severely affected by the crisis, these programmes were identified as an effort to secure long-term development processes in which donor countries would be involved for years, mainly through providing loans. The foreign stake in the form of investments and loans was too much to forgo.

With loans from the World Bank, the IMF, the Japan Bank for International Co-operation (JBIC), the Asian Development Bank (ADB), the United Nations, USAID and AusAid, the SSN programmes started in fiscal year 1998/99. These programmes have been implemented up to the third phase, to deal with the worst impact of the economic crisis. This third phase ended in fiscal year 2000. To reduce poverty in the mid to long term, the GOI has revised its policies by, for example, transferring some SSN programmes to the regular programmes in fiscal year 2001.

This chapter discusses the implementation of the programmes and the extent to which they have reached the targetted population in coping with the crisis. The discussions focus on the specific programmes of the SSN which have been implemented in fiscal year 1998/99 and 1999/2000. They are the JPS BK (Jaringan Pengaman Sosial-Bidang Kesehatan — SSN for health), JPS BP (Jaringan Pengaman Sosial-Bidang Pendidikan — SSN for education), OPK (Operasi Pasar Khusus — Special Market Operation for rice), and PDM-DKE (Pemberdayaan Daerah dalam Mengatasi Dampak Krisis Ekonomi — Regional empowerment for overcoming the impact of the economic crisis). Yet, up to May 2000 some SSN programmes had not been implemented.[2]

Objectives of the SSN Programmes

The SSN programmes have two objectives. In the short term, the programmes are designed to safeguard people's consumption. In the long term, they serve as a recovery programme to generate productive economic activities. The recovery programme will require the restructuring and refocusing of processes performed by the government. It aims to help people to get back to their normal lives, as before the crisis.

To achieve these objectives, the SSN programmes include:

1. securing the supply of basic staples at affordable prices, which is achieved through providing subsidies for various staples;
2. providing employment opportunities in economically productive and labour-intensive activities to give the people sufficient purchasing power for their basic needs;

3. guaranteeing basic health and education services at prices affordable by the general public;
4. reinvigorating public economic activities, especially small and medium enterprises, and increasing the participation of co-operatives to promote economic activities which are not only productive but also incorporate the spirit of co-operatives.[3]

The SSN programmes have commonly targetted three groups: first, the chronically poor, that is, those who had been poor even before the crisis; second, the temporary poor, those who had become poor because of the crisis; and third, those who are not necessarily poor, but whose welfare has been badly affected by the crisis. The vulnerable group, such as the disabled, children, and old people require longer-term aid, while others who were affected by the crisis may need immediate short-term aid. The SSN programmes should be able to quickly assist those requiring immediate and short-term aid.

The SSN programmes use mainly two approaches. The first is the sectoral approach, where funding is allocated through technical departments (*departemen teknis*), or non-departmental government agencies (such as the LPND, *lembaga pemerintah non departemen*). The second is the regional approach, where funding is allocated for regional (district and province) developments (DADPD, *daftar alokasi dana pembangunan daerah*) according to their needs. Yet, government agencies in the districts or provinces should also consider allocation using the sectoral approach, which has been decided by their ministries or other technical departments at the national level.

The funding of these programmes comes mainly from three sources, reflecting the two approaches mentioned above. The first is the sectoral development budget (*dana pembangunan sektoral*) which is allocated through the Mechanism of Sectoral Project (*Daftar Isian Proyek Sektoral*) from each related department. The second source is the regional development budget (*dana pembangunan daerah*) which is allocated through the Regional Development (*DADPD*) Mechanism (formerly known as *SPABP, or surat pengesahan anggaran bantuan pembangunan*). The third is a special budget which has been set up from other sources, better known as the Extended SSN Programme, or SSN-core.

It should be noted that wherever the source, the allocation of the budget has also often generated controversies on who should receive priority: those who have been affected by the crisis or those who were poor even before the crisis. Furthermore, concern has been mounting that leakages may occur during the implementation of the programmes.

The basic principles governing the SSN programme implementation are:

1. quick disbursement. This means that money (the allocated fund) has to be disbursed quickly and targetted directly to the beneficiaries;
2. transparent implementation. All activities must be openly held and easily known by the ordinary people;
3. accountable. All programme activities must be accountable, both technically and administratively, by the implementers;
4. well-targetted. Beneficiaries must be properly targetted and widely benefiting the ordinary people;
5. sustainable. The output of the programmes should be sustainable activities that people can easily develop as their own activities.

Budget Allocation

Year 1998/99: Rescue First

In 1998/99, the SSN programmes included a) the food security programme which was intended to guarantee a sufficient and affordable food supply, known as "Special Market Operation of Rice" (*OPK Beras*, or *operasi pasar khusus*); b) the social protection programme which consisted of two aspects, namely, social security in health (JPS BK, *bidang kesehatan*), and social security in education (JPS BP, *bidang pendidikan*); and c) employment creation through labour-intensive programmes (*padat karya*). These made up the so-called SSN-core, instead of supporting the SSN (*JPS Pendukung*) with many programmes.[4]

In the first year, 1998/99, the budget allocated was Rp17.966 trillion. The money was disbursed to eighteen programmes/intervention areas. The ministries received the money through both technical ministries (implementing ministries such as that of health, education, public works, agriculture, manpower, forestry, home affairs, and religious affairs, the National Food/Logistics Agency) and the regional/district government. However, it was later found that only Rp9.34 trillion was utilized.

The question was then: where did the remaining Rp8.65 trillion go? Did it disappear as leakages?" The government then explained that the Rp8.65 trillion had been used to support the SSN programmes. According to Tim Pengendali JPS, as stated by Mar'ie Muhammad at a press conference on 4 May 1999, it was a significant mistake to allocate the budget for non-core SSN programmes. It should have been allocated to the core programmes. This misallocation could have misled people to have too many expectations.[5] Thus, Tim Pengendali has asked the Badan Pemeriksa Keuangan dan Pembangunan (BPKP, a bureau under the Ministry of Finance) to investigate the implementation of the SSN programmes in 1998/99.

The discrepancy may also be due to the fact that the government was not ready to deal with the impact of the crisis. The focus of the SSN programmes in 1998/99 was on how to help poor families immediately, but the government said that it was "restructuring and refocusing" the regular programmes. It did not have appropriate policies to deal with the impact of the crisis, but received large amounts of money to help people to cope with the crisis. What happened then was that the money was just disbursed as quickly as possible without proper planning. It is not surprising therefore that they encountered problems in implementation because of the limited time spent in preparation and socialization, the lack of accurate data, and corruption/nepotism.

Year 1999/2000: New Improvements

The SSN programmes in 1999/2000 continued to help people to recover from the economic crisis. Improvements in implementation were carried out based on the suggestions and recommendations from the community, the implementing institutions, and academicians. The improvements were aimed at ensuring that the programmes were on the right track.

The SSN programmes in 1999/2000 consisted of:[6]

1. The food security programme (Special Market Operation of Rice, or *OPK Beras*, development of seed cultivation and chicken farming, or *pengembangan pembibitan dan budidaya ayam buras;* and development of public fishponds, or *pengembangan tambak rakyat*);
2. The SSN education programme, which consisted of scholarships for students (*beasiswa*) and operational assistance funds (OAF) for targetted schools (*DBO, dana bantuan operasional*), and scholarships for university students (*beasiswa*) and operational assistance funds for the universities (*DBO-Dikti*), as well as operational assistance and maintenance funds for public elementary schools (*SD, sekolah dasar*) and private elementary schools (*MI, madrasah ibtida'iyah*);
3. The SSN health programme through assistance in community health service, nursery, and medicines, as well as supplementary

nutrition through food assistance (supplementary food for school children, or PMT-AS, *pemberian makanan tambahan-anak sekolah*);
4. The employment creation programme through urban labour-intensive activities (Urban-Labour Intensive or PKP, *padat karya perkotaan*), and Special Initiatives for Women Unemployment (PKPP, *prakarsa khusus bagi penganggur perempuan*); and
5. The people empowerment programme through Regional Empowerment to overcome the Impact of the Economic Crisis (PDM-DKE, *pemberdayaan daerah dalam mengatasi dampak krisis ekonomi*).

The budget for the SSN programmes in 1999/2000 was Rp5.65 trillion. This amount was revised from Rp9.34 trillion (from the SSN-core in 1998/99) as a result of negotiation between the GOI and the World Bank within the SSN-AL (Social Safety Net Adjustment Loans) framework. The SSN-AL provides for (1) the consolidation and simplification of SSN programmes; (2) development of monitoring and evaluation systems; and (3) refocusing on target groups in line with recent surveys.[7] The budget was targetted at education intervention (Rp2.05 trillion), health intervention (Rp1.7 trillion), food security intervention (Rp5.323 trillion), PKP (Rp850 billion), PKPP (Rp150 billion), and PDM-DKE (Rp792.0 billion).[8]

The National Co-ordinating Team for Social Safety Net Programmes (TKPP-JPS, or *Tim Koordinasi Pelaksanaan Program Jaring Pengaman Sosial*) has carried out the following improvements:[9] first, to upgrade the information dissemination mechanism through the SSN National Information Centre(PIN-JPS) and the Information Centre at the district level; second, to set up a special unit to manage public complaints, that is, a complaint resolution unit (UPM, *unit pengaduan masyarakat*); third, to establish a regular reporting system based on performance indicators; fourth, to verify TKPP-JPS monthly reports independently by Tim Pengendali JPS; fifth, to encourage people involvement in the SSN programmes through establishing stakeholder forums at the national and district levels; and finally, to refocus SSN programmes based on a targetting mechanism and geographical allocation, using the latest data.

These improvements, including a revision of fund allocation, are responses to many criticisms from the society with regard to mistargetting and leakage. Many have pointed out the weaknesses of the SSN programmes. For example, as quoted from *Kompas* daily newspaper, dated 17 May 1999, a study on some SSN programme implementation in Java conducted by the Monetary and Financial Agency (*Badan Analisa Keuangan dan Moneter*) and the Ministry of Finance has shown the presence of mistargetting and leakage in almost all districts. The SSN-core leakage at the national level was roughly estimated at about Rp411.746 billion, and mistargetting at about Rp518.096 billion. The total sum of the national leakage and mistargetting almost surpassed Rp1 trillion. Yet, this study did not include other SSN programmes such as the PDM-DKE, some areas of SSN health-care, and other economically productive programmes of the Ministry of Co-operation and Small Scale Enterprises. Therefore, the overall sum of the leakages and mistargetting might far exceed Rp1 trillion for fiscal year 1998/99.

Evaluation

SSN Controlling Team Study

The evaluation of the implementation of the SSN programmes reported here is based on the research findings of the SSN Controlling Team (Tim Pengendali) study report 1999/2000 which was done during August–December 1999 and early 2000, as well as the SSN Implementation Report by Tim Pengendali and the Demographic Institute, Faculty of Economics, University of Indonesia, and other relevant documents and publications. This evaluation takes into account the problems that have arisen since the preparation and during the implementation of the SSN programmes. It is focused on the targetting mechanism, socialization, implementation, and monitoring and reporting of programmes.

Targetting Mechanism

The targetting mechanism was the first step in the allocation and disbursment of funds to beneficiaries. However, the problem was how to obtain representative and reliable data that reflected the real situation. With limited time and in the absence of reliable data, the SSN programme targetting mechanism used the BKKBN (National Family Planning Coordinating Board) data as the main source of information.[10] However, it should be cautioned that each SSN programme implementer had a different way of interpreting the data.

SSN Health Programmes (JPS BK)

The targetting mechanism consisted of a number of steps: first, the identification of targets by a village team — comprising integrated health services post (*posyandu*) cadres, the village midwife (BDD), a public figure, and the head of the village — based on the classification of the family (whether pre-prosperous or prosperous family-1) from the BKKBN or National Family Planning Coordinating Board. The second step was the submission of results by the head of the village to the local health service centre (*puskesmas*); third, the review of data by the head of the local health service centre and submission to the district health office; and finally, the approval of the data by the district co-ordinating team. Based on these data, a health card (*kartu sehat*) was distributed to each poor family.

Though implementers have attempted to fully follow the steps of the mechanism, some inappropriateness has been observed. The main reason is the inaccuracy of the BKKBN data, which do not reflect the real situation. The BKKBN data are based on some criteria of the "welfare" concept, but the SSN health programmes are based on the "poverty" concept. The poverty concept mainly asks how many meals the family can eat in a day, and how many calories they consume, while the welfare concept includes how many times members of the family go to the mosque or church. The Tim Pengendali report,[11] using the information from a survey conducted from November to mid-December 1999, has shown that the number of poor families in the field, according to the BKKBN's criteria, is 10–20 per cent more than those measured by the SSN health programme.

SSN Education Programmes (JPS BP)

In general, target groups for scholarships were selected from students who were considered as potential drop-outs because of failure to pay school fees, and the socio-economic condition of the family. Students who had dropped out from school one year earlier were not eligible for the scholarships.[12] In reality, the district or sub-district committee found that drop-outs were also among the recipients. The implementers may not have understood well who the target was. They should have given higher priority to students who might eventually drop out, instead of those who had already dropped out.

Another problem was the limited number of scholarships compared with the number of students who needed it. This has forced the school committees to share one scholarship with more than one student. For the same reason, the district committee has allocated one unit of the Operational Aid Fund (OAF) to more than one targetted school.[13]

Special Market Operation of Rice (OPK Beras)

The *OPK Beras* is a subsidized rice programme for those belonging to the pre-prosperous and prosperous family-1 categories. The distribution is specially directed to the beneficiaries, rather than through the public market system, at a very low price. The rice is distributed by Dolog/Sub-Dolog, the district food logistic agency, directly to the sub-district level. In this programme, the implementers, who are mainly Dolog and village office persons, also use BKKBN data as information to sell subsidized rice to the poor families. Although the BKKBN data are not accurate, they are the only data available in the village. The implementers should discuss the BKKBN data with public figures or the village team to find more relevant and accurate information. In practice, the discussions were held in some areas only.

A worse situation was when rice was allocated to targetted beneficiaries by Dolog/Sub-Dolog without using the updated data that had been discussed and approved by the head of the village and the Family Planning Field Officer/PLKB (*Penyuluh Lapangan Keluarga Berencana*). The allocation of rice was based on the quota that had been decided at the provincial or even national level. This is the reason why disbursements did not match the updated data from the village.

The Tim Pengendali report[14] has revealed three weak areas: first, the number of recipients was still far below the total number of targetted beneficiaries. The data at the district and provincial level were not accurate because the updated data derived from the villages were inappropriate. The discussion at the village level among the head of the village, the PLKB, *posyandu* cadres, and public figures might not have taken place.

Secondly, the actual recipients were not only the targetted beneficiaries. A case in Wonogiri district in Central Java province can be used as an illustration. The subsidized rice was distributed to all families in the villages, regardless of whether they were the targetted beneficiaries or not. A similar case was found in Tuban district in East Java.

People believed in *gotong royong* (working together) within the society in performing some public work or even private activities. Building a school or a private house, for example, was to be done in the spirit of *gotong royong,* and everybody in the village would work together on that project. Thus, when they came under the subsidized rice programme, they also felt that all members, not only the poor, of the village should benefit from the programme. *Gotong-royong requires the spirit of "sharing in the same fate"*. Finally, the funding was also allocated to areas that had a rice surplus and the average people did not have difficulty in buying their foodstuff. Examples include Solok district, West Sumatra, and Maros district, South Sulawesi province.

Regional Empowerment to Overcome the Impact of the Economic Crisis (PDM-DKE)

The targetted beneficiaries of this programme are poor people in both villages and cities who have been affected by the economic crisis. The programme has two types of activities, namely, physical activities, and economic activities (revolving fund). The revolving fund is a mechanism through which loans are given to people who are engaged in productive activities, such as home industries or small traders, for a specific period of time (usually one year). They have to pay back a certain amount every month. After two or three instalments (usually after three months), other people would have the opportunity to receive the same amount of loan. The selection process of this programme originally used a need-driven approach, that is, from the people, by the people, and through the people. Through village meetings, the villagers decide on what kind of economic activities they need.

This reflects the basic principle of the government, that is, to empower the community. Through this programme, the community groups are encouraged to plan for themselves with the assistance of facilitators who help them in designing, implementing, and monitoring the activities they themselves propose.

Socialization

Socialization is an effort to disseminate information to raise the people's awareness of their rights to obtain assistance through the SSN programmes. Socialization of the programmes is conducted from the provincial to the village level. An evaluation of the SSN implementation[15] shows that the lower the level of the bureaucracy the more informal is the socialization. At lower levels, socialization is included in other routine activities, such as the village weekly meeting.

SSN Health Programmes (JPS BK)

In the SSN health programme, socialization is conducted hierarchically, from the highest to the lowest level. However, the implementation guidelines (*petunjuk pelaksanaan*) from the Ministry of Health 1998/99 did not clearly mention how to socialize and who were responsible for financing the socialization.[16] The funding was not allocated at the lowest level, from the village midwife (*Bidan di Desa/BDD*) to the village people (beneficiaries). Yet, at the district level, the funding was integrated with the budget of the district health office for routine activities.[17]

The results of the study on SSN by Tim Pengendali JPS show[18] that programme socialization was carried out using three approaches: namely, formal, informal, and a combination of both. The formal approach was used at monthly or special meetings among district health officers and the village midwife at the local health service centre (*puskesmas*) at the sub-district level for discussing SSN health issues. The formal approach was also used in cross-sector meetings at the sub-district level in co-operation with other institutions, such as agricultural and animal husbandry agencies.

Informal socialization was carried out through daily meetings, interaction with people at *posyandu, arisan* (regular or social gatherings at which members contribute to and take turns at winning an aggregate sum of money or goods), or talking with neighbours (*gethok tular*).

Many districts used a combination of the formal and informal approach. The results were better than in districts which only used either the formal or informal approach. The differences were attributed to the following three factors: the different roles and level of activities of the village midwife and *posyandu* cadres; the different number of working hours as well as the activities of the village midwife and *posyandu* cadres; and the type of media and frequency of socialization.[19]

Although there were different ways to socialize the programme, the results were still limited. The understanding of the implementers of the programmes was poor, especially among the lowest level. They did not capture the essence of the messages of the SSN health programmes on socialization. For example, the implementers did not know the purpose of the health card (*kartu sehat*) and the duration of validity of the card. They did not know how to use it.[20] How could they inform the people, if they themselves did not understand the programme well?

SSN Education Programmes (JPS BP)

The degree of socialization of the SSN education programmes among the people was relatively very low, compared with the degree of socialization among the implementers.[21] The roles of the district and sub-district committees, the public figures, and school committees in the process of socialization were limited. Co-ordination between committee members and public figures often did not exist. On the other hand, school principals and committees tended to target only the beneficiaries.[22] They did not realize that they had a responsibility to inform non-beneficiaries too. Yet, non-beneficiaries, who were presumably better off economically, should understand that their children were not entitled to scholarships. Their understanding would contribute to better relations among the people, and avoid jealousy.

Implementers had more knowledge than the public, especially about scholarships. However, with regard to the operational aid fund (OAF), only the school principal and school committee members knew this programme well. Teachers who were not involved in the school committee would not fully understand.

A study of the programme[23] shows that the total percentage of beneficiaries who knew about the scholarships programme was 99.62 per cent. In other words, almost 100 per cent of the beneficiaries understood the programme. This indicates that socialization among the targetted beneficiaries was very good.

Special Market Operation of Rice (OPK Beras)

The implementers of the rice programme admitted that they did not conduct socialization properly because of the limited time in 1998/99. However, in the year 1999/2000 this was also not conducted properly, although they had more time to do it. This inadequate socialization affected both the public and especially the implementers at the forefront. They did not fully understand the meaning of the *OPK Beras*. Worse, the understanding of the people was not in line with the government's objectives and goals. People perceived that this programme meant a free distribution of rice.[24] Another issue was that some people felt that the rice was of low quality.[25] A study of the programme[26] shows that the percentage of beneficiaries who did not receive rice (under *OPK Beras*) because "they don't know the reason" was 34.0 per cent in December 1999. It decreased to 28.3 per cent in January 2000.

Regional Empowerment to Overcome the Impact of the Economic Crisis (PDM-DKE)

Like other SSN programmes, socialization of the PDM-DKE was also very limited. As a result, people perceived that the fund was a pure grant, instead of a revolving fund which they had to repay. Therefore, the aim of the revolving the fund was never achieved.

Implementation

The discussion on implementation will focus on how the activities were conducted and how the funds or services of the SSN programmes were distributed.

SSN Health Programmes (JPS BK)

The flow of funds can be divided into two stages. First, the funds will flow from the central (national) authorities to the district entities. Secondly, the funds will then be distributed by the district authorities to the payer post-office (*kantor pos bayar*), then to the local health service centres (*puskesmas*), and the village midwife. The common problem experienced was the delayed flow of funds from the national to the district entities. As found by Tim Pengendali,[27] the delay occurred in all study locations (eight districts in eight provinces), and this delay might last three to six months, or even one year. For example, in Solok, West Sumatra, the first phase of the funding of 1998/99 was received only in March 1999, although the programme was supposed to have started in August 1998. This delay caused the death of a malnourished infant who had been waiting to get aid (supplement food nutrition/PMT).

A similar situation occurred in Wonogiri district in Central Java province. The first phase of the funding for 1998/99 was received between six and twelve months after the programme began.[28] In the case of food supplement services for babies and under-five children, the village midwives should have disbursed the funds in advance to cover pregnancy services.

In the fiscal year 1998/99 almost 50 per cent of the targetted beneficiaries did not receive the funds or health cards on time. As reported by the National Coordinating Team for the Social Safety Net Programmes, the funds for fiscal year 1998/99 were disbursed up to December 1999. The results were that 66 per cent of targetted households received health cards, 81.4 per cent of health-card holders received services, 61 per cent of the targetted pregnant mothers received services from the local health service centres and village midwives, and 69 per cent of the targetted babies and children of the poor received supplementary food. Though there was a significant improvement in the following fiscal year, only 50 per cent received free health services. In the period January–December 2000, of the 14.06 million targetted households, 13 million households received health cards, of which 50.7 per cent received free health services.[29]

SSN Education Programmes (JPS BP)

One of the important factors contributing to efficient fund distribution for scholarships and the OAF is good co-ordination among districts, sub-districts, and school committees, as well as the payer post-office.[30] Generally, the authorizing school principals would collectively disburse the scholarships by collecting the funds from payer post-offices and then distributing the money to the recipient students, in order not to disrupt the class learning process,[31] and the post-office's daily activities.[32]

The report by Lembaga Demografi FE-UI and Tim Pengendali[33] shows that the use of this mechanism grew from 1998/99 to 1999/2000. More and more students received scholarships from their school committees. The scholarships were distributed in three phases each year. In 1998/1999, 41.9 per cent was disbursed in the first phase, and 53.1 per cent in the third one. In the first phase in 1999/2000 almost all students received scholarships from the school committees. An examination of the programme[34] confirms this finding. The percentage of students whose scholarships were managed by the school was 100 per cent for elementary schools, 92.0 per cent for junior high schools, and 100 per cent for senior high schools.

There are two ways in which the scholarships are managed. First they are managed by the school. After receiving funds for the scholarships, the school keeps the money and allocates to students according to their needs, such as for school payments, books, and uniforms. The disadvantage of this is that schools are free to channel the funds to other things that may not be urgently needed by the students. Even worse is that an "administration fee" might be collected for this kind of management by the school, especially if no report of fund usage is required.[35]

The second way is management by the student's family (in the targetted groups). The school allocates the money to the student's family, and the family manages the funds themselves. However, sometimes the family would use the money to buy foodstuffs especially when they have had a poor harvest.[36]

The negative impacts may have occurred because of the limited socialization among implementers and the public. There is no social control over the programme. However, generally, the SSN education programme is the best managed, compared with the other programmes. The World Bank has awarded the "President's Award for Excellence" in 2000 for good management of the programme, as it has effectively maintained students' participation at the primary and secondary levels.[37]

Special Market Operation of Rice (OPK Beras)

In regions seriously affected by the economic crisis, *OPK Beras* was very beneficial. In 1998/99 the poor were allowed to buy 10 kg of rice at cheap prices and they could afford to buy this amount (July–November 1998). In 1999/2000 (December 1999–March 2000), they were allowed to buy 20 kg at cheap prices but some of them could not afford to buy this amount.[38] The decision to increase the quota for cheap rice was problematic. On one hand, the benefit of the subsidy had been too small for each household in the previous year so that the government felt the need to increase it. On the other hand, in many areas of both Java and outside Java, the targetted beneficiaries could not even afford to buy rice at the cheap price. In other words, the cheap rice was still too expensive for them.

This explains why the proportion of families receiving the full amount of 20 kg of rice was less than 6 per cent, as verified by Tim Pengendali in the December 1999 and January 2000 distribution. An LP3ES study which conducted an evaluation of *OPK Beras* implementation during October 1999–January 2000 in the rural areas showed that about 80 per cent of the beneficiaries did not receive the full amount of rice they were entitled to. They only received an average of 11 kg per month. A study by CEFFNAS (Centre for Food Nutrition and Agricultural Studies and Services) also confirmed similar findings for the urban areas, that the targetted beneficiaries only received 13.3 kg per month, on average.[39] However, as a result of the decentralization of the *OPK Beras* mechanism to local governments, in the period April–December 2000, the monthly provincial average rose to 15.1 to 16.7 kg per household per month.[40]

Furthermore, a study by SMERU[41] showed that the quality of rice was low to medium, but the targetted beneficiaries found the quality acceptable. They were more concerned about the lack of distribution points assigned by Dolog/Sub-Dolog to distribute the cheap rice to beneficiaries.

Regional Empowerment to Overcome the Impact of the Economic Crisis (PDM-DKE)

As quoted by Tim Pengendali,[42] the research on the SSN programme that was conducted by SMERU-World Bank (Social Monitoring and Early Response Unit) in April-May 1999 has concluded that the results of the programme are mixed. The labour-intensive programme was unsuccessful in accommodating the poor people and creating employment opportunities, but the extension of the credit programme had assisted villagers to run businesses. The government claimed that Rp1.45 trillion of the Rp1.70 trillion in the total allocated budget had been disbursed to about 4 million beneficiaries.[43]

Tim Pengendali has reported that the physical part of the programme had contributed to improving the people's income by 11.25 per cent.[44] The infrastructure built as the physical part of the programme had also helped people to gain access to the market. However, this programme has created a relative dependency on the government both in terms of funding and management assistance. This programme has also aroused social jealousy between the beneficiaries and non-beneficiaries.

The National Co-ordinating Team for Social Safety Net Programmes has also identified some weaknesses of the programmes. There is a low level of commitment by the village community organization to assume responsibility for programme implementation at the local level, and little intervention by the village head and local government officials. Other weaknesses include corruption and mistargetting,[45] administrative problems, bureaucracy bottleneck, wide geographic coverage, and lack of understanding of distribution procedures among local implementers.[46] These major problems have prompted the donor agency, the World Bank, to hold back the funding for the fiscal year 1999/2000 until some improvement has been made by the Government of Indonesia.

Monitoring and Reporting

This activity is related to public accountability, especially by the implementers. The quality of the monitoring and reporting system reflects the accountability of the implementers.

SSN Health Programmes (JPS BK)

The major findings of some studies show that the local health service centre has been too busy with routine activities to handle the reporting system of the SSN health programme.[47] It has to concentrate full-time on working to serve poor families (health-card holders and others), including helping in birth delivery. In addition, the implementers have to perform administrative work which may be beyond their capability to do. Some village midwives said that they needed incentives for their additional work.

Management complaints about the programme had been mostly ignored. The people or institution also did not know who to complain to because the public complaint units (*UPM*) had not been effective. The public was still unfamiliar with this mechanism and therefore needed intensive socialization.

SSN Education Programmes (JPS BP)

The purpose of monitoring the activities was to observe whether socialization had been effective or not. In some cases, monitoring the activities conducted by the committee had been limited and not effective. The involvement of public figures and post-office personnel had also been minimal. The report of Lembaga Demografi FE-UI and Tim Pengendali JPS[48] has concluded that this monitoring is only a formality.

On the other hand, to transfer fund distribution from the post-office to the regional offices of the treasury (KPKN) is problematic. This is because KPKN officers have complicated the activities by collecting a 1 per cent "administration fee" from each school for the disbursement of funds.[49]

Special Market Operation of Rice (OPK Beras)

In reality, monitoring activities have never been conducted in this area. Reports from the implementers were mostly incomplete. Thus, the reports were few and of poor quality, containing just enough information to meet administrative purposes.[50] The implementers only reported on the distribution of rice to the people. Therefore, the information did not cover the rising aspirations of the people.

The SMERU[51] has found that the administration of *OPK Beras* has not been well managed, partly because of the unavailability (or inadequacy) of an operational budget and inconsistent, inaccurate, and ineffective public information. As an illustration, local implementers in Kampar district, Riau Province, said that they needed more incentives to operate this programme.[52] Interestingly, the chairman of the district food agency (Kasubdolog VII) and the chairman of the Regional Development Planning Agency (BAPPEDA), South Sulawesi province, recommended that the programme should be terminated because South Sulawesi is one of the rice-surplus regions in Indonesia.[53] Therefore, the programme should be selectively implemented, so that the rice-deficit districts within a region could be given more.

Regional Empowerment to Overcome the Impact of the Economic Crisis (PDM-DKE)

With regard to monitoring and reporting, the main problem of this programme was the absence of post-programme evaluation, programme monitoring, and lack of capable village facilitators. Monitoring was carried out by sub-district facilitators (FK, *fasilitator kecamatan*), village facilitators (FD, *fasilitator desa*), the TPKd/k(*tim pelaksana kegiatan desa/ kelurahan*) or the LKMD (*lembaga ketahanan masyarakat desa)*. The lack of capability resulted in incomplete reports.[54] The task was then performed by the sub-district facilitator.

Post-programme evaluation was also not carried out properly by the sub-district officers and other institutions at the district level. The low quality of human resources for implementing the programme and reporting had led to difficulty in carrying out the monitoring mechanism.[55] Consequently, there was no guarantee that the funds used for economic activities were distributed as part of a revolving fund. Many villagers had borrowed money and did not intend to return it. In this sense, the revolving fund programme was considered unsuccessful.

In 1998/99, as a result of many criticisms, suggestions and comments on the PDM-DKE's divergence and inappropriateness, the government was forced to stop the programme. In 1999/2000, there was little effort to restart the programme because the Government of Indonesia was waiting for budget disbursements from the World Bank.

In mid-July 2000, as a result of negotiation between the government and the World Bank, it was decided that the PDM-DKE programme would be restarted from October to December 2000. However, the allocation was reduced to Rp455 billion, including an allocation of Rp20 billion for safeguarding the programme. As part of the negotiation, this programme would be relaunched only if some conditions were met. The conditions were based on a main indicator and target performance, and an additional indicator and target performance. The "main indicator" involved financial (fund) absorption, village community meetings (*musyawarah desa*), and the total number of targetted beneficiaries.

The rate of financial absorption should be at least 7.5 per cent in October, 50 per cent in November, and 95 per cent in December. By October, at least 90 per cent of the village community meetings I and II should have been completed, and at least 30 per cent of poor families (beneficiaries) should have attended one meeting, and at least three village community elements should have participated in that meeting. By November, at least 90 per cent of the village community meetings III and IV should have been completed, and at least 15 per cent of poor families should have attended one of the meetings, and at least three village community elements should have participated in that meeting. In December, at the end of fiscal year 2000, 1.3 million targetted beneficiaries should have been reached.

The "additional indicator" was that 40 per cent of the total budget allocation for wages should be used to pay workers in infrastructure activities. The target should be to create jobs equivalent to 40 person-working days (HOK) for each infrastructure activity worth Rp1 million. The national average participation rate of females in infrastructure activities to total workers should be 15 per cent; the national average for female participation in revolving fund activities, compared with total targetted beneficiaries, should be 40 per cent; and every public complaint should have been attended to within 21 working days.

It was not an easy task for the GOI. Tim Pengendali JPS's *Annual Report of Fiscal Year 2000*[56] explains that financial (fund) absorption by the end of November 2000 was only Rp15.23 billion, compared with the total budget of Rp435 billion. This comprised only 3.5 per cent, far from the 50 per cent financial absorption target for that period. Three months might have been too short for implementing these programmes, including the PKP and PKPP. Considering this, Tim Pengendali JPS recommended to the Ministry of Finance and the National Development Planning Agency to negotitate with the World Bank to extend the period of implementation of these programmes to March 2001.[57]

Women-Sensitive Programmes

In 1999/2000, the SSN employment creation programmes were planned to be implemented through two labour-intensive schemes with a budget of about Rp1 trillion, namely, the urban labour-intensive (PKP) scheme, and the special initiatives for female employment (PKPP) scheme. However, as for the PDM-DKE programme, the political uncertainty and major corruption cases delayed the disbursement of several loans which were to support the budget deficit. The allocated budget for the PKP scheme in 1999/2000 was Rp850 billion, and that for the PKPP was Rp150 billion.[58]

However, the funds were not allocated until the end of fiscal year 1999/2000, and thus the activities performed only covered programme preparations, such as drawing up implementation guidelines, setting up implementing institutions at the district and provincial levels, and establishing monitoring institutions with NGOs. In early 2000, the government (through the National Development Planning Agency/

BAPPENAS) had not decided whether to launch the programmes or not.

The delay in the implementation of these programmes became a controversy. A TKPP-JPS officer said that there was uncertainty concerning these programmes. One source said that the programme was being discussed by the Ministry of Finance, but the Directorate of Budget said that it was still with BAPPENAS.[59] This uncertainty gave rise to misgivings among the people and the implementers at the forefront, leading even to unrest.

An illustration of the unrest in the field was found during spot-checking carried out by Tim Pengendali JPS in early July 2000. In a sub-district in South Sulawesi, people had been ready to implement PKP. They urged the sub-district officers to implement the programme and warned them that they would burn the sub-district hall if the programme was not implemented quickly.

Finally, in line with the PDM-DKE programme, it was agreed that these two schemes would be launched in the last quarter of fiscal year 2000 with smaller allocations. The budgets for the PKP and PKPP were reduced to about half of the 1999/2000 allocation, with Rp366 billion for PKP, and Rp75 billion for PKPP.[60]

The PKP was designed to provide job opportunities to about 400,000 unemployed people, with an 80:20 male-female composition, and compensation equal to the regional minimum wage in all provinces. On the other hand, the PKPP was designed to cater especially to the poor and unemployed women in the urban areas through economic activities proposed by them. Its target was to create 70,000 jobs, with an 80:20 female-male composition, covering six provinces with large urban cities: North Sumatra, DKI Jakarta, West Java, Central Java, East Java, and South Sulawesi.[61]

The National Co-ordinating Team for Social Safety Net Programmes seemed to be happy with the results of both programmes. Their report of December 2000 showed that 226,321 persons (204,029 of which were eligible to participate) were registered for the PKP at the registration unit opened at the sub-district level. This number was already 101.3 per cent of the target of 8.1 million person-working days. The programme also met the target for female participation, at 24.5 per cent of total employment/person-working days.[62] A similar result was reported for the PKPP. It had absorbed 83,800 unemployed women (145 per cent of the target, or 7.28 per cent of the total unemployed women). This programme had been conducted in 143 districts in six provinces.

The two programmes may represent success stories of women empowerment during the crisis. However, in South Sulawesi the case was different. The public figures and local implementers said that they preferred not to implement the PKPP in their areas. In their perception, culture and social values do not allow women to do the "3 D" (dirty, dangerous, and difficult) jobs, such as in public work projects. This type of work is not commonly done by women in their society. They agreed that it was a good idea to give women opportunities to work, but not in public work projects. Women need to be modest and to work in appropriate jobs and the programmes should take into account the culture, identity and local values of the people. Similarly, AKATIGA (1999) has found that women in Java felt that public work projects were not appropriate for them. The women proposed jobs involving "female skills", such as cleaning community facilities.

Whereas a gender approach to development is limited, the delay in implementation of the PKPP is unproductive. Yet this programme has increased women's participation in the economy. In other words, it has benefited and given appropriate positions to women compared with men, especially in the urban areas. As quoted by Setiawan,[63] gender issues have been covered sporadically in the design and development of responses to the crisis, such as *Padat Karya*, mentioned above. In general, however, women and girls have shared the impacts of the crisis, but they have not always shared the benefits of the response programmes. That is why these two programmes should be highly appreciated as an initial step in creating appropriate access for women.

Not all the SSN programmes have been concerned about women, although women's involvement has been initiated. Their access to the programme remains limited. The SSN health programmes, however, have contributed to an improvement. Women's involvement is important as seen in the participation of village midwives. The targetted beneficiaries in the SSN health programmes are also mostly women. They play important roles not only as beneficiaries but also as implementers.

The question of gender is not just a matter of being women or men. It is far more than this, because it involves human rights — gender is a development issue.[64] It has been shown in many instances that the delivery or implementation of programmes, including the SSN and aid programmes, would have been more effective if they had been done by women.[65]

A gender approach to development helps to ensure quality in three ways. It ensures, firstly, that the benefits of development are equally shared by men and women; secondly, that the different issues faced by men and women are addressed in the course of development; and finally, that the negative impacts of development are not borne disproportionately by either men or women.[66] As found in some areas, it is not easy to encourage women to participate in development, and at the same time to benefit equally from the development. Therefore, a determined effort to consider the gender aspect should be made.

Safeguarding the Programme

Safeguarding the SSN programme should be undertaken by the Government of Indonesia.This involves an effort to establish programme implementation monitoring activities. In general, it consists of improvement in the quality and coverage of information dissemination (through the PI/*pusat informasi*, or SSN Information Centre), establishment of a complaint resolution mechanism (UPM/*unit pengaduan masyarakat*, or SSN Complaints Resolution Unit), application of a performance-based reporting system, independent verification (conducted by Tim Pengendali JPS, or SSN Controlling Team), and enhancement of civil society participation.[67]

Information dissemination is closely related to socialization activities. In order to measure how effective the information dissemination is, one should analyse whether the intended beneficiaries have received the appropriate information. For the SSN programmes, the extent of information dissemination is still low.

According to the report of the National Co-ordinating Team for Social Safety Net Programmes, 73 per cent of the complaints of the SSN-core programmes had been resolved by October 2000, and the remaining were under investigation.[68] Interestingly, the findings of Tim Pengendali were that the recorded complaints received by the SSN Complaints Resolution Unit at the district level do not necessarily reflect the actual complaint resolution activities in the field. At the lowest level, that is, the targetted beneficiaries, the local implementers solved almost all the complaints directly, especially those concerning technical aspects of the programmes. In some areas, people did not know where and how to lodge their complaints because the SSN Complaints Resolution Unit was not well known.[69] Tim Pengendali has recommended that in future this institution could be an embryo of the government's accountability to the public.

The performance-based reporting system was generally unsuccessful. The number of complete and timely reports of the programmes received by the National Co-ordinating Team for Social Safety Net Programmes was very low. During December 1999 to March 2000, only 13–39 per cent completed the report and 4–40 per cent were submitted on time.

The PDM-DKE, one of three programmes implemented in the last quarter of fiscal year 1999/2000 could not satisfy the minimum report coverage. However, the PKP and PKPP, and the scholarship programme performed well because of their strong nationwide management structure.[70]

One of the tasks of Tim Pengendali JPS was to conduct an independent verification of the programme. In order to do this, Tim Pengendali worked closely with the Demographic Institute, Faculty of Economics, University of Indonesia, and the results were used as the basis of this chapter. At the same time, independent monitoring was conducted by several institutions, such as SMERU with strong financial support from the World Bank, ASEM, AusAid, and USAID.

The last element of the safeguarding activities was to enhance civil society participation. The government supported the establishment of a stakeholders' forum (FLP, *forum lintas pelaku*) in every district. By December 2000, not less than 226 districts had formed stakeholders' forums. They are autonomous forums where all civil society elements, such as public figures, academicians, journalists, religious leaders, the private sector, NGOs, targetted beneficiaries, and even ordinary people and government officials may discuss complaints, issues, and problems, especially concerning SSN programmes. In some areas, these forums may have functioned as a "watchdog" of the government. At the national level, however, the stakeholders' forums seemed more difficult to establish since some NGOs had their own standpoints and negative perceptions towards the forums.[71] Finally, the regular meetings among Tim Pengendali JPS, the National Co-ordinating Team for Social Safety Net Programmes, and some NGOs can be seen as a reflection of the spirit of the national stakeholders' forums.

Lessons Learned

The SSN programme is an example of a confusing and complicated social policy taken by the government, supported by international loans. The Indonesian Government did not have an appropriate warning system and therefore was not prepared to deal with any crisis. The Indonesian economy had been so buoyant that they did not think it necessary to prepare an emergency programme in case of crisis. A crisis did not even cross their minds.

The lesson to be learnt is that the government and related agencies, such as Parliament, universities, and non-governmental organizations should prepare an emergency programme. This should include how to allocate budgets, how to earn or raise the budgets in appropriate ways, and how to choose activities as appropriate responses to a crisis.

When preparing this emergency programme, the values of the local people should be considered. People often have their own ways of coping with the crisis. The spirit of *gotong royong* (working together within society for a public purpose, or even for a private purpose) is an example. Indonesians have a built-in SSN programme in their daily lives. Hence, the emergency programme should be directed to maintain, develop, and enhance local values to empower a self-help mechanism, especially for people in the villages and the urban poor. It should be noted, however, that *gotong-royong*, for example, can also be interpreted that all members of the village, regardless of whether they are poor or not, should receive the benefits of the SSN programmes.

The second lesson is to note the existence of a "project mentality" among bureaucrats. Funds from donor agencies are often taken as "grants", even though they are really loans. The bureaucrats would initiate projects and disburse the money. For them, it is not important that foreign debts continue to rise. The large amount of funds available to the SSN programmes has created a vested interest in getting part of the funds. Tim Pengendali has indicated that the bureaucracy still practised the "old way", such as bribing or cutting the budget allocations of the SSN programmes.[72]

It is not surprising that government officers and implementers do not try hard to plan emergency-type activities. Rather, they simply modify the existing regular programmes. Regular policies have even been passed off as emergency programmes. They simply try to disburse the money quickly. Setiawan[73] has also underlined the phenomenon that in the case of Indonesia, it is difficult to determine what is included or excluded under the Social Safety Net programmes. He has argued that the entire design of the Social Safety Net programmes in Indonesia suffers from a lack of clarity and transparency regarding which groups should receive how much, and what forms of assistance. This finding clearly supports the argument that even the government is confused about what is to be classified as SSN programmes. Therefore, it is not surprising that leakage and mistargetting in the implementation of the SSN programmes occurred.

The third lesson is that as a rescue programme, to some extent, the SSN programmes have helped poor people affected by the economic crisis. The programmes have benefited people in their struggle to survive during the crisis. A comparison between the number of poor people during the crisis and after three years illustrates this, even though the difference may not necessarily be due to the programmes. The number of poor people decreased from 49.5 million people (24.2 per cent of the Indonesian population) at the end of 1998 to 37.5 million people (18.2 per cent) in August 1999.[74] However, it is still significantly higher when compared with the conditions before the crisis.

After three years of crisis, Indonesia has started to recover. Therefore, in dealing with transient and structural poverty, the programmes need to be focused on poverty alleviation. The Controlling Team of the Task Force for SSN Improvement (Tim Pengendali JPS) has developed some long-term activities to alleviate poverty that take into account decentralization, autonomy, and democratization. Activities for coping with the crisis, people empowerment, and permanent social security programmes could be established as alternatives.

The fourth lesson to be learnt is that the success or failure of the SSN programmes depends very much on the degree of socialization. The limited time, the lack of understanding by the implementers, and inappropriate targetting were a few of the problems that occurred in 1998/99. To some extent, these problems still occurred in 1999/2000. This was mainly because of limited or unwilling socialization.

The fifth lesson involves the targetting mechanism. Accuracy of data about the conditions of the poor in every region is a must. Therefore, there is a need to create a mechanism that can capture development data in the whole of Indonesia immediately. The sixth lesson is that the participation of the people in the programmes was limited. They did not have a say in what they actually needed, except in the PDM-DKE through the village community meeting.

The SSN programmes, as discussed above, reflect the efforts of the Government of Indonesia to cope with the impact of the crisis. In order to improve these programmes or similar ones in future, six recommendations are put forward. First, the SSN programmes should be formulated for people empowerment through capacity-building. Secondly, the SSN health and education programmes should be transferred to the regular programmes. Thirdly, the PDM-DKE should be developed into productive business and capital support, managed by a community-based organization in the village. Fourthly, labour-intensive programmes should be focused on activities that give positive influences to improve the economic capacity of the people. The community should plan activities that can be sustained. Especially in the case of PKPP, the government should consider carefully the culture, social and local values in planning activities targetted at women. Fifthly, the *OPK Beras* programme should be implemented more selectively, to target especially the areas of scarcity. Sixthly, the establishment of a public complaint unit in each district would be important. The stakeholders' forums also need to be improved to encourage co-operation between various sections of the people.

Notes

1. Gunawan Sumodiningrat, "Economic Stabilization and Social Safety Net: Achieving Public Prosperity" (Paper presented at a seminar on Social Safety Net Programmes in Indonesia, JICA, Tokyo, 16 February 1999b), p. 11.
2. The programmes include Urban-Labour Intensive (PKP — *Padat Karya Pekotaan*) and Special Initiatives for Women Unemployment (SIWU or PKPP — *Program Khusus bagi Penganggur Perempuan.*
3. Gunawan Sumodiningrat (1999b), pp. 16–17.
4. In fiscal year 1998/99, there were many supporting SSN programmes, such as the National Food Security Programmes through Farmers Empowerment, Development of Poultry Rural Rearing Multiplication Centre, Rehabilitation of Brackish Water Shrimp Culture Infrastructure, Social Welfare, Labour-Intensive Programme to Eradicate Crisis Impacts, Labour-Intensive Programme for Trained Work Forces, Labour-Intensive Programme in the Forestry Sector, and so on. See also National Coordinating Team for Social Safety Net Programmes, "Indonesia's Social Safety Net Programmes and Its Safeguarding: An Expression of People's Right to Development" (Paper presented at a Seminar on Financial Crisis and the Right to Development, Jakarta, 27 February 2001), p. 4.
5. http://www.jps.or.id/proyek/pers4-5-99.html
6. Tim Pengendali JPS, *Annual Report of Fiscal Year 1999/2000.*
7. Gunawan Sumodiningrat (2000), p. 85. The GOI (inter-departmental team) and the World Bank have been developing details for this system since fiscal year 1998/99.
8. Tim Pengendali JPS, *Annual Report of Fiscal Year 1999/2000.*
9. Herman Haeruman Js, "Jaring Pengaman Sosial dan Implementasinya di Masa Mendatang", at http://satunet.com/artikel/isi/00/03/06/8480.html, p. 1–3.
10. With the data, BKKBN classified four groups of households: pre-properous households, prosperous household-I, prosperous household-II, and prosperous household-III. A household is defined as pre-prosperous if it cannot satisfy even one of the following criteria: all household members practise their religions; all members can eat at least twice a day; all members have different clothes for home, office, or travel; most of the floor area of the home is not made of earth; and that the household can find modern medical assistance for sick children as well family planning services for contraceptive users.

11. Tim Pengendali JPS (2000), p. 59.
12. Lembaga Demografi FE-UI (LD FE-UI), and Tim Pengendali JPS (2000), pp. 49–50.
13. Ibid., pp. 32 and 50.
14. Tim Pengendali JPS (2000a), p. 72.
15. Lembaga Demografi FE-UI, and Tim Pengendali JPS, *Buku V: Laporan Umum* (Jakarta, 2000b), p. 17.
16. Lembaga Demografi FE-UI, and Tim Pengendali JPS, *Buku II: Program JPS BK* (Jakarta, 2000c), p. III-1.
17. As shown in the Juklak SSN health programme 1998/99. See also Lembaga Demografi FE-UI and Tim Pengendali JPS (2000c), p. III-3.
18. Tim Pengendali JPS (2000a), p. 61.
19. Ibid., p. 62.
20. Lembaga Demografi FE-UI and Tim Pengendali JPS (2000c), p. III-4–III-5.
21. Lembaga Demografi FE-UI and Tim Pengendali JPS (2000a), p. 49.
22. Ibid., p. 19.
23. Study of the SSN education programme based on the report of TKPP-JPS conducted by Tim Pengendali JPS in February 2000.
24. Tim Pengendali JPS (2000a), p. 75.
25. Lembaga Demografi FE-UI and Tim Pengendali JPS (2000b), p. 84.
26. Verification of *OPK Beras* based on the report of the TKPP-JPS that was conducted by Tim Pengendali JPS in February 2000.
27. Tim Pengendali JPS (2000a), p. 67.
28. Tim Pengendali JPS (2000c), p. 29.
29. National Co-ordinating Team for the Social Safety Net Programmes, "Indonesia's Social Safety Net Programs and Its Safeguarding: An Expression of People's Right to Development" (Paper presented at a Seminar on Financial Crisis and the Right to Development, Jakarta, February 2001), p.10.
30. Lembaga Demografi FE-UI and Tim Pengendali JPS (2000a), p. 34.
31. Tim Pengendali JPS (2000a), p. 56.
32. Lembaga Demografi FE-UI and Tim Pengendali JPS (2000a), p. 51.
33. Ibid., p. 30.
34. Study of the SSN education programme based on the report of the TKPP-JPS, conducted by Tim Pengendali JPS in February 2000.
35. Lembaga Demografi FE-UI and Tim Pengendali JPS (2000a), p. 35.
36. Ibid., p. 37.
37. National Coordinating Team for Social Safety Net Programmes (2001), p. 9.
38. Lembaga Demografi FE-UI and Tim Pengendali JPS (2000b), p. 84.
39. National Coordinating Team for Social Safety Net Programmes (2001), p. 7.
40. Ibid., p. 8.
41. Puguh Irawan, Erman Rahman, Haning Romdiati, and Uzair Suhaimi, *Social Safety Nets Analysis and Recommendation: Prospects in Indonesia* (Report presented at the National Workshop on Social Safety Net Program in Indonesia, Jakarta, 6–7 February 2001, organized by BAPPENAS-UN ESCAP), p. 13.

42. Tim Pengendali JPS (2000a), p. 18.
43. National Coordinating Team for Social Safety Net Programmes (2001), p. 13.
44. Tim Pengendali JPS, *Hasil Pemantuan dan Evaluasi JPS TA 1998/1999* (Jakarta, June 1999), p. 42.
45. National Co-ordinating Team for Social Safety Net Programmes (2001), p. 13.
46. Puguh Irawan et al. (2001), p. 26.
47. Lembaga Demografi FE-UI and Tim Pengendali JPS (2000c), p. VII-5.
48. Lembaga Demografi FE-UI and Tim Pengendali JPS (2000b), p. 91.
49. Lembaga Demografi FE-UI and Tim Pengendali JPS (2000a), p. 52.
50. Lembaga Demografi FE-UI and Tim Pengendali JPS (2000b), p. 86.
51. Puguh Irawan et al. (2001), p. 13.
52. Tim Pengendali JPS, *Annual Report of Fiscal Year 2000* (2001), p. 21.
53. Ibid., p. 21.
54. Lembaga Demografi FE-UI and Tim Pengendali JPS (2000d), p. 81.
55. Puguh Irawan et al. (2001), p. 26.
56. Tim Pengendali JPS, *Annual Report of Fiscal Year 2000* (2001), p. 27.
57. Ibid., p. 26.
58. Tim Pengendali JPS, *Annual Report of Fiscal Year 1999/2000.*
59. This happened at the co-ordination meeting between Tim Pengendali JPS and TKPP-JPS on 11 May 2000.
60. National Co-ordinating Team for Social Safety Net Programmes (2001), p. 4.
61. Puguh Irawan et al. (2001), p. 24.
62. National Co-ordinating Team for Social Safety Net Programmes (2001), p. 12.
63. Bhakti Setiawan, *Poverty Reduction at "Intermediate" Level: The Roles of Local Government* (Proceedings of a Seminar on Renewing Poverty Reduction Strategy in Indonesia, Jakarta, 1 August 2000), p. 45.
64. Elizabeth Frankenberg, Duncan Thomas, and Kathleen Beegle, "Gender Dimensions of the Crisis: Evidence from the Indonesian Family Life Survey", *SMERU Indonesia*, No. 06 (June–July 1999), p. 1.
65. Ibid.
66. Gillian Brown, "Why Gender?", *SMERU Indonesia*, No. 06 (June–July 1999), p. 3.
67. National Co-ordinating Team for Social Safety Net Programmes (2001), p. 16.
68. Puguh Irawan et al. (2001), p. 42.
69. Tim Pengendali JPS, *Annual Report of Fiscal Year 2000* (2001), p. 46–47.
70. Puguh Irawan et al. (2001), p. 40–41.
71. Tim Pengendali JPS, *Annual Report of Fiscal Year 2000* (2001), p. 69.
72. Tim Pengendali JPS' Press Conference, 4 May 1999, at http://www.jps.or.id/proyek/pers4-5-99.html
73. Bhakti Setiawan (2000), p. 50.
74. Central Bureau of Statistics, Jakarta (1999), p. 591.

References

Akatiga. "Factory Unemployment: Gender Issues and Impacts". Mimeographed. Jakarta, 1999. Cited in Susan Horton and Dipak Mazumdar, "Vulnerable Groups and the Labor Market: The Aftermath of the Asian Financial Crisis". In *East Asian Labor Markets and the Economic Crisis*, edited by Gordon Betcherman and Rizwanul Islam. Washington, D.C.: The World Bank and Geneva: The International Labour Office, 1999.

Brown, Gillian. "Why Gender?", *SMERU Indonesia*, No. 06 (June–July 1999).

Central Bureau of Statistics. *Statistical Pocketbook of Indonesia*. Jakarta: Central Bureau of Statistics, 1999.

Frankenberg, Elizabeth, Duncan Thomas, and Kathleen Beegle. "Gender Dimensions of the Crisis: Evidence from the Indonesian Family Life Survey". *SMERU Indonesia*, No. 06 (June–July 1999).

Haeruman, Herman. "Jaring Pengaman Sosial dan Implementasinya di Masa Mendatang". Article in http://www.satunet.com/artikel/00/03/06/8480.html. Jakarta, 2000.

Irawan, Puguh, Erman Rahman, Haning Romdiati, and Uzair Suhaimi. "Social Safety Net Analysis and Recommendations: Prospects in Indonesia". Report presented at the National Workshop on Social Security Net Programmes in Indonesia. Jakarta: Bappenas-UN ESCAP, 6–7 February 2001.

Lembaga Demografi FE-UI and Tim Pengendali JPS. *Kajian terhadap Implementasi Program Jaring Pengaman Sosial, Buku III: Program JPS BP* [Studies on Implementation of the Social Safety Net Programme, Book III: Social Safety Net Programme on Education]. Jakarta: Lembaga Demografi Fakultas Ekonomi Universitas Indonesia and Tim Pengendali JPS, 2000a.

———. *Kajian terhadap Implementasi Program Jaring Pengaman Sosial, Buku V: Laporan Umum* [Studies on Implementation of the Social Safety Net Programme, Book V: General Report]. Jakarta: Lembaga Demografi Fakultas Ekonomi Universitas Indonesia and Tim Pengendali JPS, 2000b.

———. *Kajian terhadap Implementasi Program Jaring Pengaman Sosial, Buku II: Program JPS BK* [Studies on Implementation of the Social Safety Net Programme. Book II: Social Safety Net on Health]. Jakarta: Lembaga Demografi Fakultas Ekonomi Universitas Indonesia and Tim Pengendali JPS, 2000c.

———. *Kajian terhadap Implementasi Program Jaring Pengaman Sosial, Buku IV: Program PDM-DKE* [Studies on Implementation of the Social Safety Net Programme, Book IV: Social Safety Net Programmes on Regional Empowerment to Overcome the Impact of the Economic Crisis]. Jakarta: Lembaga Demografi Fakultas Ekonomi Universitas Indonesia and Tim Pengendali JPS, 2000d.

———. *Kajian terhadap Implementasi Program Jaring Pengaman Sosial, Buku I: Program OPK Beras* [Studies on Implementation of the Social Safety Net Programme. Book I: Programs on Special Market Distribution of Rice.] Jakarta: Lembaga Demografi Fakultas Ekonomi Universitas Indonesia and Tim Pengendali JPS, 2000e.

National Co-ordinating Team for Social Safety Net Programmes National Development Planning Agency. "Indonesia's Social Safety Net Programmes and Its Safeguarding: An Expression of People's Right to Development". Paper presented at the Seminar on Financial Crisis and the Right to Development. Jakarta: BAPPENAS-UN ESCAP, 27 February, 2001.

National Development Planning Agency. *Renewing Poverty Reduction Strategy in Indonesia*. Proceedings. Jakarta: National Development Planning Agency, 1 August 2000.

Setiawan, Bhakti. "Poverty Reduction at 'Intermediate' Level: The Roles of Local Government". In *Renewing Poverty Reduction Strategy in Indonesia*. Jakarta: National Development Planning Agency, 1 August 2000.

Sumodiningrat, Gunawan.. "Jaring Pengaman Sosial dan Pemberdayaan Masyarakat"[Social Safety Net and Society Empowerment]. Paper presented at the National Seminar on Social Safety Net and People Empowerment. Jakarta: BAPPENAS, 30 March 1999a.

________. "Economic Stabilization and Social Safety Net: Achieving Public Prosperity". Paper presented at JICA, Tokyo, 16 February 1999b.

________. *Pemberdayaan Masyarakat dan JPS* [Society Empowerment and SSN]. Jakarta: PT. Gramedia Pustaka Utama, 1999c.

________. *JPS: Pengalaman dan Pertanggungjawaban*. Forthcoming, 2000.

Tim Pengendali JPS. *Laporan Tahunan Tim Pengendali JPS Tahun Anggaran 2000* [Fiscal Year 2000 Annual Report of Tim Pengendali JPS]. Jakarta: Tim Pengendali JPS, 2001.

________. *Laporan Tahunan Tim Pengendali JPS Tahun Anggaran 1999/2000* [Fiscal Year 1999/2000 Annual Report of Tim Pengendali JPS]. Jakarta: Tim Pengendali JPS, 2000a.

________. *Hasil Studi JPS Tahun Anggaran 1999/2000* [Social Safety Net Study Report on Fiscal Year 1999/2000 SSN]. Jakarta: Tim Pengendali JPS, 2000b.

________. *Hasil Studi Evahrasi JPS: Kabupaten Wonogiri-Jawa Tengah*. Jakarta, February 2000c,

________. *Laporan Tahunan Tim Pengendali JPS Tahun Anggaran 1998/1999* [Fiscal Year 1998/1999 Annual Report of Tim Pengendali JPS]. Jakarta: Tim Pengendali JPS, 1999a.

________. *Hasil Pemantauan dan Evaluasi JPS Tahun Anggaran 1998/1999* [Results of Monitoring and Evaluation of Fiscal Year 1998/1999 SSN]. Jakarta: Tim Pengendali JPS, 1999b.

________. *Hasil Studi JPS: Kabupaten Wonogiri — Jawa Tengah*. [Results of Studies on SSN: Wonogiri (Central Java) district]. Jakarta: Tim Pengendali JPS, 2000d.

________. *Verifikasi OPK Beras* [Verification of Special Market Operation of Rice]. Jakarta: Lembaga Demografi Fakultas Ekonomi Universitas Indonesia, 2000e.

________. *Verifikasi JPS BP* [Verification of SSN on Education]. Jakarta: Lembaga Demografi Fakultas Ekonomi Universitas Indonesia, 2000f.

11

STATE-CREATED SOCIO-CULTURAL POVERTY
Lessons from Some Micro Studies

Sukamdi and Setiadi[1]

Introduction

There is great variation in the perceptions and evaluations on the economic crisis in Indonesia made by academicians and practitioners. How did the crisis affect the people's lives and how could it be solved? How was the socio-economic situation during 1998 and 1999? How vulnerable and miserable were the people at that time?

Mubyarto (2000) has shown that there are roughly two different views on the conditions during the crisis in 1997–99. The first is the doomsday view, which perceives the situation as being catastrophic and devastating. The second is the "not that bad" view, which sees Indonesians suffering but not that much.

The doomsday view is usually macroeconomic in nature. The drastic drop in the value of the rupiah, the sky-rocketing prices, the collapse of the banking system, the fall in foreign reserves, the high rate of unemployment, and its drastic increase are some examples of indicators often cited as signs of the collapse of the macroeconomy. Policy-making, including recommendations by foreign institutions such as the International Monetary Fund (IMF), is also often based on this macroeconomic point of view.

On the other hand, the "not that bad" view is reflected in the almost "business as usual" activities of many people, especially among the middle and lower income groups. Both traditional markets and modern supermarkets are as crowded as before. Traffic in Jakarta is as bad as before the crisis. Small and medium-sized firms, including those in the informal sectors, continue to make profit. The poor, who had been poor even before the crisis, may not have noticed the difference between the crisis and non-crisis periods.

This chapter argues that the doomsday view was the underlying factor in policy-making (by both Indonesian and international institutions) during at least the first half of 1998. With this assumption, the Government of Indonesia, helped by international donor agencies, established the SSN (Social Safety Net) programme, to help people cope with the crisis. However, this chapter attempts to show that the SSN programme has created socio-cultural poverty among the people. This discussion is based on anthropological research carried out in some rural areas in Central Java and Yogyakarta. The results may not be applicable for other areas in Indonesia, but it can provide important lessons in formulating programmes to help the people.

Crisis Overblown

One of the topics frequently discussed by experts concerning the economic crisis since 1997 is the impact of the crisis on the people's economic life. The discussions often use two indicators: poverty and unemployment.

Many estimates have been made on the incidence of poverty during the crisis in Indonesia. Interestingly, estimates produced in 1998 (especially in the first half of the year) were mostly very pessimistic. The crisis seemed to have brought doomsday for Indonesia. As quoted by Feridhanusetyawan (2000), the International Labour Organization (ILO), for example, estimated that 50 per cent of the Indonesian population lived under the poverty line in 1998. The Central Board of Statistics produced an estimate of 39 per cent for mid-1998. If these estimates were accurate, the conditions in 1998 would have resembled those of the 1970s. Yet, these figures have been widely quoted by journalists, policy-makers, and even scholars, both in Indonesia and other countries as indicators of the effects of the crisis, at least for the first half of 1998.

As more data and observations became available, estimates were revised. The situation during 1998 was not as bad as was earlier estimated. Using 1998 standards, Badan Pusat Statistik (2000) has reported that the poverty rate in 1996 (before the crisis) was 17.7 per cent. It rose to 24.2 per cent in December 1998, but declined to 23.5 per cent in February 1999, and further declined to 18.17 per cent in August 1999.

The rate in the urban areas was 13.6 per cent in 1996. It rose to 21.9 per cent in December 1998, and then declined to 19.5 per cent in February 1999, and 15.09 per cent in August 1999. The rural rate had risen from 19.9 per cent in 1996 to 25.7 per cent in December 1997 and then 26.1 per cent in February 1999, before it declined to 20.22 per cent in August 1999. In absolute terms, the number of poor increased from 34.5 million in 1996 to 49.5 million in December 1998. It then declined to 48.4 million in February 1999 and to 37.5 million in August 1999.

Mubyarto (2000) has argued that the inaccuracy in estimating the rate of poverty in the first half of 1998 was because of the misconception about poverty and the pessimistic view among experts, policy-makers, and the international donor agencies. The *Asahi Shimbun* (26 January 1999) even mentioned that the estimation of poverty and unemployment level had been exaggerated simply to get aid.

Furthermore, the increase in the incidence of poverty (both in terms of percentage and absolute numbers) in 1998 seems to have occurred in all economic sectors, with the agricultural sector being the worst-hit sector. The agricultural sector had the highest percentage and absolute number of poor people because of two reasons. First, the people in the agricultural sector are usually poorer than those working in other sectors. Secondly, the skills needed to work in agriculture are very minimal, and hence it can easily absorb those who lose their jobs in other sectors. Therefore, the agricultural sector, which had experienced a labour surplus even before the crisis, had to share a heavier burden to accommodate "refugees" from other sectors. Worse, the "absorption" simply meant "sharing poverty", and did not necessarily help the "refugees"; it even reduced the welfare of the "locals". In other words, the agricultural sector experienced a severe involution.

In short, the above discussion has shown that the impact of the economic crisis penetrated all economic sectors, although the impact varied according to the sector, but was not as dramatic as first thought in early 1998.

Crisis as the Dynamics of Life

Many socio-cultural-economic studies focus on social order, normality, disruption, conflict, and change. Yet, Frans and Keebet Von Benda-

Beckmann (2000) have argued that the dominant aspects in socio-cultural-economic issues are uncertainty and insecurity, rather than conflict and disruption. The life of the Javanese in certain regions in Central Java may illustrate this debate.

Kutanegara (1998), in his study on the socio-economic conditions during the first two years of the crisis, examined the conditions according the people's subjective experiences. He saw how people put the crisis within the context of their life-long experiences. It is interesting, for example, to find that people who had lived through the Dutch and Japanese occupations (before 1945) maintained that the current crisis was nothing compared with those periods under the Dutch and Japanese.[2]

The finding of Kutanegara reveals that the perception of the poor can be quite different from that of the policy-makers. The policy-makers may perceive that the poor people had really suffered during the crisis, yet the people might not feel the same way. This is simply an illustration of the contrast between the doomsday view, mostly shared by the policy-makers, and the "not that bad" view held by the people. The policy-makers may have been influenced by the poor macroeconomic indicators, although these indicators may also reflect the negative perception of the policy-makers themselves. On the other hand, the rural people might perceive the condition as nothing extraordinary. They had been poor and suffering even before the crisis. They knew how to survive in such conditions. Their survival instinct and ability might have been much better than those involved in policy-making, who might have panicked because they themselves had never experienced such a drastic fall in their financial welfare. It is not surprising that Noteboom (1998) has found that the impact of the crisis was not visible among the rural people. Perhaps the economic system among the poor is more flexible than that for the rich and/or the policy-makers.

Mubyarto (2000) has stated that the crisis affected the modern sector more than the rural-traditional sector, and the poor adjusted much better to the crisis. The question is how they coped with the crisis. Hadi Soesastro (2002) has pointed out that during the crisis the economy shifted from a domination by large corporations and state enterprises to small- and medium-sized firms and the informal sector.

Hirzt (1995) has mentioned that people struggled through the economic crisis, overcoming the constraints they faced and attempting to increase their quality of life. Abdullah (1999) has found that the depression and misery felt by the rural people had been managed by the people themselves, either through the household, or the community.

In essence there are two survival strategies. The first strategy is a subsistence effort, to simply fulfill daily needs. The second is an accumulation effort, consisting of the first strategy, but also including an effort to accumulate capital to ensure individual and group survival in the future (Saptari 1997). This strategy depends on economic, social, political, and demographic formations. Any strategy adopted to survive will influence not only the people's own lives, but also the long-term dynamics of the community.

Coping Mechanism

The Population Studies Centre at Gadjah Mada University (Abdullah 1998; Kutanegara 1999; and Faturochman 1998) has conducted an analysis of the survival strategies in the rural areas in Yogyakarta, Central Java, and East Java, covering both agricultural and non-agricultural sectors. Table 10.1 shows the levels of the people's difficulty in coping with the crisis in three different rural areas. The first is Sriharjo (Yogyakarta) where people live in an agrarian context; the second is Kalitengah (Klaten, Central Java) where people (especially females) survive partly on small-sized industries; and the third is Kaboansikep (East Java) where most spouses, especially the wives, work as factory

TABLE 10.1
Difficulties Faced by the People of Three Villages as a Result of the Economic Crisis
(In %)

Type of difficulty	*Sriharjo (DIY)*	*Kalitengah (Klaten)*	*Keboansikep (Jatim)*
Revenue	26	52	16
Daily needs	39	20	29
Education	9	7	20
Housing	6	9	11
Health	13	7	18
Social expenses	7	5	5
Other	0	0	1
Total	100	100	100

Source: Dwiyanto (1999).

workers. The different environments can be expected to produce different strategic survival behaviours. There are two types of responses to the crisis — one related to consumption; and the other to production.

It is interesting to observe how people in Ceper (Central Java) adjusted their consumption behaviour. They reduced their allocation for non-food necessities to maintain their consumption of food. People in Srihardjo (Central Java) reduced the frequency of eating rice, from thrice a day to twice a day. They also changed from drinking a sweet drink, such as tea or coffee, to drinking fresh water. However, this change may be seen as a silver lining, as they have adopted a healthier life-style by reducing or stopping sweet drinks.

The silver lining in the change towards better food consumption was also found in the villages of Waringin Jaya and Mekar Jaya in Bekasi, West Java. CIDA (2000) found that since the crisis the people have consumed less meat and eggs and eaten more *tempe, tahu,* kangkung leaves, and legumes. Yet, we do not know whether these people realize that their change in consumption pattern during the crisis was for the better. Perhaps, these healthier foods were still regarded as inferior goods, which they would avoid if they had more money. Kutanegara (1998) has found that people in Ceper and Srihardjo did not really understand the importance of the quality of food. The most important thing to them was that there was something to eat. They said:

> *Sing penting iso mangan, mangan ya sak anane, ora usah neka-neka apa maneh enak-enakan* (the most important thing is to eat, just to eat anything we can, and not to worry whether it is delicious).

The study by Abdullah (1999) has found that the people's attitude towards life was much influenced by how they coped with the crisis. In Jatinom (Central Java), people accepted the crisis as something normal. They saw it simply as a recurring cycle they could not avoid. They had experienced crises from time to time and they knew very well how to adapt to such a situation. For them, the crisis did not make any difference. One said:

> *Padha bae......sithik dicakake sithik, akeh dicakake akeh* (It is the same...if we have a little, we have to consume little; if we have much, then we can consume much)

Another respondent said:

> *Nek cara kula....kenging moneter ya wis men. Nek kula mung ngoten... soale ora ijen kok. Kabeh dha ngalami.* (In my way... suffering from monetary

crisis is okay... that is the way I am.....I am not alone. Everybody suffers.)

Yet, Faturochman (1999) has found a different way to cope with the crisis. Those who had been used to the rise and fall of their incomes had no problem in adjusting their consumption patterns. They might concentrate on their main necessities (such as food), pawn their possessions such as a sewing machine, borrow money, sell some other assets, or try to find other jobs. Among the 331 respondents in the Kalitengah village, 7 per cent just accepted their fate and 87 per cent worked harder to overcome the fall in their purchasing power. From these 87 per cent who worked hard, 30 per cent chose to be more frugal in their spending, 30 per cent chose to open new businesses, and 27 per cent chose to make more efficient use of household resources.

However, a different picture emerges if we look at the production side. Faturochman (1999) has shown that those directly related to the modern economic sectors, especially those at the lower levels, had suffered much. Low-level workers in the modern sectors, for example, experienced a drastic fall in their welfare. One said:

> *Tidak ada pendapatan sama sekali selama enam minggu ini.* (There is no income at all during these six weeks.)

Another respondent mentioned:

> *Krisis menyebabkan "tek sek", nggak tahu lah* (The crisis causes a "sudden death", I don't know)

A better coping mechanism was seen among those working in the garment sector. They found other business opportunities, such as looking for casing debris to sell. The employer responded to the crisis by diversifying his business, by doing things which were not within his specialization (Yuarsi 1999). They became individualistic and had less concern for others. The most important thing was how they themselves could survive. One respondent (Faturochman 1998) explained:

> *Di masa sulit seperti ini yang penting kita sendiri hidup....sulit untuk mencari bantuan pihak lain. Makanya...Orang lain bukan menjadi urusan kita* (During a difficult period like this, the most important thing is our own life...it is difficult to seek help from others. Thus...other people are not our concern.)

Those who worked in the agricultural sector seemed to cope by selling goods and services in *warung* (simple stalls selling cheap daily needs). Faturochman (1998) explained that though the price of agricultural products rose, the terms of trade of agricultural products were still declining. Some said that they could not depend on agricultural products alone. They leased out their land but the rental income was not enough to satisfy their daily needs. The earnings from agriculture were spent on tuition for their children. Others said that their earnings from agriculture were used for emergency purposes only, and they depended on the pension they got from their father and by trading at a *warung*. In general, it seems that the people did not use their earnings from agriculture as a source of money to finance their daily activities. Agriculture was sometimes only a part-time activity.

Only a few respondents reported that they survived by working mainly as farmers. They were those who could diversify their agricultural activities. The landless could also survive because the demand for their labour remained high throughout the year.

In short, the people in this village had great financial resilience. The high productivity achieved on their land and the *nrimo*[3] culture contributed significantly to this relatively high financial resilience.

In difficult times, there were five types of coping mechanisms. The first was the *pasrah*, including those who stopped their activities, patiently understanding the situation and drawing them closer to God. The second type was expansive, including those who started new activities, expanded their geographical market, and increased their capital by borrowing from outside the family. The third type was the explorative. This was similar to the second type, but they used more resources from the family. The fourth type dealt with management. They optimized their resources by, for example, moving the business location, changing jobs, and being thrifty. The last type was long-term in nature, and sometimes not related at all to immediate daily tasks such as preparing food for the children. The third and last types of coping mechanisms were commonly used by the people.

In Jatinom, Abdullah (1999) also did not find much impact of the crisis. There are three possible reasons for this absence of a decline in the welfare of the people here during the crisis. The first is that there was a flow back to rural subsistence production. The people intensified the use of their land by planting more productive plants. The second reason was that they diversified their businesses, rather than continued with just agricultural activities. For example, they looked for river stones to sell for construction material. In other words, they allocated their time more productively than they did before the crisis. The strong economic "fundamentals" in Jatinom might have provided many opportunities to respond to the crisis.

People were also more willing to work in less attractive jobs, the so-called 3D (dirty, dangerous, and difficult) jobs. Tukiran and Sutanto (1999), for example, found that people in Gunung Kidul, Central Java, besides spending more frugally, worked as hard and diligently as possible, regardless of the type of jobs they could get. People in the rural areas might not regard status as an important thing in their lives, and they might not need much government support.

The above discussion has shown the differences in response with regard to consumption and production. For consumption, especially in the rural areas, people still depended on others; but, for production, they had to help themselves.

Government Intervention: A Long-term Economic Trap

As mentioned before, the monetary crisis caused the government to panic because it was not prepared to face the events. Thus, people lost confidence in the government, and it has had to apply sound macroeconomic management to regain the confidence of the people (Nopirin 2000).

Nevertheless, the monetary crisis grew into an economic and political crisis, which culminated in the collapse of then President Soeharto on 21 May 1998. The succeeding government then attempted to manage the non-monetary sectors. It introduced some breakthrough programmes to cope with rising poverty. It instituted the so-called Social Safety Net (SSN) programme. Principally, the SSN programme was one of the inter-ministerial programmes aimed at solving the problem of poverty during the crisis. The programme tried to help those who suddenly fell into poverty and to bring the economy back to recovery, towards sustainable growth and stability (Mubyarto 1999).[4] Unfortunately, it was not clear who were poor because of the crisis (or the new poor) and who were poor even before the crisis (the old poor). Worse, it was not easy to decide who should be prioritized from the two groups of the poor.

Through the SSN programme, the government has been successful in obtaining funds to create job opportunities both at the local and sectoral levels, and for emergencies. The government provides free services for health-care and family-planning, especially for those classified as poor according to the "*pra-sejahtera*"[5] measurement, and scholarships to ensure that all children under nine years old are enrolled in school.

Finally, the government supplies cheap staple food-stuff (Tukiran and Sutanto 1999.) Indeed, the programmes have been implemented regardless of whether the recipients are new or old poor. However, the implementation has not necessarily achieved the goals of the programme, which is to help the poor (new or old poor) to cope with the crisis. The following are some findings from micro-studies done in Yogyakarta and Central Java.

Darwin (1999) has found that the SSN programme was not relevant to the people's needs in some villages in Java. The government carried out the programme simply because it was a government programme, without regard for the aspirations of the society. Some resistance in the form of protests emerged because it was seen that help had gone to those who did not deserve it.

Mubyarto (2000) has mentioned that in identifying the recipients many "mistakes" were made. Instead of providing the money to those who were really in need, the money was often distributed to those who were more "vocal" in the society. Those who were really poor often could not fight to get the money. In other words, the recipients of the funding were often those who did not really need the money. Furthermore, it was difficult to avoid political interests in the distribution of the funding.

An example of the government's disregard for conditions in society was the rice distribution programme in Ngampilan village. Bulog (the institution in charge of stabilizing the national stockpile of rice) had calculated that there were 339 households eligible to buy cheap rice. However, 625 households turned up. The head of the neighbourhood administrative unit, Rukun Tetangga, was *ewuh-pekewuh* (feeling uneasy, uncomfortable, and reluctant) to refuse to sell cheap rice to neighbours who were actually not eligible to buy. The head treated everyone equally, both poor and non-poor. Each of the poor households was actually allowed to buy 10 kg of rice at the cheap price of Rp1,000 per kg. (The market price was about Rp3,000 per kg.) However, because the head could not refuse to sell cheap rice to everyone, each household (the poor as well as the rich) was allowed to buy only 5 kg.

An example of the success of lobbying by the élites was that of a village in North Semarang subdistrict. Soetrisno (1999) found that 18 per cent of the funds allocated to help jobless people and poor households was distributed to the business people and government employees.

Cheap *sembako* (nine essential foods), which were supposed to be sold to the poor only, was made available to all members of the local society, regardless of whether they were poor or not (*Kompas*, 10 February 1999). Some people who were not eligible to receive aid also benefited from the programme simply because they could get the *kartu sehat*.[6] In Boyolali, the recipients of money as aid were taxed. These recipients were supposed to be poor and hence should not be taxed. If they were rich, they should not receive aid. It is possible that the recipients were not poor, and hence were taxed. Yet, this practice was a violation of the objective of the SSN programme.

Soetrisno (1999) has found that the programme in the health sector did not really reach the poor. It did not take the local conditions into account. It could have invited the participation of housewives to identify the poor families, because they would know better. Furthermore, there was a lack of effective social marketing of the programme. As a result, people did not know the existence and purpose of the programme.

Jelinek (1999) found that a blacksmith in Gunung Kidul could earn Rp 20,000 per day. However, the government perceived that he needed help. He was then forced by the head of the *kecamatan* (sub-district) to participate in a prescribed labour-intensive programme designed by the government. He subsequently earned only Rp5,000 per day.

Soetrisno (1999) found that problems in Banyumas were related to factors such as a delay in scholarship disbursement, unequal distribution of labour-intensive projects, and delay in the delivery of rice aid. Frustration and social jealousy resulted in such cases. In Boyolali, the problems were related to misuse of funds (for physical construction), the existence of "red-plate"[7] NGOs, delay in funding disbursement, cancellation of the food supplement programme for school-children, non-transparancy in the distribution of scholarships, fake activities,[8] and coercion to join the labour-intensive projects.

People have also been spoilt by the SSN programmes. For example, moral hazard was found in the health sector. Because of the relatively cheap, and even free, health-care services, people used the services excessively. When the "crisis" is over and there is no longer cheap and free health-care services, these people may feel frustrated that economic recovery has reduced their welfare.

The programme had "determined" that some parts of the society were poor and thus ought to receive the entire support programme. Interestingly, more people "admitted" that they were poor. Even the heads of the local regions were happy to say that they were poor so that they could get help from the SSN programme. The money for the poor became the target of fighting among those who were in charge of the distribution. This is evidence of the low sensitivity and lack of compassion among those who were not poor.

What was worse was that the help was a kind of charity, which did not help the people to solve their own problems. The condition of being poor was a blessing, because by being poor, they could receive money. If they were not poor, they had to work hard to convince others that they were poor. They were not embarassed to receive this charity. This phenomenon thus produced new social and political problems.

The intervention of the government in the SSN programme actually created the feeling that the crisis had overwhelmed the people and that they had not been fairly treated. It created an impression that being poor was a state where other people (and the government) should help. The poor was defined as the needy who should receive charity. Instead of educating the people to help themselves, the government has given them an incentive to get charity. Thus, the programme has produced a feeling of dependence and killed the creativity of the people. They feel that it is their right to demand aid, at least in terms of the *sembako*, from the government or from other sectors of the society (Darwin 1999). Although the "poor" have acknowledged that the condition is *belum apa-apa* (nothing, just trivial), they still insist on their "right" to get the help. Thus, they rationally responded to the SSN programme.

Following Kleden (1987), the conclusion is that the government has actually introduced a feeling of socio-cultural poverty by implementing the SSN programme. The intervention just increased the isolation and marginalization of poor households, both socially and politically. Economically, the poor had been marginalized. With aid which does not respond to their aspirations, they have basically become subordinated to a lower position. It has become more difficult for them to solve their basic needs in social services (such as education and health-care), job opportunities, and purchasing power. Furthermore, the help to the poor has also aroused "jealousy" on the part of those who did not get the help, regardless of whether they deserved it or not. The programme has brought about social division, a lack of identity, and no control over their lives.

Concluding Remarks

The statement *"krisis ya biar, semua kan mengalami..."* (Crisis is okay. Everybody experiences it.) which has been expressed by many rural people, on the other hand, may show the resilience of the rural people in adjusting to crisis. Yet, the statement may also reflect the inability to change the situation, and hence they become "numb" to the conditions, a fatalistic attitude towards life.

The crisis conditions and the pattern of managing the crisis developed by the government have contributed to a socio-economic vulnerability among the poor people to both external influences and internal social conflicts. This vulnerability in turn has influenced greatly the poverty status among the rural people themselves. Much of the chaos and horizontal conflicts among the villagers and the recent social turbulence reflect an economy that has been improperly managed and controlled.

The economic crisis has resulted in many programmes designed to overcome the impact of the crisis on the welfare of the people, especially the poor. However, these programmes have produced new problems among the rural poor in the form of social poverty. These phenomena were not seen before the crisis, because the poor had always had some productive ways to cope with their poor economic situation.

Nevertheless, the government still feels compelled to help the poor through their programmes of direct intervention, without really understanding the aspirations of the poor. The crisis had created confusion and panic among government bureaucrats and international donor institutions, and the SSN programme is an outgrowth of such confusion and panic (Chalid 2000). In contrast, the people whom the government has attempted to help, often already possess coping mechanisms in the form of productive-microeconomic efforts at either family or institutional level.

The question then is how to manage the economy during the crisis, so that local aspirations can be well integrated with government programmes. It is not easy to formulate such a programme. Yet the people's freedom to participate in determining the programmes to help themselves will be of paramount importance in managing the crisis at the family, community, and institutional levels.

The programmes should co-opt individuals of high integrity as the key performers in policy-making and leadership. Secondly, the top-down approach should be replaced with one incorporating the aspirations of the people. Thirdly, the policy-makers and leaders should stop treating the poor simply as an object of their projects. It is time to decentralize authority to the regions and to have bottom-up planning involving the grass-roots. In this context, there have been many integrated programmes based on a community system. The local institutions can be organized to overcome the excessive domination of the bureaucrats' roles (Suryadi 1999).

Notes

1. The writers would like to thank Wulan Astuti for her contribution in finalizing this chapter.
2. Indonesia was under the Dutch for about three hundred and fifty years before Indonesia fell under Japanese occupation in 1942, and won independence in 1945.
3. *Nrimo* has a very deep meaning. It is related to observing and understanding whatever is happening. People with *nrimo* culture will always be happy with whatever they have. It is of course debatable whether *nrimo* is good or bad. After all, what is good and what is bad?
4. More discussion on the concept of SSN can be found in Chapter 9 of this volume.
5. This is the definition of poverty by the BKKBN(Badan Koordinasi Keluarga Berencana Nasional or National Family Planning Coordinating Board). The welfare of the population is classified into *"pra-sejahtera"*, *"sejahtera 1"*, *"sejahtera 2"*, and *"sejahtera 3 plus"*. The *pra-sejahtera* is the lowest level of welfare. They are families which have not been able to satisfy their socio-psychological needs. The *sejahtera* families are those which have been able to satisfy their socio-psychological needs, but have not been able to save and to get information. The *sejahtera 2* families are those who have fulfilled their socio-psychological needs and have been able to save and to get information. The families with the highest welfare, the *sejahtera 3 plus*, are those *sejahera 2* families who have been able to contribute significantly to society. This definition is very broad, and it has been difficult to measure each level with precision.
6. *Kartu sehat* (literally "healthy card") is a card for the poor to get free health-care services.
7. "Red plate" is literally the number plate for motor vehicles used by state-run institutions. NGOs are not supposed to be related to the government. Therefore, "red-plate" NGOs refer to those NGOs which are managed by government officials. These NGOs only started after the government launced the SSN programme. In addition to the "red plate" NGOs, there are also many "private NGOs" which were just established during the crisis to take advantage of opportunities arising from the availability of money in the SSN programme. These NGOS often disappeared quickly after they completed the projects.
8. "Fake" activities refer to those activities which never really existed but money had been allocated and disbursed for those activities.

References

Abdullah, Irwan. "Social Security: Dari Solidaritas Mekanis ke Formalisasi Mekanisme Sosial" [Social Security: From Mechanical Solidarity to Formalisation of Social Mechanism]. Paper presented at the seminar on Social Security and Social Policy, in Yogyakarta, 28–29 December 1998.

———. "Krisis Ekonomi, Daya Tahan Penduduk, dan Social Security: Kasus Jatinom di Jawa Tengah" [Economic Crisis, Population Resilience, and Social Security: A Case of Jatinom, Central Java]. *Populasi* 10, no. 1 (1995): 15 – 26.

Aji, Gutomo Bayu. "Studi Mengenai Jaminan Sosial di Indonesia: Suatu Reproduksi terhadap Konsep-konsep Pertukaran" [A Study on Social Security in Indonesia: A Reproduction on Exchange Concepts]. Paper presented at a seminar on Social Security and Social Policy. Yogyakarta: Population Studies Center, 28–29 December 1988.

Badan Pusat Statistik. *Laporan Perekonomian Indonesia 2000: Angkatan Kerja, Konsumsi, dan Kemiskinan Penduduk* [Report on Indonesian Economy 2000: Labour Force, Consumption, and Population Poverty]. Jakarta: Badan Pusat Statistik, 2000.

Benda-Beckmann, Franz Von, and Keebet Von Benda-Beckmann. "Coping with Insecurity". In *Coping With Insecurity: An "Underall" Perspective on Social Security in the Third World*, edited by Franz Von Benda-Beckmann, Keebet Von Benda-Beckmann and Hans Marks, pp. 7–31. Yogyakarta: Pustaka Pelajar (Indonesia); and Focaal Foundation (The Netherlands), 2000.

Chalid, Pheni. "Dari JPS ke Penanggulangan Kemiskinan" [From SSN to Poverty Alleviation]. *Republika* daily, 13 September 2000.

CIDA (Canadian International Development Agency). *Coping Strategies of Poor Households in Indonesia. Report of a pilot survey testing qualitative methods to describe food security and poverty dynamics in three provinces.* Jakarta: CIDA, 2000.

Darwin, Muhadjir. "Krisis Nasional: Respons Penduduk Miskin dan Pemerintah" [National Crisis: Response of Poor People and the Government]. *Populasi* 10, no. 1 (1998): 1–14.

Dwiyanto, Agus. "The economic crisis, social security, and the government program failure: The study of three villages in Java." Paper presented at a workshop on the economic crisis and social security in Indonesia. Berg-en-Dal, the Nederlands: Neihmegen Universiteit, CASA Amsterdam and PCS GMU, 7–9 January 1999.

Faturochman and Agus Dwiyanto, "Validitas dan Realibilitas Pengukuran Keluarga Sejahtera" [Validity and Reliability in Measuring *Keluarga Sejahtera*]. *Populasi* 9, no. 1 (1998): 37–49.

Faturochman, "Bertahan Hidup di Masa Krisis: Kasus Kalitengah" [Surviving during Crisis: A Case in Kalitengah]. Paper presented at a seminar on Social Security and Social Policy. Yogyakarta: Population Studies Centre, 28–29 December 1998.

———. "Krisis dan Nasib Buruh di Perdesaan" [Crisis and the Condition of the Rural Labourers]. *Populasi* 10, no. 1 (1999): 27–42.

Feridhanusetyawan, Tubagus. "The Social Impact of the Indonesian Economic Crisis". Report prepared for the Thailand Development Research Institute (TDRI), 2000.

"Hasil Survey: JPS Timbulkan Perpecahan" [Survey Result: SSN Results in Conflict]. *Kompas* daily, 5 February 1999.

Hirzt, Frank. *Managing Insecurity State. Social Policy and Family Networks in the Rural Philippines*. Saarbrucken: Verlag Fur Entwicklungspolitik Breitenbach Gmbh, 1995.

Irawan, Puguh, and Haning Romdati. "The Impact of Economic Crisis on Poverty and Its Implications for Developing Strategies". Paper presented at a workshop on National Food and Nutrition VII. Jakarta: National Institute of Science, 1–2 March 2000.

Ismawan, Bambang. "Pemulihan Keberdayaan Masyarakat melalui Pembiayaan Mikro dan Pendampingan Mandiri" [Recovery of Society Empowerment through Micro and Self Financing]. In *Pemulihan Ekonomi Rakyat menuju Kemandirian Masyarakat Desa* [Recovery of People Economy through Self-Sustaining Rural Society], edited by Mubyarto, pp. 171–86. Yogyakarta: Aditya Media/YAE, 2000.

Kleden, Ignas. "Masalah Kemiskinan Sosial-budaya di Indonesia". *Prisma* 16, no. 8 (1987): 15–28.

"Kucuran JPS Macet di Sana-sini" [Disorganized Distribution of SSN Funding]. *Kompas* daily, 11 February 1999.

Kutanegara, Pande Made. "Sriharjo pada Masa Krisis" [Srihardjo during Crisis]. *Populasi* 10, no. 1 (1999): 55–72.

Kutanegara, Pande Made et al. *Dampak dan Respon Penduduk Terhadap Krisis di Sriharjo* [Impact and Response of the Population on Crisis in Srihardjo]. Yogyakarta: Population Study Center, University of Gadjah Mada, 1999.

"Masih Ada Saja yang Tega Gerogoti Rezeki Orang Miskin" [People Still Dare to Corrupt the Fortune of the Poor]. *Kompas* daily, 9 February 1999.

Mubyarto. "Krisis Ekonomi, Ekonomi Rakyat, dan Optimisme Menghadapi Pemulihan Ekonomi" [Economic Crisis, People Economy, and Optimism facing Economic Recovery]. Speech at the Opening of a Workshop on Youth in West Nusa Tenggara. Denpasar: Collaboration Agro Economic Foundation (YAE), and Pemda se-gugus Nusa Tenggara, 15 February 2000.

________. "Krisis ini Belum Seberapa... (Dua Pertiga Penduduk desa Di Klaten Tidak Merasakan Penurunan Kesejahteraan, Tujuh Persen Pasrah)". Unpublished paper, 3 February 1999.

Nooteboom, Gerben. "Food Security, Labour and Mixed Farming Strategies in an Upland Area, Desa Krajan Bondowoso, East Java. A preliminary field report on rural people's livelihoods and food security strategies in the context of the current economic crisis". Paper presented at a seminar in the Population Studies Center, University of Gadjah Mada, Yogyakarta, 22 October 1998.

Nopirin. "Krisis Ekonomi Indonesia: Apa Yang Telah Terjadi, Pelajaran Apa Yang Dapat Diperoleh Dan Langkah Apa Yang Harus Ditempuh" [Indonesian Economic Crisis: What Has Happened, What Lessons Can be Learned, and What Must be Done?]. Speech at the inauguration as professor in the Faculty of Economics, University of Gadjah Mada, 22 January 2000.

Pradhan, Menno, Asep Suryahadi, Sudarno Sumarto and Lant Pritchett. "Measurement of Poverty in Indonesia: 1996, 1999, and Beyond". SMERU Working Paper, 2000.

"Program JPS Bisa Menciptakan Bencana" [SSN Programme Can Produce Disasters]. *Kompas* daily,10 February 1999.

Saptari, Ratna. "Social Security and the Study of Java: Concepts, Issues and Problems". Paper presented at the workshop on Social Security and Social Policy in Java, Gadjah Mada University, Population Studies Center, 5–7 August 1997.

Soesastro, Hadi. "Indonesia under Megawati". Paper presented at the Regional Outlook Forum 2002 organized by the Institute of Southeast Asian Studies, Singapore, 8 January 2002.

Soetrisno, Loekman. "Studi Evaluasi Pelaksanaan Program Jaring Pengaman Sosial (JPS) di Beberapa Daerah di Jawa Tengah dan Daerah Istimewa Yogyakarta" [Evaluation on the Implementation of the SSN in some Regions in Central Java and Yogyakarta]. Yogyakarta: Center for Research on Rural and Regional Development, University of Gadjah Mada, in collaboration with the Monitoring Team on the Enhancement of the 1999 Social Safety Net Programme, 1999.

Statistics Indonesia. *Peta dan Perkembangan Kemiskinan di Indonesia* [Map and Trend of Poverty in Indonesia]. Jakarta: Statistics Indonesia, 1997.

———. *The 1998 Revised Poverty Incidence Based on the December 1998 Susenas: Methodological Issues*. Jakarta: Statistics Indonesia, 1999.

Suryadi, Charles. "Perlu Dikembangkan Community Based System" [Need to Enhance Community Based System]. *Warta Demografi* 28, no. 2 (1999): 17–22.

Suryahadi, Asep, Sudarno Sumarto, Yusuf Suharso and lant Pritchett. "The Evolution of Poverty During the Crisis in Indonesia, 1996 to 1999". Paper presented at a seminar on Methodology of Poverty Calculation in Indonesia, organized jointly by the Centre for Statistical Services, World Bank, and SMERU, Jakarta, 30 November 1999.

Suyono, Haryono. "Pokok-pokok Sambutan Jaringan Pemberdayaan Sosial Social Safety Net dalam Pembangunan Keluarga Sejahtera". In *'Social Safety Net': Development, Concepts and Its Application*, edited by Yulfita Raharjo and Ingrid Kolb-Hindarmanto. Jakarta: Puslitbang Kependudukan and Ketenagakerjaan Lembaga Ilmu Pengetahuan Indonesia (PPT-LIPI) in collaboration with United Nations Children's Fund (UNICEF), 1998.

Tukiran and Agus Sutanto. "Resistensi dan Fleksibilitas Penduduk Perdesaan Lahan Kering" [Resistence and Flexibility of Rural Dry Areas]. *Populasi* 10, no. 1 (1999): 73–94.

Yuarsi, Susi Eja. "Dinamika Pengusaha Industri Cor Logam di Masa Krisis" [Dynamics of Metal Production Business during Crisis]. *Populasi* 10, no. 1 (1999): 43–54.

12

THE LABOUR MARKET IN INDONESIA DURING THE CRISIS

Tubagus Feridhanusetyawan

Introduction

One important aspect of thc economic crisis at the macroeconomic level that would affect the quality of life of the people in Indonesia at the micro level is the adjustment in household or individual income, which depends largely on the adjustment in the labour market. A sharp economic contraction by almost 14 per cent in 1998 led to declining labour demand, massive lay-offs, and shrinking formal sector employment. Earnings in the formal sector sharply declined, and labour moved to the unprotected informal sectors. At the same time, rapid inflation of more than 77 per cent in 1998 significantly reduced the purchasing power of labour. In other words, Indonesian labourers suffered both from declining employment opportunities and skyrocketing prices, which led to rapidly declining real incomes during the worst time of the crisis in 1998.[1]

The effects of the economic crisis, characterized by a massive contraction in the real sector, rapid inflation, and excessive depreciation of the currency, leading to a decline in the real income of Indonesian labourers, depended on the nature of the adjustments in the labour market. In other words, the characteristics and nature of the labour market matter in determining whether the impact of the economic crisis led to massive adjustments in quantity (or employment), or prices (or wages), or both. In most developed countries, and in a labour scarce economy in general, wages tend to be sticky and adjustments in the labour market mostly result in declining employment. In a labour-surplus developing country, such as Indonesia, where formal sector employment is twice as large as the informal sector, wages tend to be flexible, and adjustment to the shock would come from declining real wages. Workers could not afford to be unemployed in the absence of social security, safety nets, or other forms of insurance against unemployment.

While declining real incomes at the aggregate level can be observed easily by looking at real gross domestic product (GDP) growth, or real GDP per capita, the decline in real incomes at the micro individual or household level would not be obvious. One question, for example, is the impact of the crisis on the changing patterns of income distribution. In other words, who have suffered the most from the crisis: the poor, the middle-income group, or the rich? Various studies[2] have shown that the distribution of expenditure was, in fact, more even after the crisis. In other words, the expenditures of the rich declined more substantially than the poor during the worst time of the crisis in 1998–99. However, this does not explain whether a similar trend is taking place with respect to income, mainly because reliable and accurate data on income are not readily available.

People may receive their income from several different sources: labour wages for those who work, rent from rental properties, interest income from savings as well as profits, or dividends from certain investment. The experience during the crisis, at least from the data on income tax, shows that some people actually enjoyed the windfall of interest income from the high interest rate environment in 1998. This case shows that while wages and labour earnings may have generally declined during the crisis, the total income of individuals or households might have declined to a lesser extent, or perhaps even increased, especially for those who had large savings in the banks. For those who had no income other than their earnings, declining real wages and earnings would be directly translated to declining real income.

Bearing these issues in mind, this chapter aims to present the impact of the crisis on human development in Indonesia by focusing on adjustments in the labour market. It discusses adjustments in employment and labour earnings, which are among the most crucial elements in the discussion of human development. Earnings represent the value-added, or productivity, of labour, which reflects not only the purchasing power of the people but also the financial outcome of human development. It is important to note, however, that the purpose of human development is more than just to increase earnings and productivity. Human development should also include, for example, the right to be free from fear, to have good health, to acquire knowledge, and to migrate. The discussion on the labour market is, therefore, not meant to examine the results of human development in Indonesia. Rather, it simply presents the analysis of one aspect of human development, by focusing on the adjustment of the labour market during the crisis, and how the adjustment has affected the quality of life of Indonesian workers.

The data show that the labour market has been adjusting to the crisis very well. Different from the Keynesian model, where wages tend to be sticky in adjusting to employment shocks, the Indonesian experience shows flexible wage adjustments, consistent with the neoclassical model.[3] While the unemployment rate was low during the worst time of the crisis in 1998, there was a massive movement of labour between sectors in the economy, especially from the formal to the informal, from urban to rural, and from the modern to the traditional sectors. The crisis led to a reversal of the formalization process of the labour market, which took place during the economic boom years in the early 1990s, to informalization during the crisis. Labour productivity also declined very rapidly during the crisis, but the decline was less severe compared with the reduction in real wages. With some improvement in the general economic situation in 1999 and 2000, labour began to return to the urban-modern sectors, wages started to rise, and labour productivity began to catch up. Based on the current trend, the level of real wages and labour productivity are expected to return to the pre-crisis level in 2001–02.

This chapter begins with a discussion of the supply of labour by presenting the changing patterns of labour force participation during the crisis. It elaborates on the participation of people in the labour market and critically examines some key concepts commonly used in the discussion of the labour market, such as labour-force participation, open unemployment, and under-employment. The next section discusses the demand side of the labour market, by focusing on the changing patterns of employment across sectors — formal-informal, and urban-rural classifications. This is then followed by a discussion on an important feature during the crisis, namely, labour displacement from the formal sector. The final section presents a discussion on earnings and labour productivity during the 1997–2000 period. Because of the scarcity of data, the discussion on earnings is limited to the adjustments in the formal sector.

Labour Force, Unemployment, and Under-employment

During the worst time of the economic crisis in 1998, labour-force participation actually increased, especially for females, and particularly in the rural areas. The data from the National Labour Survey, or Survey Tenaga Kerja Nasional (Sakernas) show that the annual growth of the overall labour-force increased only slightly, from 2.6 per cent annually between 1990 and 1996 to 3.5 per cent between 1997 and 1998. Focusing on the rural areas alone, the growth of the labour-force increased from about 0.5 per cent a year between 1990 and 1996 to 2.9 per cent between 1997 and 1998. On the other hand, the growth of the labour force in the urban areas decreased from 7.3 per cent a year between 1990 and 1996 to 4.7 per cent during the crisis in the 1997–98 period. During the crisis, the growth of the female labour force and employment also increased. From 1990 to 1996, the size of the female labour force grew at about 2.3 per cent annually, while during the crisis in 1997–98 it grew by 4.8 per cent. The growth of female employment had also increased from 1.8 per cent annually before the crisis to 4.2 per cent during 1997–98. The size of the male labour force, however, remained relatively constant before and after the crisis. The fact that the labour force participation of women increased during the crisis may suggest increased employment opportunities for women. It could also mean that the crisis forced women to participate and work in the labour market to provide an additional income for the household.

Small qualitative studies, such as that reported by the SMERU team (SMERU Indonesia, August 1999) have shown that women (including wives, mothers, and mothers-in-law) played an important role in helping the family to cope with the crisis. When the husbands lost their jobs, the women took over the role of the family's main bread-winner. These women would go to the cities or abroad to work as domestic workers. Therefore, the second interpretation that women were forced to participate in the labour force is more plausible.

However, the data in 1999 show a slightly different pattern. Labour force participation in general continued to increase but at a slower rate compared with that in 1998. There were also changing patterns in the rural–urban and female–male classifications. After declining from 1997 to 1998, labour-force participation in the urban areas increased significantly from 1998 to 1999. Classified by gender, the sharp increase in female labour-force participation during 1997–98 in fact did not continue, and in 1999, male labour-force participation increased faster than that of females. The reversing trend of female labour-force participation in 1999 is consistent with the economic recovery starting in 1999 and the interpretation that women were forced to participate in the labour market in 1998. As economic conditions improved, the women were less likely to be forced to join the labour market.

The number of people unemployed and the unemployment rate have often been taken as indicators of the impact of the crisis on the welfare of the people. For an example, the government, through the Minister of Manpower, mentioned several times that unemployment was expected to reach about 15 to 20 million people in 1998. The official estimates of the unemployment rate in 1998 by the Ministry of Manpower and BAPPENAS (the National Planning Agency) put it at about 14.8 per cent (13.7 million) and 13.6 per cent (12.4 million) respectively. The special task force of the International Labour Organization (ILO)[4] estimated that the open unemployment rate in 1998 was about 10 per cent, or 9.3 million people.[5]

The confusion was largely due to a misunderstanding on the concept of unemployment. In a country such as Indonesia where there are no unemployment benefits, statistics on unemployment should not be used as indicators of poverty, or the severity of the crisis. It should be no surprise that the unemployment rate would even decline during bad times and increase during good times. The misunderstanding of the concept has resulted in many attempts to "enlarge" the number, or the rate, whenever the number or the rate is found to be "too" small. Yet, policy-makers seem to have accepted the concept that open unemployment is always small in Indonesia, but they still try to show that a "correct" measurement would produce a much more "desired" and larger number, or rate. They then use the concept of under-employment. If the "new" measurement still produces a low rate, they then refer to the absolute number to show the severity of the problem. It is not surprising that the number of unemployed is then "shocking", but this is simply because the absolute number reflects the large Indonesian population.

The problem is that Indonesia has only been partially following the international standard (as recommended by the ILO) in defining unemployment. On one hand, Indonesia has been using the international standard in defining the openly unemployed as those who are able and willing to work but are not working at all and still looking for work. However, a person is defined as working if he/she works at least one hour a week. With these definitions, the number of openly unemployed persons increased from 4.184 million (4.69 per cent) in August 1997 to 5.045 million (5.46 per cent) in August 1998, and 6.030 million (6.36 per cent) in August 1999.

Table 12.1

Labour Force in Indonesia, 1997–99

	Number (million)			*Percentage*			*Growth (%)*			
	1997	*1998*	*1999*	*1997*	*1998*	*1999*	*1990–96*	*1997–98*	*1998–99*	*1997–99*
General										
Working Age Population	**135.07**	**138.56**	**141.09**	**100.0**	**100.0**	**100.0**	**2.5**	**2.6**	**1.8**	**4.5**
Urban	53.35	56.09	58.98	39.5	40.5	41.8	6.0	5.1	5.2	10.5
Rural	81.72	82.47	82.11	60.5	59.5	58.2	0.6	0.9	–0.4	0.5
Labour Force	89.60	92.74	94.84	100.0	100.0	100.0	2.6	3.5	2.3	5.8
Urban	31.92	33.41	36.10	35.6	36.0	38.1	7.4	4.7	8.1	13.1
Rural	57.68	59.33	58.74	64.4	64.0	61.9	0.6	2.9	–1.0	1.8
Male	55.27	56.76	58.43	61.7	61.2	61.6	2.7	2.7	2.9	5.7
Female	34.34	35.97	36.41	38.3	38.8	38.4	2.5	4.8	1.2	6.0
Population Employed										
Total	85.41	87.67	88.81	100.0	100.0	100.0	2.2	2.7	1.3	4.0
Urban	29.40	30.30	32.32	34.4	34.6	36.4	—	3.1	6.7	9.9
Rural	56.10	57.40	56.49	65.7	65.5	63.6	—	2.3	–1.6	0.7
Male	53.01	53.90	54.90	62.1	61.5	61.8	2.4	1.7	1.9	3.6
Female	32.40	33.77	33.91	37.9	38.5	38.2	2.0	4.2	0.4	4.7
People Looking for Work	4.20	5.06	6.03	4.7	5.5	6.4	13.4	20.6	19.1	43.6
Not in the Labour Force	45.47	45.82	46.24	33.7	33.1	32.8	2.2	0.8	0.9	1.7

Source: Central Board of Statistics, Sakernas data, various years.

Although the rate and number of unemployed increased, the rise was small. Because there is no unemployment insurance and other social security benefits, the data should be interpreted carefully. A small unemployment rate means that there is a small percentage of the Indonesian labour force that actually chose to be openly unemployed during the 1997–99 periods. They had no problems financially, as they could afford to be unemployed because of their past income and wealth, good severance pay, or help from family and friends.[6] The relatively low (open) unemployment rate could also indicate that the labour force had adjusted to economic changes through the dynamics of real wages.

The unemployment rate was the highest for those between 15–24 years old, the age when secondary school graduates enter the job market. Open unemployment among those who were 30 years or older was generally not significant in Indonesia. The open unemployment rate also tended to be higher among those with secondary education or above. The rates increased from about 10 per cent in 1997 to about 12.5 per cent in 1999. This contrasts with the relatively low and stable unemployment rate (between 0.3 per cent and 0.4 per cent) among those with no schooling. Another characteristic of unemployment in Indonesia in the 1990s was urban unemployment. While the urban areas accounted for only 30 per cent of total employment, the unemployment rate was almost 60 per cent.[7] The duration of unemployment was also short, an indication of a relatively flexible labour market.[8]

On the other hand, Indonesia has not followed the international standard in defining under-employment. Badan Pusat Statistik (Central Board of Statistics) Indonesia (2000) has mentioned that under-employment is internationally defined as those who have not worked fully as defined by their capacity, and those who have worked in the wrong jobs. The first is often termed visibly under-employed, and the measurement is relatively easier. The second is the invisibly under-employed, the measurement of which is more difficult.

Because of the difficulty in measuring invisible under-employment, the Badan Pusat Statistik has measured only the first type — visible under-employment. It should be noted, however, that even the measurement of visible under-employment has its limitations. The major question is whether individuals are voluntarily or involuntarily working for less than 35 hours a week. Under-employment, or visible under-employment, should refer to the involuntarily under-employed, those who are not working fully but are still looking for work. Yet, in Indonesia, the under-employed is defined to cover all of those who work less than 35 hours a week, regardless of whether they do it voluntarily (not looking for more jobs) or involuntarily (still looking for more jobs). In other words, the measurement of under-employment is overestimated.

Badan Pusat Statistik (2000) has calculated under-employment as excluding those who work less than 35 hours a week but are not looking for more work. In other words, it excludes the voluntary under-employed. This "new" measurement is consistent with the measurement of open-unemployment, which only deals with those who are looking for jobs. As a result, the number and rate of under-employment dropped significantly from about 33 per cent (including voluntary under-employment) to about 11 per cent (excluding voluntary under-employment), as presented in Table 12.2.

Table 12.2
Under-employment in Indonesia: 1997–99

	August 1997	*August 1998*	*August 1999*
Including Voluntary Under-employment			
In million people	28.05	31.93	31.37
Percentage of labour force	31.43	34.58	33.08
Excluding Voluntary Under-employment			
In million people	10.67	8.57	11.98
Percentage of labour force	11.96	9.28	12.63

Note: Under-employment means working less than 35 hours a week.
Source: Badan Pusat Statistik (2000).

Furthermore, there was a changing trend of under-employment. With the "old", traditional criteria, under-employment increased in 1998, then declined in 1999. With the "new", internationally recommended criteria, under-employment declined in 1998 and then rose in 1999. The worst time of the crisis, in 1998, may have resulted in a rising inability to be under-employed, and hence the number of under-employed and the rate of under-employment declined that year. In other words, workers were forced to work full-time to overcome their declining incomes. The improvement of economic conditions in 1999 might have raised the ability to be under-employed, and hence, the number and rate of under-employment rose in 1999.

An interesting pattern of under-employment based on urban–rural and male–female classifications can also be observed in Table 12.3.

Table 12.3
Open Unemployment and Under-employment: 1997–99

	Aug–97	*Aug–98*	*Aug–99*
Total			
Open unemployment (in million)	4.18	5.05	6.03
Open unemployment rate	4.69%	5.46%	6.36%
Under Employment (in million)	10.67	8.57	11.98
Under-employment rate	11.96%	9.28%	12.63%
Open unemployment + Under-employment (in million)	14.86	13.61	18.01
Open unemployment + Under-employment rate	16.65%	14.74%	18.98%
Urban			
Open unemployment rate	8.04%	9.28%	10.46%
Under-employment rate	6.89%	5.84%	8.05%
Open unemployment + Under-employment rate	14.94%	15.12%	18.51%
Rural			
Open unemployment rate	2.82%	3.30%	3.84%
Under-employment rate	14.78%	11.22%	15.44%
Open unemployment + Under-employment rate	17.60%	14.52%	19.28%
Male			
Open unemployment rate	4.10%	5.05%	6.03%
Under-employment rate	10.61%	7.39%	11.41%
Open unemployment + Under-employment rate	14.71%	12.43%	17.44%
Female			
Open unemployment rate	5.64%	6.12%	6.88%
Under-employment rate	14.13%	12.25%	14.58%
Open unemployment + Under-employment rate	19.77%	18.38%	21.46%

Note: Under-employment excludes voluntary under-employment.
Source: Badan Pusat Statistik (2000).

While the open unemployment rate was generally much higher in the urban areas, the under-employment rate was always higher in the rural areas. The flexibility of jobs and the community networking in the rural areas may have explained the higher under-employment rate there. On the other hand, the higher incomes in the urban areas may have resulted in a higher rate of open unemployment here. Both open unemployment and under-employment rates were always lower for males than for females. The situation where the male is generally the main breadwinner in the family may have explained why females can better afford to be either openly unemployed or under-employed.

The data from Sakernas in 1999 show that the unemployment rate increased from 5.4 per cent in 1998 to 6.4 per cent in 1999, a greater increase compared with that in 1997–98. It is important to note that this adjustment in the labour market did not take place during the worst time of the crisis, but only two years later. The data confirm the notion that the adjustment in the first year of the crisis was that of real wages caused by inflation, with the unemployment rate increasing slightly. When inflation decreased in 1999, causing real wages to rise sharply, employment finally had to adjust, and as a result, the unemployment rate increased in 1999.

The Changing Structure of the Labour Market

The Indonesian labour market from 1990 to 1996 was characterized by its rapid transformation, followed by labour tightening, and increasing of real wages. Labour moved from the informal to the formal sector, from rural to urban, from primary sectors such as agriculture to modern sectors such as construction, manufacturing, and services. The engine of growth for the labour market tightening was broad-based growth in all sectors, especially in the labour-intensive manufacturing sector.[9]

The crisis has reversed the formalization of the labour market, that was taking place before the crisis, into a process of informalization during the crisis period from 1997 to 1998. The formalization of the labour market — characterized by the expansion of the formal sector in the economy — was rapid during the boom years of the early 1990s. The share of informal-sector employment declined from 71.4 per cent in 1990 to 65 per cent in 1996, while that of the formal sector grew from 28.6 per cent in 1990 to 36.8 per cent in 1996. This formalization of the labour market was more rapid in the urban areas and, naturally, was accompanied by a strong urbanization process. During the crisis,

Table 12.4

Employment Status of Indonesian Workers, 1990–99

	Number (million)			*Percentage*			*Growth (% p.a.)*			
	1997	*1998*	*1999*	*1997*	*1998*	*1999*	*1990–96*	*1997–98*	*1998–99*	*1997–99*
Total	**85.41**	**87.67**	**88.81**	**100.0**	**100.0**	**100.0**	**2.2**	**2.7**	**1.3**	**3.8**
Formal	31.74	30.33	31.93	37.2	34.6	36.0	5.6	–4.4	5.3	0.6
Employer with permanent employee	1.47	1.53	2.55	1.7	1.7	2.9	11.7	4.1	67.2	42.5
Employee	30.28	28.81	29.38	35.5	32.9	33.1	5.3	–4.9	2.0	–3.0
Informal	53.66	57.34	56.88	62.8	65.4	64.0	0.6	6.9	–0.8	5.7
Self-employed with no employee	19.86	20.52	21.71	23.3	23.4	24.4	3.5	3.3	5.8	8.5
Self-employed with temp/ family worker	17.98	19.69	18.91	21.1	22.5	21.3	2.8	9.5	–3.9	4.9
Family worker	15.81	17.13	16.26	18.5	19.5	18.3	–4.6	8.3	–5.1	2.7
Female	**32.40**	**33.77**	**33.91**	**100.0**	**100.0**	**100.0**	**1.9**	**4.2**	**0.4**	**4.4**
Formal	9.66	9.62	10.18	29.8	28.5	30.0	5.2	–0.4	5.8	5.1
Informal	22.74	24.16	23.73	70.2	71.5	70.0	0.8	6.2	–1.8	4.2
Male	**53.01**	**53.90**	**54.90**	**100.0**	**100.0**	**100.0**	**2.4**	**1.7**	**1.9**	**3.5**
Formal	22.09	20.71	21.76	41.7	38.4	39.6	5.7	–6.2	5.0	–1.5
Informal	30.92	33.18	33.15	58.3	61.6	60.4	0.5	7.3	–0.1	6.7
Rural	**56.05**	**57.37**	**56.49**	**100.0**	**100.0**	**100.0**	**0.3**	**2.3**	**–1.5**	**0.8**
Formal	14.95	13.88	14.40	26.7	24.2	25.5	3.7	–7.2	3.8	–3.8
Informal	41.10	43.49	42.09	73.3	75.8	74.5	–0.6	5.8	–3.2	2.3
Urban	**29.35**	**30.30**	**32.32**	**100.0**	**100.0**	**100.0**	**6.9**	**3.2**	**6.7**	**9.2**
Formal	16.80	16.45	17.53	57.2	54.3	54.2	7.4	–2.0	6.6	4.2
Informal	12.56	13.85	14.79	42.8	45.7	45.8	6.3	10.3	6.8	15.1

Source: Central Board of Statistics, Sakernas data, various years.

the share of the informal sector in general increased from 63.3 per cent to 65.4 per cent. This annual increase during the crisis was much larger than the annual growth of the informal sector, of about half a per cent, during the preceding decade. At the same time, the growth of formal-sector employment declined by minus 4.4 per cent. The fact that total employment grew by 2.7 per cent in 1997–98, higher than the annual rate of about 2.0 per cent before the crisis, was in fact due to the sharp increase in employment in the informal sector.

The informalization process has been stronger in the rural areas, especially during the crisis. Prior to the crisis, during 1990–96, people were leaving the informal sectors at the rate of 0.6 per cent in the rural areas. The trend shifted sharply during 1997–98, when there was a substantial growth of 5.8 per cent going into the informal sectors. A similar trend was seen in the urban areas — not as salient, but nevertheless, quite significant. During 1990–96, informal sector employment grew by 6.3 per cent annually. Following the crisis, the growth increased to 10.3 per cent. Meanwhile, formal-sector employment in the rural and urban areas contracted by 7.2 per cent and 2.0 per cent respectively.

By looking at the employment status within the informal sector, it can be surmised that the crisis had increased the share of family workers. The increasing number of employed in the informal sector was expected, but the fact that the number of family workers increased significantly during the crisis suggests that people looked for jobs within their family unit as part of the coping mechanism to survive the crisis. The number of women working as family workers increased more significantly than that of the men during the crisis. From 1986 to 1996, before the crisis, the number of female family workers decreased by 1.8 per cent annually. However, from 1997 to 1998, the number of female family workers increased by 6.5 per cent.

The most recent data in 1999 suggest a reversal of this pattern. With early signs of economic recovery, the labour force moved back to the formal sector. After declining by more than 4 per cent from 1997 to 1998, the number of workers in the formal sector increased by 5.3 per cent in 1998–99. In two years, from 1997 to 1999, informal-sector employment increased by 5.7 per cent while that of the formal sector increased by 0.6 per cent. This means that additional employment during that period was created in the informal sector. The recent movement back to the formal sector, however, also suggests that labour absorption in the informal sector is limited. In fact, the recent move to the formal sector took place for both male and female workers, and also for urban and rural categories.

There was a rapid movement of labour out of the agricultural sector in the seven years from 1990 to 1996, before the crisis hit. Agricultural employment declined rapidly from 56 per cent of total employment in 1990 to about 44 per cent in 1996. The rate of employment in the manufacturing sector grew from about 8 per cent in 1990 to about 13 per cent in 1996. The construction sector absorbed a large proportion of the unskilled labour moving out of the agricultural sector, as employment in this sector grew by almost 11 per cent a year from 1990 to 1996. The share of the trade, restaurant, and hotel sectors also increased sharply from almost 15 per cent in 1990 to almost 19 per cent in 1996, and became the second largest sector (after agriculture) in absorbing labour.

The economic crisis seriously affected the non-tradable sectors, especially construction, the inefficient financial sector, and the highly import-dependent manufacturing sector. Labour from these sectors were laid off and moved to other sectors — especially the surviving agricultural sector. Through terms of trade effects, the sharp currency depreciation led to the collapse of highly import-dependent sectors. In contrast, some export-oriented manufacturing, such as textiles, shoes, and garments, largely benefited from the crisis. The Sakernas data have shown that during the crisis in 1998, employment in the utility (electricity, gas, and water) sector declined by 37 per cent, followed by mining (23 per cent), construction (15.9 per cent), and manufacturing (10 per cent). These reductions were drastic changes from, for example, 10.7 per cent annual growth of employment in the construction sector, and 6.6 per cent annual growth in the manufacturing sector from 1990 to 1996. The collapse of the financial sector during the crisis also reduced employment to minus 5.8 per cent in 1997–98. Again, during the economic slowdown, agriculture turned out to be the saviour of the economy in labour absorption, with an increase of 13.3 per cent in employment during the crisis period. After declining from 56 per cent in 1990 to 41 per cent in 1997, the share of employment in the agricultural sector increased to 45 per cent in 1998.

The movement to the agricultural sector during the crisis, however, did not last long, suggesting the fact that labour absorption in the agricultural sector was limited. The data in 1999 show that labour started to move out from the agricultural sector and to go back to the other modern sectors, especially manufacturing and public utilities. After growing by almost 10 per cent from 1997 to 1998 at the peak of the crisis, employment in agriculture declined by 2.6 per cent from 1998 to 1999. Employment in other sectors started to increase from 1998 to 1999, such as 7.7 per cent in mining, 15.9 per cent in

Table 12.5

The Changing Pattern of Sectoral Employment, 1990–99

	Number (million)			*Percentage*			*Growth*			
	1997	*1998*	*1999*	*1997*	*1998*	*1999*	*1990–96*	*1997–98*	*1998–99*	*1997–99*
Total	**85.41**	**87.67**	**88.81**	**100.0**	**100.0**	**100.0**	**2.0**	**2.7**	**1.3**	**3.8**
1. Agriculture	34.79	39.41	38.38	40.7	45.0	43.2	–1.9	13.3	–2.6	9.3
2. Mining	0.88	0.67	0.73	1.0	0.8	0.8	6.4	–23.0	7.7	–20.6
3. Manufacturing	11.01	9.93	11.52	12.9	11.3	13.0	5.6	–9.8	15.9	4.4
4. Utilities	0.23	0.15	0.19	0.3	0.2	0.2	3.2	–37.0	28.1	–23.9
5. Construction	4.18	3.52	3.42	4.9	4.0	3.8	10.2	–15.9	–3.0	–22.5
6. Trade	16.95	16.81	17.53	19.9	19.2	19.7	6.3	–0.8	4.2	3.3
7. Transport & Communication	4.13	4.15	4.20	4.8	4.7	4.7	8.9	0.7	1.3	1.9
8. Financial Services	0.66	0.62	0.63	0.8	0.7	0.7	6.1	–6.0	2.7	–3.6
9. Services	12.57	12.39	12.22	14.7	14.1	13.8	4.3	–1.4	–1.4	–2.9

Source: BPS, Sakernas data, various years.

manufacturing, and 28 per cent in electricity, gas, and water. Employment in the construction sector still decreased by about 3 per cent during the same period.

The movement of labour to the informal sector and to the traditional sectors, such as agriculture, forestry, and fisheries, in 1998, was accompanied by the movement of employment opportunities to the rural areas. The crisis reduced the growth of urban employment from more than 6 per cent per annum during the boom years in 1990–96 to about 3 per cent in 1997–98. The annual growth of rural employment, on the other hand, increased from almost 0 per cent before the crisis to more than 2 per cent after the crisis.

However, the data in 1999 again show a reversal of this urban–rural pattern. From 1998 to 1999, employment in the urban areas grew by 6.7 per cent while that in the rural areas declined by 1.6 per cent. In fact, this reverse movement was so strong that within two years after the crisis, employment in the urban areas still increased by more than 9 per cent, compared with less than 1 per cent in the rural areas. In other words, the movement to the rural areas during the crisis was a temporary phenomenon.

Tracing the Patterns of Labour Displacement[10]

While the additional increase in unemployment was small, this does not mean that there were no serious lay-offs or employment reduction in the labour market. The small increase in the unemployment rate in 1998 at the aggregate or average level clearly shows that those who lost their jobs in one sector managed to find another job or were absorbed by other sectors. Economic adjustments caused by the crisis led to both booming and shrinking sectors and industries. Many displaced workers from the shrinking sectors were forced to work in other industries, or in the informal sector. Because the labour market in Indonesia has been flexible, real wages easily adjust to the changing supply and demand conditions. These smaller-than-expected unemployment figures once again show the flexibility of the Indonesian labour market, allowing the large reduction in real wages that it has to bear as a result of the crisis. In other words, the price of this smaller-than-expected unemployment rate in 1998 was a sharp correction in real wages.

This adjustment of the Indonesian labour market can be scrutinized in more detail with the help of several of the added questions in the 1998 Sakernas data. Designed to measure the impact of the crisis, the Badan Pusat Statistik included additional questions on labour displacements that happened after July 1997 — that is, the beginning of the crisis. The questions included reasons for displacement, the sectoral classification of the previous job, and the status of the previous job.

The results confirm the notion that the crisis immediately induced the informalization of the labour force, and a move from the more modern sectors of manufacturing and services to the more traditional sectors, such as agriculture. The results also provide an interesting insight into the gender-differentiated impact of the economic crisis.

Overall, about 4.3 million workers — men and women — were displaced after July 1997. This accounted for roughly 4.9 per cent of the 87.5 million people working in 1997.[11] From the 4.3 million displaced workers, one million dropped out of the labour force, while another million struggled to find work. In the end, about 2.2 million, or 2.5 per cent of the total workers in 1997 managed to find work, leaving 2.1 million (2.4 per cent) as the real employment reduction occurring after the crisis.

Nevertheless, it is not clear that the job displacement that occurred after July 1997 was *a consequence* of the crisis or was simply a natural phenomenon of turnover. Since in previous years there were no data on labour displacement, it is difficult to judge the extent of the impact of the crisis with regard to displacements. Hence, the question on the reasons for displacement might provide an idea of the extent of the impact of the crisis on employment reduction. The reasons for job displacement were put into five categories: (1) insufficient wages; (2) incompatible working environment; (3) dismissal; (4) going out of business; and (5) others.

The third and fourth categories can be grouped together under "involuntary job displacement" while the other three categories can be grouped as "voluntary job displacement". Hence, about half of the 4.3 million were involuntarily displaced, while the other half quit their jobs voluntarily. Men were more likely to be forced out of their jobs.

Table 12.6
Reasons for Job Displacement, 1997/98

Gender	*Involuntary*	*Voluntary*	*Total*
Male	1,562,874	1,245,388	2,808,262
Female	575,379	895,480	1,470,859
Total	**2,138,253**	**2,140,868**	**4,279,121**

Source: Calculated from raw Sakernas data, 1998.

Meanwhile, as mentioned before, the crisis had induced a process of informalization. Table 12.7 illustrates how the crisis caused a shift of labour from the formal to the informal sector. Of the 4.3 million displaced workers between July 1997 and August 1998, 3.2 million came from the formal sector while about 1.1 million were from the informal sector. Meanwhile, among those displaced from the formal sector, only 1.6 million managed to find work and a substantial share of them (59 per cent) found jobs in the informal sector. Among the 1.1 million displaced from the informal sector, about 0.6 million managed to find work. Most of them remained in the informal sector. Overall, the informal sector absorbed about 63.0 per cent (1.4 million) of those who found work after job displacement, while the formal sector absorbed only about 37.0 per cent (0.8 million).

Table 12.7
Labour Displacement in the Formal and Informal Sectors, 1997/98

August 1998 Survey / *Before July 1997*	*Employment*			*Looking for Work*	*Not in the Labour Force*
	Informal	*Formal*	*Total*		
Informal	441,469	160,705	602,174	106,341	346,842
Formal	935,384	649,560	1,584,944	979,350	659,470
TOTAL	**1,376,853**	**810,265**	**2,187,118**	**1,085,691**	**1,006,312**

Source: Calculated from raw Sakernas data, 1998.

The patterns of displacement and adjustment also confirm the notion that the crisis reversed the trend towards the more modern sectors, such as manufacturing and services, and instead moved away from those sectors towards the traditional sector of agriculture. In absolute terms, the sectors that displaced the most workers were, in order of magnitude, manufacturing, agriculture (probably because of drought and El Niño), services, trade, and construction. Even though agriculture displaced a relatively large number of workers, it simultaneously absorbed a substantial number who had recently been displaced (see Table 12.8).

A high proportion of those who lost their jobs found work in agriculture (39.3 per cent). A smaller proportion found work in trade (19.2 per cent) and manufacturing (12.1 per cent). This movement out of the modern sectors into agriculture — the sector that absorbed the

Table 12.8
Displacement of Workers by Sector, 1997/98

Sector	*Displaced from Sector*		*Absorbed by Sector in 1998*	
	Number	*As % of 1997 Employed*	*Number*	*As % of Total Displaced*
1. Agriculture	782,603	2.2	859,142	20.1
2. Mining	63,833	7.1	45,566	1.1
3. Manufacturing	1,094,249	9.8	264,995	6.2
4. Utilities	24,144	10.4	2,221	0.1
5. Construction	562,736	13.4	208,092	4.9
6. Trade	676,113	3.9	420,511	9.8
7. Transport & Communication, etc.	235,071	5.7	165,398	3.9
8. Financial Services	61,757	9.4	9,348	0.2
9. Services	778,615	6.2	211,845	5.0
TOTAL	**4,279,121**	**4.9**	**2,187,118**	**51.1**

Source: Calculated from raw Sakernas data, 1998.

largest number of displaced workers from every major industry in the economy, except trade (see Table 12.8) — signalled an important trend of movement back to agriculture and, consequently, to the rural areas.

In terms of gender, the Sakernas data show that the crisis reduced employment opportunities in the formal sector for male workers relative to female. Total employment in the formal sector decreased from 30.3 million in 1997 to 28.8 million in 1998. Male workers accounted for 1.4 million, or 98 per cent, of this reduction in employment in the formal sector. This is not surprising given the fact that the economic sector that suffered the most — and would be the slowest to recover — was the construction sector, which was male-dominated. Meanwhile, the sectors that survived well during the crisis were the female-dominated labour-intensive export-oriented industries, such as those in textiles, garments, and footwear.

Nevertheless, a more detailed observation of the displacement data offers an interesting insight into the process of labour market adjustment. The fact that females contributed only 2 per cent to the total employment reduction does not imply that they did not experience labour displacements. In fact, the number of females displaced from their work was comparable to that of males. Females accounted for about a third

Table 12.9
Displacement by Gender, 1997/98

Gender	Displaced			1997 Total Employment
	Number	As % of Total Displaced	As % of 1997 Total Employed	
Male	2,808,262	65.6	5.3	53,005,502
Female	1,470,859	34.4	4.5	32,400,027
TOTAL	**4,279,121**	**100.0**	**5.0**	**85,405,529**

Source: Calculated from raw Sakernas data, 1998.

of those displaced between July 1997 and August 1998 (see Table 12.9). Compared as a percentage of total employment in 1997, by gender, the difference between males and females was less than a percentage point (5.2 and 4.4 per cent respectively). This implies that the effects of these displacements were as substantial for females as it was for males. The majority of males who were displaced came from the manufacturing sector (22.6 per cent of total displaced), construction sector (18.9 per cent), and services (17.3 per cent). A majority of females were displaced from the manufacturing sector (31.2 per cent) and trade (22.0 per cent).

If women accounted for a third of those displaced, yet contributed a relatively miniscule share of employment reduction, does it mean that the labour market absorbed the majority of these female workers? Interestingly enough, that was not really the case. As a matter of fact, a majority of women (about 69 per cent) who were displaced in 1997 were not working at the time of the August 1998 labour survey. In fact, a significant number of them were "discouraged", and left the labour force as a result of the crisis — the number was much higher for women compared with men in both absolute and relative terms. Most of those that dropped out of the labour force returned to their domestic role in housekeeping.

Again, even though the number of displaced female workers who left the labour force was much higher than male workers, overall, there was actually a decrease in the number of women not in the labour force, while there was an increase in the number of men not in the labour force. The number of women not in the labour force decreased from 34.44 million to 34.35 million — a drop of 0.3 per cent — while the number of males increased from 11.03 million to 11.47 million — an increase of 4 per cent.

Table 12.10

Labour Displacement for Males and Females

Status on July 97 \ *Status on Aug 98*	*Labour Force*			*Not in the Labour Force*				*Total Displaced after July 97*
	Working	*Looking for Work*	*Total*	*Going to School*	*Housekeeping*	*Others*	*Total*	
Male								
Informal	459,809	76,706	536,515	2,696	11,690	94,966	109,352	645,867
Formal	1,264,326	643,672	1,907,998	4,676	29,884	219,837	254,397	2,162,395
TOTAL	**1,724,135**	**720,378**	**2,444,513**	**7,372**	**41,574**	**314,803**	**363,749**	**2,808,262**
Female								
Informal	142,365	29,635	172,000	3,418	205,939	28,133	237,490	409,490
Formal	320,618	335,678	656,296	6,891	329,587	68,595	405,073	1,061,369
TOTAL	**462,983**	**365,313**	**828,296**	**10,309**	**535,526**	**96,728**	**642,563**	**1,470,859**

Source: Calculated from raw Sakernas data, 1998.

These seemingly contradictory numbers show that the workers being absorbed into the labour force were often not the same workers leaving the labour force. Even though the exit of women from the labour market was balanced by a significant number of women entering the labour force, the crisis caused many women who were previously working to get out of the labour force and return to their domestic role. This implies that the crisis caused significant, albeit unknown, negative effects towards previously working women.

Earnings and Productivity

One important aspect of adjustments in the labour market is the change in labour earnings and productivity during the crisis. Because the data on earnings in the informal sector are unavailable, this section presents the changes in labour earnings and productivity in the formal sectors to illustrate the adjustments made in the labour market. Similar to the situation in other developing countries, accurate data on earnings are generally hard to obtain in Indonesia, but the Sakernas has reported the total monthly earnings in the formal sector, which at least present the picture of monthly wages in that sector before and after the crisis.

For several decades before the crisis, nominal and real wages had generally moved along the same pattern because inflation was relatively constant at about 8–10 per cent a year. However, during the peak of the crisis in 1998, as shown in Table 12.11, nominal wages still increased, but real wages declined very sharply because of skyrocketing inflation. The Sakernas data show that nominal monthly wages in all sectors, measured as monthly earnings[12] in the formal sector, increased by 16.2 per cent from 1996 to 1997, and by 17.2 per cent from 1997 to 1998. After being corrected using GDP (gross domestic product) deflators, real wages still increased by about 3.2 per cent in 1997, but then sharply declined by 33.1 per cent from 1997 to 1998. The new level of real wages in 1998 was comparable to that of 1989/90, meaning that the increase in real wages during the seven years before the crisis was wiped out within one year. Compared with the decline in personal consumption in the GDP data, which was only about 3 per cent, the data again suggest that people maintained their consumption level by using their savings. Real wages quickly recovered in 1999 and 2000, mainly because of lower inflation, but by comparing with those of 1997, real wages in 2000 was still about 20 per cent lower. Considering the rapid growth of real wages recently, the level prior to the crisis could be reached in 2001/02.

The size of the decline in real wages varied between sectors, with construction experiencing the largest shock in real wages early in the crisis, with a decline of more than 44 per cent. Trade, mining, and manufacturing sectors also experienced a substantial drop in real wages, by more than 30 per cent. A smaller decline in real wages in 1998 was seen for utilities, and the transport and telecommunication sectors, but the decline was still large at more than 22 per cent. It is also clear from Table 12.11 that the real wages in some sectors recovered faster than others. By tracing the growth from 1997 to 2000, it can be seen in the table that wages in the transport and telecommunication sectors already reached the pre-crisis level in 2000, while those in the utilities, manufacturing and agriculture sectors also caught up to a lesser extent. Wages in the construction sector recovered very slowly, as the level of real wages in 2000 was still about 60 per cent of the pre-crisis level.

Table 12.11 also shows that the real wages data in the formal sector from Sakernas tend to suggest that this crisis was one that affected urban workers especially. A quick estimate by using a non-agricultural GDP price deflator shows that the decline in real wages in the urban areas from 1997 to 1998 was about 33.1 per cent. By using the agricultural GDP deflator, a similar calculation resulted in a real-wage decline of 29.8 per cent in the rural areas.[13] By comparing the real wages in 1997 and 2000, it was obvious that those in the rural areas recovered faster than those in the urban areas. Real wages in the rural areas remained relatively flat in 1998–99, but then started to increase rapidly by more than 21 per cent in 1999–2000. This is not surprising because the movement of labour from the urban to the rural areas in 1997 and 1998 prevented a rapid increase in real wages in the rural areas in 1998–99. However, the movement of labour back to the urban areas resulted in a sharp increase in real wages in the rural areas in 1999–2000. The increase in real wages in the urban areas was relatively more stable, at about 6.3 per cent from 1998 to 1999, and 8.6 per cent from 1999 to 2000. Overall, real wages in the urban areas in 2000 were 25 per cent lower than the pre-crisis level, while those in the rural areas were about 13 per cent lower.

Classified by gender, the data do not suggest any real difference between male and female wage adjustments. The data only suggest that male wages seemed to take a longer time to rebound than those for females. Classified by the level of workers' education, the data clearly show that the wages of those with high school education tended to increase faster in 1999–2000, compared with those with lower or higher education.

Table 12.11
The Growth of Real Wages, 1997–2000
(In per cent)

Classification	*1997–98*	*1998–99*	*1999–00*	*1997–00*
All Sectors (deflated by GDP deflator)				
Agriculture	–24.6	0.4	22.1	–7.6
Mining	–37.2	31.1	–21.8	–35.6
Manufacturing	–30.8	3.2	31.0	–6.5
Utilities	–22.5	16.8	7.5	–2.7
Construction	–44.7	–0.1	7.5	–40.6
Trade	–33.6	–1.1	15.1	–24.4
Transport & Comm. Etc.	–22.8	10.2	21.2	3.1
Financial Services	–29.9	–2.1	24.4	–14.6
Services	–22.4	4.4	10.0	–11.0
By Region				
Urban (deflated by non-agriculture GDP deflator)	–35.1	6.3	8.6	–25.1
Rural (deflated by agriculture GDP deflator)	–29.8	2.4	21.5	–12.7
By Gender (deflated by GDP deflator)				
Male	–32.8	6.1	12.9	–19.5
Female	–32.8	8.6	9.0	–20.5
By Education (deflated by GDP deflator)				
Primary school or less	–28.0	0.9	9.2	–20.6
High school	–35.3	13.8	20.2	–11.4
Higher than high school	–28.9	–5.3	3.3	–30.5
Overall Average Wage (deflated by GDP deflator)*)	**–33.1**	**6.7**	**11.7**	**–20.2**

Note: The growth of average wages is different from the average growth of wages.
Source: Calculated from Sakernas data.

Labour productivity, measured in this chapter as real GDP divided by the number of employed, also declined sharply in 1998 because of economic contraction. During the early period of the crisis in 1997, labour productivity still increased by 3.1 per cent, but then sharply declined by 13.7 per cent in 1998 because of the massive economic contraction in 1998. During the same period, real wages increased by about 3.3 per cent in 1997, and then declined sharply by 33.1 per cent in 1998. It is interesting to note that while the real wages of labourers during the crisis was comparable to that in 1989/90, the level of labour productivity overall was similar to that in 1993/94. In other words, real wages declined faster than labour productivity during the crisis, which may indicate an undershooting of wages. The data also clearly show that after the sharp decline in 1998, real wages tended to catch up faster than labour productivity in 1999 and 2000.

The comparison between the growth of real wages and labour productivity in this section, however, has to be treated with caution. First, the real wage is derived only from the formal labour market, while labour productivity is calculated for the whole economy, that is, for both the formal and informal sectors. On the one hand, data on GDP classified by formal and informal sectors are unavailable, while on the other hand, data on wages or earnings in the informal sectors are also unavailable. In other words, the movement of labour from the formal to the informal sector during the crisis certainly complicates the analysis on labour productivity.

By looking at the trend from 1997 to 2000, when the decline in labour productivity was still below that of real wages, there seems to be some room for real wages to increase without affecting the competitiveness of the economy. However, the fact that real wage growth was higher than labour productivity growth in 1999 provides an indicator that the surplus in the labour market was only temporary.

There were differences in labour productivity and real wage adjustments across sectors. The data from Sakernas suggest that the adjustment in the manufacturing sectors was larger or faster than in other sectors, reflected by the larger correction in real wages, and no correction in labour productivity in 1998. Real wages in the manufacturing sector declined by 31 per cent in 1998, compared with 21 per cent in services, and 25 per cent in agriculture. Labour productivity in manufacturing remained constant while that in agriculture and services declined by 10 per cent and 2 per cent respectively. Again, a sharper reduction in employment and real wages in the manufacturing sector shows that the biggest labour market adjustment in 1998 took place in the manufacturing sector. The

Table 12.12
The Growth of Real Wages and Productivity

Year	*95–96*	*96–97*	*97–98*	*98–99*	*99–00*	*97–00*
All Sectors						
Labour Productivity	5.5	3.1	–13.7	–0.4	3.6	–11.1
Nominal Wages	15.7	16.2	17.2	22.9	24	78.7
Real Wages	6.5	3.3	–33.1	6.7	11.7	–20.2
Agriculture						
Labour Productivity	3.3	6.3	–10.3	5.5	–3.8	–8.9
Nominal Wages	13.9	11.4	30.7	22.7	20.9	93.9
Real Wages	3	–1.1	–24.6	0.4	22.1	–7.6
Manufacturing						
Labour Productivity	11.9	1.1	0	–10.5	4.9	–6.1
Nominal Wages	17.7	18.4	11	19.7	32.6	76.2
Real Wages	5.6	1.1	–30.8	3.2	20.6	–6.5
Services						
Labour Productivity	–2.9	–2.9	–1.9	0.1	5.4	3.5
Nominal Wages	18.1	8.4	20.8	18.2	28.6	83.5
Real Wages	7.3	–7.1	–20.8	–5.8	13.3	–10.7

Note: Deflated by sectoral GDP price deflator.
Source: Calculated from data collected by the Central Board of Statistics.

Indonesian economic crisis started as a financial crisis but the adjustment in the manufacturing sector was generally faster than that in the financial sector.

It is interesting to see that a sharp decline in labour productivity in the first year of the crisis (1998) took place in the agricultural sector, while productivity in manufacturing was relatively constant. In the latter part of 1999, however, labour productivity in manufacturing declined rapidly by 10 per cent, while that in agriculture increased by more than 5 per cent. This pattern of adjustment was generally caused by the movement of labour from the manufacturing sector to agriculture at the beginning of the crisis, and then back to the manufacturing sector in the following year. What presumably happened was that because of the drastic decline in real wages, people moved out of the manufacturing sector faster than other sectors in 1998. This rapid movement out of the manufacturing sector (compared with other sectors) prevented a drastic decline in labour productivity per worker in that sector. However, in 1999, real wages in the agricultural sector declined and people moved again out of agriculture. This created an increase in labour productivity in agriculture. Those leaving agriculture entered the manufacturing sector, causing a further decline in the labour productivity of the manufacturing sector.

To some extent, the changes in minimum wages during the crisis contributed to the trend in wages. During the worst time of the crisis in 1998, the annual increase in the minimum wage was delayed. The annual increase, which usually falls due on 1 April, was delayed until August 1998 when the minimum wage was increased by 15 per cent, smaller than the inflation rate of 77 per cent. This partly explains the sharp decrease in real wages in 1998. However, when the overall inflation rate in 1999 was only 2 per cent, and the cumulative inflation up to May 2000 was less than 1 per cent, the minimum wage was increased twice, by 16 per cent in April 1999 and then by 25 per cent in April 2000.

The loosening labour market weakened the bargaining power of labour in determining wages in 1998, but the bargaining power of labour is expected to increase in the coming years. Political reform and democratization have given more freedom to workers to set up labour movements and trade unions recently. As a result, the pressure for higher wages, for example, an increase in the minimum wage, is expected to be stronger. However, because of the slow process of economic recovery, the increase in productivity and employment could not keep up with the accelerating pressure for higher wages. It would therefore not be surprising if the incidence of labour disputes, strikes, and other labour problems would increase in the coming years.

Conclusion

During the crisis, the adjustment in the labour market was remarkable. The labour market was flexible in adjusting to the massive shock of the crisis. The data during the peak of the crisis in 1998 suggest that the crisis reversed the process of formalization to informalization, and from urbanization to ruralization. The increase in unemployment was small but the correction of real wages was drastic. In other words, labour market adjustments took place mostly in wages rather than in employment because workers could not afford to be unemployed or underemployed. After the crisis struck, unemployment increased slightly from 4.7 per cent in 1997 to 5.5 per cent in 1998, and the rate has been relatively constant at about 6 per cent since 1999. While unemployment and under-employment changed only slightly, the adjustment in real wages was drastic. Real wages declined by 33.1 per cent from 1997 to 1998 during the worst time of the crisis, and then increased by 6.7 per cent in 1998–99, and 11.7 per cent in 1999–2000. Overall from 1997 to 2000, real wages declined by 20.2 per cent.

Labour productivity also declined during the crisis, but the adjustment was less drastic than that of real wages. Labour productivity on average declined by 13.7 per cent from 1997 to 1998, but the overall decline from 1997 to 2000 was about 11 per cent. The flexible movement of labour across sectors played a major role in determining labour productivity. At the beginning of the crisis, labour moved out from the manufacturing to the agriculture sector so that labour productivity in the manufacturing sector could be maintained at the expense of declining productivity in agriculture. In later years, this trend was reversed together with the reverse movement of labour out from agriculture.

There are several contributing factors to the specific nature of the labour market adjustment in Indonesia. The first is the flexible nature of the labour market itself, as the labour turnover rate is generally high. Combined with the labour-surplus nature of the economy, weak labour unions, and low reservation wage, the flexible nature of the labour market led to flexible real wages. The second factor that played a major role in sharp wage adjustments is the specific overall macroeconomic condition, where excessive monetary expansion led to a high inflation and a sharp depreciation of the currency. Because of the labour market flexibility and the absence of any unemployment benefits or other forms of social security, displaced workers would have to find other jobs — mostly with lower wages — to survive the crisis. The data confirm the notion that many people in the formal labour market lost their jobs during the crisis, but soon found another one at a lower wage, or moved to the informal sector to get some additional income.

The process of informalization and ruralization in the labour market, however, did not last long. The data in 1999 indicate a movement out of agriculture back to the manufacturing and more urban-based sectors. There was also a movement out from the informal sector, but by looking at the data for the two years from 1997 to 1999, the pattern of labour market informalization during the crisis is still clear. Finally, the trend towards stronger labour unions and rising minimum wages may eventually reduce the labour market flexibility observed during 1997–99. This trend may then benefit those in the formal sector, and hurt those in the informal sectors, particularly the less-educated workers.

Notes

1. Feridhanusetyawan (2000) has documented the social impact of the Indonesian economic crisis.
2. For example, Frankenberg et al. (1999).
3. This result is similar that of Manning (2000), which also shows that a large change in relative prices from the exchange rate depreciation had a smaller impact than expected on the employment structure.
4. See ILO (1998).
5. From February to May 1998, the Minister of Manpower, representatives of labour unions, and other observers announced large and overestimated unemployment figures, ranging from 13 to 20 million people unemployed. They might have used these large numbers to show the severity of employment problems in Indonesia. See,for example, *Jakarta Post,* 14 April 14 1998; and *Suara Karya,* 14 May 1998.
6. An unemployed high-level manager with a large savings account would be able to maintain his/her quality of life by consuming his/her savings. In contrast, an uneducated daily factory worker who had lost his/her job had to find another job in other factories or work in the informal sector to survive. In other words, this unemployed factory worker could not afford to be unemployed.
7. See Manning and Jayasuriya (1996); and also Manning and Junankar (1998).
8. See Agrawal (1996).
9. The impact of rapid economic growth on the labour market is discussed, for example, in Agrawal (1996) and also in Manning (1998).
10. Much of this section is taken from Feridhanusetyawan and Gaduh (2000).
11. Note, however, that the data on displacement formed part of the 1998 Sakernas data, while the data on the number of workers in 1997 formed part of the 1997 Sakernas data. Although the two are not perfectly comparable, they are deemed to be precise enough for the purpose of this exercise.
12. Monthly earnings consist of monthly wages plus other benefits.
13. Other data suggest that the decline in real wages in the rural areas, represented by real wages in agriculture, declined by about 40 per cent from 1997 to 1998. A similar trend took place in the outer islands, such as Sulawesi, Nusa Tenggara, and Sumatera (Cameron 1999).

References

Agrawal, Nisha. "The Benefit of Growth for Indonesian Workers". World Bank Policy Research Working Paper, no. 1637. Washington D.C, 1996.

Badan Pusat Statistik. *Pengembangan Metode Penghitungan Pengangguran: Pengangguran Terbuka Dan Setengah Pengangguran di Indonesia 1997–1999* [Development of Methods of Estimation of Unemployment: Open Unemployment and Underemployment in Indonesia 1997–1999]. Jakarta: Badan Pusat Statistik, 2000.

Cameron, Lisa. "Survey of Recent Developments". *Bulletin of Indonesian Economic Studies* 35, no. 1 (1999).

Feridhanusetyawan, Tubagus. "The Social Impact of the Indonesian Economic Crisis". In *Social Impacts of the Asian Economic Crisis in Thailand, Indonesia, Malaysia, and the Philippines.* Thailand Development Research Institute (TDRI) with support from the Ford Foundation, Bangkok, December 2000.

Feridhanusetyawan, Tubagus, and Arya B. Gaduh. "Indonesia's Labor Market During the Crisis. Empirical Evidence from the *Sakernas,* 1997–1999". *Indonesian Quarterly* 28, no. 3 (2000).

Frankenberg, Elizabeth, Duncan Thomas, Kathleen Beegle. "The Real Cost of Indonesia's Economic Crisis: Preliminary Findings from the Indonesian Family Life Surveys". Labor and Population Program Working Paper Series 99–04. Rand Corporation, March 1999. Also available at the homepage of Rand Corporation, http://www.rand.org).

ILO. *Employment Challenges of the Indonesian Economic Crisis.* Jakarta: ILO, 1998.

Manning, Chris. *Indonesian Labor in Transition: An East Asian Success Story?* Cambridge University Press, 1998.

________. "Labour Market Adjustment to Indonesia's Economic Crisis: Context, Trends and Implications". *Bulletin of Indonesian Economic Studies* 36, no. 1 (2000): 105–36.

Manning, Chris, and P.N. Junankar. "Choosy Youth or Unwanted Youth? A Survey of Unemployment." *Bulletin of Indonesian Economic Studies* 34, no. 1 (April 1998).

Manning, Chris, and Sisira Jayasuriya. "Survey of Recent Developments". *Bulletin of Indonesian Economic Studies,* August 1996.

SMERU. "The Labor Force Dimension of the Economic Crisis. Case Studies of Four Industries". *SMERU Indonesia,* no. 7 (August 1999).

PART IV

Emerging Issues

13

POLITICAL ECONOMY OF BUSINESS RELATIONS BETWEEN INDONESIA AND SINGAPORE

Linda Low

Introduction

Indonesia and Singapore easily stand at two ends of a continuum in the Association of Southeast Asian Nations (ASEAN), ranging from physical size and per capita national income to, most starkly, their responses to globalization and governance. Both the Indonesian state and government, synonymous with the dominant Golongan Karya (Golkar) since independence in 1945, tightened under Soeharto's New Order in mid-1960s, and the People's Action Party (PAP) in Singapore since 1959 bears resemblance. However, the similarity ends as soon as the strategies and policy options to run the largest ASEAN economy and a mere city-state are put in a practical perspective.

While the historical and traditional symbiosis between Singapore and Malaysia with the British legacy is pervasive, a contention of this chapter is that the political economy of business relations between Indonesia and Singapore has far more potential and opportunities. Paradoxically, national rivalry has emerged between Malaysia and Singapore as a consequence of converging development paths in industrialization and in the level of prosperity and standard of living, especially between Kuala Lumpur and Singapore. The same competitive strain may not, or would take a much longer time to surface for Indonesia as it is a much larger agriculture-based economy and there is more scope for complementarity with Singapore.

Much depends on the evolving political economy of relations and alliances at both the state and private levels, and these prospects are assessed here, beginning with a brief overview of economic relations before and after the financial crisis in 1997. The issues and problems facing Indonesian–Singapore relations are discussed in the following section, first in the context of their respective domestic constraints before translating them into the regional and global environment. The concluding section notes some policy implications, and suggests how business relations can be further synergized between the two countries.

Economic Relations Before and Since the Crisis

Two crucial related areas define economic relations between Indonesia and Singapore: the historical entrepôt trade, and networks of Chinese capital and enterprise. The true magnitude of trade between the two countries has been officially blacked out on the Singapore side since Indonesia's confrontation during Singapore's merger with Malaysia and never restored because of extant smuggling trade. Indonesia must be as important as Malaysia in Singapore's trade relations.

Table 13.1 shows Indonesia's main export and import markets in 1996. Singapore accounted for the third largest in exports and fourth in imports. Thus, Singapore was the top ASEAN market for Indonesian exports and imports.

Table 13.1
Indonesia's Main Export and Import Markets
(In US$ million)

Exports	*1994*	*1995*	*1996*	*1997* [e]
Japan	11711	12627	12885	13976
US	6382	6852	6795	8150
Singapore	3605	2898*	4565	Na
South Korea	2584	2888	3281	3880
Germany	1684	1535	1489	1984
China	1445	1817	2057	2400
Hong Kong	1150	1579	1625	1468
Others	11499	15222	17119	21595
Total	40060	45418	49816	53453

Table 13.1 (*continued*)
Indonesia's Main Export and Import Markets
(In US$ million)

Imports	*1994*	*1995*	*1996*	*1997*[e]
Japan	8441	10735	8504	11056
US	3092	4572	5060	4976
South Korea	2794	2949	2411	4192
Germany	2408	3052	3001	2802
Singapore	2045	1288*	2875	Na
Australia	1597	2156	2535	2862
UK	617	1013	1118	892
Others	10886	14864	17365	14889
Total	31880	40629	42869	41669

[e] BMI estimates.
* Non-gas and oil only.
Source: Bank Indonesia, *Business Monitor International* (Indonesia, 1998), p 66.

Table 13.2 shows Indonesia's top investors on a cumulative basis from 1967 to July 1996. Singapore was fourth after Japan, the United Kingdom, and Hong Kong, but first among the ASEAN countries.

Table 13.2
Indonesia's Top Investors, 1967–July 1996, Cumulative
(In US$ billion)

Japan	32.1
UK	28.7
Hong Kong	18.3
Singapore	13.3
US	12.3
Netherlands	10.5
Taiwan	9.2
South Korea	7.1
Australia	6.2
Germany	5.1

Source: Investment Co-ordinating Board of Indonesia, *Business Monitor International* (Indonesia, 1997), p. 45.

Tables 13.3 and 13.4, showing direct foreign investments (DFI) in Singapore and Singapore's DFI, respectively, in the ASEAN countries reveal that Indonesia is the second largest ASEAN partner after Malaysia.

Table 13.3
Stock of Foreign Equity Investments by Singapore in ASEAN
(In US$ million)

	1986	*1991*	*1992*	*1993*	*1994*	*1995*	*1996*
ASEAN	1669.6	2889.8	3041.9	3843.5	4928.6	5677.3	6400.8
Malaysia	1379.9	2106.4	2220.7	2462.5	2910.9	3523.9	3953.6
Indonesia	137.1	91.6	61.3	170.6	575.0	788.2	950.9
Philippines	34.3	157.2	150.3	167.8	351.0	356.7	380.5
Thailand	37.4	485.7	516.9	951.0	904.3	801.8	903.2
Brunei	80.0	48.7	92.7	91.5	187.4	206.2	211.4
Vietnam	—	—	—	—	—	0.4	1.1
Indonesia % ASEAN	8.2	3.2	2.0	4.4	11.7	13.9	14.9
Total	24702.8	54563.2	56660.9	62766.9	74605.2	84267.0	96484.8

Source: Singapore, Department of Statistics, *Yearbook of Statistics 1998* (Singapore, 1998), p 69.

Table 13.4
Stock of Singapore's Equity Investments Abroad in ASEAN
(In US$ million)

	1991	*1992*	*1993*	*1994*	*1995*	*1996*
ASEAN	3996	4897	6107	9680	12993	13371
Malaysia	3121	3917	4619	6500	7715	7573
Indonesia	267	328	620	1997	3305	3340
Philippines	90	106	202	382	619	869
Thailand	448	457	591	723	977	1077
Brunei	69	89	75	77	35	27
Vietnam	—	—	70	127	342	486
Indonesia % ASEAN	6.7	6.7	10.2	20.6	25.4	25.0
Total	15184	17741	22181	29765	39145	44837

Source: Singapore, Department of Statistics, *Yearbook of Statistics 1998* (Singapore, 1998), p 69.

By 1996, Indonesia had accounted for a quarter of Singapore's investments abroad in the ASEAN countries, as shown in Table 13.4.

By sheer proximity and size, Indonesia is increasingly a core parameter in Singapore's map and economic space. The relationship reached a peak in 1989 with the formalization of the Singapore–Johor–Riau growth triangle, which was later renamed the Indonesia–Malaysia–Singapore growth triangle when more Malaysian states and Indonesian provinces were added (Low 1998). When the growth triangle concept was extended to the regionalization policy in 1993 to take advantage of the demand and supply sides of the regional boom in Asia, Indonesia remained an important destination even when the fever was in China.

Before the financial crisis reached its full-blown proportions in both economic and socio-political aspects (Low 1999), Singapore intuitively offered financial and material assistance to its ASEAN neighbours. As soon as Thailand and Indonesia indicated they were seeking financial assistance from the International Monetary Fund (IMF), Singapore offered US$1 billion and US$5 billion respectively as part of the IMF rescue plan. Specifically, Singapore and Japan each committed US$5 billion (S$8 billion) to supplement the IMF package even as the IMF and multilateral agencies agreed to a US$23 billion package for Indonesia as well as bilateral pledges of another US$15 billion. Joint statements were issued by the finance ministers of Singapore and Japan to that effect to help restore confidence (*Straits Times*, 20 November 1997).

Singapore Finance Minister, Richard Hu, clarified that the sum was not a gift but a five-year facility which could be drawn down in tranches of US$1 billion, carrying a commercial interest rate of an average of six months U.S. dollar inter-bank interest rate plus a premium, and loan repayment within five years. This together with the earlier pledge of US$1 billion for Thailand were sovereign loans and would remain part of Singapore's foreign assets, which would not affect the official reserves of the Monetary Authority of Singapore (MAS). The Indonesian loan was offered after Prime Minister Goh Chok Tong discussed Jakarta's request with senior government ministers. The decision was subsequently cleared by the Cabinet (*Straits Times*, 29 October 1997).

A second contribution to Indonesia was the offer to purchase rupiah to support Indonesia's currency alongside the efforts of the Japanese and Indonesian central banks. The amount of intervention by Singapore and Japan was not predetermined and would depend on developments in the foreign exchange markets. Singapore also proposed a multilateral loan guarantee, or trade-financing guarantee for Indonesia in early February 1998, with participation from the West and Japan. It admitted to being new as a benefactor after some misunderstanding over an exchange of documents it had expected from Indonesia as a formal request. Indonesia was somewhat upset, a clear demonstration of "big brother" politics after its humiliation with the IMF (*Straits Times*, 4 November 1998). Indonesia was dissatisfied with Singapore's apparent "wait-and-see" attitude instead of driving its promise forward more expediently. Deputy Prime Minister Lee Hsien Loong cautioned against drawing up a wrong scheme which might damage Singapore's reputation and the government had to be answerable in Parliament.

Relations appeared cordial initially, with further in-kind assistance beginning in 1998. Education Minister Teo Chee Hean paid a three-day visit to meet with army chief Wiranto when the Singapore navy delivered 10,000 metric tonnes of rice (*Straits Times*, 6 August 1998). The government partnered with Indonesia's largest Muslim organization, Nahdlatu Ulama (NU), with a gift of 500 metric tonnes of rice and supply of medicine worth US$12 million (S$20 million) for the poor. The biggest consignment in the humanitarian aid project was by way of 36,000 food cartons shipped to Indonesia by the Singapore Red Cross Society in January 1999, the third of a four-phase project co-ordinated by the Society. The following consignment in June 1999 achieved the target of S$5 million, with S$4.3 million raised in all (*Straits Times*, 11 January 1999).

A few incidents may have tilted bilateral relations between Indonesia and Singapore somewhat. First, when President Soeharto named B. J. Habibie as his Vice-President in February 1998, Lee Kuan Yew had remarked, without naming Habibie, that the financial market might be "disturbed" that the criteria and choice had been on the appointee's expertise in science and technology, with a proclivity to high spending on such projects. President Habibie probably neither forgot nor forgave Singapore for this remark. He later said that he did not see the friendship as falling under the category of "a friend in need is a friend indeed" (*Asian Wall Street Journal*, 4 September 1998). To him, Singapore was just a "dot" in his office map, much as he expected the wealthy city-state to have helped more.

To Indonesia, particularly President Habibie, humanitarian assistance was charity and made Singapore a fair-weathered friend (*Straits Times*, 21 February 1999). Being the fourth most populous country in the world, Indonesians are a proud and nationalistic people. As much as Singapore sees itself as a reputable international financial centre, it would have been more appropriate to help Indonesia with investments and its external debt financing. Lee Kuan Yew's warning to Singaporeans "to prepare for more heat" as leaders in the region came under stress, making more accusations and threats (*Straits Times*, 24 February 1999) was perceived as paranoia because Indonesia did not view Singapore as a threat (*Straits Times*, 21 February 1999). The ethnic problems in Indonesia should alert Singapore, with its large Chinese enclave, of the inextricable link they share. Whether it is resentment of a small city-state's success, or even if it is not a zero-sum game, "small brother" should be beholden to "big brother" instead of appearing highhanded and arrogant. In such circumstances, both Malaysians and Indonesians can easily accuse Singaporeans of having rule and efficiency-based thinking rather than trying to build relations from the heart.

A more grievous misunderstanding occurred because of Habibie's mistaken notion that there were no Malay officers in Singapore's Armed Forces, once similarly conjured by Malaysia, and he called Singaporeans racists (*Straits Times*, 10 and 14 February 1999; *International Herald Tribune*, 14 February 1999). His attack on Singapore was driven by residual ill-feeling arising from Lee's subtle remark about Habibie's suitability as Vice-President, and he wanted respect and validation from Lee. His advisers from the Association of Muslim Intellectuals were also unhappy about Singapore's invitation to opposition leader Amien Rais to speak in Singapore (*Far Eastern Economic Review*, 25 March 1999, p. 31). Abdurrahman Wahid, as leader of Nadhlatul Ulama, later criticized Habibie for his lack of political sense which caused unnecessary problems with Singapore. The remark shows not just "big brother politics" but also dangerous connotations of intolerance of Singapore's success. Thus, while Singapore may have no domestic Chinese problems, its Chinese characteristics as perceived externally are perhaps not as benign.

In spite of its superlative efficiency based on international competitiveness, rule of law, overall good governance, and relatively less corrupt capitalism, Singapore is quintessentially a small, open city-state which needs the political goodwill of its much larger neighbours to give it both physical sustenance and economic space. As a virtual capital of overseas Chinese, Singapore may not be as easily forgiven for being a safe haven whenever there is capital flight caused by political instability in nearby Malaysia or Indonesia, even if it did nothing to attract such refuge. The majority in Indonesia wants to see a people's economy with equal opportunity for small and medium-sized enterprises and local concerns, and not capital flight to nearby Singapore as aiding and abetting huge Chinese conglomerates.

While Singapore does not expect potential requests from others in ASEAN, it would have to think hard if there were because of these extensive commitments. Lee Kuan Yew has denied that Asian countries with large reserves have been tight-fisted in helping floundering neighbours recover. His view was that he could not see how any Asian government could impose conditions with financial assistance which was best channelled to organizations such as the IMF with the capacity to confront governments (*Sunday Times*, 31 January 1999). Goh Chok Tong also expected verbal attacks from Indonesia but refused to be drawn into its domestic politics (*Straits Times*, 5 March 1999). Singapore chose to say "the minimum" so as to avoid any provocation for neighbours are "sometimes like husbands and wives".

The emotions and candour prompted by these incidents indicate that a deep rethinking on both sides would be helpful. While one can easily dismiss the rhetoric as a way of externalizing the domestic pressure faced by the Indonesian President during the crisis and in his new term of office, the recurring ethnic factor underlining the distrust is of concern. Business between the two countries is conducted mainly by Chinese business enterprises even if some government-linked companies (GLCs) and state enterprises are also involved. Although there has been no noticeable adverse effects other than the expected drag caused by the crisis and the general uncertainty in Indonesia itself, the crisis has been insightful.

Singapore is studying Indonesia's request to sign a mutual extradition treaty as many Indonesians had fled to the Republic and were seeking permanent resident status (*Straits Times*, 14 February 1999). Foreign Minister S. Jayakumar commented that it was too early to accede and Singapore would probably not want to because it was not an entirely innocent bystander as a safe haven for Chinese capital. An interesting policy change in immigration, effected in September 1998, was not as innocuous as it seemed (*Straits Times*, 25 July 1998). In delineating three categories of migrants as P for professional and highly skilled, Q for semi-skilled and R for unskilled and manual workers, the extension of dependent privileges to parents and parents-in-law for P immigration passes is telling. Only Asian migrants would find this attractive as Anglo-Saxon foreign talent would be concerned only for their immediate family, defined as spouse and children. That the immigration law was changed at the height of the ethnic and social disturbances cannot be a simple coincidence.

Habibie had to retract his statement that ethnic Chinese are not vital to Indonesia when he asked them to return, as Chinese capital had fled to Singapore and Hong Kong. Liem Sioe Liong and Eka Tjipta Widjaya were among some tycoons who pledged to bring back some US$16 billion parked in Singapore and elsewhere, with security guarantees from Wahid when he was elected President in October 1999

(*Business Times*, 2 November 1999). The Bank of Indonesia has estimated that a total of US$80 billion, including foreign investors' funds, has flowed out, and only US$30–50 billion belong to Indonesians.

Although Wahid, Megawati, and Amien Rais regard Singapore in a more friendly manner than Habibie, there are outstanding wrinkles in a few business deals. One involves Singapore Power and Pertamina in a natural gas agreement valued at US$8 billion which stumbled over prices (*Straits Times*, 18 June 1999). It was concluded under a memorandum of understanding (MOU) signed in September 1997 for the importation of gas via a pipeline from West Natuna Sea to Jurong island (*Straits Times*, 17 July 1999). The deal was further complicated by Indonesia's investigation into alleged irregularities in the tender awarded to U.S.-based McDermott International Inc. for the gas pipeline project (*Business Times*, 27 August 1999).

The most recent incident of social violence occurred in the resort island of Lombok, where Muslims attacked ethnic Chinese, which spread to Ujung Pandang in Sulawesi just like other sectarian violence. The cause of the violence in Lombok was over land sold to the Salim group and other investors, including Singapore companies, in 1991 at very low prices. Higher payments were being demanded by the exploited owners (*Asian Wall Street Journal*, 20 January 2000; and *International Herald Tribune*, 21 January 2000). While Singapore was not implicated, it seemed that there was guilt by association.

The most positive turn in bilateral relations came with President Wahid's first official visit to Singapore, and it is significant that he made this his first stop. Singapore promised help and Lee Kuan Yew agreed to join an international advisory council that Wahid proposed to set up (*Straits Times*, 11 November 1999). Singapore was obviously well prepared as Goh specifically proposed two investment funds to jump-start investment by Singaporean firms in Indonesia (*Asian Wall Street Journal*, 14–15 January 2000; and *Straits Times*, 14 January 2000). A GLC will invest up to US$500 million by buying minority stakes in distressed assets held by the Indonesian Bank Restructuring Agency (IBRA). It would give incentives to the original owners who had the expertise to turn the companies around with foreign investment, and be willing to bring in Singapore companies as comfortable partners. Singapore's stake would be limited to 10 per cent to avoid any misunderstanding that it was acquiring cheap assets when Indonesia was in distress — a lesson learnt from previous occasions, no doubt. An additional S$400 million (US$239.8 million) facility would be set up in conjunction with banks based in Singapore to finance investments by Singapore companies in

Indonesia. A team of ministers from both sides would flesh out these concepts.

The success of the Singapore-based consortium led by Cycle & Carriage for Indonesian's 45 per cent stake in PT Astra, held by IBRA, over the other two bidders led by Newbridge Capital and Singapore's Government Investment Corporation (GIC) is a result of the pact. That Singapore's GIC was involved in all three bids and that it was the one led by Cycle & Carriage which won, is significant. It includes the Lazard Asia Fund and PT Bhakti Investment, in which Soros has shares. The idea of government involvement through the GIC may be off-putting to some, as witnessed by Singapore Telecommunications' failed bid for Hong Kong's Cable & Wireless. The Cycle & Carriage group's success in buying Astra is the largest deal of its kind in Indonesia, involving a 40 per cent stake amounting to US$506 million (*Asian Wall Street Journal*, 27 March 2000; and *Far Eastern Economic Review*, 6 April 2000). It was also perfect timing for the Cycle & Carriage group which had lost its sole distributorship of Mercedez-Benz cars since January 2000. The involvement of the GIC as a member of the consortium helped, with Cycle & Carriage holding 23 per cent of the shares, the GIC 7 per cent, and the remaining 10 per cent held by Lazard Freres & Co and Bhakti Investment. If it were a purely Singapore or GIC effort, the image and results might have been less desirable.

The Singapore Government is matching dollar-for-dollar the loans granted by the Singapore-based banks for two years (*Straits Times*, 14 January 2000). Another proposal is to showcase joint projects in Batam, Bintan, and Karimun by designating all or some areas as special economic zones (SEZs). The Singapore Tourism Board is also helping to lure some of Singapore's seven million visitors over to Indonesia and is willing to invest S$2 million to promote joint destinations. As much as these are not altruistic projects, Singapore is heeding Indonesia's call for financial and investment assistance from its vantage point as a financial centre and investment hub. Singapore is relaxing its policy on official development assistance which is usually given in humanitarian form or as technical assistance in education and training.

Issues and Problems

Before identifying specific issues and difficulties in economic relations since the crisis, it is germane to have a brief overview of domestic and diplomatic perspectives from both sides. Starting with Indonesia, the first 100 days of the Wahid regime would challenge any younger and more able-bodied President, and the general consensus is that while he was obfuscating at times, he held Indonesia together in his own way. The most crucial tasks were more economic than political and social although they were all highly interrelated and dependent. The economic driver remained foreign investment to create jobs and income, and to fill the capital and foreign exchange gaps. The necessary conditions for investor confidence include corporate and financial restructuring, which in turn require legal reforms and genuine and consistent enforcement. There is no shortage of meaningful laws to promote corporate governance, but enforcement lies with the weak patrimonial nature of government and governance.

Economic reforms and liberalization are not new to Indonesia (Battacharya and Pangestu 1996; and Soesastro 1999). Liberalization had started with the New Order government to change from a state-led to a market-oriented initiative. The first phase, from 1966 to 1982, did achieve total reform because of a reversal in the latter half of the period when the oil boom in 1973–74 provided the state-owned enterprises (SOEs) with abundant resources. The second phase, from 1982 to 1993, was driven by the need to reform when oil prices dropped. The third phase, since 1994, was in response to the regional environment, characterized by heightened competitive liberalization. The 1997 crisis may have provided a new stimulus for further deregulation, representing the fourth phase under IMF tutelage, with its conditionalities and pledge extracted from the government for central bank autonomy.

The increased pace of democratization in Indonesia since the crisis is a welcomed surprise which should filter down to the labour market and industrial relations (Hadiz 1997; and Manning 1999). The negative effects of government intervention include high rates of urban unemployment and the associated rapid urban–rural migration. The failure to take advantage of the low cost of labour to expand labour-intensive manufacturing aggressively was also an opportunity missed. However, this can be redeemed because new technology has changed production methods and strategies in a knowledge-based economy (KBE). The traditional industrial relations based on Pancasila emphasized co-operation and conciliation centred on "family" principles and tripartite co-operation. In practice, however, the gap between the government's ideology and the practice of industrial relations is due to the dynamics of political economy during the New Order period since 1965. The involvement of the government and the military in business has yet to be unshackled, and this has to come with economic reform and corporate and financial restructuring.

The political format of the New Order had emphasized the primacy of Indonesian culture to achieve economic development and political stability (Sukma 1999). As a consequence, the state was stronger than society as politics changed the nature of linkages between domestic politics and foreign policy. Foreign policy was no longer subject to the power game in domestic politics, to be used by the opposition to discredit the government's implementation of its economic development programme. Since the transformation of Indonesian society in the 1990s, reflecting the ruling elite's determination to protect and sustain core political values, foreign policy seemed to have resisted global values. Foreign elements were seen as exacerbating domestic tension. Foreign policy remained subordinated to the regime's domestic interests and was used to contain unwelcome aspects of globalization to preserve dominant values as defined by the ruling élite.

Indonesia and Singapore may be similar in their cautious attitude and response to society's growing demand for democracy, but they are diametrically opposite in their views of globalization, governance, and the ongoing contest of values in the domestic and global domains. For Singapore, its best option is an assertive foreign policy which gives it the right image to survive as a sovereign city-state (Sebastian 1999). It tried foregoing independence to integrate with Malaysia, which turned out to be a failure. Opting for independence and relying on a great power might prove risky if the example of the United States abandoning its ally, South Vietnam, when domestic needs came first, is any lesson. A small state needs an image which must be credible to others. The various episodes with Indonesia since the 1963 confrontation and being designated " a little red dot" are demonstrative.

As a largely Westernized society, Singapore is in a difficult position to champion Asian values and to be a credible Asian country among equals. It has moderated this by projecting an image as a bridge between East and West in order to avert a clash in civilization (Huntington 1996) and also avoid the risk of becoming an international pariah when democratization and human rights issues are raised. Clearly, it is controversial and difficult to be definitive about what Asian values represent, and so it is best for Singapore to strive to balance its diplomatic relations in such a way that it neither alienates the United States nor a rising China. No state, much less a city-state, can be a unitary actor in the political economy of international relations, but must play to more than one audience at all times.

Singapore has institutionalized its value system to maintain national unity and motivate economic attainment in a soulful search for a national ideology and national values. The ensuing political culture governing political and policy debate is premised on these parameters of survival. It might have given itself a restricted and suppressed state image, notwithstanding the opening of a "speakers" corner modelled on London's Hyde Park (*Far Eastern Economic Review*, 6 April 200, p. 30). Political stability and economic security, which shape values and policies in the authoritarian style, is borne out of a belief that political leadership is the most critical parameter to actualize these goals. Its model of governance may be vindicated by its proven resilience in the crisis, which earned it IMF praise (*Straits Times*, 18 March 1998). However, its exposure to the region in general, and Indonesia in particular, could drag it into turmoil if its values and *modus operandi* cannot square with the rest of its neighbours.

A specific example before the crisis was the city-state's strategy of creating growth triangles based on the principle of "prosper thy neighbour", as resources were tapped and complementarities strengthened. With Singapore at the higher end of the industrial ladder, the benefits of the growth triangle were perceived to be reaped by it at the expense of others. Thus, Malaysia in particular, saw it as a "beggar-thy-neighbour" policy, and thus competes with Singapore for the same industries, using more or less similar incentives and concessions. At the same time, Singapore worries whether helping its neighbours would enable them to leapfrog ahead and generate no value-added for Singapore despite its incentives to multinational corporations (MNCs) to situate their overseas headquarters here. It recognizes that with or without its assistance, relocation will take place and it is wiser to be part of the alliance in order to have some influence to safeguard its interests.

On balance, Indonesia and Singapore have less of the historical baggage that the latter has with Malaysia. Lee Kuan Yew's friendship with Soeharto may not be replicated between the current sets of leaders in terms of intensity and duration, but Wahid and Goh have been sufficiently sincere and open in their views, principally because their economic needs have been complementary. In and of itself, the need can almost be a guarantee that many aspects of the political economy can be worked out with all the tribulations learnt during the crisis. Indonesia may appear to still lack a good team of economists and planners not because they are scarce but surfacing them with the right political and ethical labels could be a daunting task. While the tasks ahead are clear and indisputable, unlike Singapore which is more homogenous in decision-making, the numerous factions and heterogeneity in political styles and personalities in Indonesia make the policy environment tenuous.

Besides misreading the students' protests as transitory, as part of the crisis, the Soeharto regime simply did not recognize the dynamics of globalization, new information and communication technology, and the resulting competition. The financial crisis, as a product of a globalized capital market and weak financial institutions and regulatory systems in the afflicted economies was as much a symptom as an endemic feature of global capitalism. Indonesia is woefully behind and blind to systemic risks, with electronic highways taking over traditional modes of communication and delivery of goods and services, types of labour skills and talents needed, and mindset changes which go with the new economy. Languishing in such oblivion, relying on traditional agriculture and oil resources to power the economy, has proved to be inadequate to satisfy its rising mass of socially and economically alienated and dissatisfied voters. Its seasonal haze spewing over to the region is another classic case of benign neglect that the old system can continue to be repaired and nursed along without a paradigm shift.

While Singapore has caught on with globalization, new technology, and the knowledge-based economy much earlier and initiated policies to respond to the challenges, in truth, it may not be able to help Indonesia as quickly and decisively as a much stronger and larger economy could. Singapore is experiencing its own difficulties in terms of attracting the requisite foreign talents, invoking creativity and innovativeness into its education system, and liberalizing its political culture and environment in tandem with such mindset changes. In terms of scale, three to four million people can only do so much for over 200 million in Indonesia.

Jointly as a pact, however, the prospects are quite the contrary, provided Singapore can convince its American, European, and Japanese MNCs that Indonesia and Singapore can be a duo to be exploited together. The big push must still come from outside — the sale of Astra to the consortium led by Cycle & Carriage is a case in point. Confidence-building is crucial to attract more foreign investors, with Singapore interests taking a role as part of the team and part implicit guarantor. Singapore can work on the political economy aspects if Indonesia is more diffident and wary of Western investors, with nationalism still a force to contend with.

Conclusion and Policy Implications

Indonesian–Singapore bilateral relations have been traditionally strong despite the Indonesian confrontation. The city-state poses less of a rivalry and threat to a big economy. The growth triangle experience has been a good one even if not resoundingly successful, which is hard to measure in tangible terms in any case. Confidence has been generated by the pact of initiatives since Wahid's visit to Singapore, reciprocated by the Singapore team in Indonesia to explore ideas and seek mechanisms.

The Chinese connection can be put to positive use because the network has always been there, and Singapore's version of *quanxi*, or Chinese business networking, is relatively cleaner and more transparent than elsewhere. The GLC presence may be shunned elsewhere, much as in China or Malaysia, but seem to matter less in Indonesia. MNCs in Singapore are always on the look-out for opportunities, and they have good working relations and understanding of Singapore's business culture to co-operate with it outside the city-state.

These are positive factors but the business environment in Indonesia must first be put in order. This means incisive economic reform and corporate and financial restructuring, as promised to the IMF, and there is no shame in conformance, as proven by both Thailand and Korea. On its own, Singapore can only do so much to influence thinking and decisions in Indonesia as it essentially has neither the political clout nor the desire to have anything except economic dividends from its alliances. Its alliance with Indonesia may also spur the biggest country in ASEAN to regain its leadership in regional matters. Since Soeharto's departure, Indonesia has taken a hiatus in ASEAN matters, and so has Malaysia, embroiled in managing the crisis. The task has fallen almost by default onto Singapore, not that it was not ready to take a higher profile in regional and global matters, but the blessing of its bigger ASEAN partners, explicitly or implicitly, is important.

Whether they are big or small countries, Indonesia and Singapore have to face globalization, new technology, and the new economy squarely as these have arrived and it is no longer a choice to accept these dynamics or not. As a team, the odd couple can do much for each other, especially when there is as much interest from the private sector as from the top. More massive industrial restructuring is needed in Indonesia with its large agricultural and resource base, and Singapore business may have limited experience there. However, its expertise in trading, finance, distribution, and logistics, and networking on a global scale can be of some assistance. The presence of MNCs in Singapore and the confidence they have in working with Singapore enterprises can be a useful bridge that Indonesian business can fruitfully tap.

However, the most important ingredient is the comfort level and confidence which both Indonesia and Singapore must first have with each other before they can team up to seek other alliances. Despite being in close proximity and in ASEAN for so long, there is more in history, politics, sociology, and culture in Indonesia that the average Singapore businessman may still be ignorant of. This is especially true of the younger generation which is more electronically network-based and believe that efficiency and speed are more virtuous than spending time to know each other in a more well rounded manner before doing business. Political leaders and bureaucrats can only do so much in initiating projects, and the reliance on such initiatives from the top must be supplemented and replaced gradually from the bottom. More knowledge and information of each other can be important building blocks to this relationship as bilateralism or regionalism is ultimately geographically based.

References

Barlow, Colin, ed. *Institutions and Economic Change in Southeast Asia: The Context of Development from the 1960s to the 1990s*. Cheltenham and Northampton: Edward Elgar, 1999.

Battacharya, Amar, and Mari Pangestu. "Indonesia: Development Transformation and the Role of Public Policy". In *Lessons from East Asia*, edited by Danny M. Leipzeiger. Ann Arbor: University of Michigan Press, 1996.

Hadiz, Vedi R. *Workers and the State in New Order Indonesia*. London and New York: Routledge, 1997.

Han, Sung-joo, ed. *Changing Values in Asia: Their Impact on Governance and Development*. Singapore, Tokyo and New York: Institute of Southeast Asian Studies, and Japan Center for International Exchange, 1999.

Huntington, Samuel P. *Clash of Civilizations and the Remaking of World Order*. New York: Simon & Schuster, 1996.

Lee Kuan Yew. *The Singapore Story: Memoirs of Lee Kuan Yew*. Singapore: Singapore Press Holdings, Times Editions, 1998.

Low, Linda. "Overall Assessment of IMS-GT". In *Indonesia–Malaysia–Singapore Growth Triangle: Borderless Region for Sustainable Progress*, edited by Agman Awang, Mahbob Salim and John F. Halldane, pp. 43–58. Johor Bahru: Institute Sultan Iskandar, 1998.

________. "The Economics of the Asian Crisis: A Diagnostic and Prescriptive Attempt". *Asia Pacific Journal of Finance* 2 (1999): 93–110.

Manning, Chris. "Labour Institutions: The Case of Indonesia". In *Institutions and Economic Change in Southeast Asia: The Context of Development from the 1960s to the 1990s*, edited by Colin Barlow, pp. 42–54. Cheltenham and Northampton: Edward Elgar, 1999.

Prakash, Aseem, and Jeffrey A. Hart, eds. *Globalization and Governance*. London and New York: Routledge, 1999.

Sebastian, Leonard C. "Values and Governance Issues in the Foreign Policy of Singapore". *Changing Values in Asia: Their Impact on Governance and*

Development, edited by Han Sung-joo, pp. 219–54. Singapore, Tokyo and New York: Institute of Southeast Asian Studies, and Japan Center for International Exchange, 1999.

Singh, Bilveer. "Challenges Confronting the Foreign Policy of a 'Developed Singapore". *Singapore: Towards a Developed Status*, edited by Linda Low, pp. 271–89. Singapore: Oxford University Press, 1999.

Soesastro, Hadi. "Government and Deregulation in Indonesia". In *Institutions and Economic Change in Southeast Asia: The Context of Development from the 1960s to the 1990s*, edited by Colin Barlow, pp. 105–17. Cheltenham and Northampton: Edward Elgar, 1999.

Sukma, Rizal. "Values, Governance, and Indonesia's Foreign Policy". In *Changing Values in Asia: Their Impact on Governance and Development*, edited by Han Sung-joo, pp. 115–45. Singapore, Tokyo and New York: Institute of Southeast Asian Studies, and Japan Center for International Exchange, 1999.

World Bank. *World Development Report 1998*. New York: Oxford University Press, 1998.

14

DRUG ABUSE IN INDONESIA
An Increasing Problem During the Economic Crisis

Joyce Djaelani Gordon and David Djaelani Gordon

Introduction

Indonesia is in the midst of a full-blown drug abuse and addiction crisis. From being practically unheard of in the past decade, drug abuse has suddenly become a major problem in the country. Years of denial with regard to drug abuse problems in Indonesia, or more importantly, reports that never stated the truth about the drug problem, have cost Indonesia much in more ways than one.

With an estimated 1.3 million drug abusers and addicts in the country in the year 2000, Indonesia has more than it can intelligently and effectively handle. Still debilitated by the pressures of the economic crisis and increasing poverty, as well as ongoing political problems, the issue of drug abuse has to compete with many other issues occupying the minds of the government and the masses. On the other hand, addiction and the economic crisis have lured people into the lucrative drug business.

Problems related to drug abuse and addiction have definitely increased the incidence of HIV/AIDS, Hepatitis C, economic problems, crime, and violence in the country. The lives of millions of families have been affected by these problems. They have become dysfunctional, with most of them not knowing what to do or where to go to seek qualified help. Indonesia has also seen a steady increase in violent student brawls, bloody and senseless riots, and an increasing crime rate, worsening within these past few years, escalating with the problem of drug abuse and addiction. Unfortunately, all these problems will continue to escalate unless the country takes a firm stand against drug abuse.

However, the system of control has not been set up properly, and it is still in its infancy. Indonesia failed to carry out any effective drug abuse prevention programmes when it mattered most, and now it is too late for prevention. Money had been wasted in the past, and now Indonesia has to stretch whatever resources it has to deal with this now monstrous issue. The need for firm intervention is crucial.

The biggest problem is that many people in Indonesia, including professionals, are mostly ignorant about the strategies needed to battle these problems. Most are still calling for intervention to reduce supply only, with the naive expectation that a reduction in drug supply will stop the people from using and abusing drugs. Intervention programmes for reduction in drug demand and in drug-related harm are not given much thought. Information and education is critical at this stage, together with interventions that can make a difference. Indonesia has run out of time, and this will be costly for Indonesia in terms of money and lives.

No Longer a Transit Point

> *"Indonesia is no longer a transit point for drugs. It has become a market as well as producer of some drugs"*, warned Habibie, the Indonesian ex-President in his "World Anti-Drugs Day 1999" keynote address at the Palace (28/6). Declaring a battle against drugs, President Habibie added, *"Dealers are especially targeting young people, causing drug abuse to spread rapidly among the young. This situation does not seem to be the least affected by the economic and political crises."*

Drugs have become increasingly easy to find, if you know where and what to look for. Drugs are also easily available in schools throughout Jakarta. Students report that there are many pushers who haunt school and university grounds, just waiting for young students to walk out from schools. Some pushers even sell "hard drugs" in the school canteen, and toilets. "Pushers also often sell drugs, posing as 'street vendors', they tape the drugs under mineral water bottles. You take the bottle, pay for your drink and drugs, and simply walk away," says Budi (17), a student from a private school in South Jakarta. He added that, "many teenagers also used drugs prior to student brawls, to drone out their fear. Under the influence of drugs, they don't even fear the police." This pattern will spread to other cities throughout

Indonesia, unless certain steps are taken to prevent it. Rina (23), a student from a local university in Central Jakarta, also reported that there were places in her university where people go to shoot drugs.

> I once found an *insul*[1] above the ceiling panel of my school toilet, when I was looking for one. That's normal practice for Junkies to stow their *insul*. What the heck. I used it!
>
> — T, HIV+, HCV+ male addict, 18

Bars and discotheques are of course still the easiest places to find drugs. The most popular drugs used in these settings are *Cimenk* (marijuana), and *Ineks* (Ecstasy). *Cimenk* is normally sold for Rp100,000 per envelope. The prices of locally made Ecstasy may vary from Rp35,000 to Rp75,000 per tablet. The better the quality of Ecstasy, the more expensive it is. Imported ones may fetch up to Rp.150,000 per tablet, and are usually targetted at the more affluent crowd.

The areas of Baturaja, Tanah Abang to Kampung Bali, and Jalan Jaksa are dubbed by local addicts as the "Golden Triangle" for *Putaw*[2] (heroin) and other drugs. Located within the heart of Jakarta, the "Golden Triangle" has become the heart of the addict community. However, sales are not limited to the "Golden Triangle", and neither is *Putaw* the only drug sold in these areas. Delivery orders can also be made. Jatinegara, Cipinang, Gudang Peluru, and Senayan are other areas where users can easily buy drugs. Generally, a gram of *Putaw* costs around Rp150,000 to Rp300,000, depending on the quality. The same goes for a gram of *Shabu-Shabu* (methamphetamine) which is beginning to gain popularity among the young. These drugs also come in small affordable packages costing Rp30,000 to Rp50,000, which is enough for novices to get high on, and share a little with others. Peppy (27), a recovered addict, said that he had used 0.5 grams of *Putaw* a day. It is easy to calculate how much he had to spend per month on his drug habit. He used to inhale (drag, chase the dragon) *Putaw*, but then turned to injections as they gave him a better high, on a smaller amount of drugs, thus wasting less.

The fact that drugs are easily available and also affordable is enough to make parents worry that their children's pocket money will be used to buy drugs. They should! Pills such as Rohypnol and Nipam (barbiturate) only cost Rp2,500 to Rp3,000 a strip, and many young people pop these pills as they would candies, creating a cheap high. They can also easily afford locally made Ecstasy.

The easy availability of drugs in Indonesia, more so in Jakarta, is a clear indication that the country has become a target for drug-marketing, while also becoming a centre for drug production. Ecstasy is now locally manufactured in great quantities, although the quality cannot be guaranteed. The newspapers and media have often reported the uncovering of small and large factories around Indonesia by the police. Some of these factories have modern and sophisticated equipment for producing Ecstasy. *Kompas*, Indonesia's leading newspaper, reported that a few Indonesians had been caught trying to smuggle Ecstasy to Hong Kong! Marijuana, for example, is a weed native to the land, grown especially in Aceh and many parts of Sumatra. Therefore, Indonesians can no longer say that, "Indonesia is just a transit point". Indonesia has started to manufacture, and distribute its own illegal drugs. The Indonesian drug business is huge today, and the drug lords can certainly, and easily buy their way out of any trouble with the amount of money they are handling.

The fact is that the economic crisis in Indonesia has boosted the drug market in Indonesia. In the midst of the economic crisis in Indonesia, with massive layoffs and high inflation rates, drug dealing provided a quick way up and out of poverty. It would be naive to think that the drug business would be adversely affected by poverty. No country, rich or poor, is immune to drug abuse and addiction problems. The availability of money only affects the types of drugs that people would use.

The economic and political crises have thus aggravated the drug scene. Selling drugs is a very lucrative business. The Indonesian economic crisis, if anything, has only spurred people to turn to drug dealing as a source of income, and this has helped to encourage more abusers and addicts. Drug dealers use various marketing strategies to grab customers, alluring them with the promise of *fun and escape from worries and stress*. The amount of money wasted on this is huge. If an abuser or addict spends about Rp100,000 a day, and recognizing that Indonesia has reportedly 1.3 million drug abusers and addicts, the amount spent on drugs here would be about Rp130 billion *each day*. It could have been better spent to help others during the times of political and economic crises.

The Lucrative Business

With the amount of "hard drugs" available throughout Indonesia, there is no question that Indonesian drug cartels and drug lords are in firm control of the Indonesian drug market. The illegal drug market in Indonesia is unquestionably a multimillion dollar a day business. With an estimated number of 1,300,000 active abusers and addicts (not including recreational users) in the country (and growing daily), the amount of money that filters down through the Indonesian drug market is phenomenal. A small calculation will prove the point.

Using a low estimate of a million addicts in Indonesia, and then conservatively estimating that approximately 600,000 of these individuals are abusing or addicted to *Putaw* and *Shabu-Shabu*, and if the amount of drugs they use individually is an eighth (⅛) of a gram per day, this would translate into a staggering 75 kilograms of *Putaw* and *Shabu-Shabu* transacted on a daily basis. If each gram is sold at an average of Rp250,000 per gram, the amount of money that filters through the drug business daily is approximately Rp18,750,000,000. This is a conservatively low figure.

Many people (carriers, mules) have been caught at the Soekarno Hatta International Airport for smuggling heroin and Ecstasy. They are mostly Africans, and people from other developing countries. They are always small-time carriers, looking for easy money. Yet nothing is ever heard about drugs being discovered/uncovered in Indonesian shipping ports where the large containers arrive in Indonesia! With its vast shoreline, it would be more than easy for boats to dock unnoticed anywhere along the remote beaches of Indonesia.

The Dealers

People become dealers because it is an easy and quick way to make money. It is also an easy way for addicts to support their drug habit.

A drug habit can be very hard on an addict's pocket after a while, and therefore, many addicts turn to stealing. Some progress to become pushers to support their personal drug habit. By turning others to their drug of choice, pushers can negotiate a better deal, sell some and have enough left over to use for themselves. However, this happens only with the less serious dealers. The serious dealers are hardly ever addicts, and are calculating and cunning business people. They recruit chosen people, who in turn recruit other people to put the drugs on the streets. Chosen people are those who need money, yet do not need the drugs for themselves. Addicts are not a good choice as they are hard to trust and often steal and use their own merchandise to support their habit.

> I got fired during the crises. I used drugs to escape from the painful reality. I used, and later began dealing drugs because I have no more money and have stolen or sold everything I could! As I began selling drugs, I made good money. Then I began using the drugs more for myself. It got me into trouble with my connection and they hounded me,

said Donny (37), who is struggling to recover, after realizing that his drug habit was becoming increasingly more painful than staying clean.

As shown in Table 14.1, there is a significant increase in drug dealing committed by people as they become addicts. There are addicts who were dealers first before becoming addicted, but this is not common. Most addicts took drugs first, before becoming dealers, as reported by the addicts in the Yayasan Harapan Permata Hati Kita Recovery Centre (January 2000).

Table 14.1
Drug Dealing, by Addiction

Did you ever deal in illicit drugs?	*Never*		*Once*		*More than Once*	
N = 127	*N*	%	*N*	%	*N*	%
Before Drugs	115	90.55	3	2.36	9	7.09
After Drugs	44	34.65	9	7.09	74	58.26
Difference	–71	–55.91	+6	+4.73	+65	+51.17

Source: Database, Yayasan Harapan Permata Hati Kita (Addiction Treatment and Recovery Community Centre), Ciawi, Bogor, 2000.

During the economic crisis, many people took on other jobs besides keeping their profession, such as dealing in drugs. One mother said:

> My tailor is now a *BD*![3] I was so shocked when I went there to get my dress done, and found some young kids were on the floor in *pedaw*.[4] Little kids were everywhere, ignorant of the going-on around them. They had the *BR*[5] on the glass table top, and a piece of cutter blade there, and tin foil pieces scattered on their filthy floor. I pretended to be ignorant, and asked my tailor … 'these boys look tired, why don't you tell them to sleep inside?' And she just laughed at me without saying anything.
>
> — SE, mother of an addict, 38

Dealers are not a distinguishable group of people. Dealers come from all walks of life, from addicts themselves, to university students, high school students, mothers and fathers, unemployed people, employees and workers, young and older executives, sex workers, police, and those in the military, high-ranking officials, and their children. Anyone can be a dealer.

Often after a drug bust (which happens all the time), many members of the police force steal the drugs for themselves, and are known to deal in the drugs that they confiscate, selling them back in the streets at very reasonable prices. This is a common crime here, committed by the police themselves. (Destruction of drugs by the police is nearly unheard of.... Every once in a while, a small amount of "drugs are burned for public appeal". But ... the tons of drugs confiscated by the police and military mysteriously disappear all the time!)

> I was once offered to buy drugs at KOMDAK... I thought they (his friends) were just pulling my leg. It turned out to be true ... , and the drugs were cheap! And they (the policemen) were so easily manipulated. We managed to get a lot of drugs for less money!
>
> — R, male addict, 22

The following article, from *Kompas* daily newspaper, is only one of the many stories that we know happen regularly here, although not always causing casualties, as in the following incident.

> First Sergeant (Sertu) Fikri Zakaria (25) died with 3 bullets shot into his body. First Sergeant I Gusti Ketut Putra, member of Pomdam Jaya (Military Police) was suspected to be the person who shot Fikri. The incident took place in Kelapa Gading, North Jakarta, Sunday evening (2/1). Sertu Fikri, a member of the traffic police department, Polda Metro Jaya, was shot following an incident where he attempted to extort money from a drug dealer, while Sertu Putra positioned himself to back the drug dealer. Head of the Metro Jaya, Maj. Gen. (Police) Noegroho Djajoesman said that; "the incident started with an ambush done by the police, on New Year's Eve, in a house located in Pulomas, East Jakarta. There, police were able to confiscate a huge quantity of Shabu. In the ambush, Fikri, used the name Iwan Syah, and claimed to be a Second Lieutenant. Negotiations were made, and it was agreed that the Shabu dealer would pay Rp.15 million to him. He was able to pay Fikri Rp.13 million that night, and promised that the remaining Rp.2 million would be paid in Kelapa Gading, Sunday night (2/1). In the second transaction, however, the shabu-shabu owner brought a military police member to back him up. (rts/yns — *Kompas*, Tuesday, 4 January 2000, p. 6)

This is a fact, and as painful as it is, we must learn to accept this truth. Money seems to ensure the smooth operation of the drug business. It is common knowledge among addicts that they can buy confiscated drugs, seized by the police in their drug raids, and that these drugs can be bought cheap. The more drug raids are conducted, the richer these people (police) become.

> We know this, because they sell them (drugs) to us. The 'police' also stand behind the drug lords, so that the drug lords become untouchable by law.
>
> — AB, female addict, 21

Those who are caught are always the "small fries". They are people who do not have the courage, or connections, to go against the drug lords, or police, and risk their wrath when they disobey. It is also no secret that police protection is still only a word. It usually costs a lot to have real police protection! However, to many, this is not an option for they have no money. They are the ones who go to jail, until someone in the family, or someone they know, can pay the police to release them:

> She was nabbed by the police for selling drugs, also her husband and her daughter. They could minimize the charge if they only would say who the big dealers behind them were. Until now, they are keeping their mouth shut, and just would not talk! I wonder if it is too risky for them to open up. And I wonder if the police would really provide them with police protection, if they do open their mouths?
>
> — SE, mother of an addict, 38

Since many drug dealers have been released from police custody, especially those who happen to be the children of high officials or important people, or in the police and military, many question whether anyone is really serious in dealing with the drug problem? Users, abusers and addicts are the ones who get the worst deals, when faced with the law enforcers. When caught carrying a pill or two on the person, they are arrested, and have to pay a bribe, or go to jail.

Distribution

The network for drug distribution is not very complex, as it uses a standard multi-level marketing procedure. However, the network is not always easily uncovered, because of protection of the business by the police, the military and the syndicate. Those who have the money to conduct this business, the drug lords, do not actually touch the drugs. They have certain "paid people" who do the actual buying and the dealing for them. The profit from the drug business is sent straight to their bank accounts.

Usually, a drug lord will have two or three people in the upper levels of the organization next to him/her to manage the drug business (they have others who manage their "legal businesses, paid for by profits from the drug business"). These chosen people under the drug lord will each have about three others under them who contract the larger transactions, transport the drugs, process the drugs, and conduct the flow of the distributions in large quantities down to the next level of dealers, who deal in kilograms. These people in turn would have a group or gang to sell the drugs in small quantities on the street. The junkie dealers will then buy and sell small amounts of drugs to friends and clients, and usually use the rest of the drugs themselves.

The dealers at the lower rung of the ladder would deal with anyone and therefore run the highest risk of getting caught. Some also use little children (around ten years old) to sell the drugs to clients. There are also addicts who "travel, and buy drugs for their own circle of friends". They can also be added to the distribution line.

Addicts, however, are often not the people heading the business. Most of them deal in drugs just to support their own use. If they can do the *run*[6] for their friends, they can often make better deals, and earn a little profit from it — at least, get enough free drugs to use for a while. Often, the problem arises when addicts themselves do the dealing, and end up using all the drugs themselves rather than sell the drugs. Some people in the business can also slip and become addicts themselves. It is rare that addicts can make a meaningful profit, when they are addicted to the very drugs they are trying to sell.

Drug dealing is now commonly found around Jakarta, and even elsewhere in Java for sure. The interesting thing is that these deals are often blatantly open. Many lay people think that deals are done secretly, just like in the movies, but for addicts, it is like buying candies. Just go to an area where you know there are dealers, knock on a door, and they will show you where you can get what you want. Compared with other countries, Indonesian dealers at the lower levels are really sloppy.

> There was a time when I needed *pakawan*.[7] And a Junkie friend and I just decided to go to Baturaja, although we did not personally know any dealers there. We just knew that Baturaja was where we could find some stuff. So we went. After looking around some we saw two guys coming out from a house, we could see they were Junkies. We just went in and asked whether they had some stuff. They did!
>
> — A, male addict, 23

> I was on Angkot[8] today in Bogor, and the driver whispered to me if I wanted to buy some ganja!"
>
> — RC, male addict, 16

HIV/AIDS/Hepatitis C and Drug Abuse

Hepatitis and AIDS are a serious threat to drug users. According to UNAIDS, 700,000 young people aged 10–24 are infected with HIV in Asia yearly. United Nations officials have reported that heroin addiction is responsible for 65 per cent of new HIV infections nationwide in Vietnam. The greater Jakarta area has about 150,000 drug users with an average age range of 15–24 years old. Experts say that 50 per cent are estimated to be injecting drug users (IDU).

HIV and Hepatitis C viruses are becoming a grave concern. It is estimated that 80 per cent of HIV/AIDS cases come from the IDUs. The trend in Indonesia seems to be that HIV/AIDS cases will mostly be among the IDUs, compared with heterosexuals, as in Malaysia, New Jersey, Hanoi, and New York (*Republika* newspaper, 20 September 2000). In August 2000 alone there were 98 newly reported cases (73 with HIV and 25 new AIDS cases) in Indonesia. Of this, 72 cases of HIV/AIDS (61 new HIV infections and 11 cases of AIDS) were IDUs.

Yayasan Harapan Permata Hati Kita (Yayasan Kita), an addiction recovery centre in Bogor, West Java, for residents coming from Jakarta and other areas in Indonesia, has seen a jump in Hepatitis C (dubbed the *Dragon*) prevalence rates among the IDUs. In October 1999, the rate of Hepatitis C among the more than 100 residents who came for treatment was 70 per cent. In September 2000, their test results showed a 92 per cent prevalence rate among new residents. HIV, on the other hand, has climbed from 10 per cent in October 1999 to 40 per cent in September 2002. It is true that this is the report of only one recovery centre. However, other drug recovery centres are currently not providing counselling and testing for these two viruses. Or if they are, they are not doing it openly and are keeping the results to themselves (not disclosing this even to the addicts themselves). Others are not confirming their findings, and hence are not included in the national statistics. The number of IDUs is increasing among the population of drug addicts, especially during the economic crisis. "Shooting drugs" rather than "chasing the Dragon" (burning and inhaling) can stretch what little amount of drugs that addicts have to get high on. However, since needles are not easily available, most Indonesian IDUs share needles and thus pass on viruses among themselves, and then, to their sexual partners. Many IDUs report sharing needles with 2–5 people daily, and most do not know anything about cleaning needles. Tables 14.2 and 14.3 show the responses of addicts at Yayasan Harapan Permata Hati Kita.

However, when the addicts were asked whether they practised what they knew about cleaning needles, the answer tended to be no.

Table 14.2
Number of Persons Sharing Needles

How many people do you 'usually' share needles with (daily) when you use drugs?	*No.*	*%*
Never shared needles	44	32.12
2–5 people	93	67.88
6–10 people	0	0
>10 people	0	0
Total	137	100%

Source: Database, Yayasan Harapan Permata Hati Kita (Addiction Treatment and Recovery Community Centre), Ciawi, Bogor, 2000.

Table 14.3
Knowledge on Cleaning Needles

Did you know how to clean your works (needles) so you would not get diseases or viruses before coming to Yayasan Kita?	*No.*	*%*
No	85	62.04
Yes	52	37.96
Total	137	100%

Source: Database, Yayasan Harapan Permata Hati Kita (Addiction Treatment and Recovery Community Centre), Ciawi, Bogor, 2000.

Needle and syringe educational programmes are still not openly available and sanctioned in Indonesia, although these programmes could do much to keep HIV and Hepatitis C infections from rapidly increasing. Advocates for harm reduction programmes still have problems in making the needle awareness programme a reality. Most lay people see these programmes as promoting the culture of drug abuse rather than preventing the spread of the two deadly diseases, with arguments reminiscent of condom promotion for sexually transmitted diseases and HIV/AIDS prevention. The only difference is

Table 14.4
Practice of Safe Methods

Did you practise safe methods when using needles?	*No.*	%
No	77	56.20
Yes	48	35.04
Other	12	8.76
Total	137	100%

Source: Database, Yayasan Harapan Permata Hati Kita (Addiction Treatment and Recovery Community Centre), Ciawi, Bogor, 2000.

that one needs a doctor's prescription to buy needles, while condoms are more easily accessible. Most people have yet to understand the cost of high rates of HIV/AIDS and Hepatitis C among the productive age population, and what this can potentially mean to Indonesia. The direct cost of the loss of productivity, loss of employment, health care costs, just to name a few, can be huge, not to mention other indirect costs.

Peter Piot, of UNAIDS, in a press release (2 April 1999) stated that the economic crisis had caused nearly 20 per cent of young Indonesian girls to drop out of school in 1998/99. His biggest concern was these young girls, without education and employable skills, would drift into high-risk behaviour, such as drug use and prostitution. In addition, in drug circles, young girls often sell sex to get drugs, or simply exchange sexual favours for drugs. This would of course contribute to the rapid spread of HIV/AIDS and Hepatitis C among the young people of Indonesia.

The Mass Media and Public Information on Drugs

There have not been any significant mass media reports that teach Indonesians about drugs. Most of the information in the mass media have been reports about drug raids and confiscation of drugs by the police or immigration officers. Thus, they were only able to create an impression on the people that law enforcement was what Indonesia needed to fight against drugs.

In the Jabotabek area of Jakarta, one can see banners in the residential areas that are not very friendly and not very educational either. These banners, made by the local neighbourhood, would say:

> "Berantas *Narkoba*[9] dan *Togel*[10]!" (Destroy Narcotics and Gambling Lotto.)
> "Awas, Bahaya NAZA[11] Mengancam kita" (Beware, the Danger of Drugs Threatens Us!)
> "Sehat atau Wafat, Berobat dan Bertobat. Remaja Sehat Simbol Bangsa Sehat" (Health or Death. Get Treatment and Repent. Healthy Teens Symbolizes Healthy Nation)

The money used to make these banners could certainly have been put to better use. At least, those banners could have been made more educational. It is doubtful that people who read the banners would be empowered to do anything about drug abuse in their own area. The irony is that these banners are often found in the very same areas where addicts buy their drugs. In some instances, these banners are placed just above the houses of the drug dealers, without the people in the neighbourhood even knowing that they are the houses of the dealers. How can anyone help to keep drugs from the area they live in, if they do not even know who their enemy is, or where the drug addicts or dealers live?

Information and education regarding the dangers of drugs are very limited and shallow. For example:

> "Don't use drugs ... it's dangerous!"
> "Don't use drugs ... it's *haram*!"[12]

Which teenager, looking for acceptance, for a place to belong, for fun and excitement with their friends and peers would pay attention to such slogans. It is thus easy to understand why there is misinformation and myths among the public with regard to drugs. Among these myths are:

- — *ganja* is not dangerous because it is a natural substance;
- — to get off from *Putaw* addiction, use *Shabu* because it is not addictive;
- — if you smoke marijuana once you will automatically become addicted;
- — good kids do not use drugs;
- — Moslems do not drink, and thus they do not become drug addicts;

— Addicts are from broken homes
— you can get off drugs if you pray to God for help

These are the information that parents and teachers continue to share with the young. However, the young know better from reality. Most Indonesians do not! Most parents do not even know what marijuana looks or smells like. Most have never even seen *Putaw* or *Shabu*. The signs go unrecognized by parents. At the same time, the young have different things in mind. Among their own myths are:

— Using *Putaw* (or *Shabu*) can help overweight people lose weight
— Using ganja can increase your creativity
— *Shabu* is less dangerous than *Putaw*
— *Shabu* is good for increasing sexual stamina

School provides some (a little) information about drugs, especially for those who have studied abroad. Most of those from the countryside have never received any information about drugs. They only get a lecture about the various types of drugs. Little, if any, is shared on the psychological and problematic aspects of drug use, abuse, and addiction. Even less information is given on HIV/AIDS, Hepatitis C, and sexually transmitted diseases. The police would lecture the young people about drugs, usually carrying some visuals with them, or samples of drugs. However, they would talk about the illegal aspects of drug use more than anything else.

Sometimes the police would show an outdated documentary film, made in the 1970s, about *morphine addicts.*[13] The drug addicts featured in the film were shown in the process of *sakaw*, wearing bell-bottom trousers of the 1970s, and sporting Beatles-style long hair. The young people are amazed that the police still use this outdated film after thirty years. The information is considered *basi*[14] by the young people, and therefore none would pay attention to the film, and would laugh at it.

> For me, I was already wet (using)... so what the heck ... I might as well swim (continue using).
>
> — A, male addict, 22

Quite often, these school presentations become the source of jokes among the young students. Information about the effects and the impact of drug use on a person's life is never provided in the schools. Much real information is needed for everyone. Parents and teachers cannot talk to the young about drugs, mostly because they themselves do not have the information. From the report of the addicts themselves, it is clear that people do not have any information on how to detect drug use early enough to save them from unnecessary misery. People really do not have information on addiction, let alone the more complex issues such as AIDS and Hepatitis C, and sexually transmitted diseases, and other illnesses that can be contracted from the use of illegal drugs.

Because of this lack of information, even among people who are supposedly knowledgeable about drugs and drug addiction, it has been easy for those addicted to keep their drug habit a secret. Many addicts manage to hide their addiction for years before being caught. When parents, family or teachers finally find out, it is usually too difficult to help.

Thus, many parents bring addicts to hospitals or clinics for treatment and medication numerous times before they understand that it is not the right way to help them overcome their drug problem. Many people have been led to believe that addiction is simply a physical problem, but this is not so.

There are parents who isolate their children who have problems with drugs in faraway places or in small cities because they do not know how to handle them. They also wrongly believe that their children will be safe from drugs that way, but there are drugs in faraway places and small cities too. Geographical moves would not change addicts. If addicts cannot find their favourite drugs, they will switch to anything that is available, as long as it can get them high.

There is no place in Indonesia that we know of that is free from drugs anymore, not even in the small villages. As some addicts shared:

> I was sent to Purworejo, because my mother thought that I would not find drugs there. Wrong! Not only I could continue using there, I became a dealer there, and the money was good.
>
> — T, male addict, 23

> I was already an addict in high school, then I moved to Batam. While I was there back then, all I could find was alcohol, so I used a lot of alcohol. When I came back to Jakarta, I simply took off from where I left off. I got on *Shabu-Shabu*, soon I became violent at home. I ended up in a holding cell, until I agreed to get treatment for my addiction.
>
> — PD, male addict, 37

> I was sent to Yogyakarta, because my parents thought Yogyakarta was different, and that I would have difficulty in finding *Putaw*. The first day I was there, I got into *sakaw*, so I set out to find *Putaw*. I went to Malioboro. I saw a guy who seemed like a user, and I asked whether he had some stuff. He did. When there is a will,

> there is a way. Moreover, I had more freedom in Yogyakarta to use drugs than I did here in Jakarta, without having to look over my shoulder!
>
> — DK, male addict, 20

People do not have clear information on what to do when they find that someone close to them is addicted. This type of drug and crisis information about addicts is not available in Indonesia yet. Even those who boast hotline services do not know how to handle the addict's need for information. As an addict also shared:

> I saw this advertisement on television last night (*Hotline Service for drug abuse), and I decided to call them. I told them that I was a Junkie, and that I needed help. They did not know what to tell me! They did not know what to do with me! There were lots of, ... hm ... uh ... well ... ehm ... ahs coming from them. That blew my mind! How could they open a Hotline Service when they don't even know what they are doing, or talking about!"
>
> — A, male junkie, 24

Better Information, Education, and Communication

People need clear and precise suggestions and information on the steps they need to take when they find anyone abusing, or is addicted to drugs, information that would empower individuals to take firm action with more confidence, and save people from unnecessary tragedy and misery. This kind of information should be made available in:

- — government and private offices;
- — schools and educational institutions, from elementary school to universities, and including the international schools in Indonesia (there are many abusers and addicts in the international schools);
- — public places such as shopping malls, business centres, transportation depots, which can display posters and brochures;
- — public seminars, workshops, and lectures for the general public where talks should include reformed addicts and their parents as speakers to share what they know as true, and how real recovery works.

Teachers often do not know what to do with their students who have problems with drugs. Many are simply asked to leave school when found to be abusing drugs. It is naive to think that expelling students using drugs would solve the problem and teach the students a lesson. This would not solve the bigger problem that Indonesia is facing.

There are, however, a few schools that have responded appropriately when they found their students to be using, abusing, or addicted to drugs. They have sent the students to drug abuse professionals for counselling and rehabilitation. When the students are deemed to be clear of their addiction, they can return to school under tight supervision by the school staff. Unfortunately, other schools simply refuse to deal with the addicts.

Information on rehabilitation and recovery should also be disseminated, as well as the "process" of helping drug abusers and drug addicts to recover from addiction. If information is well disseminated, people could help to reduce the number of abusers and addicts. It would also help to cut down the length of time needed to help drug abusers and addicts out of their addiction. If people knew what to do, *including the so-called professionals,* the level of success in combatting addiction would be greatly increased. These people seriously need training on how to handle addicts and their addiction!

That is why recovered addicts should be selected as facilitators, who together with other "drug specialists" can play a larger role in sharing information about addiction and recovery (and HIV/AIDS and Hepatitis). The best way to effectively disseminate information is by:

— Having honest and factual information included in all school curriculums (starting at the junior high school level);
— Having more seminars for various groups of people;
— Having professional training for various groups of people;
— Having more NARCOTICS ANONYMOUS and ALCOHOLICS ANONYMOUS meetings in the community, together with their counterpart groups, NARANON and AL-ANON.
— Having effective and thoughtful campaigns that apply to addiction, HIV/AIDS, and Hepatitis throughout Indonesia.

Drug abuse campaigns in Indonesia have so far not been effective. People seem to be bumping into, and overlapping with one another, without any unity in their goals and objectives. None seems to have clear and definite priorities, or provide any strong statements, and all seem ignorant about the need to have nationwide campaigns to make a stand against addiction, AIDS, and Hepatitis C.

> Why can't people here make a national campaign? You know, kind of like the World AIDS Day campaign thing ... You know, where everyone in the world works together, and everyone is sent an outline of what the campaign or theme will be, then everyone works towards the same thing? A Committee could make a common statement poster, brochures or whatever, then have everyone adapt it to their local language and needs. That makes more sense to me.
>
> — Z, male addict, 16

Campaigns should have the same theme in their programmes, targetting different groups of the population. Many are targetted at prevention, and none at intervention. In other words, most campaigns are not targetted at the drug abusers and addicts. Materials should also reach out to professionals to inform them on what they can do; to teachers on what they should know; to politicians on what they can accomplish; to RT/RW[15] on what they can do locally, as well as to parents, friends, etc. None of this is being done at the moment. Everybody seems to be just screaming "Say No to Drugs" or "Abolish Drugs". That is an outdated scream! If "Say No to Drugs" worked, the drug culture would never have arisen in the first place, and the most powerful countries of the world would not be spending billions of dollars on trying to stop drug addiction.

> For more than 5 years, I lived as a Junkie. That time, I never knew about the dangers and how easy it would be for me to get infected with HIV/AIDS. In certain times, I saw posters, brochures, but they never really caught my attention and I never cared. I continued to use needles and have sex with multiple partners. I was so goddamn sure that I would never catch any diseases ... HIV/AIDS, Hepatitis A, B, C and STDs ... while in reality the possibility of me becoming infected with all these diseases was just huge.
>
> — M, male addict, 22

Conclusion

The economic crisis has incapacitated Indonesia from taking a real stand in the prevention and curbing of drug abuse and its related problems. Mass and public education has been limited by the unavailability of funds, and the low priority that drug abuse seems to have been given during the crisis in Indonesia. This has caused much losses, and more will be lost in the coming years, economically, socially, politically, and also in terms of human lives. Those who die would likely be those in the productive ages, and this could ensure the continuing economic crisis and cause other future problems in Indonesia.

The drug abuse culture has already taken a grip on Indonesia, while prevention and intervention efforts are still limited to slogans, which are far from effective. Cases of addiction and HIV/AIDS/HCV have been increasing, and once they have grown they will be here to stay, never to be totally eradicated. Will Indonesia be like Africa which now reports a 25 per cent prevalence rate of HIV/AIDS in their general population? Will the Indonesian economy be taken over by drug lords? These are questions that need to be considered seriously and urgently if a difference is to be made.

Notes

1. *Insul*: slang for syringe; also called *insulin*.
2. *Putaw*: heroin, slang for *putih*, or white.
3. *BD* (read bayday): Bandar; dealer; the person who oversees deals.
4. *Pedaw*: high; that moment of rush after shooting drugs.
5. *BR*: abbreviation for *barang*; literally "stuff"; drugs.
6. *Run*: to do courier service; to buy, carry.
7. *Pakawan*: stuff to use; drugs; from the word *pakaw*.
8. *Angkot*: *ANGkutan KOTa*, city transportation.
9. *Narkoba*: *NARkotik dan OBAt*; narcotics and drugs.
10. *Togel*: *TOto GELap*; gambling lotto.
11. *NAZA*: Narkotik, Alkohol, Zat Adiktif (Narcotics, Alcohol and Addictive Substances)
12. *Haram*: against the law of religion; strongly prohibited by religion.
13. *Morphine* addiction was rife in Indonesia in the 1970s, with the upsurge of the flower generation.
14. *Basi*: mouldy; old; used to signify food that is already spoilt and can no longer be used.
15. RT/RW: Rukun Tetangga/Rukun Warga; RT is the smallest unit of a neighbourhood area consisting of 15–20 households; while RW is larger and consists of several RTs.

References

Gordon, Joyce Djaelani, and David Djaelani, et al. *Rapid Assessment on HIV/AIDS/HCV: A Study Done by Drug Addicts in Recovery*. Bogor, Indonesia: Yayasan Harapan Permata Hati Kita (Yayasan KITA); Addiction Treatment & Recovery Community Centre, January 2000.

Kompas daily. "Peras Bandar Narkotika, Seorang Polisi Tewas". 4 January 2000, p. 6.

Republika daily. "DPR, Kurang Sense of Emergency Hadapi HIV/AIDS" [Parliament lacks sense of emergency in managing AIDS]. 20–24 September 2000, p. 14.

"Semiloka Nasional Menanggapi Masalah NAZA" [National Workshop on Overcoming NAZA Issues]. Puncak, West Java: KerlipNAZA, 20–24 September 2000.

15

MANAGING THE ELDERLY IN A CRISIS SITUATION

Santo Koesoebjono and Solita Sarwono

How old are you?

Age is quality of mind
If you have left your dream behind
If hope is cold
If you no longer look ahead
If your ambition's fires are dead
Then you are old

But if from life you take the best
If in life you keep the jest
If love you hold
No matter how the years go by
No matter how the birthdays fly
You are not old

— H. S. Fritsch
(*Warta Demografi*, no. 1, th. 24, 1994)

Introduction

In many societies, the old people form a vulnerable and financially weak group in the population. They are vulnerable because of their poor health and physical condition, disabilities, social isolation, poor housing, and lack of care. They are financially weak because they do not have enough savings or their pension is too little to support their lives at old age. Many of them have to depend on their children or relatives or are forced to continue working to make ends meet. The economic crisis has presumably worsened the condition of the elderly although the impact differs because senior citizens are not a homogenous group.

The number of elderly persons will increase rapidly in the coming half century. The trend of population ageing is confirmed since future senior citizens are already there and their survival can be forecasted with accuracy, barring unforeseen calamities. The impact of two decades of fertility and mortality decline is shown in the rapid growth rates of the older age groups and the low growth rates of children. In Indonesia, the population aged 65 years and older more than doubled between 1971 and 1990, from 2.97 million to 6.75 million, or from 2.5 to 3.8 per cent of the population (Hugo 1996, p. 15). By the year 2025, some 13 per cent of the population will be 60 years or older, a rise from about 7.6 per cent in 2000. Ageing is a global event and will spare no country. The United Nations considers ageing as one of the urgent issues in the coming decades (UN 1992b, 1993; and UNFPA, 1998). Consequently, public policies should be oriented towards a permanent aged society. Concern about the sub-population of senior citizens is therefore justified.

The conjunction of ageing and the economic crisis has dealt a severe blow to the position of senior citizens. Generally speaking, the elderly are confronted with two types of crises. The first is an external crisis, that is, the economic crisis that hit Indonesia in 1997/98, and the second is an internal crisis, that is, crisis in the family with regard to care.

These crises have serious effects but at the same time they can stimulate new ways of setting up a care system and of producing new devices designed to help the elderly to better cope with their handicaps, to participate in economic and social activities, and to enjoy life.

This chapter is based on general observations regarding the condition of elderly people, with special attention given to Indonesia. It discusses the consequences of population ageing, the implications of the economic crisis on the elderly, how the elderly cope with crisis situations, and anticipation of a greying society in Indonesia.

Rising Grey Population

The twin processes of low fertility and low mortality underlie the process of population ageing (UN 1993). The number of youngsters has been declining and the populations of the new generations are becoming smaller. At the same time, the number of persons at advanced ages has been growing because of a longer life-span. People are living longer because of better public health services, medical advancement, and improving economic conditions. More people will reach higher ages and the number of the "80 plus" will also increase. The United Nations' long-range population projections estimate an ultimate life expectancy at birth of 84.7 years for both sexes by the mid-twenty-first century (82.5 years for men, and 87.5 years for women in 2045–50) (UN 1992a). The maturing of the age structure has resulted in a rising concentration of the population at the middle and high ages of 65 and older. Ageing will affect the total population, especially the working-age sub-population.

Great disparities in the age structures between countries prevail since the stages of the ageing process vary. Ageing has a long history, taking place over approximately a century for most Western European countries (Sauvy 1966). Many developing countries are still at the early stages of ageing but some are already facing the consequences of an ageing population, such as labour shortage (for example, Republic of South Korea and Singapore). As it is the case with population growth, population ageing demonstrates that it is incorrect to assume a one-world population (De Beer and Van Wissen 1999).

Within a country, ageing also varies between regions. Regions most affected by out-migration to other regions because of organized migration (transmigration) or moves of individuals and families on their own initiative will experience rapid ageing since migration is mostly age selective. The young, more energetic, and educated tend to leave, moving to centres of bustling economic activities or less crowded and undeveloped rural areas. Considering that population moves are to a large extent driven by economic motives, the real or perceived better living conditions in other places may trigger moves that in the course of time may take the shape of mass migration (Petersen 1958). By then migration becomes an established pattern, shored up by the presence of a social network that links migrants and those left behind, and is therefore instrumental to a chain migration of follow-up moves (Massey et al. 1993). The continuous flows from rural to urban as well as to empty rural areas can be witnessed in Indonesia in recent decades (Hugo 1997). The persistence of such outflows forms a relevant cause of ageing at the regional level, next to the trend of mortality and fertility.

The United Nations' publications (1999a,b) show that all countries will experience population ageing and face its consequences. In early 2000, about 600 million persons all over the world were 60 years and older. This is 10 per cent of the world population. This number will be almost doubled (1,181 million) in 2025 to attain the estimated 15 per cent of a plausible world population of 7.8 billion (Table 15.1). The population aged 60 years and older is growing more rapidly than the growth of the total population. By 2025, one out of four persons in the more developed countries will be 60 years and older, whereas in developing countries the ratio will be one in approximately eight persons. The contrast between the present and future populations can be visualized by comparing the present populations of developing countries, where the youths are well represented, with the actual populations of the Western European countries where senior citizens are common in the society's daily life. The experience of these countries could be used as a reference in developing measures to anticipate the ageing problem in Asia without necessarily copying the procedures.

It goes without saying that Indonesia will not be exempted from this population ageing process. In 2025, Indonesia will have an

Table 15.1
Total Population and Population Aged 60 Years and Older.[1]

Region	*Year*	*Total Population (in million)*	*Number of 60+ (in million)*	*% 60+*
World	1975	4,074.7	346.3	8.5
	2000	6,055.0	605.5	10.0
	2025	7,823.7	1,181.4	15.1
More developed countries	1975	1,048.4	161.5	15.4
	2000	1,188.0	231.7	19.5
	2025	1,214.9	336.5	27.7
Less developed countries	1975	3,026.3	184.6	6.1
	2000	4,867.1	374.8	7.7
	2025	6,608.8	845.9	12.8
Indonesia *	1975	135.7	4.3	5.3
	2000	212.1	15.9	7.6
	2025	311.9	34.6	13.2

[1] According to the United Nations the term "aged" or "elderly" refers to the group of population aged 65 years or older, whereas in Indonesia 60 years is commonly used as the start of ageing (*Warta Demografi* 24, no. 1 [1994]: 5).

Source: UN (1999a and 1999b); * Biro Pusat Statistik (1993) and Ananta and Arifin (1991).

estimated 35 million elderly persons, or 13.2 per cent of the population, a rise from 16 million, or 7.6 per cent of the population in 2000. Indonesia will then be categorized as "aged", since a population is considered "aged" if 10 per cent or more of its population are elderly (Cowgill and Homes 1970). The total population will rise by 99.8 million, or 47.1 per cent between 2000 and 2025, whereas the population aged 60 years and older will grow by 18.7 million, or 117.6 per cent. Within the context of the ASEAN countries, Indonesia's position is between the extremes of the less-aged and advanced-aged societies (Table 15.2). In 2000, elderly persons in Brunei, Cambodia, and the Lao PDR represent about 5 per cent of the respective total populations. At the other extreme, over 10 per cent of the population of Singapore are 60 years or older. In 2025, the range will vary between 7 per cent for Lao PDR, 11 per cent for the Philippines, and over 28 per cent for Singapore. For comparison, by the same year senior citizens will form 33 per cent of the population of Japan, and 22 per cent of the population of the Republic of Korea. Given that in 2025 the majority (60.4 per cent) of the world population will reside in Asia, this continent will house more than half (59.6 per cent) of the world's population over sixty.

The question is: will Indonesians live long in poor health or in good health? Will old women then "suffer" more than old men? (Ananta et al. 1997).

Table 15.2
Proportion of Persons Aged 60 Years and Older to Total Population in ASEAN

	% of 60+ in		
Country	*1975*	*2000*	*2025*
Brunei	5.6	5.2	17.8
Cambodia	4.7	4.9	8.5
Indonesia	**5.3**	**7.6**	**13.2**
Lao P.D.R.	4.6	5.3	6.8
Malaysia	5.6	6.6	13.7
Myanmar	6.2	7.5	13.5
Philippines	4.3	5.7	10.9
Singapore	6.7	10.5	28.4
Thailand	4.7	8.7	18.1
Vietnam	6.4	7.4	12.3

Source: UN (1999a).

Consequences

The main consequences of population ageing are the needs for care, financial resources, facilities, and tools for elderly persons. The lengthening of the life-span is not necessarily accompanied by improvements in the quality of life for all (World Bank 1993; and INSERM 1994). Progress in medical sciences and technology provides the opportunity for individuals to function actively in daily life, who otherwise would not be able to do so — for instance, the disabled and elderly persons. In other words, the people who stay alive but become disabled might have died if they had lived some decades earlier, when the average life-span was lower and medical technology was still in its infancy. The growing number of elderly persons will be accompanied by an increase in the numbers of elderly disabled, since the level of disability rises from about the age of 50–54 years (Yu 1991).

The relevance of disability can be illustrated by the 1988 figures from the United Kingdom. The prevalence of disability rose steadily from 38 per 1,000 for children aged 5–9 years to 79 per 1,000 at ages 45–49 years, and 205 per 1,000 at ages 60–64 (Pickin and St. Leger 1993). Experiences in the OECD countries, on the other hand, have shown a reversing trend — namely, there are more and more healthy and fewer disabled old people because of the advances of medical technology for early detection and treatment of diseases (Ananta et al. 1997). Despite this positive trend, the life-span of the disabled continues as progress in medical technology lengthens people's lives much faster than progress in restoring the patients' health. All these disabled people thus need (health) care.

What does the changing age structure mean in terms of burden and care? Various measures are presented to assess the burden of an ageing society in demographic terms, such as the ratio between the age group 65 and older to the age group 15–64, the supposedly working age population. This ratio will rise in all countries. By 2025, it will attain about 12.5 per 100 for Indonesia, or for every elderly there will be eight persons in the working age group, a rise from one to 14 in 2000 (Table 15.3). To illustrate the seriousness of ageing, the ratio is about one to two for Japan and Western Europe. If other indicators are used, such as the ratio between 65 plussers to youngsters under 15 years, or between 65 plussers and people aged 15–24 just entering the work force, the result will be similar, namely, a rising ratio for the coming period. In other words, the burden will continue to rise and so will the need for and efforts to provide care.

Table 15.3
Ratio between Elderly and Working Age Population (in %)
(% 65+ to 15–64 years)

Country	*1975*	*2000*	*2025*
World	9.9	10.9	15.7
More developed countries	16.4	21.4	33.0
Less developed countries	7.1	8.2	12.8
Indonesia*	5.8	7.4	12.5

Source: UN (1999a); * Biro Pusat Statistik (1993); and Ananta and Arifin (1991).

Are old people only a burden to the society? Or do they also contribute to societal activities? Ageing translates to a demand for financial resources, care-sector professionals, and special devices/equipment to meet the needs of senior citizens for social security and health care. The costs of the social security systems will rise as a consequence of ageing. This will use up a larger share of the nation's budget and can become a heavy burden for many countries in the post-economic crisis period. The change in the age structure will also affect the private savings of the society since a high dependency ratio would mean lower savings rates as a result of the inability of elderly persons to save, and rising deficits for governments because of the social security systems (Heller 1998; Parant 2000).

On the other hand, the sprouting of new technologies and medicines for the elderly is evidence that senior citizens are also a driving force behind new research and products, creating specialized employment opportunities. Because of their disabilities, aged persons need devices that have to be developed and produced (a decline in fertility and an increase in ageing have generated the motto: reduce baby-chairs, add more wheelchairs). The demand for new products not available some forty years ago is a clear example. Recently, Japanese companies developed a gadget to track straying senior citizens by a satellite-based global positioning system and a cellular phone network. The production of these tools and devices and the need for services for the elderly, varying from health and mental care to financial and daily household support and elderly persons' switchboard, create ample job opportunities and stimulate new economic activities.

Another aspect of ageing that needs attention is the lengthening of the average age, although serious diseases and malnutrition are still widespread in Asia (Knowles 1999). Not only is the number of elderly rising but they are also living longer. Thus, resources for care (financial, manpower, material, and know-how) need to be extended over a longer period. Besides, since the life expectancy of women is longer than that of men, there will be an excess of women at the higher ages. In 2025, about 62 per cent of persons aged 80 years and older in the world will be women. Such imbalance in the sex ratio is a common feature in all countries (64.5 per cent in the more developed countries, and 61.3 per cent in less developed countries, according to United Nations projections). This means that crises will hit women disproportionately, and that care needs to be given to this category of aged persons, given the fact that women generally have unequal access to basic services (FNUAP 1998).

The longer life span also means that societies will witness the rise of multi-generation families that could become a source for a family-centred care system (intra-family transfer of wealth/resources). On the other hand, the declining fertility and even the frequent occurrence of childlessness will pose problems in the future, as old people will have fewer family members to care for them. The declining family size means that there will be fewer children to live with and to assume the economic, social, and emotional burdens of caring for their parents. In the last half of the twentieth century, the average number of children in Indonesia dropped from over 6 in the early 1950s to less than 2.5 per woman (Caldwell 1997; and UN 1999a). At the same time, there are also parents who have their own social network and may not like to move and stay with their offspring. Many elderly people in Western Europe, for example, express their wish to live independently.

The lengthening of the average age and improved public health conditions yield a growing number of elderly people who are still fit to work. The life expectancy of the elderly in the less developed countries is not much lower than those living in the more developed countries. Upon retirement at 60 years, each senior citizen has, on average, 15–20 more years to live, equivalent to a third of their adult life or a quarter of the life expectancy at birth (Tan 1999, p. 178). These senior citizens form a group of capable and experienced persons who can potentially boost the available human resources. As noted by Ogawa et al. (1994, p. 371), in Asia there has been an acute shortage of young workers as a result of expanded enrolment in higher education and a decline of fertility, and the demand for elderly workers is likely to rise considerably. Continuing to work after retirement also gives dignity to these elderly persons as they feel part of the society and therefore have status in their community (Palmore 1975).

It is pertinent to realize that not all elderly people are in need of care and assistance from others, and that not all of them face the hardship of the economy. Many elderly in the urban areas cannot be categorized as needy persons. Many retired persons in developing countries are in good health and sometimes they are forced to continue working as their pension is far from sufficient (OECD 1998). Their expertise and long years of working experience can be a valuable contribution to the functioning of organizations, companies, and factories. Even in small enterprises, these senior citizens can give practical but valuable advice to their successors. Senior citizens will become a familiar part in all societal activities. In the rural areas, senior citizens can function as respected members of the society, maintaining and passing on tradition and societal norms, giving advice with regard to community work, and so on.

Rapid ageing increases the demand for health services and, therefore, health expenditure, particularly the costs of long treatment for the older group (Höhn 1999). Yet health budgets for the developing countries, where the population growth rate is high, do not increase proportionately (WHO 1990). In industrialized countries, health expenditures accounted for 9.2 per cent of the gross national product (GNP) in 1990 compared with 4.7 per cent in the developing countries, and 8.1 per cent for the whole world. In the industrialized countries, some US$1,860 per person was spent on health compared with US$41 per person in the developing countries (World Bank 1993, pp. 52, 211). In the case of Malaysia, the share of total government medical expenditure in GNP increased from 1.51 per cent in 1970 to 3.53 per cent in 1980, owing to the high cost of hospital use and technology in the care of an ever increasing elderly population. As a result, the Malaysian Government has started exploring the possibility of privatizing medical care services. Similarly, the privatization of medical care services is one of the policy options being considered by the Thai Government, which allocated 1.43 per cent of its GNP for health expenditure in 1983 (Ogawa et al. 1994, p. 372).

As is the case in Thailand, the budget allocated for health programmes as a proportion of the Indonesian national budget (APBN) has in general shown no increase over the last fifteen years (Iskandar 1997). It varied from 2.4 per cent in 1982/1983 to 2.2 per cent in 1992/1993. The portion for health-care for the elderly is only a small fraction of this amount. There is no doubt that resource constraints have a negative effect on the development of general public health, quality of care improvement, utilization of services, and development of health personnel (Iskandar 1997). The concurrence of ageing, deteriorating health conditions, and the economic crisis illustrates the need for a long-term strategy to finance and organize social security systems (such as pension schemes and health care) for the care of the aged.

Life of the Aged in Indonesia

The definition of "old" is determined not only according to the biological factor (age) and political consensus among scientists and governments throughout the globe but also by culture and by the individuals themselves. In other words, the meaning of "old" or "elderly" is subjective. In the Indonesian context, "old" refers to a situation when a person's physical as well as mental well-being is diminishing and, hence, his/her dependency on other's assistance is increasing (Hatmadji et al. 1999, p. 1). One can feel old at 40 years of age, whereas another may still feel young at 60. By consensus, the average retirement age is fixed at 55, and for practical reasons, the age for the "elderly" is fixed at 60. However, with 55 taken as the general retirement age, many Indonesians tend to feel old upon nearing 50.

The proportions of people aged 60 and older living in the urban and rural areas are 7.6 per cent and 8.3 per cent, respectively (Hatmadji and Pardede 1999). In 1990, the province of Yogyakarta had the highest proportion of inhabitants aged 65 and older, at 7.3 per cent (Niehof 1995, p. 425). Urban areas attract and retain more older females than males because older women, especially widows, are inclined to join their children living in the cities (Niehof 1995, p. 427). Half of the elderly in Indonesia are still productive (8.7 per cent are in full-time employment), mostly in the informal sector (86.3 per cent, mainly in the agrarian sector) because of their low education and limited skills (80.3 per cent did not complete primary school and 14.0 per cent did not go further than primary school). This generation of elderly spent their childhood and youth in colonial times, with very little access to public education. This explains their low level of education.

The illiteracy rate among the elderly was 41.5 per cent, according to the 1995 inter-censal survey, with the rate for women being more than double that of men (56.2 per cent and 25.4 per cent respectively). It is hence easy to assume that more unskilled jobs are given to women than men. Looking at the difference in the percentage of completely retired elderly in the urban and rural areas (65 per cent in the urban and 76 per cent in the rural, according to Hatmadji et al. 1999, p. 10) it can be concluded that rural people work longer than their peers in the cities.

Better economic conditions, better family support, or better care and housing facilities for the aged may explain why the urban elderly stop their productivity at an earlier age.

Despite the hard work, one-third of the elderly in Indonesia have difficulties in supporting themselves, with an average income of 500,000 rupiah (or US$250) per year (Hatmadji et al. 1999, pp. 12–13), 60 per cent of which are spent on food (Dwiyanto 1999, p. 48). With a pension far from sufficient, most of them (45 per cent) have to rely on family support, while 31 per cent are self-employed. Their only asset is their house (78 per cent) and/or piece of land (80 per cent) (Hatmadji and Pardede 1999). A survey done by the Indonesian Epidemiological Network (JEN) in 1993 has indicated that the vast majority (82.4 per cent) of the elderly in the rural and urban areas owned the house in which they lived, and some 53 per cent of the interviewed elderly aged 60–69 were still providing for their children. Only 1.5 per cent were living on their own (Niehof 1995, p. 430).

As in many other developing countries, this asset or control of resources is often used by the elderly as a measure of power over their kin (UN 1994, p. 97), particularly when it is increasingly difficult for the younger generation to buy a piece of land and a house owing to the rapidly escalating population density, mainly in the urban areas. The prospect of inheriting parental assets used to induce many adult (and married) children to live in the parent's home and provide the care needed by the elderly and ailing parents. However, when the significance of land diminishes because other labour alternatives are available to the children, the resources and power are likely to shift from parents to the children, and co-residence will decline or will change in character (Keasberry 1998, p. 41).

Three-quarters of the elderly population suffer from chronic diseases, such as hypertension, arthritis, ulcers, and back pain. Only a small percentage (less than 10 per cent), however, perceive themselves to be in poor health, and it is interesting to note that 29 per cent of elderly women in the study in West Java were stated to be in poor health (Hatmadji et al. 1999, pp. 14–16). Most elderly people (70 per cent) perceive themselves to be in good health (Niehof 1995, p. 431) as long as they can still function in daily life, in the family, social life, and at work. Even when they are suffering from chronic back pain or cough, they still feel healthy. They only feel ill when they have to stay in bed. This perception of health and illness, however, is also shared by the younger generations in Indonesia (Sarwono 1996, p. 84).

In general, the elderly in Indonesia show an acceptance (*nrimo*), with a tendency towards a fatalistic attitude (*pasrah*), in dealing with the problems of ageing. As an illustration, here is what was said by an old man in Yogyakarta (Dwiyanto 1999, p. 41):

> *Kula wis tutug .... nek dipundhut .... aja gawe repote anak-anak. Nek kula dipundhut, kepengin ora usah nganggo mondok, 'ra 'sah lara"* (I am nearing my end .... when I die .... I don't want to bother my childern. When I'm dying I don't want to be hospitalised, don't want to get ill or suffer).

Up to the present there has been little evidence relating to the well-being of the elderly in Indonesia, let alone time series information on shifts in the levels of well-being. Moreover, measurement is difficult in semi-subsistence economies and situations where there are complex community and family support mechanisms (Hugo 1996, p. 16).

Although many elderly are economically under-privileged, they still hold a respectable position and high status in the family and community. Some 57 per cent are heads of the family and the majority of them (70–75 per cent) make important decisions in family affairs, such as deciding the education for their children, determining family expenditure, selecting the children's partners, and performing wedding ceremonies. Only a few of the elderly are assigned domestic work, especially when the family can afford to employ domestic help. As a care-giver, the task of the elderly woman is to supervise the work or to teach the young (Hatmadji et al. 1999, p. 10). Rural elderly women are predominantely care-givers in spite of their age, whereas the urban elderly tend to be more on the receiving end (Niehof 1995, p. 430).

A frequently mentioned problem for old people is loneliness (Niehof 1995, p. 431) or social isolation (Dwiyanto 1999, p. 60). To the elderly in Indonesia, family support is very important and much desired. Kinship is a key factor in determining the life situation of elderly people. The benefits of kinship relationships, which are based on trust, are comparable with those of insurance schemes (Niehof 1995, p. 433). Although most of the elderly in Indonesia (70 per cent according to Hatmadji et al. 1999, pp. 16–17) have three children or more, family support for them is, nevertheless, diminishing. According to a survey conducted in Java in the late 1980s, in the urban areas some 10 per cent of the elderly had no living children, and 28 per cent had only one or two children. The equivalent proportions in the rural areas were 8.7 per cent and 28.6 per cent respectively (Hugo 1996, p. 17).

Ailing and deteriorating in their physical strength, elderly persons increasingly need care. They become more and more dependent on their children and family. Unfortunately, modernization and concentration of investments in the urban areas are changing the pattern of family support. Two socio-demographic developments, namely, urbanization and increased female participation in the labour force, contribute significantly to the declining family support (Niehof 1995, p. 427). Young people (men and women) move out from the parent's home, sometimes to other cities, to take up employment and live independently. With higher levels of migration, the likelihood that an elderly person will have a child living close by will be reduced. Similarly, with increasing participation of females in the work-force outside the home, the availability of care-givers in the family house is declining (Hugo 1996, p. 17). Moreover, modernization brings an individualistic attitude into society. Accordingly, the type of support for the elderly is shifting from personal to financial. In other words, personal, emotional and physical contacts with the elderly are diminishing and substituted by financial support. Thus, there is a shift from family care to community care. This brings up the issue of the roles of the government and the younger generation in providing resources to care for the elderly because the "greying is paying" (Peterson 1999).

According to tradition, the role of the care-giver is assigned to female members of the family, namely, the wife and daughters. Sons, on the other hand, have never been assigned the role of providers of day-to-day (physical) care (Niehof 1995, p. 427; Afrizal 1998, p. 67; and Hugo 1996, p. 18). Increased female employment outside the house enables daughters to provide financial support. At the same time, this prevents them from performing the traditional role of care-giver (Niehof 1995, p. 427). Personal care is replaced by financial support or substituted by other persons or institutions, such as hiring nurses, domestic help, or putting the elderly and/or young children in care institutions.

As on average, women live longer than men, most Indonesian women spend the latter years of their lives as widows, while most men can rely on the support of their wives as they become frail (Hugo 1996, p. 21). Old widows or spinsters living alone get the least support from the family and the social environment (Niehof 1995; and Dwiyanto 1999). Many people and various charity groups are willing to help orphans and poor children but few give donations to poor widows. Almost 15 per cent of these widows and unmarried women living in the cities have no offspring (in the rural areas, the proportion is 11 per cent) (Hugo 1996, p. 17). In order to survive they keep working until their physical strength can no longer tolerate it. Hugo was struck by the loneliness, poverty, and deprivation of older widows and unmarried women who lived on their own and often had to rely on the charity of the community to survive (Hugo 1992, p. 214).

Realizing the problem of maintaining family care for the elderly, the Indonesian Government and private initiatives have started to provide institutions for the elderly. Studies indicate mixed feelings about this alternative care (Dwiyanto 1999, pp. 56–58; Niehof 1995, p. 432). Elderly people view homes for the aged as good alternatives but they are reluctant to use that service. According to Hugo, half of the older people believe that nursing homes are important, but only 15 per cent indicate that they would be willing to live in such an institution (Hugo 1996, p. 18). A study in Jakarta has shown that almost 70 per cent of the aged living in the homes for the elderly come from the lower socio-economic strata, and the main reason for their moving to institutional care is conflict with a son or daughter-in-law with whom they were living prior to moving to the home. After moving to the institution, their economic situation improved and they generally felt happy and satisfied (Niehof 1995, p. 432).

Hatmadji et al. have observed that the demand for institutionalization and professional care for the elderly is low. The main reasons are social preference for family support and lack of funds or financial support. Some families in the urban areas tend to hire in-house nurse-aid, whereas in the rural areas, the elderly are taken care of by the children and grandchildren (Hatmadji et al. 1999, pp. 16–17). To share the burden of caring for their elderly parents, it is common practice for the sons and daughters to invite the parents to stay with them in turn. The parents would then move from one child's house to another after a short stay. Naturally, this method does not apply to the elderly with only one living son or daughter.

The findings from different studies have indicated that the current generation of elderly people in Indonesia are highly dependent on the family or local community for support. If the situation of the elderly in Indonesia has not deteriorated in recent decades, then at the very least they have not shared proportionately in the increased prosperity of the nation in the last two decades (Hugo 1996, p. 25).

Implications of the Economic Crisis

The economic crisis has affected the elderly, although not in the same ways or degree of severity, since the elderly do not form a homogeneous group in the population. It is easy to assume that the poor elderly, who receive the least support from the family, community and government, receive the hardest blow, particularly the poor homeless, childless, and poor widows who are still supporting their offspring (Tan 1999, p. 178).

A study in West Java during the crisis has shown that 25 per cent of the elderly had considerable difficulties with their finances, whereas

2.3 per cent (the majority lived in the cities) were in serious financial difficulty (Hatmadji et al. 1999, p. 13). Indeed, the recent economic crisis has had a greater impact on the urban population in Java than in the outer islands. The rapidly increasing cost of living, especially in the urban areas, associated with the immense pressure being placed upon housing, land, services, food, and so forth, are especially felt by the aged. This is because many of them do not have independent power to compensate for such increases through obtaining higher incomes (Hugo 1996, p. 21).

The impact of the economic crisis can be grouped into different categories, following the theoretical model developed by Keasberry (1998, pp. 38–43). The first category includes those under intergenerational co-residence. Urbanization, increasing population density, decreasing housing supply, and rapidly increasing prices of land and goods have resulted in a reduced living space for each family. Families live in smaller houses. This makes the living arrangement for three or four generations sharing the same house less common (Tan 1999, p. 178; and Keasberry 1998, p. 39). All the same, although housing conditions do not always permit co-residence, according to JEN's survey, the overwhelming majority of the elderly still live with their children (Niehof 1995, p. 430).

The second category includes those who are more economically dependent. The economic crisis has forced hundreds of companies, factories, and organizations to lay off their employees. When this happens, the management tends to retrench the more senior employees nearing their retirement. Many people lost their jobs and people (young and old) were forced to sell their houses and properties as well as to use their meagre savings to continue living. Many could not continue to maintain their standard of living. Within the family, support for the elderly is therefore reduced. With reducing incomes, families set priorities, often sacrificing the elderly and giving them the lowest priority.

The economic dependence of the elderly is determined by the extent to which they have been able to accumulate wealth and assets during their more active working years, access to support provided by the government and community groups, and the amount of support received (Hugo 1996, pp. 22–23). As the economy of the working group worsens and the priority for supporting the elderly becomes lower, it is logical to assume that during and after the crisis most elderly in Indonesia become even more dependent economically.

With regard to the economic status of the elderly, some significant gender differentials have been identified. Older women have fewer resources and lower levels of well-being than their male counterparts (Hugo 1996, p. 21; and Dwiyanto 1999, p. 29).

The third category involves those who need less personal care, and more financial support. As a consequence of decreasing co-residence, more elderly persons tend to be physically separated from their children. This physical separation is usually compensated by remittances (support in the form of money or in kind) and long-distance communications, at the expense of losing emotional ties, thus causing loneliness.

Could children take care of their parents during the period of the crisis and in the future? What would they do if their parents needed their help? Lay-offs resulting from the economic crisis have reduced the support and remittances to parents. The cost of transportation may also hinder them from frequently visiting their parents, and the commitment to their jobs may keep them from visiting at any time they want. Before the crisis, only 34.2 per cent of the urban elderly received visits more than once a week, and 40.4 per cent received visits infrequently, hardly ever, or never. In the rural areas, the equivalent percentages were 54.6 per cent and 26 per cent (Hugo 1996, p. 18). It is easy to imagine that the frequency of visits would have declined since the crisis.

What has already been noticed in the urban areas is that to assist the elderly who do not want to live with their children, the children would pay for the professional help of a servant or a nurse. In this way, the elderly can live independently in their own homes (Keasberry 1998, p. 40). This substitute ensures physical care but reduces emotional care. As the crisis seems to have less impact on the urban well-to-do families, the urban elderly continue to receive this substitute support.

The fourth category includes female care providers. As in many other countries, the role of the family care provider is traditionally given to female members of the family, particularly the wife, daughter, or daughter-in-law. With the reduction in family incomes, the lower-middle income families might have to lay off the people who helped them with domestic work, or baby-sitting. This means that the woman of the house has to take over these duties, which takes up perhaps half of her day. Being not in a position to add hours to her day, she has to take time off from her productive tasks to do house-work (reproductive role). In other words, she must reduce her working hours or hours of study (if she is enrolled in an education programme) or stop entirely the productive tasks. Quitting the job means a further cut in income.

To help ease the burden on the younger women, elderly women often come forward to give a hand. The mother comes to live with her daughter or son and grandchildren. This has a double effect. The elderly woman is assured of physical care and economic as well as emotional support from her family to help her survive the worsening condition of life, while at the same time she provides the family with her services in caring for the young children and doing domestic work. Since part of her duties have been taken over by her mother or mother-in-law, the younger woman can regain her productive role (fully or partly). This mutual help, which is more applicable in the rural setting, gives satisfaction to both parties. Nonetheless, women, young and old, clearly suffer more from the increasing demand for care.

Poor widows (young or old) with dependants are the hardest hit by the crisis. Their small income is reduced, leaving very little money to live and to support the entire family. This condition has forced them to work harder and longer hours. Some have even become beggars. Their children have to leave school as they cannot afford to pay the school fees or for transport to go to school. Besides, their mothers can use an extra pair of hands to help them with work that generates some income.

The fifth group includes those needing more professional care. Another relevant impact of the economic crisis was on the state of health of elderly persons. In times of economic crisis, many people lose their incomes. As a consequence, they reduce their nutritional intake and cannot afford to buy medicines or visit a doctor for treatment when they are sick. For example, the fees for heart surgery (*tubing*) has increased fourfold, from 10 million rupiah in 1995 to 40 million rupiah in 2000. This jump in fees applies to other types of surgery and medical treatment too. As a consequence, people revert to self-medication and traditional medicine. Although this situation affects all groups, the weakest among them, such as the elderly, children, and disabled, are the worst hit. Considering the naturally frail health of the elderly, this drawback could have serious consequences in terms of mortality. Professional care is therefore needed.

In addition, apart from diminishing contacts and visits because of lack of time and migration, the younger generation is becoming less capable of providing the needed care for the elderly when they succumb to various chronic diseases and disabilities. The variety of diseases and health problems found among the elderly population is larger than the problems encountered half a century ago. The development of medical technology has provided cures or methods to make a person's life more comfortable. To apply and administer the treatment and technology, however, trained professionals are needed. Numerous new professions in the fields of gerontology, diet, nutrition, physiotherapy, and so forth have developed and advanced in recent decades.

The sixth category are those requiring less reciprocal relationship/ support. Traditionally, the young are obliged to help and care for their elders and in reverse, the elderly are also obliged to care for the young, although societal and economic developments have transformed the life-styles and way of living of the people (Wongsith 1996). Regardless of their economic condition, many elderly people want to continue supporting their offsprings, as reflected in the following quotation:

> *Anak saya rumahnya nggak kecil, nggak besar .... untuk ke sana agak sulit mencari. Suami isteri bekerja, menantu saya karyawan rumahsakit. Saya tidak mengharapkan apa-apa dari anak-anak. Kalau bisa malah ngasih. Anak saya kalau dengan saya respek, begitu sopan, takut dan ngajeni.*
>
> [My daughter's house is not large but also not small .... it is quite difficult to find that house. Both my daughter and her husband work, my son-in-law is a hospital employee. I do not expect to get anything from my children. If possible I want to give and help them. My children respect me, very polite, obedient and acknowledge my authority].
>
> (Dwiyanto 1999, p. 45)

The quotation confirms the conclusion drawn by Koentjaraningrat that Indonesian children are supposed to show respect to their parents and to acknowledge their authority and it is an obligatory duty to take care of them in their old age (Keasberry 1998, p. 42).

The elderly persons' desire to live independently and give support to the family has, nonetheless, become increasingly more difficult to realize as a result of the worsening family economy. There will probably be fewer care-givers available for the elderly, and inter-generational support and mutual aid will decline. In cases where the elderly have more assets, the younger will ask for and receive more assistance from their parents. However, when parents are in a weaker position, they will become more dependent on their children.

Migration may also change the frequency and type of contact in relationships between elderly parents and their children, the role of primary care-givers, the care activities provided by the elderly and the feasibility of reciprocal care (Keasberry 1998, p. 43).

The seventh category is inter-generational conflict. It seems that the elderly have a high status within their families and that the majority of the children strongly reject the notion of ever permitting their parents to be placed in an old age home (Keasberry 1998, p. 42).

Confronted with the pressing problem of financial support for the old, one pertinent question arises: is the younger generation prepared to put aside an increasing portion of their income to finance the social security system? In Japan, one of the most rapid ageing populations in the world, for every retired person there were 4.4 working persons in 1997. This ratio will change drastically in 2005: one retired person versus 1.5 working persons, meaning that a smaller number of persons will have to put aside a greater sum of money for the care and pension of elderly persons. The number of economically active contributors to social security will decline whereas the number of elderly persons will increase. Such a shift in the ratio between elderly persons and the working age population will take place in Indonesia too, and this could put a strain on the solidarity between generations.

As noted by Keasberry (1998, p. 43), in Indonesia the forces strengthening family solidarity by Islamization on the one hand and the breakdown of traditional values and norms by the processes of differentiation of the family and community, individualization and schooling, on the other hand, may probably cause conflicting relationships between elderly parents and their children.

Coping with the Crisis

> *Wong niku kudu ngukur carane dhewe. Biyen piye, saiki piye .... dadi nggih nrima. Sedaya niku ming kantun nglampahi ... (manut) napa dhawuhe Gusti Allah. Kula mboten duwe ... trima pun ... pun mboten duwe pikiran macem-macem.*
>
> [One should know his/her own capacity. How it was then, how it is now .... so one can accept it. You just need to do everything .... (obey) what is commenced by Allah the Almighty. I am poor .... I just accept it ... I don't think much about it.]
>
> (Dwiyanto 1999, p. 40)

The above quotation from an elderly man in Yogyakarta reflects the accepting attitude of what is happening to him when confronted with economic problems. This seems to be the general attitude of the elderly in Indonesia.

Like their peers in most developing countries, many elderly persons in Indonesia have little pension, others have no pension at all, or their income is not sufficient to save for their own support later. Many white-collar workers do get a pension but the amount and their savings are not sufficient to make ends meet. The economic crisis has forced many elderly to continue working, often by taking a job much below their standard, as long as their physical condition allows them.

Along this line, Hugo has stated that in the urban and rural informal sectors, in which the extended family is often the unit of production, there is no concept of a mandatory retirement age, and elderly people are readily incorporated, although their specific roles in the production process may change as their physical capabilities decline (Hugo 1996, p. 20). To most of these people, retirement age has no practical meaning. Elderly women work longer than the men to earn an income (mostly as self-employed workers) as well as to care for the grandchildren. Older workers find it especially difficult to compete in the formal sector of the labour market because they are generally less educated than the younger generations. A retired schoolteacher becoming a *becak* driver is just one illustration. This weak situation makes aged persons vulnerable during a downturn in the economy.

Besides continuing to work and postponing retirement, the elderly also take several other strategies to cope with the crisis situation. The first strategy is by reducing expenses and borrowing money. The most common strategy taken by people (young and old) is to cut down the family expenses. In so doing, the family often cuts a large proportion of their support for the elderly (money or in kind) and gives a higher priority to the needs of children. To make ends meet, the elderly also cut their expenses, such as stopping their subscription for newspapers and buying them only occasionally, replacing their medicines with local traditional medication (*jamu*), and cutting down on entertainment/recreation, such as going to the cinema or traditional plays, eating out, etc. (Dwiyanto 1999). If reducing expenses is not enough to support their daily life, the elderly tend to borrow money from family members, friends, or neighbours, but not from the bank because they may not be able to pay it back.

The second method is inter-generational transfer of wealth. When borrowing money is not sufficient to support their daily life and when there is little assurance of long-term support, the elderly tend to use the last resource, which is renting out or selling their property, that is, valuables (jewellery, gold, etc.), house, and land. As most of these properties are inherited, they need their children's approval to sell them. The children are better informed about the market price and usually have a larger network to obtain the best price.

Since it is a family property, the money received from selling or renting it out will not be used by the elderly alone but will be shared with the children and grandchildren. Authority to manage the money may be given to one of the younger generation. In this way, the transfer of wealth makes the elderly more dependent on their offspring.

The third method is by transferring the responsibility for care. When the chance for living with adult children (co-residence) or having them living close by diminishes, many elderly seek emotional (and among the poor, also financial) support from their social network, such as their relatives, neighbours, friends as well as ex-colleagues. In the urban areas, groups or clubs are formed to accommodate the needs of the elderly to maintain social contact and to keep them active. Apart from maintaining economic independence, mental and physical fitness, keeping the elderly involved in various social and economic activities will give them dignity and a chance to contribute to the welfare of the society. This feeling of dignity is particularly important when they have already lost economic power, position, and status, and their physical condition is deteriorating. With a sense of dignity they can continue living and being well accepted in their family, community, and society at large.

The need to keep elderly people active stimulates individuals in non-governmental organizations (NGOs) or the private sector to create various types of activity involving old people. One example is to provide continuing education for the elderly. The Medical Faculty of Trisakti University in Jakarta, for instance, has developed a programme called "University of the Third Age", an education programme especially designed for retired persons (Sarwono 1997).

The fourth method is by strengthening solidarity or social cohesiveness. Managing the elderly does not differ from managing any other groups of the population. In this matter, two elements are important to consider, namely, equity and solidarity (Koesoebjono and Sarwono 1997). *Equity* can be described as full and equal access for all people with regard to income, resources, and social services, including health services. By narrowing the gaps in health status between the highest and lowest income groups, it is expected that distribution of material benefits can be made more equitable, resulting in a higher degree of self-reliance. To reach equity, solidarity is needed. *Solidarity* can be achieved, if not encouraged, between generations and different socio-economic categories through favourable political, economic, social, and cultural environment. Governmental as well as non-governmental organizations and private enterprises should stimulate and co-operate to meet the basic human needs of all people, including the poor and vulnerable groups, especially the elderly.

Solidarity can be promoted through inter-sector co-operation within a country and international co-operation between countries to ensure universal access to basic needs and health services. Solidarity can be achieved through the improvement of the social safety net and people's health through the action of individuals, families, and the community for the care of elderly persons.

Inter-generational solidarity is instrumental for the creation and provision of services for all people, and equity enhances a sense of solidarity among the peoples within a country. Mutual interrelationship between equity and solidarity contributes to the promotion of equality in the people's economic and health status. Solidarity forms a social net to muffle the impact of socio-economic crises.

Anticipating a Greying Society in Indonesia

It is inevitable that in the coming decade a larger proportion of the Indonesian population will become "aged", when the proportion of 65 plussers will reach 10 per cent or more. In anticipation of this situation, let us take a look at the potential problems arising from this ongoing ageing process and how to prevent or resolve the problems.

Changing Values in Treating the Old

In a general sense, ethnicity provides a cultural context that includes values and norms with regard to old age, the relationship between the old and the young, and obligations and responsibilities towards elderly people (Niehof 1995, p. 433). Indonesia's largest ethnic group, the Javanese, have a bilateral kinship system, with a network of kin to draw upon for old-age support. The elderly must be respected, thanked and cared for by the young. Family support is essential for the elderly. Reluctance to care for the elderly is socially sanctioned. These expectations or beliefs are very much shared by the elderly, as indicated in different case studies in Java (Hatmaji et al. 1999; and Dwiyanto 1999, p. 53). The relationship between expressed beliefs and action with regard to family responsibilities, however, is very complex in practice. Family obligations are redefined in the course of time. Mutual support between kin, which is affected by social change, can no longer be taken for granted. The ongoing process of socio-cultural change, migration, urbanization, increasing participation of women in the labour force and decline in the average household size can have a profound influence on the nature and degree of support between kin (Niehof 1995, p. 433).

That the values relating to the care of the old are changing and the role of kin is diminishing is illustrated in case studies in Yogyakarta (Dwiyanto 1999, p. 59). As a realization of obedience, parents expect their children to visit them at least once a year (40.3 per cent), or send them money or other things (28.2 per cent), or send them news (11.2 per cent). These findings show clearly the importance of the role of children in supporting their parents at old age. Parents hope to get economic assurance, psychological, and social support from their children. In reality, the urban elderly receive visits infrequently, hardly ever or never, whereas their peers in the rural areas receive more frequent and regular visits from their kin. Financial support is often insufficient, as the children's financial situation is also suffering. In Yogyakarta, the average income of the elderly is 168,000 rupiah per month and they get an additional 59,000 rupiah from family members. This amount is still not enough to cover the average monthly expenditure per capita of 249,000 rupiah (Dwiyanto 1999, p. 48).

Tan speculates that these changing values with regard to the elderly relate to modernization and the increasing level of education of the younger generations. Moreover, demand for care and support for the elderly will require greater commitment of time and financial resources from the young. Failure to meet these demands will create inter-generational conflicts (Tan 1999, p. 174).

Weakening Social Cohesion

A crucial aspect of support for the elderly is family solidarity, which can be differentiated into six types (McChesney and Bengtson 1988). They are (1) associational solidarity: the frequency and patterns of interaction in various types of activities; (2) affectional solidarity: the type and degree of positive sentiments held about family members and the degree of reciprocity in these sentiments; (3) consensual solidarity: the degree of agreement on values, attitudes, and beliefs among family members; (4) functional solidarity or exchange: the degree to which family members exchange services or assistance; (5) normative solidarity: the perception and enactment of norms of family solidarity; (6) inter-generational family structure: the number, type, and geographic proximity of family members.

The last aspect is often considered the most important factor in looking at the position of the elderly in a family, as families constitute a meeting place for members of different generations.

As discussed in the previous sections, it appears that solidarity among family members in Indonesia, particularly between the young and old, is loosening. Changing values, norms, life-styles, increasing individualism, and declining family incomes have made the younger generation less attentive and less supportive of their elderly parents. The elderly, on the other hand, are not in a position to enforce their demands for respect and support from the young as it will only create or add to conflicts between the different generations.

A shift from a multiple-generation household towards a single-person household, and waning loyalty and obedience on the part of the young are also becoming more apparent in South Korea, Hong Kong, and China. An exception, however, can be observed in the advanced urbanized economy in Japan, where traditional family life and values are still maintained despite decreasing incomes of the elderly (Tan 1999, p. 178). Family solidarity among the Japanese is still strong, but in other areas of Southeast Asia and East Asia, there is considerable doubt about the continued importance of the family as a support system in the future. Reliance on alternative support and the accumulation of personal wealth would be a prudent if not necessary response (Mason 1999, p. 44).

Ageing: A Neglected Issue

The issue of ageing in Indonesia has not been given serious attention. Despite the growing number of elderly, ageing is still a neglected area of policy concern, as the government is preoccupied with other pressing population issues, such as the consequences of the continuing high overall annual population growth, uneven population distribution and under- and unemployment (Hugo 1992, p. 207). By and large, the care for the elderly is the responsibility of the family and relatives.

In Asia, care for the elderly seems to have developed through four stages (ESCAP 1994, p. 73), namely:

1. support comes entirely from family or relatives;
2. establishment of private or charitable institutions for the elderly as an alternative to family care;
3. government provision of social services as a necessary supplement to family support;
4. attempts are made to adapt an integrated approach towards the provision of support for the elderly, including a balanced development of cash assistance, in-kind services, and a combination of public and family efforts.

Furthermore, it has been observed that in the development and implementation of community programmes for the elderly, people in developing countries are hindered by numerous constraints (ESCAP 1994, p. 74): care for the ageing receives a lower priority in policy making; there is an absence of a national policy; the problem of ageing is focused on financial resources; there is a lack of insight on the growing gap between normal care and the availability of facilities; voluntary organizations are usually working on a small scale and there is a lack of co-ordination in their work; and there is a lack of manpower to mobilize the elderly to play a positive role.

As a consequence of this lack of political support, efforts to improve care services cannot be optimized. To tackle the growing problems of ageing, it is crucial that the government's concern be raised and larger resources be allocated for elderly care.

Suggestions for Elderly Care

Considering that the ageing process will proceed and cannot be stopped, we need to search for alternatives to make the distribution of care services more equal for the elderly of various socio-economic strata and to develop strategies to utilize the elderly as a human resource.

Improving the Care for the Elderly

Care begins at home and involves inter-generational participation. Hence, individuals and families can contribute to this service. Care comprises more than just medical care as people experience and react differently to illnesses. Illnesses are frequently accompanied by symptoms of anxiety and distress caused by external factors (for example, economic crisis) as well as internal factors (such as, family circumstances), which require counselling, comfort, and emotional support (King 1996). For that purpose, training programmes are needed to equip individuals and families with the basic knowledge and skills to help the sick/homebound, aged, or disabled family members. These training programmes can be developed and implemented by the local NGOs, thus extending the scope of support and care from families to community groups.

As mentioned before, women will live longer than men. Therefore, health services and social care need to be aimed at this group. One might say that by living longer, women pose a burden to society. On the other hand, old women can help ease the economy of their family by taking care of their grandchildren. Particularly during the economic crisis, when many young families lost their jobs and their incomes became too little to hire a baby-sitter or a servant, or to send the young children to a day-care centre, the grandmother could help to solve this problem by providing child-care. By allowing the grandmother to do this, the mutual relationship between generations would be strengthened, and affectional and functional solidarity in the family would grow. The grandmother, who has to live with her child and is dependent on the family, will then not consider herself a burden in her child's family. Elderly women need not only seek care but they can become care-givers too.

The idea of involving individuals, families, and community groups in providing care for the weak (the aged and sick/disabled) will stimulate community members to take responsibility for their own welfare and health, including self-care. Involving community members in providing care will promote the community's self-reliance in social welfare. To stimulate self-reliance among the families and communities, public-private initiatives in the area of social provisions is, therefore, an essential alternative.

The government's efforts and non-governmental community-based activities should go hand-in-hand in providing social needs and care services (King 1996). Non-governmental organizations can establish care institutions and provide all kinds of activities aimed at helping the aged and disabled to better function in society in times of crisis and prosperity. Voluntary as well as paid services can enhance the provision of this care service. At village or neighbourhood level, a voluntary organization could provide care for elderly persons and assist them in their daily life.

Shifting the Retirement Age

In order to maximize the utilization of an old-but-useful work-force, appropriate policy measures and programmes designed to keep the elderly in the labour force should be implemented in developing countries. A gradual shift in retirement age is an example. At present, it is common practice that most elderly people with low incomes have to work to support their lives and to depend on family support during the later years, namely, in housing, food and other needs (Tan 1999, p. 178). The future generation of elderly will be well educated, and most jobs involving modern technology, such as in the service sectors, will not require physical strength. As the ageing process advances, the health condition and education of the elderly will improve, and consequently, the retirement age should be raised. This shift, however, requires changes in various factors related to the labour market, including the wage system (Ogawa et al. 1994, p. 371). Besides shifting the retirement age, the elderly can also be used as reserves in case of labour shortages (Tan 1999, p. 184).

An arrangement has to be designed to enable senior citizens to continue participating in the economic and social activities, for financial reasons as well as for sustaining their mental and physical condition (Koesoebjono 1997). An effort to keep the elderly active can be observed in Jakarta. A doctor has organized at a health centre (*puskesmas*) a monthly get-together session for senior citizens. The aim is to maintain their mental and physical health. The programme consists of physical exercise/gymnastics, group discussions on current social topics, and trips to various places. Apart from joining the sessions, a few members of this group also do odd jobs, such as helping a daughter or niece in a catering service, giving advice to younger people with regard to managing business, and the like.

Establishing a Permanent Social Safety Programme

It is one of the government's tasks to develop a social security system for pensions and health-care. At present, there are three major pension schemes provided by the Indonesian Government (Hugo 1996, pp. 24–25):

1. a pension plan for government workers, covering 4.21 million employees;
2. a pension plan for the members of the armed forces (data for its coverage is not available); and
3. a "pay-as-you-go" social security scheme (ASTEK) that obliges large and medium-sized enterprises to join in. In 1993, this programme covered almost six million employees.

Hence, at best, Indonesia's pension schemes cover only about 10 million of Indonesia's more than 70 million workers (Hugo 1996, p. 24). Confirming this finding, Ihromi has reported that some 11.5 per cent of Indonesia's work-force are covered by pension or old-age assurance provisions. These are almost exclusively civil servants, army personnel, and city-based employees of large private sector organizations, especially industrial companies (Hugo 1996, p. 25; and Niehof 1995, p. 432). The amount of money received from the pensions is rarely sufficient to meet the living costs of elderly persons, and they are predominantly provided to males. Moreover, more than half of Indonesia's workers are employed in the informal sector. It is difficult to develop a formal pension scheme that incorporates this group.

During the economic crisis, the Indonesian Government attempted to assist the poor elderly by providing financial support through the Social Safety Net or SSN (*Jaringan Pengamanan Sosial/JPS*) programmes. Priority was given to the very poor elderly in the rural as well as urban areas. This effort, however, was only temporary, in response to the emergency situation following the crisis. To ensure long-term support and care for the elderly, this kind of programme needs to be institutionalized. As stated by Booth, the implementation of the Social Safety Net programmes, however inadequate the targetting, has built up a set of expectations, namely, that the government should provide basic needs (such as food, health, and education) for all sections of the population. Future governments will have to transform the emergency SSN/JPS programmes into more comprehensive social programmes aimed at giving all citizens access to basic needs and services (Booth 2000, p. 161).

There is clearly a need for social provision for the aged. Moreover, new research has to be done to develop appliances for the elderly to function in their daily life so that they can live independently. The funding of these activities is a burden on the budget of most developing countries but a public-private initiative could be envisaged, as social security systems need not be entirely supported by the state. Such an experience could stimulate and strengthen the role of the traditional and community-based social safety network (local charities, local safety net) (Einhorn 1998). It would be a mistake to postpone this action, as the effects of population ageing will become more pressing.

Socializing Old-Age Homes

The provision of care for the elderly differs according to socio-economic categories, as elderly persons are a heterogeneous sub-population. Not all families are incapable of providing care for their parents in combination with their daily activities. The majority, however, cannot afford a big house and a domestic worker to take care of the parents. Alternatives need to be developed. An old-age home for elderly persons, such as in industrialized societies, may become an alternative to consider. This prospect may sound harsh for people in more traditionally oriented societies but it is becoming inevitable as the ageing process advances.

There is an increasing need for homes for the elderly in Indonesia (Dwiyanto 1999, p. 67; Hatmadji and Pardede 1999, p. 11; and Niehof 1995, p. 432). To motivate the elderly to live in such homes, it is necessary to provide better services and facilities than what is available at present. This improvement will change the stigmatization of the idea that a home for the elderly is only for the poor or neglected old, and to convince people that living there is not necessarily distressing.

An education and information campaign has to be developed to create awareness and to change the attitude of the population about this non-traditional prospect. It is inevitable that health education and information will become an indispensable component of a caring society (Koizumi 1985). Comprehensive health information can help people to be better prepared to care for themselves, their families, and others.

Suggested Policy for Developing Countries

In anticipation of the problems in the care of the elderly, a policy based on an integrated approach needs to be developed. The following aspects should be considered (ESCAP 1994, p. 74): encouraging social integration and support for the elderly; determining minimum standards of living conditions; and appreciating the position of older people in the context of interdependencies between family members of all ages.

Family support and community programmes can be strengthened in the following ways (ESCAP 1994, p. 75). The first is by strengthening or supporting families who provide care for the elderly and institutionalizing the mechanism for support. Accordingly, Hatmadji and Pardede suggest financial support or incentives (such as subsidy for house rent or fiscal tax reduction) for families who provide care for their aged parents (1999, p. 12), as there is no substitute for the emotional security that a family can provide for the elderly. In addition, to alleviate the burden of caring for the elderly, following the Dutch example, temporary institutionalization of the elderly may be arranged to enable their family/care-givers to enjoy a short holiday.

The second is by providing administrative support for co-ordinating community services, and the third is by ensuring minimum standards of services and care through legislation or guidelines and monitoring procedures.

The fourth way is by increasing education and instilling a sense of responsibility among family members to care for the elderly. To promote family solidarity in Malaysia, people celebrate Family Day, besides Mother's and Father's Days. Such an initiative has been taken in Indonesia as well and needs to be further promoted.

The fifth way is by encouraging the elderly to form self-support groups where mutual reliance could be engendered. Such a support group is especially necessary for old widows and unmarried women who receive the least support from their surroundings.

The sixth way is by training professionals and para-professionals to organize and promote family support and community-based programmes for the elderly. In the Indonesian context, this training can be integrated in the training of health cadres at village and neighbourhood levels.

The seventh way is by reducing obstacles hindering the participation and integration of the elderly in socio-economic activities, and the eighth way is by promoting a positive image of being old that would in turn provide confidence in the elderly themselves, and develop better acceptance and understanding of the elderly in the community.

As most developing countries cannot afford the costly investments of institutional care for the elderly, it is essential to develop a correct perspective of population ageing in society, and the policies needed in national expenditure and allocations, investments, consumption patterns, labour, and employment. These policies should encompass the young as well, and should emphasize healthy lifestyles and appropriate financial security for old age (Tan 1999, p. 184).

Conclusions

New Paradigm:[1] Aged Society

No country will be exempted from the ageing process. The number of elderly persons will more or less stabilize after 2050. Ageing is a global process that will shift the structure of societies and the shape of economies. Ageing forms a social and economic challenge. Senior citizens will be a familiar picture in the society and daily life. More aged persons will live independently on free will and because their children live and work elsewhere. The care for the elderly will shift from family to community and network of friends and neighbours.

Government and non-government, private and non-profit organizations should prepare well ahead for the advent of a greying society in which elderly persons can still contribute in activities. Health care for senior citizens will possibly be more concentrated in specific areas such as in small towns and villages. New types of housing for the elderly (old age homes) will arise. A social security system needs to be devised to support the elderly in times of crisis and prosperity. Thus, funds will have to be allocated for the social security system and it is hoped that the group's participation in social activities will increase too. During the transition period, ways and means need to be explored and developed to meet the rising demand for care and pension, and for income generating activities for the elderly.

Paradoxes

A discussion of the elderly as a rising sub-population contains some paradoxes. Elderly people demand more support from society in the form of finance, facilities, and care. At the same time, they are a driving force underlying new research and products. They can be used as reserves for manpower in case of labour shortages. They also contribute to the rise of new economic activities and change in life-styles. They are not merely a burden.

Demographic trends show differences in survival rates by sex. Women live longer than men. This may mean that women are more of a burden to society. However, it is also a fact that women work longer than men (self-employed or at home) and they are care-givers for the family, especially for young children. Increased female participation in the labour force has strengthened women's independence and economic position in the family. At the same time, this has reduced their role as care providers in the family, and also the average number of children per woman.

Traditional societies, including Indonesians, want to maintain and promote respect for the elderly. This norm is not consistent with the reality. The proportion of the national budget spent on health-care for children under five years is much higher than the budget for the elderly (10 per cent and 7.5 per cent respectively, according to Hatmadji and Pardede [1999]). For various reasons also, more and more young people leave their parents and do not care for them.

The need for old-age homes is increasing following the cracking up of family solidarity, migration, urbanization, and declining fertility, but the attitude towards institutionalizing the elderly remains ambivalent. There is some cultural and social reluctance in sending the elderly to old-age homes, despite the increasing need for institutional care. Both the younger generation and the elderly themselves share this ambivalent feeling.

It would be interesting to explore further the extent to which these paradoxes will affect the economic and social conditions of the society. A research on this topic is therefore recommended.

Notes

1. Paradigm is defined as "the entire constellation of beliefs, values, techniques and so on shared by the members of a given community" (T. S. Kuhn, *The Structure of Scientific Revolutions* [Chicago: University Press, 1970], p. 175).

References

Afrizal. *Elderly health care in contemporary matrilineal Minangkabau*. Proceedings of the Health Social Science Action & Partnership — Retrospective & Prospective Discourse, presented at the fourth Asia-Pacific Social Science and Medicine Conference (APSSAM). Yogyakarta: Population Studies Centre, Gadjah Mada University, 2000.

Ananta, Aris, and Evi Nurvidya Arifin. *Projection of Indonesian Population: 1990–2020*. Jakarta: Demographic Institute, Faculty of Economics, University of Indonesia, 1991.

Ananta, Aris, Evi Nurvidya Anwar, and Diah Suzenti. "Some economic demographic aspects of ageing". In *Indonesia Assessment. Population and Human Resources*, edited by G. W. Jones and T. H. Hull, pp. 181–204. Canberra/Singapore: Australian National University/Institute of Southeast Asian Studies, 1997.

Biro Pusat Statistik. *Proyeksi Penduduk Indonesia per Propinsi 1995–2005*. Jakarta: Biro Pusat Statistik, 1993.

Booth, Anne. "The Impact of the Indonesian Crisis on Welfare: What Do We Know Two Years On?" In *Indonesia in Transition*, edited by C. Manning and P. van Diermen, pp. 145–62. Singapore: Institute of Southeast Asian Studies, 2000.

Caldwell, J. C. "Population and Human Resources: Indonesia's demographic place in the larger scene". In *Indonesia Assessment. Population and Human Resources*, edited by G. W. Jones and T. H. Hull, pp. 59–66. Canberra/Singapore: Australian National University/Institute of Southeast Asian Studies, 1991.

Centraal Bureau voor de Statistiek (CBS). *Maandstatistiek voor de Bevolking 2000/1*. Voorburg, 2000a.

________. *Statistical Yearbook of the Netherlands 2000*. The Hague: SDU Publishers, 2000b.

________. *The year 1999 in figures and a look back at the century*. Voorburg, Statistics Netherlands, 2000c.

Centraal Informatiepunt Ouderen (CIPO). *Oudereninformatie in zakformaat*. The Hague, June 2000a.

________. *Doe jezelf niet te kort*. The Hague, June 2000b.

Cowgill, D. O., and L. D. Homes. "The demographic ageing". In *The Daily Needs and Interests of Older People*, edited by A. M. Hoffman. Springfield, Ill., Charles C. Thomas, 1970.

De Beer, J., and L. Van Wissen. *Europe: One Continent, Different Worlds. Population Scenarios for the 21st Century*. The Hague, European Population Conference, 30 August–3 September 1999, Vol. 2.

Dwiyanto, A. *Household and Family Care for the Elderly — and the Socio-economic Position of Elderly People in the Region of D.I. Yogyakarta, Indonesia*. Yogyakarta: University of Gadjah Mada, Population Studies Centre, 1999.

Economic and Social Commission for Asia and the Pacific (ESCAP). "Ageing and the Family in the Developing Asian and Pacific Countries". In *United Nations, Ageing and the Family*. Proceedings of the United Nations International

Conference on Ageing Population in the Context of the Family, Kitakyushu (Japan), 15–19 October 1990, pp. 73–75. New York, 1994.

Einhorn, B. "Asia needs a safety net. But what kind?" *Business Week*, 12 October 1998, p. 28.

FNUAP. *Population Mondiale. Les générations nouvelles*. New York, 1998.

Fritsch, H. S. "How old are you?" In *Lansia: Modal ekonomi masa depan. Warta Demografi* 24, no. 1 (1994).

Hatmadji, S. H. and E. L. Pardede. "Sturktur demografis dan sosio-ekonomis penduduk lanjut usia di Indonesia". Paper presented at the seminar on Struktur Rumah Tangga dan Penduduk Lansia di Indonesia. Jakarta, 6 March 1999.

Hatmadji, S. H., Mundiharno and E. L. Pardede. "Penduduk lanjut usia Indonesia: Gambaran umum dan studi kasus di Kabupaten Bogor dan Cirebon". Paper presented at the Seminar on Nasional IPADI: Melembagakan pendekatan pembangunan bangsa dengan wawasan kependudukan, Jakarta, 23 March 1999.

Heller, P. S. "Ageing in the Asian Tiger Economies". *Finance & Development* (June 1998), pp. 26–29.

Höhn, C. "The issue of population ageing in Germany: An invention of demographer". *Europeople,* a special bulletin published on the occasion of the European Population Conference/EPC 99, 1999, p. 2.

Hugo, G. "Ageing in Indonesia". In *A Neglected Policy Concern in Ageing in East and South-East Asia,* pp. 207–31. London: Arnold, 1992.

———. "Intergenerational wealth flows and the elderly in Indonesia". Paper presented at the Continuing Demographic Transition seminar, Canberra, 14–17 August 1996.

———. "Changing patterns and processes in population mobility". In *Indonesia Assessment. Population and Human Resources,* edited by G. W. Jones and T. H. Hull, pp. 68–100. Canberra/Singapore: Australian National University/ Institute of Southeast Asian Studies, 1997.

INSERM. *Statistical Yearbook on Health Expectancy. Retrospective 1993 Issue.* Montpellier, 1994.

Instituut Sociaal Raadslieden (ISR). *Ouderen en inkomen. Wat gaat er veranderen als men 'op leeftijd' komt?* The Hague, August 1999.

Iskandar, M. B. "Health and Mortality". In *Indonesia Assessment. Population and Human Resources,* edited by G. W. Jones and T. H. Hull, pp. 205–31. Canberra/ Singapore: Australian National University/Institute of Southeast Asian Studies, 1997.

Project Mantelzorg. "Zorgen voor een ander". *Mantelzorg, Uw zorg, onze zorg.* Rijswijk, 2000.

Keasberry, I. N. " The implications of social change for elderly care in rural Java: A theoretical framework". *Journal of Population* 4, no. 1 (1998): 21–54.

King, S. "Role and functions of non-governmental organizations: Provision of community-based services for the elderly; enhancing national capacity". Paper presented at the Expert Group Meeting on the Implications of Asia's

Population Future for the Family and the Elderly. UN-ESCAP, Bangkok, 25–28 November 1996.

Knowles, J. C. "The Social Crisis in Asia". Paper presented at the 12th Workshop on Asian Economic Outlook. Manila: Asian Development Bank, November 1999.

Koesoebjono, S. "Manula sebagai sumber daya yang berpotensi". *Republika*, 1 October 1997.

Koesoebjono S. and S. Sarwono. "Towards a Care Society". *Majalah Kesehatan Perkotaan* 4, no, 1 (1997): 37–44.

Koizumi, A. "Health problems of the year 2000 and beyond". *Health Policy* 4 (1985): 307–19.

Mason, A. "Population change in East Asia". In *Population economics, demographic transition, and development*, edited by A. Mason, T. Merrick and R. P. Shaw, pp. 21–47. WBI Working Paper. Washington: World Bank, 1999.

Massey, D. S., J. Arango, G. Hugo, A. Kouaouci, A. Pellegrino, and J. E. Taylor. "Theories of International Migration: A Review and Appraisal". *Population and Development Review* 19, no. 3 (1993): 431–66.

McChesney, K. Y., and V. Bengtson. "Solidarity, Integration and Cohesion in Families: Concepts and Theories". In *Measurement of Intergenerational Relations*. Beverly Hills, California: Sage Publications, 1988.

Niehof, A. "Ageing and the Elderly in Indonesia: Identifying Key Issues". *Bijdragen tot de Taal-, Land- en Volkenkunde*, pp. 422–37. Leiden: KITLV, 1995.

NRC Handelsblad. *Ruim 44.000 mensen krijgen nog geen hulp*, 10 July 2000.

OECD. *Maturing Prosperity in an Ageing Society*. Paris, 1998.

Ogawa, N. et al. *Health Status of the Elderly and their Labour Force Participation in the Developing Countries along the Asia-Pacific Rim*. NUPRI Reprint Series, No. 51. Tokyo: Nihon University Population Research Institute, 1994.

Palmore, E. *The Honourable Elders. A Cross-Cultural Analysis of Ageing in Japan*. Durham, North Carolina: Duke University Press, 1975.

Parant, A. "Les revenues des retraités". *Population & Sociétés*, No. 356 (April 2000).

Petersen, W. "A general typology of migration". *American Sociological Review* 23, no. 3 (1958): 256–66.

Peterson, P. *Gray dawn: How the coming age wave will transform America and the world*. New York: Times Books, 1999.

Pickin, C. and S. St. Leger. *Assessing health needs using the life cycle framework*. Buckingham: Open University Press, 1993.

Prihastuti, D. "Model pertumbuhan penduduk lanjut usia (lansia) di Indonesia dengan pendekatan multiregional". Master's thesis. Program Studi Kependudukan dan Ketenagakerjaan. Program Pascasarjana. Universitas Indonesia, Depok, 2000.

Sarwono, S. "Personalistic belief in health: A case in West Java". *Health Care in Java*, edited by P. Boomgaard, R. Sciortino & I. Smyth, pp. 81–94. Leiden: KITLV Uitgeverij, 1996.

________. "Perawatan Lansia di Negeri Belanda". Paper presented at the seminar on Membina Kemandirian di Usia Ke Tiga, at Trisakti University, Jakarta, 27 November 1997.

Sauvy, A. *Théorie générale de la population*. Vol. 2, *La vie des populations*. Paris: Presses Universitaires de France, 1996.

Sociaal en Cultureel Planbureau (SCP). *Sociaal en Cultureel Rapport 1998. 25 jaar sociale verandering*. Rijswijk: SCP, 1998.

Tan, P. C. "The role of the elderly and their support within changing family structures in developing countries in United Nations: Population growth and demographic structure". Paper presented at the United Nations Expert Group Meeting on Population Growth and Demographic Structure. Paris, 16–20 November 1992.

United Nations (UN). *Long-range World Population Projections. Two centuries of population growth 1950–2150*. New York, 1992a.

———. *Demographic causes and economic consequences of population aging*. New York, 1992b.

———. *Demographic Yearbook. Special Issue: Population ageing and the situation of elderly persons*. New York, 1993.

———. "Overview of recent research findings on population ageing and the family". In *United Nations, Ageing, and the Family*. Proceedings of the United Nations International Conference on Ageing Population in the Context of the Family. Kitakyushu (Japan), 15–19 October 1990. New York, 1994.

———. *World Population Prospects. The 1998 Revision. Vol 1. Comprehensive tables*. New York, 1999a.

———. *World Population Prospects. The 1998 Revision. Vol 2. The sex and age distribution of the world population*. New York, 1999b.

UNFPA. "Population ageing. Improving the lives of older persons". Report of the ICPD+5 Technical Meeting on Population Ageing, Brussels, 6–9 October 1998. New York, 1998.

Voorlichtingscentrum Sociale Verzekering (VSV). *De kleine gids voor de Nederlandse sociale zekerheid 2000*. Deventer: Uitgeverij Kluwer, 2000.

Warta Demografi, year 24, no. 1 (1994).

World Bank. *Development Report 1993. Investing in Health*. New York: Oxford University Press, 1993.

WHO/World Health Organization. "Primary Health Care. Towards the Year 2000". A report of the Consultative Committee on Primary Health Care Development. Geneva, 9–12 April 1990.

Wongsith, M. "Family Structure and Care of the Elderly in Thailand". Paper presented at the Expert Group Meeting on the Implications of Asia's Population Future for the Family and the Elderly, UN-ESCAP, Bangkok, 25–28 November 1996.

Yu, Y. "Demography of Disability". *Population Bulletin of the United Nations*, No. 30 (1991): 61–78.

16

THE INDONESIAN CRISIS IN AN ALTERNATIVE PERSPECTIVE

Views from Outer Indonesia[1]

Maribeth Erb and Yosep Jelahat

Introduction

> Were the achievements real? ... Why have things gone wrong? Is it because Indonesia has been pursuing a wrong development strategy?
> (Soesastro 1999, p. 1)

What is referred to as "the Indonesian crisis" is commonly depicted as having started in July 1997, when the devaluation of the Thai bhat led other Asian currencies into a tailspin. The "monetary" crisis that ensued, the collapse of the financial sector, the loss of many industrial jobs, the austerity measures imposed by the International Monetary Fund (IMF), the difficult economic conditions for many, and intensifying protests, eventually led to the end of the 32-year presidency of, at that time, the longest reigning Asian leader. Just a year before, in 1996, despite escalating protests and unrest in Indonesia, articles in *Asiaweek* had pointed to the "economic fundamentals" as being still strong (Suh and Shameen 1996), and there was no "danger of collapse" (Berfield and Loveard 1996)[2]. Prominent economists also, even though they pointed out some of the misfits between macro-data and micro studies (Hill 1996, p. 195), as well as the difficulties in assessing the number of people living in "poverty" (Booth 1993), still had great praise for New Order Indonesia, which they had described as having gone, during

Soeharto's reign, from a "basket case" to one of "Asia's success stories" (Hill 1996, pp. 1–3), or from a "drop-out" to a "miracle" (Booth 1999, p. 113).

Indeed, the conventional assessment still seems to be that even though Indonesia is now in economic ruins, the years of development were still beneficial to the population; one cannot undervalue what has been done, even though disaster has struck. For example, looking back over the New Order one analyst has painted the following picture:

> Enormous progress was made in health, education, agriculture and poverty eradication, to mention a few of the most important fields. From 1969 to 1994 GDP (Gross Domestic Product) growth averaged 6.8 per cent and real GDP per capita increased more than threefold. From the early 1970's up to 1997 this economic development formed the basis for the regime's main claims to legitimacy. Suharto personally could claim a large share of the credit as being the leading proponent for development and economic modernisation. The fruits of the development also trickled down to Indonesia's thousands of villages and urban neighbourhoods in the form of new schools, roads, health-care centres and irrigation plants... This was at the heart of Soeharto's and the New Order's legitimacy (Eklof 1999, p. 3).

This idea of "trickle-down" is an important component of conventional economic theory, about which more will be said later. However, the view that the masses benefited generally from Soeharto's reign is one commonly held by economists and well-to-do Indonesians alike. For example, one Florenese woman, whose family prospered under the Soeharto regime, recently made the comment:

> People in Indonesia just don't know how to say thank you. Here I am riding in a car, I have experienced flying in an airplane, all of these things because of the last government and the last president. We never had all this in the past. People just don't know how to say thank you.

Economists too seem to regret the end of the New Order economic boom, and feel that the way out of the crisis is to return to the policies of the New Order (if not to the corruption, collusion and nepotism), to the "economic growth" that was directly responsible for the "dramatic decrease in poverty from 1970 to 1996" (Jacquand 1999, p. 398). A return to that growth, according to that observer, will lift a large percentage of the "poor", especially those made poor by the crisis, above the poverty line again.

This chapter suggests that it is worthwhile taking a step back from these conventional interpretations of the achievements, and subsequent "crisis" in Indonesia. Most assessments of the achievements of the New Order and the subsequent monetary and financial "crash" are, we think, primarily from a Java-centric, and perhaps an urban-centric, perspective. Some analysts have recognized that there are places in Indonesia where "the crisis" was experienced differently from industrial Java (see, for example, Potter 2000), where dependency on jobs created by foreign investors meant devastation when foreign capital was frightened away by the political collapse triggered by Soeharto's withdrawal from power. In this chapter, one of the aims is to contribute additional reflections on how the "crisis" has affected people outside Java, particularly in the eastern province of Nusa Tenggara Timur. Secondly, the crisis in Indonesia is put into a wider, global perspective, considering it against the background of much critical recent literature looking at the wider issues of development, "economic growth", neo-liberalism and the devastating effects these have had on many people, especially the poorer ones, and the environment.

For, although it might be argued that much "development" had taken place during the years of the New Order, the very fact of the sudden collapse of part of the Indonesian economy questions, as one critical commentator did about the history of Third World development in general, whether much of it was "appropriate" development (Trainer 1989, pp. 489–93). Trainer has argued, and his ideas are used here to look at the situation in New Order Indonesia, that it is a mistake to identify development with growth. Market forces have produced the development of the wrong kinds of industries, not those needed in the developing countries, but instead those demanded by the developed countries. In addition, indicators of "growth" measure the wrong things. As one astute commentator has suggested, "symbolic or artificial wealth ... grow[s] by means of the destruction of the real wealth of all the world" (Berry 2001, p. 7). Thus, capital is accumulated and invested by some, and this measures growth; yet the destruction and displacement resulting from the growth is not measured in economic statistics. It has been argued that, in fact, growth, in the free market economic model pushed onto the Third World, "became dependent on constricting and depressing wages, that is, on increasing poverty and repression" (Bello 1999, p. 225). This begins to answer the question why, if Indonesia's "fundamentals" were so strong, they could so easily be wiped out almost overnight. Certainly, the economic collapse itself raises the question about the "fundamentals" that were supposed to have indicated a "healthy economy".

Hence, it is suggested here that the conventional view of the Indonesian crisis is based on a faulty estimation of the achievements of "development" and "aid", and what they can do for "the poor", not only in Indonesia but throughout the Third World. Thus, the questions raised by Soesastro, quoted at the opening of this chapter, need to be addressed. Has Indonesia been in fact pursuing a wrong "development strategy"? Could it not be that perhaps there was a "crisis" that started much earlier, a crisis due to this faulty view of what "development" is?

It is suggested here, as other scholars have, that the system of "development" and "growth" has been constructed to impoverish, to weaken previous systems of community co-operation and sustainability and to create dependency, fragility and vulnerability (Escobar 1995; Trainer 1989, 1996; Danaher 2001; Bello 2000a; Boucher 1999; and Petras and Veltmeyer 2001). Development, suggests Escobar, is a hegemonic "discourse" that constructs the Third World as "backward" and the "developed" world as "modern". This construction of the world creates a set of power relations that contribute to underdevelopment and poverty (Escobar 1995, pp. 21–54). Wealth is produced for some in the Third World, but only those who allow the financial institutions and corporations of the First World access to the process of "development". For ultimately, the wealth and benefit of "aid" and "development" are controlled by the leaders of institutions of the developed world, who choose the projects to be aided, who send out the experts, who lend the money, and who are the ones who make the fortune from this major industry (George 1992; and Hancock 1989). This recent literature questions whether there can be "sound foundations and fundamentals", "strong pillars and structures" in a market system controlled by the rich countries, who are primarily the ones profiting from "development" and "growth".

By addressing these issues, this chapter will attempt to view the Indonesian crisis in the context of this alternative perspective, which is based on a different assessment of the accomplishments of development, and focuses more on the "peripheral" areas of Indonesia. In this era of *reformasi* (reformation/change) and "local/regional autonomy", there should be more localized assessments of the economic situation in Indonesia, as well as a local-led movement to "develop" those economies in the future.

The Creation of Poverty

> Vernacular societies had developed ways of defining and treating poverty that accommodated visions of community, frugality, and

> sufficiency. Whatever these traditional ways might have been, and without idealizing them, it is true that massive poverty in the modern sense appeared only when the spread of the market economy broke down community ties and deprived millions of people from access to land, water, and other resources. With the consolidation of capitalism, systemic pauperization became inevitable (Escobar 1995, p. 22).

> Let us remember that the main purpose of aid is not to help other nations but to help ourselves (Richard Nixon, 1968, quoted in Hancock 1989, p. 71).

As suggested above, most assessments of New Order Indonesia praise the efforts to "alleviate" poverty (Tjiptoherijanto 1997; Manning 1999, p. 122; Hill 1996, pp. 191–99; Booth 1999, p. 129; and Eklof 1999, p. 3). Granted that some of these scholars have their reservations about what had actually been achieved, and how it was done, but in general their assessments are positive about the reduction of poverty, and the improvement in the material conditions of a large percentage of the population in Indonesia during the New Order period. Given the devastating conclusion of the New Order, they still prescribe a return to a strategy of market-led growth and export dependency; the neo-liberal strategy that further integrates local economies into a global, corporate controlled economy. Poverty, according to this view, will eventually be eradicated because "a bigger pie will be created for all".

One assessment, as stated above, even suggests that a large percentage of those who have slipped below the poverty line during the crisis, "the easy poor", will regain their place above the poverty line when economic growth returns. His concern, therefore, is with "chronic poverty", the "very poor", those who had been poor despite the "miracle" boom in Indonesia, and the various New Order programmes designed to alleviate that poverty (Jacquand 1999).

The use of the term "chronic poverty" is misleading in a number of ways. "Chronic" represents poverty as a static condition. It gives the impression that the percentage of the "very poor" or "chronically poor" (between 10–15 per cent, depending on whose statistics are used, referring to those who "remained" poor despite all the New Order's best efforts), have been the same people all along. In addition, the use of the term "chronic" suggests that there is something about them, their intransigence, that keeps them poor, and hence they are "chronically" so. It allows us to believe that maybe it is their fault.

Reading the "statistics" of poverty this way obfuscates a whole history — a history of the consequences of colonialism, and of development policies that displaced and impoverished people, stripping them of their land and other resources. The use of the word "chronic poverty" disguises and ignores a whole history of the creation of poverty through various development programmes, and through the various discourses associated with development.

As Escobar relates in his review of "development" in the Third World, what he calls the "globalization of poverty" took place after World War II, when two-thirds of the world were discovered to be not living according to the standards of wealth of the "more economically advantaged nations" (1995:23). He goes on,

> Almost by fiat, two-thirds of the world's peoples were transformed into poor subjects in 1948 when the World Bank defined as poor those countries with an annual per capita income below $100 (ibid, p. 24).

The problem of this definition and assessment of poverty is that it reduces everyone in the Third World to the same general category of being "poor" without asking what their living conditions were really like. Most of those people probably did not rely on a wage-labour or monetary income for survival, but these models of "wealth" and "poverty" stated that these people were "poor", and the prescription was that they would have to "modernize" and follow the path of the "developed" countries. And, "... if the problem was one of insufficient income, the solution was clearly economic growth" (ibid, p. 24).

So was born in one breath, two modernization theories. One set out stages of development that the impoverished nations would have to pass through in order to "progress". This enshrined "development" as the supreme goal, placing the "First World" countries at the pinnacle, the imitation of which was the hoped for aim of all those in the other "worlds". Another one maintained the need for the development "industry", which gave free reign to developed countries through "aid" and "expertise" to capitalize on others' "backwardness". This may sound a rather strong accusation, but quite a lot of research in recent years has indicated that "aid" was never really meant to be that.

For example, Lappe, Collins and Kinley (1999) have written tellingly of the U.S. food aid programme, actually designed to rid the U.S. markets of surplus wheat without depressing global prices. At the same time, this aid gave an opportunity for various U.S. corporations to extend their reach into foreign markets. Monies paid for food aid were in local currencies that were then lent at low interest to U.S. corporations that wanted to expand into the receiving countries' markets, and also served U.S. military interests (pp. 187–88; and Lee 1999, p. 200, 203) These combined tactics, instead of being aid to the underdeveloped, led to massive underdevelopment and poverty. Food aid, they claim, was basically a disguised form of dumping, which lowered the prices of agricultural goods to the extent that local farmers could not compete. Farmers, who were bankrupted by this food aid, later had no choice but to become the cheap labour in the newly opened American transnational businesses (see also Lee 1999). Hence, in this instance, it can be seen how "development" impoverished and served the aims of the wealthy and powerful. In fact, Indonesia was one of the top five recipients of U.S. food aid in 1980 (Lee 1999, p. 197).

Granted there were places in the "Third World" where people's lives had earlier been devastated by colonialism and war, where the exploitation over centuries had already led to what might be characterized as "underdevelopment". Modernization theory did not recognize the difference, however, and constructed all the "Third World" as being mired in poverty because of the lack of productivity, capital, and technology.

In looking at the claimed "progress" to alleviate poverty in Indonesia's New Order, however, it is important to differentiate among the 60 per cent labelled as "poor" before the New Order "miracle" took off. In Java and other parts of western Indonesia, for example, many farmers had been dramatically affected by the Dutch colonial "cultivation system", which had systematically exploited the labour of tenant farmers and resulted in their impoverishment (Arief and Sasono 1980, pp. 59–70). Therefore, some of the "poverty" measured in Indonesia during the immediate post-colonial era was the result of colonial exploitation and the underdevelopment produced by it. However, others in more "peripheral" areas in Indonesia had not experienced Dutch colonialism in the same way.

Slave-raiding since the seventeenth century, that had been triggered by Dutch trade and control in western Indonesia, did have an impact on western Flores, in what is now the province of East Nusa Tenggara, but the Dutch did not directly occupy the island until the beginning of the twentieth century, when colonial policies had shifted to more "ethical" ones. In consequence, quite a few older Florenese during the New Order period expressed a longing for a return of Dutch colonial rule. There were those who experienced a fairly positive impact of Dutch colonial rule, because of the attention to education and health, and there were also quite a few who were affected very little by it. Hence, by the end of Dutch colonialism, there were a substantial number of people in Western Flores, and it may be true for other places outside Java as well, that had not been drawn too tightly into the colonial world system.

This was clearly to change during the years of independence, most particularly during the New Order. This has been expressed rather poignantly by quite a few elders in western Florenese villages, who compared the Dutch civil servants to the New Order ones.

> At least, those administrators always brought their own food, their own horses, their own necessities. They never asked for anything from the local people,

unlike administrators under the New Order government. Thus was New Order rule characterized as a new, more virulent, more destructive, form of colonialism.

During the colonial era, and until the 1970s, very little money was used in the Florenese economy. Thus, the measurement of poverty in Flores during that time has to be understood in relative, not absolute terms. One can compare the situation to that described by Stephanus Djuweng (1996) for the Dayak people of Kalimantan:

> In 1970 when I was still a small boy, we had zero population growth and no income per capita. There was no investment or services, but we were very happy. We had good quality food and everything we needed from nature.

With "no income per capita", according to conventional means of assessing the Dayaks, they would be "below the poverty line", and yet, were they really poor? The same question can be asked of many other communities in Indonesia during the 1950–70 period, often held up as being characterized by 60 per cent of the people living "below the poverty line". It is this period that is used to compare unfavourably with the major "progress" made by Soeharto's New Order, bringing, so the statistics tell us, a large proportion of the population above this poverty line.

Yet, what did New Order "development" give to those people brought into the statistics of poverty during the post-1970 period? Certainly, the situation of these "poor" was not a static one. Many who were "happy" before New Order policies were implemented, found that they were the targets of programmes of development that affected them in very adverse ways.

Hancock, in his vast critique of aid to the Third World, has related how the World Bank rather indiscriminately offered assistance to various resettlement programmes around the world, including the transmigration programme of Indonesia, first funded by the Bank in 1976 (1989, p. 133). Resettlement of Javanese and Madurese to the less populated islands of Sulawesi, Sumatera, and Kalimantan, as well as the politically sensitive areas of Irian Jaya and East Timor, over the decades has systematically ignored indigenous land tenure systems, and in some cases has led to the use of brutal violence by the military towards local inhabitants if they show resistance (Hancock 1989, pp. 133–34).

As in other parts of the world, resettlement into tropical forest lands has led to severe environmental damage on land not suited to sustained agriculture. Not only has this been ecologically disastrous, but it also means that the transmigrants, the direct recipients of these programmes designed to help them improve their economic conditions have also ended up in worse situations than when they started. More often than not, they are forced by circumstances to abandon the transmigration sites and to flock to urban centres looking for work and living in squalid conditions. By and large, their living conditions are worse than what they left behind in Java (ibid, p. 136). This points to one way that two distinct populations can be, and have been thrust into "poverty" by one New Order "development programme".

The World Bank and other agencies that have been supporting these kinds of development schemes to foster "progress" and "modernization" in Indonesia hold the view that people should not be allowed to get in the way of development, that governments should "sustain reforms against the opposition of those who are adversely affected" (Hancock 1989, p. 129), and that "economic growth is treated as an end in itself, rather than a means to an end" (ibid, p. 130). Hence, the kinds of projects and developments supported by the development agencies and the Indonesian Government systematically ignore the environmental damage that takes place and the rights of the indigenous peoples living on the land that gets damaged. This has been painfully clear not just in the transmigration programme, but also in other programmes supporting "economic growth" and "development".

Another programme, perhaps what could be considered the flip-side of transmigration, is the resettlement of "isolated" peoples considered to be "backward" and undeveloped as a way of civilizing and developing them. If transmigration was meant to be aid to the landless from overpopulated areas, then resettlement of the "isolated" was meant to bring the landed into more populated areas, and under the paternal eye of the Indonesian Government. Li contends that these resettlement programmes persisted despite their patent failure (similar to transmigration programmes), because of their implicit logic of "social engineering" and "governmentality" (1999, p. 301). In this case, she argues, we can see clearly that the aims of "development" were about negotiating the extension of state control. Interestingly, she suggests that although resettlement, and development in general, was presented as "giving generously" to needy peoples, it often ended up as a taking away (pp. 313–14).

The way that "development" pretends to give, but often takes away, can be illustrated in numerous cases where projects dealing with mining, logging, plantation and tourism in various places, such as Irian Jaya, Sulawesi, Kalimantan, and Lombok, have taken away the rights of local residents, and have often ended up being disastrous ecologically. Compensation for the land, if any is offered, is usually insufficient, and people displaced by these developments are thrust into situations of poverty, exploitation and abuse (IRIP New Service 1996; Moody 2000; and Robinson 1986, 2000).

But what about agriculture? What about some of the glowing reports given to the development of agriculture during the New Order? For example, Booth (1999, p. 114) praises the attention paid to agriculture by the Soeharto government, which brought Indonesia from an importer of rice, to self-sufficiency in rice within the period 1979–85. Without this priority given to agriculture, despite its diminishing place in the Indonesian economy overall, industrial development could not have taken place, this economist tells us. Between 1967 and 1973, programmes of the "green revolution" brought in high-yielding rice:

> Rice harvest yields began to increase, especially on Java, laying a basis for future industrialization by feeding prospective factory workers in towns and cities, enlarging rural buying power to consume these factories' products, and reducing inflationary pressures by keeping the prices of key foodstuffs stable (p. 114).

This conventional view, taken from a macroeconomic approach, ignores what actually happened to individual farmers at that time, and twists the facts in a peculiar way. This agricultural expansion, the "green revolution", certainly led to higher yields of rice production. However, the introduction of the technology and materials necessary for this "revolution" resulted in the pauperization of quite a few land-holders, who were subsequently squeezed out of agriculture. Between 1963 and 1983, the percentage of landlessness in Java rose 16 per cent (Fakih 2000, p. 11). This laid the foundation for future industrialization in Java by, first and foremost, creating a captive pool of cheap labour, forced to move to the towns and cities in search of work[3]. The businesses that expanded were not primarily those that produced things that people in the rural areas needed, but instead for export.

This is part of the logic of economic growth (Trainer 1988, 1989, and 1996). This shift out of agriculture is illustrated clearly by the estimations given by Sunanto, taken from research done in Desa Argomulyo (where Soeharto was born), that in 1993 only 6.8 per cent of a farmer's yearly earnings were from agriculture (2000, p. 97). The majority of the farmers, because of poor earnings from farming, were forced to work in the cities to supplement their income. This situation was to be explained by New Order policies that kept the price of rice low (euphemistically called "keeping the prices stable" by Booth). Sunanto explains that the increase in prices was traditionally announced in October, at which time the cost of fertilizer and pesticides actually went up, but rice prices were only allowed to increase in January the following year (Sunanto 2000, pp. 95–96). In this way, farmers were paying more for production, before they could enjoy an increase in the price of rice.

Sunanto gives examples of other tactics that allowed the bureaucracy to profit at the expense of the farmers, such as keeping the costs of their produce artificially low, exacting various payments to the government by forcing the farmers to sell their rice, sugar, and cloves to various "co-operative" institutions, and of course the various costs for the "signatures" of bureaucrats, which raised the overall cost of production (Sunanto 2000, pp. 96–102).

We witnessed a similar kind of situation in East Nusa Tenggara. Farmers have been captive producers for the government programme, Koperasi Unit Desa (KUD). KUD was designed as a safety net for the villagers in times of poor harvest. The idea seemed a good one for the people of East Nusa Tenggara, who frequently experienced "hunger times", when in some villages the harvest of the past year was not good enough to see the village through until the next harvest. The KUD storage barns, located in the *kecamatan* (district) capitals, were meant to acquire, at a low price, extra harvests that could be made available to those who needed it in difficult times, at a low price. In practice, however, KUD was a monopoly in the hands of corrupt officials, who did not allow farmers to sell their produce to other buyers. *Kecamatan* officials would force the farmers to "sell" their produce to the KUD (though often they would not be paid for it for a long time, if ever), at a price even lower than that set by the government. The additional money was pocketed by the officials. The officials were so keen to force the farmers to hand over their produce that they often had no adequate places to store it, and the rice paddy would get mouldy and go bad.

Other KUD "projects" were meant to "encourage" farmers to plant crops for sale, such as coffee, green beans, and onions. However, the officials in charge of KUD would not allow the farmers to sell their harvest to other buyers, setting the army and police on them if they tried to, and controlling the fields that they planted. They would give the farmers a very low price for their produce, and then sell it at higher prices, splitting the profit with higher level officials. Instead of encouraging farmers to be more industrious in their planting, these kinds of programmes often discouraged them, and turned them away from putting in any extra effort.

An additional government control over farmers' produce was the *retribusi,* a duty paid on all goods crossing over *kabupaten* (regency) borders. School-children leaving their regencies to attend school in another regency — a very common practice, especially at higher levels of education — were forbidden to take more than 20 kilograms of rice with them for their daily food consumption needs. This meant that they would have to purchase rice during their school term, benefiting the government and the middlemen, who made the profit by selling rice in the urban centres (often coming from the KUD stores, bought at cheap prices and sold at a higher price). Livestock, used universally in East Nusa Tenggara as marriage gifts to affinal kin, would be taxed if brought over a regency border, no matter what the purpose of the transport of the animal was. Thus, a Manggaraian (in the farthest west of Flores), who needed to bring a pig, for example, to affinal kin in Eastern Flores, would have to cross over four regency boundaries, paying a tax each time even though the pig was meant to be a gift, and would consequently be forced to pay a high price on a pig, that was in fact the produce of his own efforts. In this way, farmers were squeezed for a lot of extra tax on their produce, as well as forced to purchase food that, in fact, they could provide for themselves.

Control over trade both by tax and the KUD meant that farmers were never getting the prices that they, in fact, could have, given a more "free trade" environment. Therefore, despite all the talk about "economic liberalization" in the restructuring of the Indonesian economy during the 1980s and 1990s that led to the "boom" of the Indonesian economy, in fact, this "liberalization" did not penetrate to the villages. It was a good example of rules being lifted for rich investors, but being applied more strictly to the poor in the "informal sector", as discussed for tourism developments in Lombok and Bali by Dahles and Bras (1999).

In this way, developments of the New Order reflected the kinds of developments happening in agriculture all over the world. Even though production went up and there was a "quantitative" leap in the ability of Indonesia to feed its people, the "qualitative" ability of individual farmers to survive by farming decreased. In this very important way, dependency was created and the context for a crisis was produced.

What was the Crisis?

> Development projects in Indonesia, as around the world, only marginalise the local peoples and deprive them of their own land and resources (Djuweng 1996).

> It is not surprising ... that in many countries the poor now see development ... as an alien process, something done to them and a waste of effort (Hancock 1989, p. 128).

In searching for the "source" of the Indonesian financial crisis, Feridhanusetyawan (2000) has described New Order Indonesia as a "shiny house", with "fragile foundations". Soeharto's Indonesia was like "a house, which looked good and shiny from outside, but was built on rather fragile construction and foundation". No one seemed to care in good times, but then it "collapsed when an earthquake hit" (Feridhanusetyawan 2000, p. 156). This economist suggests that "solid foundations" are important for "sustainable economic growth". Although his analysis goes some way towards hinting that there was something fundamentally wrong with the New Order economic policies, perhaps it does not push the criticism far enough.

It is necessary to return to an important concept of the conventional economic view: trickle down. What were some of the things "achieved" by the New Order government that led Berfield and Loveard in *Asiaweek* magazine to say in 1996: "Not for nothing is Soeharto known as Bapak Pembangunan — the father of development". As quoted above, Eklof mentions "new schools, roads, health-care centres and irrigation plants" (1999, p. 3).

Despite these achievements, it is possible still to query how helpful they really were in the lives of many Indonesian people. Often, the development projects that "trickled down" to the masses ended up more than anything else as sources of revenue for civil servants, and not really sources of aid to the poor. Thus, as one astute Florenese observer suggested, "civil servants managed to get rich due to other people's poverty". Projects to "help the poor" were primarily siphoned off by the rich.

In Western Flores, from observations and experiences, it is possible to suggest, using an alternative lens, that these "trickle down" projects themselves created a crisis situation for the masses. Partially, this had to do with corruption; partially, it had to do with poor planning; partially, it had to do with the poorly conceived idea of development in the first place.

Projects from Jakarta over the decades of the New Order created what people are now referring to as a "project mentality", which many see as a hindrance to real, appropriate kinds of development. This, one could argue, is the real crisis. For example, quite a number of INPRES schools, funded in the 1970s and 1980s by the government, fell down before the students ever entered the door. This was because contractors that were awarded the project by the local government heads, first "contributed" a hefty percentage of the project money back to the person who awarded it to them, then took out their own profit, before even starting to plan construction. With what was left they were forced to skimp on materials so much that the final construction fell down almost before a picture could be taken to be sent to Jakarta.

This "project mentality" is closely associated with the "civil servant orientation" of the education system, and the apparent New Order structuring of the main goal of education to create members of the national bureaucracy. This clearly is closely associated with other forms of the creation of "dependency" and the destruction of village self-sufficiency in food production and reproduction. Being a waged labourer is to be dependent on a larger system and to be far more vulnerable than the villager who, although perhaps involved in cash crop production, is still importantly involved in subsistence agriculture, as is true in Western Flores to a large extent. Being a civil servant during the New Order meant also becoming part of a vast system of patronage links and the accompanying corruption that ate into the projects at various levels. "Civil-servantism" tended to foster a highly egotistic style of interaction, wherein each person was out for themselves to get as much profit as possible from the "system" of projects and development.

Very few educational facilities claimed to prepare the student to go back to the village and become involved in useful "real" developments there, for example, to improve agricultural production or village life in general. There was little money in that. Instead, the orientation was up and out. Hence, the New Order education policies led to a tremendous "brain drain" of many of the best and brightest out of their areas of origin, and into the urban centres, ultimately to Jakarta. Recently, one Western Florenese woman complained:

> There are so many Manggaraian (western Florenese) people who are wealthy living in Jakarta. What have they done for their homeland? Nothing. Most of them leave and they never come back. Why is this?

Again we see this as part of the New Order crisis.

Even those who left were not well prepared by the Indonesian educational system to compete globally. Anderson remarks that one of the major shortcomings of Southeast Asian societies was that the leaders did not use to good advantage the "miracle" years of boom to, among other things, develop a skilled, well-educated work-force; not least of these was Indonesia. The reasons for this, he argued, were that the authoritarian regime saw students as a potentially politically volatile group, and hence education was not used to instil initiative or creativity, but loyalty. A key backdrop to this was foreign investment. Foreign corporations did not want potentially high-wage, demanding workers, but low-wage, submissive and non-unionized ones (1998).

As for health, it is true that clinics were built and health-care workers, doctors, and nurses trained. What we observed during the New Order period was that villagers were often better off without going to the clinics. In one *desa* that one of the authors lived in for three years (1983–86), health-care workers would indiscriminately administer the same three medicines for every ailment — chloroquine, penicillin, and vitamin B complex — often without explaining to the patient what they were being given. Recently, there have been educated villagers who have questioned the administering of penicillin in this way, which often ignored the completion of the prescribed dosage. One health-care worker reported that tuberculosis was reaching epidemic proportions in his area, because people had not been using the prescribed medication in the proper way, a sign of earlier neglect by medical practitioners. By the early 1990s some villagers were complaining that "modern" medicine was no good (the European priest who had been the real source of medication during the 1970s and 1980s had since left), and they were reviving their traditional "magic" in search of cures for their ailments.

Another detrimental effect of the health-care system for Florenese was the way that health-care workers were rewarded for the number of IUDs that they introduced into the village communities. Women were forced to use these birth-control devices and there was little follow-up, or discussion about the long-term effects of wearing them. More than one woman had died from internal bleeding because of improper use of IUD, while the detrimental effects of the use of other questionable forms of birth control, such as pills and injections, without proper supervision, and even forced vasectomies, can only be guessed at. As with many other New Order policies, birth control was a means to an end. Development discourse had constructed "population" as a "problem" that needed to be attended to, and if it were not, then "aid" would not be forthcoming. So it is clear that the "end" had in fact nothing to do with the supposed subjects of its prescription.

Irrigation was a major concern of New Order projects in Western Flores. All the irrigable land designated for big projects — often uninhabited grasslands near the coast — was divided up among individuals in neighbouring villages, and then dams were built to make water available for the growing of wet rice. Of the three large grassland projects that we are familiar with, two in Eastern Manggarai and one in southern Manggarai, only one, in the plain of Gesing in northeastern Manggarai, could be deemed "successful" from the point of view of the resident population. The other Eastern Manggarai project totally failed because the corruption of the local government officials, who saw this as a "project" to profit from, ensured that a proper dam that could survive even one rainy season was never built. The other project was a massive success story by New Order standards, having become the major "rice basket" for the whole of Western Flores. However, the land that had originally been divided among the local villages, by means of various "green revolution" tactics resulting in bankrupting the poor, had long ago been taken over by well-to-do civil servants in the towns.

Finally, the roads built by the New Order government are perhaps the most devastating of all the crises created by "development", since they have led, and will continue to lead to major social and cultural displacement. For two decades of the New Order, Manggaraians (the people of Western Flores) waited patiently, with great anticipation, for roads. Money sent from Jakarta to build them was systematically misused (the massive amount of extortion practised by the *Bupati* "serving" Manggarai in the 1980s was considered so excessive even by New Order standards, that he was arrested and tried at the end of his term.)

Nevertheless, in the 1990s roads began to be built with a vengeance. However, as with many other development projects of the New Order, the objectives were never carefully planned out. What were the roads really for? Who was supposed to benefit from them? When, in late 1997, one of the authors visited a village on the northern coast that she had known in the 1980s, the changes wrought by the road were shocking.

The northern trans-Flores road had been opened officially by President Soeharto in 1990. By 1997, the villagers, who had never seen motorized transportation in the 1980s, had started to take it for granted in an unhealthy way. This was part of a wider dependency on a monetary economy that had begun years earlier. However, in the late 1990s, this was beginning to look like a "cultural crisis". In the earlier years in the north coast, people had made a lot of money by collecting the tiny fish that swarm up the streams to breed, and selling them to Chinese Indonesian traders who exported them to Japan. Because of the ready cash that could be received from catching these fish, people gave up planting rice and maize. These fish, however, had started to disappear by the end of the 1980s, forcing people to return to farming. Once the road was built, however, a new innovation, the kiosk, appeared. Selling cigarettes and other consumer goods along the roadside seemed an easy way to make a living instead of farming.

At about the same time, in a programme that was supposed to help backward villagers in the mid-1990s, called "ABRI *masuk desa*", the army arrived with the road, and built for the villagers a piped water system. The army personnel assured the people that they need not keep wells any longer, so most people cemented them over. However, over time the water system broke down, and people did not know how to fix it. The army was no longer around, and so they were left with great difficulty in obtaining water. The one man who had kept his well had to fight off his neighbours, who all wanted to use it. Many people ended up "using the road", and buying water from the town, instead of digging new wells. The catastrophe of both the road and other apparently easy means to get cash was that people no longer wanted to work for their living, but wanted it all to be delivered to their doorstep.

Roads seem to have fostered a "market mentality" — rather than making it yourself, it is better to buy it with cash; rather than working at producing anything yourself, it is better to sell someone else's produce for profit. This, according to the critical literature on development, is one of the main goals of development, to destroy self-sufficiency in production and to integrate people into a global market system. Those who were profiting by this road were the merchants in the towns. They would give credit to small traders, who would set up kiosks in the villages. People would buy products produced elsewhere, such as Indomie (probably made from U.S. wheat; reportedly, the Soeharto family pocketed 100 rp. for every package sold), sugar (the Javanese peasant who produces it will not get any profit), and biscuits (made by Kong Guan factories in Jakarta or Surabaya).

The circulation of these products fostered the growth of these New Order-controlled industries, located elsewhere, which contributed to profits for others. For the kiosk owner, more often than not there were not enough buyers, and they ended up using the products themselves, thus putting themselves into a situation of spiralling debt, and "on the road" to landlessness, for once their debt becomes large enough, and once someone decides that their land is worth something (for the development of some project), the debt will be called in, and they will have to pay it in the only way that they can. One astute observer in the Manggaraian capital recently commented:

> Roads are built for the big businesses like Coca Cola. These companies can sell their products right in the village, and other big companies can come in and buy the villagers' produce cheaply. Villagers are not the ones who profit from the roads.

Roads are a path in, but also a path out. They lead to greater and greater urbanization, as the young flock down them to the cities, hoping for better opportunities, since the roads themselves do not bring these to the village. Roads are a tool of global capital and a means of greater centralization and control for those who have it.

We suggest that development during the New Order period, though perhaps not as radical as in other Third World countries, had many detrimental aspects to it. Programmes meant to "develop" them usually ended up enriching civil servants and big business. The bureaucrats of the New Order, whom many villagers viewed as a colonial master worse than the Dutch, were one of the worst manifestations of New Order "development" and corruption for the typical Florenese villager. When civil servants came to visit the village, they would demand to be treated like kings. When they left the village, they would leave with all kinds of wealth, which the villagers would then have to carry for them.

We suggest that the New Order regime, which fostered corruption and allowed exploitation to flourish, was typical of the kind of inappropriate "development" that has been found in the Third World since the 1950s. Signs of "growth", conventional economic indicators, do not tell about the average person's experience. As Hancock suggests (1989, p. 128), "the arse-about-face logic" of bureaucrats, who reduce human beings to "capital instruments, to mere means of production", highlights the wrong indicators as signs of "success". Instead of looking at the experiences of the average people, often characterized by fear, or community life, often characterized by displacement, or social values, often eroded by economic developments, economists measured growth, which was mostly enriching only a few. To look at the "shiny exterior" is to ignore the condition of many of the people who were being displaced, exploited, and led on a path away from self-sufficiency, autonomy, and control over their own lives.

The Crisis

> If you read Indonesian history, local resistance against land acquisition by those in power has been happening for hundreds of years. Diponegoro led a revolt against the Dutch when they were taking land to build along the northern coast of Java. The same thing is happening now in Kalimantan and in Irian. Local people are protesting against land acquisition, carried out in the name of development. So I ask myself, what is really the difference between colonialism and development? It's only that the first was

> done by a colonial government, the second by our so-called independent government. And that's not a significant difference (Djuweng 1996).

Though the suffering of millions because of the financial collapse in Indonesia should not be belittled, the worst of the crisis could well be over. All in all, it is suggested that inappropriate development encouraged by the New Order policy led to a growing crisis for the average village Indonesian. Agricultural programmes left them impoverished and landless, or having no control over the produce of their own efforts; education and health, if not directly detrimental, were part of projects which allowed certain people, mostly civil servants, to gain wealth at the expense of the poor, and because they were poor. Transmigration and resettlement programmes, and mining projects led to environmental deterioration, unhealthy living conditions, and the displacement of the local people; tourism developments took land away from the indigenous inhabitants; logging, and the burning of forests led to widespread health and environmental catastrophes. These were all the growing crises of the New Order.

An analysis of the socio-economic situation during the "financial crisis" can, thus, only be understood against the background of the earlier "crises" created by the New Order. In looking, for example, at the province of East Nusa Tenggara and other places in Indonesia, it has been illustrated that development was mostly inappropriate. For some people, those less tightly connected to the bureaucracy or global capitalist industry, the end of the New Order saw an improvement in their situations. What was devastating for those who had lost their self-sufficiency in food production, turned out to be a boon to those who had not. Unfortunately, this is not likely to continue, if the prescriptions of conventional developmental economics are followed in the new "reform", local autonomy era to come. This is especially so if prescriptions of "structural adjustment" of the IMF and World Bank continue to be followed.

The monetary crisis, and the ensuing economic downfall of the financial sector in Indonesia resulted in a major windfall for many farmers in outlying parts of Indonesia. In fact, on a visit to Western Flores in June 1999, a number of people said that the farmers were looking forward to the next change of President, since it seemed that each time there was a change, the price of coffee went up. To the farmers of Flores, and other places with cash crops to sell, such as coffee, chocolate, cloves and vanilla, "*krismon*" (an abbreviation for *krisis monoter*, or the monetary crisis) was a positive thing, and not the disaster that it was to those in the cities and in the Javanese countryside. The prices of goods also went up, but the windfall in the capital was unprecedented for them. Many farmers in Flores had enough money to buy satellite dishes, and even automobiles.

The reason for this was not only the devaluation of the rupiah, and the consequent larger amounts of rupiah that would be given for a kilogram of coffee. It was also the loss of the monopoly of the Koperasi Unit Desa (KUD), controlled by the previous bureaucracy that had set the price which farmers could be paid for their cash crops. It was also the withdrawal of the regulations and duties on trade between regencies that truly freed up trade possibilities for village farmers.

Another positive outcome of the "financial crisis" was the end of New Order repression, and a freeing up of public space to voice dissent and protest. This has meant that, for example, mining companies in Kalimantan, Sulawesi, Irian Jaya, and East Nusa Tenggara, which during the Soeharto era had been able to take land away from the local people, and devastate the environment, are now being called to task. Local people are making headway in their protests against these companies, and local governments are demanding their share of the revenue, which under the highly centralized administration of the New Order was unthinkable. This is making mining operations not as lucrative as they had been in the past (Moody 2000; and Robinson 2000), and it is likely to cut into "economic growth".

One such case of protest over a mining project unfolded during 2000 in East Nusa Tenggara. The quality of the marble found on Timor Island is apparently very high. PT Karya Asta Alam had been quarrying for marble in the regency of Timor Tengah Selatan (TTS, south central Timor) for several years. Initially, the villagers there claimed that the land that this company wanted to mine was sacred land. At the insistence of the New Order government, however, and with promises by the company that they would help to develop the village of Netpala by providing schools and heath-care facilities, mining eventually began. The villagers waited for more than a year, but no construction of the promised facilities was forthcoming, and they were told that "sampling" was still going on. After a time, the villagers started to ask, what does the word "sampling" mean? They were told, by those who knew English, that it meant taking small amounts to test the quality of the marble. The villagers became angry, for large amounts of marble had already been extracted, with no benefit yet in sight for the villagers. In fact, the situation was quite the reverse. Marble dust was causing damage to crops, and polluting water sources, and the incessant noise of the equipment was making their lives very unpleasant. The villagers started to protest, and mining was stopped.

In Timor, especially in the capital of East Nusa Tenggara, Kupang, advocacy groups have gained in influence and power, and the complaints of villagers are being heard on a whole range of projects that they feel have been disadvantageous to them. The title and first sentence of one article written on the discussion page, hosted by PIAR, Yayasan Pusat Informasi Advokasi Raykat (Centre of People's Advocacy and Information) about the exploitation associated with industrial developments in Kupang, illustrates this.

> ***Pengingkaran Budaya dan Pelanggaran Hak Azasi Manusia di Kecamatan Kupang Barat***
> **(The Sidelining of Culture and the Violation of Human Rights in Western Kupang)**
> Development, it turns out, is a disaster for local village people. This is perhaps the best expression to summarize the consequences of the processes of development that have taken place in the 32 years of the New Order government (Stefanus Mira Mangngi, undated, translated freely by M. Erb)[4]

The article goes on to detail how, over the past thirty-two years, the development of various industries in Kupang have deprived the indigenous people of land through abusive, violent means, and have destroyed their culture and ways of life. The article states that if the various projects of industrialization slated to be developed in Kupang continue to follow the development strategies of the New Order, it would aggravate the crisis for the populations there.

Is Development, Growth, and Aid the Answer?

> The growth principle is the problem (Trainer 1989, p. 492).

> Aid is not bad because it is sometimes misused, corrupt or crass; rather it is inherently bad, bad to the bone, and utterly beyond reform. As a welfare dole to buy the repulsive loyalty of whining, idle and malevolent governments, or as a hidden, inefficient and inadequately regulated subsidy for Western business, it is possibly the most formidable obstacle to the productive endeavors of the poor. It is also a denial of their potential, and a patronizing insult to their unique, unrecognized abilities (Hancock 1989, p. 183).

> The indiscriminate, "sheer growth" concept of development causes immense havoc among the poor. It has stripped them from the land and moved them to urban slums, it has made large numbers poor and hungry, it has destroyed their forests to build dams and in many

> cases it has replaced rich cultures and supportive social networks with the alienation and shallowness of 'modernization' (Trainer 1989, p. 491).
>
> Some people might argue that we can make development sustainable. But in my opinion it cannot be sustainable, and cannot bring justice or prosperity to the people. Instead, it has brought two big global crises: an environmental crisis, and a crisis of social justice. In the US, although the GNP has increased, the index of social welfare has declined. People have no leisure, no community life, no extended relationships or friendships. People are just in a hurry to make money (Djuweng 1996).
>
> At present I don't think development can bring a prosperous and just society. There is no sustainable development, it's an absurd notion (Djuweng 1996).

What has been suggested here is that the economic "fundamentals" and "growth" of the New Order, as they are read at a macroeconomic level, actually hid various crises that were taking place at the micro-level. If the local communities, the villagers, and the vast majority of the population of Indonesia are to really experience a level of economic prosperity, a major change in the strategies of development needs to be made. In our view, a move towards local autonomy in this reformation era would be a good start, but it would depend on the level of the "local" to be acknowledged and how this would work out in practice.

Is "sustainable development" an "absurd notion"? It is if it follows the precepts of conventional economic theory and the kind of policies suggested by the IMF and eager foreign investors. Expecting Indonesia to recover because of foreign investment, the "free hand" of the market, and the eventual "trickle-down" of prosperity to the masses, will mean returning to some of the strategies of New Order "development", and this would be "absurd". In fact, it has been suggested by some commentators that the "growth" that Indonesia did enjoy during that period was not because of the neo-liberal policies and structural adjustments that are now being prescribed as a remedy, but because the worst of these measures had not yet penetrated to Southeast Asia because of its privileged position during the Cold War (Bello 2000a). It has been suggested here that "development" pursued according to neo-liberal principles develops the wrong things, prioritizes the wrong things, and has not made, and will not make the lives of a large percentage of Indonesians better. If there is a return to economic growth and reliance on foreign investment, more Indonesians would become worse off, and continuously made increasingly vulnerable to currency devaluations, market price fluctuations, and the whims of people in far away places.

The idea itself that investors are "needed" needs to be re-examined. A good friend, a Manggaraian businessman, summed up a response to this idea recently, when he said,

> Investors are businessmen, they are looking for profits. The hopes of the local governments in the new reformasi era, that inviting investors in (to NTT, for example) to help "development", is an erroneous one. Investors will not give the money to develop the facilities that are needed in NTT; these must be supplied by the government. Education, healthcare, these must be provided by the government, and they must be provided to prepare the local population for investors, so that they will know how to protect themselves and get the most out of the relationship, the deal that is to be forged. For investors are businessmen; they are, naturally, only looking for profit.

It appears that awareness of this reality is not common, however, and as discussed above, one often hears of the bad deals that the local people have received from investors who had promised to help them "develop".

The best way to sum up this analysis of the socio-economic situation in Indonesia before and during the "crisis" is to present a brief synopsis of the radical alternative economic theories of Ted Trainer. Trainer thinks that there is such a thing as a "sustainable economy", but it is not one based on "development", the underlying philosophy and logic of the New Order regime. He categorically rejects the free market economy that has led to the situation where:

— "Scarce resources go to the relatively rich, because they can bid more for them ... "
— Only "the most profitable things are produced", so often the things needed by larger numbers of poor people are not produced.
— Inequality and poverty are becoming worse (even in the rich countries)
— "Unemployment tends to increase ... because technical advances increase the amount of work produced per worker"
— "There is enormous but unavoidable waste", since we have "an economy that cannot be healthy unless we ... constantly increase the amount of production and consumption going on"
— "There is inappropriate development".... Many things are being built in the Third World, but "these developments do not contribute to the production of the most needed things" ... "because investment goes into those areas that are most profitable".

— Large numbers of people are bored, lonely and frustrated, since priority is not placed on developing communities and relationships, but on economic turnover.
— People do "far too much work and producing"
— "We are rapidly damaging the ecological life support systems of the planet".
— "Growth is crucial in this economy" ... so that "there is no point at which people would be considered rich enough".... or "at which we would have had sufficient development". This is because those who have capital, and their quest to get more of it, drive the economy. "They make profits" ... and can only reinvest it profitably if "an increase in the value of producing and consuming takes place" (1996, pp. 4–6).

Trainer lays out an alternative, that in fact in many ways was already the kind of lives lived by many in the Third World before they were introduced to development: a "simple, self-sufficient and cooperative way of life... a zero growth economy". In fact, he argues, all people must move to a "simpler economy, highly localized, whereby small regions largely meet their own economic needs in basically cooperative and participatory ways with little need for bureaucracy, giant corporations, international importing or exporting or large state governments". There would be "local control over most development via town meetings.... small local firms mostly using local resources to meet local needs" ... "the cash economy would be a relatively minor part of a sustainable" ... or as he calls it a "conserver society" (ibid, pp. 7–8).

In essence, Trainer lays out a strategy for local autonomy that many Indonesians could well follow, because this kind of life is one essentially familiar to them, but one that the forces of development and modernization have been trying to destroy during the thirty-two years of the New Order. So that, for example, for people such as those located in the villages of Indonesia in the past, in response to the question, "What specific things is it appropriate to develop?", Trainer would answer,

> Very few! Often it is distressingly obvious that people living in largely self-sufficient ways in unspoiled ecosystems need only a few basic necessities, perhaps emergency medical care, relief from some arduous labor or improved gardening techniques, in order to enjoy a high and secure quality of life despite quite low GNP per capita (1989, p. 491).

This view can be supported by the results of the "economic crisis" in Indonesia. Those people who were less closely tied to the world capitalist system, who were not wholly dependent on it, were better off than those who had become urban labourers, bereft of land or a means of livelihood outside the market system. It is therefore suggested that it is not the best prescription for Indonesia to attempt to return to "growth" and encourage foreign investment, but instead to aim for a sustainable economy based on true local autonomy and community participation.

In conclusion, although not all readers will agree with this assessment of the situation in New Order and post-New Order Indonesia, it is hoped that some have been convinced that it is at least necessary to contemplate alternatives to the way that Indonesia has been developing over the past thirty-five years and to try to incorporate some of these alternatives into the *reformasi* of the future.

Notes

1. The material on which this chapter is based has been collected and experienced over a long period of time. The senior author started research in Flores from 1983 to 1986 and has returned numerous times since then. She would like to express her appreciation to the Lembaga Ilmu Pengetahuan Indonesia (Indonesian Council of Sciences) for permission to do this research and to Universitas Nusa Cendana, and the University of Indonesia for sponsorship. Her research was supported by a Social Science Research Council Fellowship and a National Science Foundation Grant for Improving Doctoral Dissertation Research in the early years, and the latest research has been made possible by grant number R111-000-022-112/007 from the National University of Singapore and a period of study leave. She would like to express thanks to these institutions for their support. The junior author originates from the island of Flores, and now lives in Kupang, the capital of the province on the island of Timor and has done a great deal of research work in other places in East Nusa Tenggara province. The collaboration for this chapter, and some of the research on which it was based, was done together by the two authors for four months in 2000. The junior author would like to thank the Universitas Nusa Cendana for the time given to do that research.
2. Walden Bello suggests that journalists, economists, investors, and investment analysts propped up the illusion of an eternal Asian boom because of their own self-interest in doing so, thereby ignoring any data to the contrary (2000b, pp. 185–88).
3. In other words, they were not all "prospective labourers" beforehand.
4. The original in Indonesian is as follows: *"Pembangunan ternyata malapetaka bagi masyarakat adat. Itu mungkin ungkapan yang tepat jika kita mencermati dampak dari proses pembangunan yang sudah berlangsung selama 32 tahun orde baru"*.

References

Anderson, Benedict. "From Miracle to Crash". *London Review of Books Online.* http:www.lrb.com.uk/v20n08/ande2008.htm

Arief, Sritua, and Adi Sasono. *Indonesia: Dependency and Underdevelopment.* Jakarta: Institute for Development Studies, 1980.

Bachriadi, Dianto. "Land for the landless: Why 'democrats' in Jakarta aren't interested in land reform". *Inside Indonesia* 64 (October–December 2000).

Bello, Walden. "Development Debacle". In *The Paradox of Plenty: Hunger in a Bountiful World,* edited by Douglas H. Boucher, pp. 217–26. Oakland, California: Food First Books, 1999.

———. "Building an Iron Cage: The Bretton Woods Institutions, The WTO and the South". In *Views from the South: The Effects of Globalization and the WTO on Third World Countries,* edited by Sarah Anderson, pp. 54–90. Chicago: Food First Books and the International Forum on Globalization, 2000a.

———. "The Asian Financial Crisis: Heroes, Villains, and Accomplices". In *Principled World Politics: The Challenge of Normative International Relations,* edited by Paul Wapner and Lester Edwin J. Ruiz, pp. 181–90. Lanham, Boulder, New York, Oxford: Rowman and Littlefield Publishers, Inc., 2000b.

Berfield, Susan, and Keith Loveard. "Suharto under Fire: Riots in Jakarta and a Host of Other Challenges Raise the Question: Can the Aging President Handle the Pressure?". *Asiaweek.com* 9608/09/cs1.html, 1996.

Berry, Wendell. "The Idea of a Local Economy". In *Orion On Line,* special issue: *People and Nature, 2001.* At http://www.orionsociety.org/pages/om/archive_om/Berry/Local_EconomyPR.html

Booth, Anne. "Counting the Poor in Indonesia". *Bulletin of Indonesian Economic Studies* 29 no. 1 (1993): 53–84.

———. "Development: Achievement and Weakness". In *Indonesia Beyond Soeharto: Polity, Economy, Society, Transition,* edited by Donald K. Emmerson, pp. 109–35. New York: M. E. Sharpe, 1999.

Boucher, Douglas, ed. *The Paradox of Plenty: Hunger in a Bountiful World.* Oakland, California: Food First Books, 1999.

Dahles, Heidi, and Karin Bras, eds. *Tourism and Small Entrepreneurs: Development, National Policy, and Entrepreneurial Culture: Indonesian cases.* New York: Cognizant Communication, 1999.

Danaher, Kevin, ed. *Democratizing the Global Economy: The Battle against the World Bank and the IMF.* Monroe and Philadelphia: Common Courage Press, 2001.

Djuweng, Stephanus. "Interview: Development is an Extension of Colonialism". *Inside Indonesia* 47 (July–September 1996).

Eklof, Stefan. *Indonesian Politics in Crisis: The Long Fall of Suharto 1996–1998.* Nordic Institute of Asian Studies, 1999.

Escobar, Arturo. *Encountering Development: The Making and Unmaking of the Third World.* Princeton University Press, 1995.

Fakih, Mansour. "Tijauan Kritis Terhadap Revolusi Hijau". In *Menggeser Pembangunan, Memperkuat Rakyat: Emansipasi dan Demokrasi Mulai dari Desa,* edited by Dadang Juliantara. Yogyakarta: Lapera Pusaka Utama, 2000.

Feridhanusetyawan, Tubagus. "Indonesia: In Search of the Source of Crisis". *Indonesian Quarterly* 28, no. 2 (2000): 156–70.

George, Susan. *The Debt Boomerang: How Third World Debt Harms Us All.* London: Pluto Press; and Amsterdam : The Transnational Institute, 1992.

Hancock, Graham. *Lords of Poverty*. London: Macmillan, 1989.

Hill, Hal. *The Indonesian Economy Since 1966: Southeast Asia's Emerging Giant.* Cambridge University Press, 1996.

IRIP New Service. "Beaches and Broken Bones: Tourism disrupts villagers in Lombok". *Inside Indonesia* 47 (July–September 1996).

Jacquand, Marc. "Poverty Alleviation in Indonesia Since the Economic Crisis: Beyond Immediate Relief". *Indonesian Quarterly* 27 (1999): 389–401.

Juliantara, Dadang, ed. *Menggeser Pembangunan, Memperkuat Rakyat: Emansipasi dan Demokrasi Mulai dari Desa.*Yogyakarta: Lapera Pusaka Utama, 2000.

Lappe, Frances Moore, Joseph Collins, and David Kinley. "Aid as Obstacle: Twenty Questions about our Foreign Aid and the Hungry". In *The Paradox of Plenty: Hunger in a Bountiful World,* edited by Douglas Boucher, pp. 178–94. Oakland, California: Food First Books, 1999.

Lee Kheng Poh. "New Food Aid: Same as the Old Food Aid". In *The Paradox of Plenty: Hunger in a Bountiful World,* edited by Douglas Boucher, pp. 195–207. Oakland, California: Food First Books, 1999.

Li, Tania Murray. "Compromising Power: Development, Culture, and Rule in Indonesia". *Cultural Anthropology* 14, no. 3 (1999): 295–322.

Mangngi, Stephanus Mira. "Kawasan Industri Kupang: Pengingkaran Budaya dan Pelanggaran Hak Azasi Manusia di Kecamatan Kupang Barat". www.jaringnet.org/fokus/fokus_2.html, undated.

Manning, Chris. "Poverty Decline and Labour Market Change in Indonesia: Lessons from the Suharto Era". *Indonesian Quarterly* 27 (1999): 122–45.

Moody, Roger. "Dirty Landlord: Local Views on Sulawesi's Inco Mine". *Inside Indonesia* 61 (January–March 2000).

Petras, James, and Henry Veltmeyer. *Globalization Unmasked: Imperialism in the 21st Century.* Canada: Fernwood Publishing, Zed Books, 2001.

Potter, Lesley. "Rural Livelihoods and the Environment at a Time of Uncertainty: The Situation Outside Java". In *Indonesia in Transition: Social Aspects of Reformasi and Crisis,* edited by Chris Manning and Peter van Diermen. Singapore: Institute of Southeast Asian Studies, 2000.

Robinson, Kathryn May. *Stepchildren of Progress: The Political Economy of Development in an Indonesian Mining Town.* New York: State University of New York Press, 1986.

________ . "Revisiting Inco: Reformasi hits Sulawesi's 'Freeport'. *Inside Indonesia* 61 (January–March 2000).

Soesastro, Hadi. *The Economic Crisis in Indonesia: Lessons and Challenges for Governance and Sustainable Development.* Pacific Link, http://www.pacific.net.id/pakar/hadisusastro/economic.html, 2000.

Suh, Sangwon, and Assif Shameen. "Resting on a Secure Base: The economy should survive the recent unrest". *Asiaweek.com* 9608/09/cs5.html, 1996.

Sunanto, Hatta. "Pembangunan Pertanian dan Keadilan Sosial". In *Menggeser Pembangunan, Memperkuat Rakyat: Emansipasi dan Demokrasi Mulai dari Desa*, edited by Dadang Juliantara. Yogyakarta: Lapera Pusaka Utama, 2000.

Tjipoherijanto, Prijono. "Poverty and Inequality in Indonesia at the End of the 20th Century". Paper presented at the third ASEAN seminar on Social Development, Universitas Riau, Pekan Baru, Indonesia, June 1997.

Trainer, Ted. *Developed to Death: Rethinking Third World Development*. London: Green Print, 1988.

———. "Reconstructing Radical Development Theory". *Alternatives* 14 (1989): 381–515.

———. *Towards a Sustainable Economy: The Need for Fundamental Change*. Oxford: Jon Carpenter; Sydney: Environbook, 1996.

Index